Praise for *Fooled Again*

"*Fooled Again* is a must-read for anybody concerned about the health and preservation of our democracy."

—JOSEPH WILSON, author of *The Politics of Truth*

"Mark Crispin Miller deserves the nation's thanks for drawing attention to the grave threat to democracy that comes from unreliable voting machines—and their possible abuse by unscrupulous politicians."

—ROBERT PARRY, author of *Secrecy & Privilege: Rise of the Bush Dynasty from Watergate to Iraq*

"A terrific writer with a very important message."

—TOM DASCHLE, former Senate Majority Leader

"Mark Crispin Miller makes a compelling case that the tactics used in Florida to steal the 2000 presidential election were used again in Ohio and elsewhere to steal the 2004 election, and are very likely to be used in 2008."

—DAVID MOORE, former Senior Editor of the Gallup Poll and author of *How to Steal an Election*

"A great read and a great work of scholarship. I am amazed at Miller's ability to assemble and synthesize so much information. American democracy is fortunate to have such a gifted scholar on its side."

—LANCE DEHAVEN-SMITH, Professor of Public Administration and Policy, Florida State University

"I encourage those who visit my web site to read the book *Fooled Again* by Mark Crispin Miller. This is an important and illuminating book about our seriously flawed election system."

—BARBARA STREISAND

"[Miller] makes a compelling case that virulent antidemocratic forces fueled by religious fervor are making an all-out assault on American democracy, but to my mind the most troubling aspect of *Fooled Again* is its indictment of the media, democracy's watchdog, which are letting it happen. . . . *Fooled Again* is a wake-up call." —*The Christian Century*

"Mark Crispin Miller's *Fooled Again* is a jeremiad aimed at the heart of the national Republican machine. But it's also a work of original reporting that in the end amounts to a solid case for Republican theft of the 2004 presidential election. . . . *Fooled Again* may well describe the endgame that leads to single-party dominance through the next generation." —*Chicago Reader*

"*Fooled Again* is of crucial importance in helping to thoroughly document the dangerous extremism of the Rove Republicans—and their deeply un-American aversion to democracy and their willingness to use whatever means necessary to keep or gain power."
—DON SIEGELMAN, Governor of Alabama 1999-2003

"[Miller] makes a compelling argument for the need for sweeping election reforms." —*The Columbus Dispatch*

"Miller is right. The electoral system is not a criminal case, and you don't have to prove that Bush stole the election beyond a shadow of a doubt in order to eradicate all doubts you may have about the race. And he's right, too, that we should have had a serious investigation into the flaws in the last election, and that those flaws—and the flaws we see every year—should prompt politicians to fix the entire electoral system before the next big race."
—Salon.com

"A fascinating catalogue of impeachable offenses and prosecutable crimes." —Kirkus Reviews

"In case you need more fodder to support your conspiracy theories at the Thanksgiving table, Mark Crispin Miller presents *Fooled Again*, a well-researched and wide-reaching book. . . . From old-fashioned goonery to high-tech shenanigans, Crispin adds up how individual thievery yanked the White House away from John Kerry." —*Portland Mercury*

"Miller has done his homework, and his sources are numerous and scrupulously footnoted. He comes close to convincing an open-minded reader that the 2004 election was a gigantic fraud. His exhortation to Democrats 'not to milk it for partisan advantage but to use it to promote, and realize, electoral reform' is the book's stated purpose, and Miller does make a strong case for reform. . . . Miller's call for electoral reform becomes an urgent clarion call to all Americans, one that should not be ignored." —*Florida Sun-Sentinel*

"The author of *The Bush Dyslexicon* warns that the 2000 Florida recount was just the beginning." —*The Washington Post*

"In recent days Mark Crispin Miller has reported that he heard from Kerry personally that Kerry believes the election was stolen. The dialogue has been widely reported on the internet. Kerry has since seemed to deny it. We have every reason to believe Miller." —*Columbus Free Press*

"BuzzFlash strongly recommends *Fooled Again* by Mark Crispin Miller because our democracy simply cannot afford another fraudulent or stolen election." —Buzzflash.com

"(T)here was indeed something rotten in the state of Ohio in 2004. Whether by intent or negligence, authorities took actions that prevented many thousands of citizens from casting votes and having them counted. The irregularities were sufficiently widespread to call into question Bush's margin of victory. This was not a fair election, and it deserves the scrutiny skeptics have brought to it." —*Mother Jones*

"Mark Crispin Miller has been at the forefront of watchdogging the Republican leadership for years and has recently released a new book titled *Fooled Again*. If you've read his previous works, *The Bush Dyslexicon* and *Cruel and Unusual*, you know that Miller never walks the easy path towards proving his theories. *Fooled Again* is no exception. It's brilliantly written—of course. But it also manages to organize and draw together the litany of inconsistencies; the myriad of suspicious deals, methods, and results which were largely ignored by the mainstream media—and even the losing ticket—in the days leading up to and through the election." —Bob Cesca, *The Huffington Post*

FOOLED AGAIN

The *Real* Case for Electoral Reform

Mark Crispin Miller

BASIC
BOOKS

A Member of the Perseus Books Group

New York

FOR AMY

Books published by Basic Books are available at special discounts for bulk purchases in
the United States by corporations, institutions, and other organizations. For more
information, please contact the Special Markets Department at the Perseus Books
Group, 11 Cambridge Center, Cambridge MA 02142, or call (617) 252-5298 or
(800) 255-1514, or e-mail special.markets@perseusbooks.com.

Design by Jane Raese

A CIP catalog record for this book is available from the Library of Congress.
Hardcover: ISBN-13: 978-0-465-04579-2; ISBN-10: 0-465-04579-0
Paperback: ISBN-13: 978-0-465-04580-8; ISBN-10: 0-465-04580-4

10 9 8 7 6 5 4 3 2 1

The sovereignty of a despotic monarch assumes the power of making wrong right, or right wrong, as he pleases or as it suits him. The sovereignty in a republic is exercised to keep right and wrong in their proper and distinct places, and never suffer the one to usurp the place of the other. A republic, properly understood, is a sovereignty of justice, in contradistinction to a sovereignty of will.

THOMAS PAINE, 1786

Things have come to a pass where lying sounds like truth, truth like lying. . . . The conversion of all questions of truth into questions of power, a process that truth itself cannot escape if it is not to be annihilated by power, not only suppresses truth as in earlier despotic orders, but has attacked the very heart of the distinction between true and false. . . . So Hitler, of whom no-one can say whether he died or escaped, survives.

T. W. ADORNO, 1945

No voter disenfranchisement occurred in this election of 2004, and for that matter [in] the election of 2000. Everybody knows it. The voters know it, the candidates know it, the courts know it, and the evidence proves it.

TOM DELAY, JANUARY 6, 2005

Contents

Preface

How will America vote in 2008? That is the central question raised by this book. But in asking it I am not thinking of how the election of 2006 might affect the field of candidates for '08; or how Jeb or Rudy or John or John or Hillary will try to "position" him- or herself, energize or transcend his or her "base," or raise the many millions needed to "define" him- or herself before the cameras. I am not concerned with the parties' strategies or tactics, or with any other traditional feature of political campaigning.

The crucial question of how the nation votes in our next presidential race is finally unrelated to all such theatrics. At issue, instead, is the integrity of our electoral system. Unless that system is reformed from top to bottom, and as soon as possible, what will happen is a foregone conclusion. The election of 2008 will be a repetition of 2004—and a preview of 2012, 2016, 2020 and every "presidential race" thereafter, until the gap between our dismal national condition and the ruling party's claims has grown so large that even those in power begin to notice it, and take some further catastrophic step to change the subject.

The point of looking back at the 2004 election, then, is not to throw Bush out of the White House and put John Kerry in his place. For one thing, the Constitution offers no guidance as to what should happen if it turns out that a seemingly elected president was not elected. Without doubt, the perpetrator(s) of so vast a fraud should be impeached; but even if that were feasible under this regime, the succession would not fall to Senator Kerry. And even if there were a constitutional argument for making Kerry president of the United States, it would not mean that such a switch would necessarily be desirable, considering Kerry's swift concession after having staunchly promised to "count every vote." And so a true account of the 2004 election is not a partisan endeavor; nor could it be, as any true account can shed no very flattering light on either party. While the Bush Republicans were plainly getting ready, from 2001, to sabotage the race, the Democrats, with very few exceptions, were ignoring every sign of such intent. They were apparently more worried that they might be charged with "paranoia" than they were about the state of our electoral infrastructure. In any case, the best use Democrats can make of this book would be not to milk it for partisan advantage but to use it to promote, and realize, electoral reform—a campaign in which every genuinely patriotic member of the GOP will surely join them, as America will not survive if its republican and democratic institutions are not salvaged and protected.

It is the purpose of this book to serve American democracy by pointing out the truth about the last election, for that truth alone, and not the maunderings of the punditocracy, will set us free. In this world, first of all—the world of politics and history—the truth itself is liberating, as it dispels the deadly fog of propaganda, superstition, dogma, rumor, groupthink, spin and wishful thinking that sometimes, lately, seems to cloud all minds. To assert that Bush was "re-elected handily" (or at all) is as false as all the other lies and delusions Bush & Co. has flogged over the years: that Iraq posed a grave danger to the world, and was complicit in the terrorist attacks on 9/11; that the Bush administration could not have prevented 9/11; that our troops are in Iraq today because of 9/11; that America today is safer from terrorist attacks than it was on 9/11; that the torture at Guantánamo and Abu Ghraib and elsewhere was the free-lance work of just a few sadistic men and women and not the strange fruit of administration policy; that "climate change" is not occurring, and that, even if it is, there's nothing we can do about it, and even trying to reverse it would destroy America's economy; that the universe is 6,000 years old; that Social Security is on the brink of ruin, and must be "saved" by the "reforms" proposed by Bush; that childhood obesity is not a problem; that homosexuality is chosen; that Karl Rove did not speak to certain journalists about Valerie Plame Wilson's status at the CIA; that the wars in Iraq and Afghanistan are going well, the "terrorists," "in their last throes," now getting desperate; that "freedom's on the march"; that God told Bush to smite Saddam Hussein; and on and on. To recognize that Bush & Co. stole their "re-election," or at least to open one's mind to the possibility, and to demand a new and unconstrained investigation into what went down in 2004, is a cognitive and moral action vital to the health of this republic.

And as it is crucial that we recognize Bush/Cheney's (second) theft of power, it is no less important that we grasp exactly how it was accomplished. In a nation of this size, complexity, diversity and (nominal) transparency, the theft of a presidential race is no simple matter but requires a wide array of complementary actions national and local. It cannot be accomplished by a small group of operatives convening secretly in some well-appointed bunker. In fact it cannot be done secretly at all. It requires the active participation of hundreds, even thousands of loyalists who value winning over democratic principle—because they believe that their opponents are *demonic*, beings so dangerously evil that their victory simply cannot be allowed. Such a theft requires an opposition too intimidated to speak out in its own defense, and a press too scared of seeming "liberal" (or one too deeply sympathetic to the right) to report what's plainly visible to any rational observer. Such are the pathologies required for the successful theft of an election in America today, and such pathologies are now demonstrably at work.

As this book points out, the Republican Party did whatever it could do, throughout the nation and the world, to cut the Kerry vote and pad the Bush vote. Some of its methods were exceedingly sophisticated, like the various cyber-scams pulled off in tight complicity with Diebold, ES&S, Sequoia, Triad and other corporate vendors of electoral infrastructure. Other methods were more bureaucratic: the disappearance of innumerable Democratic registration forms, countless absentee ballots and countless provisional ballots, as well as multitudes of would-be Democratic voters wrongly stricken from the rolls because of "felonies" never committed or committed by somebody else, or for no given reason whatsoever. There were vast logistical inequities in state after state. Democratic precincts got far too few machines, and those machines kept breaking down, or turning Kerry votes into Bush votes, with long, long lines of would-be voters stuck for hours (or, as often happened, giving up and not voting); while pro-Bush precincts tended to have plenty of machines, all working well, so that voting there was quick and easy. And then there were old-fashioned dirty tricks meant to scare people into staying home, or to send them to the wrong address, or to get them out to vote a day too late. There was also outright bullying, intimidation and harassment—the oldest methods of mass disenfranchisement, just as obvious in 2004 as they were in Dixie after Reconstruction, only now such methods were used nationwide (and the U.S. federal government, in this case, was behind them).

Such computer problems, bureaucratic ploys and individual misconduct were apparent not just in Ohio (and Florida, and all throughout the South), but coast to coast—a national carnival of civic crimes and improprieties, maintained by two separate but complicit groups. At the top were those orchestrating the grand rip-offs and reversals in such states as Florida, Ohio, Arizona, Minnesota and Georgia. And then there was the grass-roots soldiery: the cadre of believers who perceive the enemy as Satan's spawn, and who therefore saw it as their sacred duty to destroy as many Democratic votes as possible and facilitate as many Bush votes as they could, regardless of how many actual voters might choose either candidate. These troops often served as poll-workers and poll-watchers, or they might show up, the party paying all expenses, to threaten would-be Democratic voters on the telephone or to hand out flyers warning that all voters who had unpaid parking tickets or owed child support would be arrested at the polls. Some of them would go from door to door in Democratic neighborhoods, kindly offering to "deliver" any absentee ballots to the proper office. As in the South after the Civil War, there was a large and angry population more than willing to use guile or terror to suppress the vote, seeing such crime as patriotic, civilized, even godly.

In short, the election of 2004 was stolen by a theocratic movement, just as hostile to the promise of democracy as any Bolshevik or Nazi of the past or any fuming Islamist today. That movement has never spoken for the American majority and never will. The only proper way to fight it, then, is to defeat it at the polls—and there's the rub, for if this faction controls what we still quaintly call "the ballot box," our electoral opposition is irrelevant. The only rational response must be to break their civic stranglehold by taking back our democratic institutions, and instituting the reforms now necessary to ensure that the United States cannot be hijacked by a fierce minority of theocratic militants backed by certain corporate powers. We need to do away with electronic voting (which can never be entirely secure); use a standard paper ballot, worded and designed for easy comprehension; federalize the electoral system, so that its workers are trained civil servants, not local bigots or politicos; make Election Day a Sunday or a national holiday, or, better yet, a week devoted to the all-important choice of who will serve the people in the people's government; make Instant Run-off Voting (IRV) universal in America, to give a chance to viable third-party candidates; institute strict campaign finance reform; and not least, start comprehensive media reform—disassembling the commercial juggernaut that now dictates what we know and when we know it—so that our politics can finally be emancipated from the glittering shackles of Big Money.

But there can be no movement for reform, however badly needed, if there is no scandal driving it. Most rational Americans agree that we must have electoral reform; and yet too often we are told by these same rational Americans that we must "get over" the election of 2004, as only then will we be able to "move on" to more important matters—like electoral reform. That view is irrational, for if we just ignore the copious evidence that Bush & Co. committed vast electoral fraud in order to protract their rule, there appears to be no pressing reason to reform the system. "If it ain't broke, don't fix it," Bush & Co. will say; and there will be no adequate reply to that truism (especially in "a time of war") as long as we indulge the fiction that the system is *not* seriously "broke."

And right now, as we dawdle, Bush's party and the movement that it serves are busily advancing measures to consolidate their "victory" by making fair elections more unlikely. There are strenuous campaigns underway to get electronic touch-screen voting into California and New York, Illinois and Maryland— longtime Democratic strongholds, which will suddenly and inexplicably become depleted of their Democrats once those machines are put in place. In Georgia and Indiana, laws were lately passed requiring all those who would vote to purchase state-approved photo IDs—essentially "a poll tax in disguise," as Rep. John Conyers has put it—and nationwide there also have been various efforts to make voting still more difficult for immigrants and for the poor, among other subject populations. The point of all such stealthy actions is to rein in, control and thus in essence terminate American democracy—a plan that we believers in American democracy can foil, but only if we will acknowledge that that plan is in the works, and that it made great progress in 2004.

Mark Crispin Miller

FOOLED
AGAIN

1.

The Miracle

Whichever candidate you voted for (or think you voted for), or even if you did not vote (or could not), you must admit that last year's presidential race was pretty interesting. Maybe not as interesting, or important, as the election in Ukraine, with its bold majority refusing to be cheated of self-government by a devious authoritarian regime. And maybe our presidential race was not as interesting, or as important, as the election in Iraq, whose people bravely ventured to the polls to choose the body that will someday choose their government for them, if the Bush regime allows it. Those foreign contests must have been more interesting than ours and more important, or the U.S. press would not have so meticulously covered both those races while reporting very little on the aftermath of the election here, other than to confirm and reconfirm Bush/Cheney's startling victory. And yet, notwithstanding the comparative indifference of our press, the election here had many points of interest; for Bush's victory *was* startling. It was, in fact, miraculous, even if the U.S. press chose not to point that out.

Indeed, Bush's victory was a miracle of such proportions that our press's silence on the subject must be yet another indication of that institution's liberal bias; for if the media were not entirely hostile to the Spirit, as so many figures in the government have charged—and as some 51 percent of the electorate apparently believes—the print press and the newscasts in this country would have hailed President Bush's re-election not just as a stroke of genius by Karl Rove but as the work of God Himself, just as Pat Robertson foretold. "I think George Bush is going to win in a walk," the cleric had predicted, ten months earlier, on a broadcast of *The 700 Club*.[1] "I really believe I'm hearing from the Lord it's going to be like a blowout election in 2004." That the statement was a little crass does not make it wrong. Certainly no other worldly factor can account for that amazing win, which no human pollster could foresee, and which no mortal has been able to explain in rational terms.

On Election Day itself and shortly after, there were several signs that the whole process had been overtaken by some higher power. For instance, it was first reported that the president had won 8.56 million more votes than he had received four years before—a figure that was soon bumped up to 11.5 million.[2] This was a miracle, as Bush's disapproval ratings were too high, and his approval ratings far too low, for such a sweep to be explicable as a mundane phenomenon. His numbers had been droopy since mid-May, when Gallup had him down to a 46 percent approval rating and Pew down to 44 percent, with 48 percent disapproving.[3] "We're in that place where no presidential re-election campaign has ever been."[4] Thus Matthew Dowd, a senior adviser to Bush/Cheney, had gloomily conceded in the spring, when press reports were noting that Ronald Reagan and Bill Clinton had, in their respective reelection drives, enjoyed approval ratings well up in the 50s. As Election Day approached, Bush's numbers had not budged:[5]

Gallup Poll and CNN/USA Today/Gallup Poll (10/29/04–10/31/04)
    Approve: 48%   Disapprove: 47%   Unsure: 5%

CBS News Poll (10/28/04–10/30/04)
    Approve: 49%   Disapprove: 44%   Unsure: 7%   MoE: +/- 4%

Newsweek Poll (10/27/04–10/29/04)
    Approve: 46%   Disapprove: 47%   Unsure: 7%   MoE: +/- 3%

Kerry's numbers were considerably higher in the swing states.[6] It therefore would have been remarkable enough if, with such ratings, Bush had just squeaked by. That he could win by such a hefty margin was extraordinary, as many witnesses on the religious right were happy to observe: "George W. Bush's popular vote total of 58 million [*sic*] set a new record, exceeding the one established by Lyndon Johnson in 1964," exulted *Catholic Insight*, a website dedicated to "traditionalist Catholicism."[7]

There is no doubt that Bush was passionately favored by a multitude of true believers on the right. Were there enough of them to make so great a difference? In the election of 2000, there were some four million evangelical voters who did not come out for Bush. Throughout the last campaign, Karl Rove did everything he could to get them to the polls. Although he seems to have succeeded, at least according to some calculations, that increase cannot account for Bush's victory, nor was it near enough to "evangelicize" the president's base. The evangelical vote for Bush was 9 percentage-points higher than it had been four years earlier—a rise offset significantly by the 6.4 percentage-point increase in *total* voter turnout.[8] In the end, rightist evangelicals accounted for only 40 percent of the president's electoral support: the same as in 2000, when Bush had *lost* the popular vote.

Therefore, it would have to be a broader coalition of believers that enabled Bush's "re-election." Regular churchgoers (that is, those who go to worship once a week or more) accounted for 42 percent of voters—a constituency almost twice as large as the bloc of evangelicals.[9] We find, however, that, as the religious coalition broadens, its members are more evenly divided: 60 percent of such churchgoers cast their votes for Bush, while 40 percent supported Kerry. (Apparently, traditional Catholics went for Bush by 53 percent, with 47 percent supporting Kerry.)[10] And yet even that much larger bloc of voters only represents approximately half of Bush's vote.

There is, in short, no evidence for the contention that the Christian right extended Bush's reign. That he did so well despite his vaulting disapproval ratings is still quite a marvelous achievement, dependent on the unexpected whim of several million phantom voters.

The impression that new multitudes of evangelicals poured forth to vote for Bush may, in part, have resulted from a recent change in wording by exit pollsters.[11] In 2000, voters leaving polls were asked this question: "Do you consider yourself part of the conservative Christian political movement, also known as the religious right?" In 2004, that question was revised to wash away its partisan and/or fanatical associations: "Would you describe yourself as a born-again or evangelical Christian?" Predictably, more voters defined themselves as evangelicals in answering the latter question—23 percent, whereas 14 percent had deemed themselves evangelical *conservatives* four years before. As the *Washington Post* reported on November 4, "polling specialists said the 2004 wording virtually assures more affirmative answers." Whatever motivated the revision, its effect was to exaggerate the impact of the evangelical vote and thereby make Bush's flock seem larger than it really was. This also was the pointed message of the pro-Bush propaganda vented by the leading theocrats just after the election.

According to the leaders of the theocratic right—whose theory gloriously resonated far and wide—Bush won because the righteous hordes of born-agains encouraged Christians of all kinds to rise and vote: mainline Protestants as well as Catholics, including black and Latino believers; and their impact was further strengthened by a smattering of pro-Bush Jews (whose numbers had grown by 6 percentage-points since 2000).[12] That national crusade was spurred, allegedly, by "moral values." Gay marriage, boasted Tony Perkins, president of the Family Research Council, was "the hood ornament on the family values wagon that carried the president to a second term."[13] However rich (and strange) that metaphor, the theory that another Great Awakening put Bush back in office is unfounded. Such widespread religious zeal would certainly have registered in Bush's polls. Moreover, there is solid evidence that "moral values" mattered little to the national electorate. On November 11, Pew published an extensive post-election poll asking those who had lately voted to define the issue that concerned them most.[14] Iraq came out on top, noted by 25 percent, followed by jobs and the economy, 12 percent, with 9 percent invoking terrorism. "Moral values" was a phrase used only by another 9 percent —with only 3 percent noting specific controversies like Tony Perkins's proud hood ornament, while 2 percent referred to the candidates' personal deportment.

Further, there was a prior version of the poll, presenting each respondent with a list of seven issues, and asking him or her to rank them in importance. (In a later poll, the questioner named no specific issues.) According to that survey, "moral values" mattered most to 27 percent of the electorate—the leading issue in that less objective version of the poll, but a concern to only one in four respondents.[15] And according to another post-election poll, by Zogby International, 33 percent of voters deemed "greed and materialism" the most pressing moral problems in America, while only 12 percent of those polled cited gay marriage.[16]

Thus there is good reason not to buy the argument that Bush was re-elected by his flock. That it was they who "carried the president to a second term" would seem to be a demographic and an arithmetical impossibility—unless, of course, God worked a miracle with that minority of pious right-wing voters, multiplying them supernaturally, like Jesus' loaves and fishes.

There were yet other miracles. The national turnout was immense by current U.S. standards: 60.7 percent, the highest in 36 years.[17] (In 2000, it was 54 percent.) That the president won handily with such a turnout would appear to reconfirm the view that the electorate skewed Republican, or, more precisely, toward the Christian right. This would represent a revolutionary shift, as Democrats have always benefited most from crowded polls. "The higher the turnout, the better off Kerry is," said Curtis Gans, director of the Committee for the Study of the American Electorate (CSAE), five days before Election Day.[18] (Twelve days earlier, Gans had made the argument in more numerical detail: "This year, anything beyond 116 million or 117 million should benefit the Democrats, because most of the constituency beyond the 5 or 6 million new voters that Republicans might claim [to have registered] are likely to be Democrats." The final tally on Election Day exceeded Gans's figure by more than five million votes.)[19] It would also mean that the Republicans had registered far more new voters than the Democrats—an unlikely coup, however keen the president's religious base, as the Kerry/Edwards registration drive was noticeably stronger, especially in Ohio and Florida, both of which the president, miraculously, won.[20] The heightened *Democratic* turnout would explain that party's signal victory in state legislative races, as the Democrats realized a net gain of 76 seats nationwide, taking over the statehouses in Montana, Colorado, and John Edwards's home state, North Carolina—all three of which the president, miraculously, won.[21] (The Democrats also took control of the legislatures of Oregon, Vermont and Washington.) And yet the president won anyway—a feat particularly marvelous in light of the Democrats' extraordinary unity in 2004. The party was, for once, not split between its centrist and progressive wings, but unified by a determination that had been missing from its ranks since 1964. Ralph Nader's campaign had depended on Republican assistance, and he ended up with 411,304 votes, or 0.36 percent of the total. (The combined third-party total was the lowest since 1988.)[22]

On the other hand, the Republicans were *not* united but in fact divided, as the Democrats have largely been, between a center-right Old Guard and a wing more militant and ideologically committed—the difference being that the Democratic Old Guard runs the party, while extremists dominate Bush/Cheney's GOP; and they are infinitely farther to the right than the most liberal Democrats are to the left. (A Democrat as far left as, say, Dick Cheney is far right, would have to be an outlaw in the mountains of Peru.) Throughout the campaign, there were signs of disaffection with Bush/Cheney and their theocratic following, not only among moderate Republicans but also further right within the party, from the libertarians of the Cato Institute to reactionary firebrands like Bob Barr.

"Today's 'Republican' Party is one with which I am totally unfamiliar," wrote John Eisenhower, Dwight Eisenhower's son and a lifelong champion of the GOP in a September 9 op-ed— "Why I Will Vote for John Kerry for President"—for the rightwing *Manchester Union Leader*.[23] Decrying the regime's "hubris and arrogance" in foreign policy, its fiscal recklessness, and its authoritarian drift, Eisenhower announced that he was crossing party lines:

> Sen. Kerry, in whom I am willing to place my trust, has demonstrated that he is courageous, sober, competent, and concerned with fighting the dangers associated with the widening socio-economic gap in this country. I will vote for him enthusiastically.

He concluded: "I urge everyone, Republicans and Democrats alike, to avoid voting for a ticket merely because it carries the label of the party of one's parents or of our own ingrained habits." On October 14, a similar statement came from Ballard Morton, scion of an old Kentucky family long devoted to the GOP. His father, Thruston Morton, had been a U.S. senator, and national chairman of the RNC;[24] and his uncle, Rogers Morton, also chaired the RNC, served in the House of Representatives as a Republican, and had served in both the Nixon and Ford cabinets. In the *Louisville Courier-Journal*, Morton bid farewell to Bush:

> I cannot in good conscience vote for President Bush in this election. What he has done since his election in 2000 goes against the values I treasure both in terms of leadership and in our nation. He has not done what he said he would do. He has lost my trust and my respect.[25]

On the other hand, John Kerry "offers us a choice"—on Iraq, on global terrorism, on U.S. national security, on fiscal policy, on the environment, on healthcare. "Above all, he offers a return of decency and integrity to the White House." Others wrote with more ferocity. As early as December 1, 2003, in the *American Conservative*, Doug Bandow, a senior fellow at the Cato Institute and former special assistant to Ronald Reagan, assailed the Bush regime's Big-Brotherism in a piece called "Righteous Anger: The Conservative Case Against George W. Bush." The president, Bandow concluded, "enjoys neither royal nor religious status that would place him beyond criticism. Whether or not he is a real conservative, he is no friend of limited, constitutional government. And for that the American people should be very, very angry."[26]

Many other former allies and supporters publicly defected. On July 31, General Merrill "Tony" McPeak, former Air Force chief of staff and one-time Veteran for Bush, called the regime's foreign policy a "disaster" which has "alienated our friends, damaged our credibility around the world, reduced our influence to an all-time low in my lifetime, given hope to our enemies."[27] McPeak signed on with Kerry/Edwards. "As president," he wrote, "John Kerry will not waste a minute in bringing action on the reforms urged by the 9/11 commission. And he will not rest until America's defenses are strong." Bush, on the other hand, "fought against the very formation of the commission and continues to the present moment to give it only grudging cooperation, no matter what he says."

Founding neocon Francis Fukuyama, author of *The End of History and the Last Man*, announced on July 13 that he would not vote for the president[28]—a startling declaration from the luminary who, along with Dick Cheney, Donald Rumsfeld, Paul Wolfowitz, Jeb Bush and other advocates of *pax Americana*, had signed the war-like manifesto of the Project for the New American Century (PNAC) in 1997. (PNAC's purpose was to propagate the program for a worldwide Reaganite imperium, based on "anti-terrorism" and "free markets." Its members started lobbying for a U.S. re-invasion of Iraq in early 1998.)[29] Other rightists who opposed Bush's re-election include Paul Craig Roberts, a former associate editor of the *Wall Street Journal* and, under Reagan, an assistant secretary of the treasury; Lew Rockwell, president of the Ludwig von Mises Institute in Auburn, Alabama; and former congressman Bob Barr of Cobb County, Georgia—a member of the Council of Concerned Citizens (CCC) and one of Bill Clinton's most ferocious critics.[30] In "An Agonizing Choice," an op-ed syndicated on October 7, Barr (without endorsing Kerry) gave three good reasons not to vote for Bush: "record levels of new spending," the failure "to improve our border security" and the regime's drive to curb the "freedoms and civil liberties" of "law-abiding citizens." (In November of 2002, responding to the Patriot Act and other strokes of federal repression, Barr had joined forces with the ACLU, becoming a consultant on "informational and data privacy issues.")[31]

The president's diminished standing on the right was also evident in the complicated editorial posture of the *American Conservative*, a vigorous rightist magazine established in 2002 by Scott McConnell, Pat Buchanan and Taki Theodoracopulos as an expression of dissent from Bush & Co.'s "free trade" and pro-Israel policies.[32] The magazine's final issue before Election Day included a kaleidoscopic non-endorsement of the president, with McConnell backing Kerry, Taki coming out for Michael Anthony Peroutka of the tiny Constitution Party, Alan W. Bock endorsing Michael Badnarik of the Libertarian Party and columnist Justin Raimondo (who had helped run Buchanan's presidential drive in 1996) supporting Nader, in whom he heard "the voice of the Old Right." The president was Pat Buchanan's choice, the veteran agitator arguing, a bit defensively, that national elections call for "tribal" loyalty: "No matter the quarrels inside the family, when the shooting starts, you come home to your own."

As such examples indicate, the Republican campaign *against* Bush/Cheney was the work of no one faction but a drive as ideologically diverse as the party itself.[33] On the same side as Bob Barr—and going further—was Hillary Cleveland, the widow of ten-term congressman James Colgate Cleveland (R-NH), who was George H. W. Bush's regular paddleball partner when the two served in the House. Although close to the Bush family ("George and Barbara are very dear friends") and a lifelong party loyalist, Cleveland was so horrified by George Jr.'s doctrine of pre-emptive war that she joined the opposition, in September taking charge of the GOP Women for Kerry Steering Committee in New Hampshire. While appalled by Bush's general recklessness, Cleveland was especially concerned about the war, deeming Bush's policy illegal and disastrous. "I think he is usurping an authority he does not have. He has alienated our allies, destroyed our relations in the Muslim world, and actually invited terrorists into Iraq. I think Kerry is our best hope to get us out of Iraq and reestablish our diplomatic relations in the world."[34] "I am voting for Kerry," wrote diplomat and moderate Republican Dan Simpson in the *Pittsburgh Post-Gazette* on October 27. "America can't live in this world with a busted foreign policy."[35]

That view was far more strikingly expressed throughout the campaign season by a broad range of eminent Republicans. On

June 16, a bipartisan group of 27 former diplomats and military officials urged the president's electoral defeat. The group—Diplomats and Military Commanders for Change (DMCC)—included, among other stalwarts of the GOP, Jack Matlock, Jr., Reagan's ambassador to the Soviet Union; William Crowe, chairman of the Joint Chiefs of Staff under Reagan; H. Allen Holmes, Reagan's ambassador to Portugal; and Charles Freeman, Bush Sr.'s ambassador to Saudi Arabia. (David Thalheimer, who had been an Air Force officer—and a Republican—for twenty years, published a more personal repudiation of Bush/Cheney's military policies: "Sir, you are relieved from duty!" it concludes).[36] The group pulled no punches in its public statements.

> From the outset, President George W. Bush adopted an overbearing approach to America's role in the world, relying upon military might and righteousness, insensitive to the concerns of traditional friends and allies, and disdainful of the United Nations.[37]

Such open disapproval by so grand a body was unprecedented in our history, according to historians as ideologically diverse as Richard Kohn, the Pentagon's chief Air Force historian under Reagan and Bush Sr., and the liberal war horse Arthur Schlesinger, Jr.[38] There was another party mutiny on August 30, when Mainstream 2004—a group of seventeen former governors, senators, representatives and state and federal officials, all of them Republican—came out deploring "the extremist element that controls the Republican party" and kicked off an ad campaign intended to subvert that "element."[39] Asked if he would vote for Bush, A. Linwood Holton, former governor of Virginia and the group's prime mover, answered, "Not unless they change substantially between now and November."

On September 8, the board of the Log Cabin Republicans voted 22 to 2 against endorsing Bush—the first time since its founding, in 1993, that that *very* straight gay-advocacy group refused to back the party's presidential candidate.[40] "Certain moments in history require that a belief in fairness and equality not be sacrificed in the name of partisan politics. This is one of those moments," said Patrick Guerriero, the group's executive director. "There is a battle for the heart and soul of the Republican Party, and that fight is bigger than one platform, one zconvention, or even one President." And on October 4, an open letter to the president, signed by 169 tenured and emeritus business professors from the world's top business schools—a group by no means Marxist in their views—appeared in the *New York Times* and the *Financial Times*, informing Bush that "U.S. economic policy has taken a dangerous turn under your stewardship."[41] Conceived and drafted by members of the faculty at Harvard Business School, where Bush received his MBA, fifty of the letter's signatories taught, or had taught, at Harvard. One of them, Robert Merton, had received a Nobel Prize, as had William Sharpe, an emeritus at Stanford. Two other of the letter signatories had won Pulitzer Prizes. The letter catalogued the regime's economic failures with frightening sweep and specificity:

> Nearly every major economic indicator has deteriorated since you took office in January 2001. Real GDP growth during your term is the lowest of any presidential term in recent memory. Total non-farm employment has contracted and the unemployment rate has increased. Bankruptcies are up sharply, as is our dependence on foreign capital to finance an exploding current account deficit. All three major stock indexes are lower now than at the time of

your inauguration. The percentage of Americans in poverty has increased, real median income has declined, and income inequality has grown.[42]

The document repudiated Bush/Cheney's basic economic policy of taxing less and less while spending more and more—a wild reversion to the "voodoo economics" that distressed the nation under Reagan. The letter asked Bush to recall (or read) the textbooks that were assigned to Harvard's students in his day, which would explicate the dangers of his budgetary hedonism and send him "the clear message," as the letter put it, "that more of the same won't work." The president's economic policies were also pointedly condemned by entrepreneurial titan Lee Iacocca, who came out for Kerry in late June, and by Nobel Prize-winning economist Joseph Stiglitz, whose "Bush Is Dead Wrong" ran in the *Guardian* on October 6.[43]

There was no analogous cross-over by top Democrats. Those few who did back Bush—Zell Miller, Ed Koch—were mostly unsurprising renegades, as they had long leaned right. Startlingly, Bush had an outspoken advocate in Ron Silver, one of Hollywood's most liberal figures, who became a fervent Bush believer after 9/11. Such endorsements were based wholly on the issue of "terrorism." "While I don't agree with Bush on a single domestic issue," Koch said, "they are all trumped by the issue of terrorism, where he has enunciated the Bush Doctrine and proven his ability to fight this war."[44]

Thus Bush was no more popular with true fiscal conservatives than he was with his party's moderates or libertarians, or those authentically concerned about our national security. Although beloved by many corporate racketeers, Bush has frightened cooler capitalist heads with his "What—me worry?" economics and—

another factor bad for business—his "fuck you" foreign policy. Many of the world's financial players were put off by the president's faux-cowboy swagger, which induced a gloomy climate of foreboding at the World Economic Forum in Davos, Switzerland. "Many participants described this year's meeting as the most dismal they could remember," the *Irish Times* reported in 2003; and the mood was just as grim the following year, as Bush's trade and budget deficits grew ever larger.[45] From midsummer of 2004, the same unease inhibited Bush/Cheney's U.S. funders—a fact reported not in the U.S. media but, pointedly, by the *Financial Times*: "Some leading fundraisers of Mr. Bush's re-election bid have stopped active campaigning and others privately voice reservation," the paper noted on August 27.[46] The ticket's wealthy patrons had donated millions for the party Bacchanale in New York City—the costliest political convention in U.S. history. "But one senior Wall Street figure, once talked of as a possible Bush cabinet member, said he and other prominent Republicans had been raising money with increasing reluctance. 'Many are doing so with a heavy heart and some not at all.' He cited foreign policy and the ballooning federal deficit as Wall Street Republicans' main concerns." "Many of them may be maxed out," admitted one unnamed Republican, "but they are backing away from Bush."

A week before Election Day, there was much clearer evidence of Bush's low repute among the moneymakers. On October 25, the *Financial Times* itself endorsed John Kerry as "the better, safer choice," denouncing Bush as "a polariser," economically "reckless," dangerously given to "crusading moralism," and doubly hobbled by a "blind faith in military power" and a "stubborn reluctance to admit mistakes."[47] Although less sanguine than the *FT* about John Kerry's presidential skills, the *Economist* was just as blunt in its rejection of Bush: "Our confidence in him has been shattered."[48] The editors marveled at the "sheer incompetence and hubristic thinking" that had marked the regime's handling of Iraq, and were especially appalled by the fascistic treatment of Islamic "detainees":

> Today, Guantánamo Bay offers constant evidence of America's hypocrisy, evidence that is disturbing for those who sympathise with it, cause-affirming for those who hate it. This administration, which claims to be fighting for justice, the rule of law and liberty, is incarcerating hundreds of people, whether innocent or guilty, without trial or access to legal representation. The White House's proposed remedy, namely military tribunals, merely compounds the problem.

That a magazine so influential here, and so conservative, would render such a damning judgment on the president is further evidence of Bush's unimpressive standing in the business world.

His reduced appeal was obvious also in the nation's newspaper endorsements. According to *Editor & Publisher*, which kept a running tally during the campaign, Bush was *not* the choice of over 60 papers that had formally endorsed him in 2000, with over 40 of them switching to John Kerry while the others backed no candidate for president.[49] Throughout what seemed to be Bush Country—the so-called Red States—newspaper editors hailed Kerry as the sound antithesis to a destructive and deceptive president. "From the war in Iraq and the acidic sections of the Patriot Act to global warming and national energy policy, Bush's foreign and domestic policies have been based on secrecy, fear, distortion and misinformation," claimed the *Albuquerque Tribune*.[50] "Bush, whom the *Tribune* endorsed in 2000, has offered simplistic slogans to complex problems, while Kerry sees complicated problems and offers the promise of appropriate solutions—complex or not." "Four years ago, the *Orlando Sentinel* endorsed Republican George W. Bush for president based on our trust in him to unite America. We expected him to forge bipartisan solutions to problems while keeping this nation secure and fiscally sound," reported Florida's second-largest daily. "This president has utterly failed to fulfill our expectations. . . . We trust Mr. Kerry not to make the mistakes Mr. Bush has." (Kerry was also endorsed by the *Miami Herald*, Florida's largest daily.)[51] "One of the most troubling aspects of Bush's leadership style is his view that 'if you're not with us, you're against us,'" declared the *Billings Gazette*, Montana's largest daily. "Americans need a president who will listen to both dissenters and supporters—a president who will challenge his advisers to challenge groupthink. George W. Bush is not that president."[52] Even the newspaper in the president's ostensible home town of Crawford, Texas, shifted from his column into Kerry's: "The publishers of *The Iconoclast* endorsed Bush four years ago, based on the things he promised, not on [his] smoke-screened agenda," declared the *Lone Star Iconoclast*.[53]

> Today, we are endorsing his opponent, John Kerry, based not only on the things that Bush has delivered, but also on the vision of a return to normality that Kerry says our country needs.
>
> Four items trouble us the most about the Bush administration: his initiatives to disable the Social Security system, the deteriorating state of the American economy, a dangerous shift away from the basic freedoms established by our founding fathers, and his continuous mistakes regarding terrorism and Iraq.

"*The Iconoclast* whole-heartedly endorses John Kerry," the editorial concluded.[54] The mayor of Crawford, Robert Campbell, also favored Kerry. "I don't see where I'm better off than I was four years ago," he said. "I don't see where the city is any better off."[55]

With the Republicans at odds and the Democrats united, Bush's victory was all the more extraordinary; and on Election Day itself there were still further mysteries, which enhance our sense of wonder even more. On Wall Street, and in betting parlors nationwide, Kerry was the gamblers' pick, until at least 5:00 P.M. EST. "The Vegas oddsmakers were predicting a two-to-one Kerry victory," recalled MSNBC's Tucker Carlson, the rightist TV personality, on July 14, 2005. "The Vegas guys really know what's up," he went on, much too frankly, "because they're literally impartial and their jobs depend on getting it right." ("They were completely wrong" about Kerry, Carlson added quickly, and confusingly.)[56]

There was the unprecedented gap between the exit poll results and the official tally, the former naming Kerry as the winner in five states that finally went to Bush, including Ohio. On November 3, those exit polls were hastily dismissed as "wrong," and then conveniently revised so that they would foretell the vote instead of contradicting it. The pollsters floated some preposterous theories to account for the bizarre malfunction: women had been over-sampled; Bush voters suffered odd attacks of muteness when confronted by young persons bearing clipboards. No one would discuss the soundest explanation of the mystery, clearly posed by Steve Freeman, a professor at the University of Pennsylvania: the exit polls were accurate, and the official numbers fraudulent. (A definitive analysis depends on the raw data at the precinct level, which the pollsters and the media have both refused to make available.)[57]

As all such anomalies were played down, or laughed off, by the U.S. press, they came to seem imaginary, even to those few who closely studied them—much as Winston Smith, in *Nineteen Eighty-Four*, can never feel entirely certain even of what's right before his eyes, as no one else is willing, or able, to acknowledge that it's really there. Thus the stubborn patriots who have refused to disregard or to forget the facts of the election have felt like the celebrants of a forbidden creed, obstinate empiricists pursuing their study furtively, somewhat like the Christians under Nero or the Jews of 15th-century Spain; and like such mystics, those who study the election have long since come to see reality (that is, "the news") as an illusion, based in this case on endless spin and doublethink and crafty visuals. So Bush's "re-election" has seemed magical indeed: miraculous, perhaps, to those who've seen it as God's will, or else a bad dream come true, an unbelievable calamity that you could not prevent and that you somehow cannot finally "prove" is happening.

The uncanny aura disappears, however, the moment that we turn away from lonely supposition, merely noting all those things that don't add up, and begin a close consideration of the public record of electoral abuses, copiously documented and attested. For there is such a record of the crimes and improprieties committed by the Bush team in Ohio—just one state, and just a partial record, but Ohio was, of course, the pivotal swing state in the election, and the catalogue of wrongs is more than adequate to demonstrate that Bush's "re-election" was no miracle but a colossal fraud. Votes for Bush were invented, Democratic votes were prevented or discarded or converted into still more votes for Bush, and a "mandate" was thus concocted out of nothing just as Enron made up stellar "profits" out of massive losses.

On January 5, 2005, under the direction of Rep. John Conyers

(D-MI), the Democratic staff of the House Judiciary Committee released *Preserving Democracy: What Went Wrong in Ohio*, a 100-page report based on a month of hearings on the vast electoral shenanigans that went on in that state before and after the election.[58] "We find," the authors state at the beginning, "that there were massive and unprecedented voter irregularities and anomalies in Ohio"—a charge of enormous gravity, since, if true, it would mean that Bush, now well into his second term, is not the rightful president of the United States; and yet the authors make that very case, and make it well.[59] Their document is no mere partisan farrago of exaggerations and big lies—like, say, the Starr Report, or the anti-Kerry *Unfit for Command*—but a meticulous review of the abundant *evidence* that we, the people, just got fooled again. Nor does the report allow the thesis that those pro-Bush glitches all resulted accidentally. "In many cases these irregularities were caused by intentional misconduct and illegal behavior, much of it involving Secretary of State J. Kenneth Blackwell, the co-chair of the Bush-Cheney campaign in Ohio."[60]

This may be news to you. Despite its explosive relevance and careful detail, the report itself, like the anomalies discussed above, went almost wholly unreported by the media. With the lone exception of MSNBC's Keith Olbermann, whose general coverage of the late electoral fraud was excellent (both on his nightly program *Countdown* and his website bloggermann.com), the U.S. press—mainstream *and* left/liberal—let the story bounce around in cyberspace, where it could resonate as just another bit of seeming on-line lunacy, like most JFK assassination sites, or those that picture 9/11 as an extraterrestrial conspiracy. Throughout the media in early January, the report was *mentioned* by the way in a few hundred stories nationwide, mostly in the lesser dailies; but aside from *Countdown* and an article in the *Chicago Tribune*, not a single mainstream story in print or on TV or radio highlighted the report or paraphrased its findings. (On Pacifica's *Democracy Now!* Amy Goodman dealt with it extensively.) Most of those passing references, moreover, noted only one or a few of the report's charges against Ohio's secretary of state. Thus the entire document, as vaguely conjured by the media, seemed to be a rather narrow brief against Blackwell per se. In fact, *Preserving Democracy* is a revolutionary overview of various electoral frauds committed throughout Ohio, at all levels of the system, and not just on Election Day but over several months, starting up (apparently) as early as September (with Blackwell's various illegal efforts to suppress the Kerry vote) and continuing right up to January 5 (the committee having been stonewalled not just by Blackwell and other state officials but also by powers beyond Ohio, including the Republican National Committee, the FBI and the major TV networks).

From the continental hush that greeted it, you'd think the report had been released on Christmas Eve in Guam. In fact the document's release (in Washington, D.C., as ever) was timed for maximum publicity: the day before the election's final public ritual, which, this time, promised a rare scene of high contention—the very thing TV loves above all else. According to the United States Code (Title 3, Chapter 1, Section 15), the president of the Senate—that is, the U.S. vice president—must announce each state's electoral results, then "call for objections." Objections must be made in writing, and "signed by at least one Senator and one Member of the House of Representatives." A challenge having been submitted, the proceedings are suspended so both houses can retire to their respective chambers to debate the question, after which they reconvene and vote on whether to accept or to reject that state's results.

Thus was an unprecedented civic drama looming on the day Conyers's report appeared. First of all, electoral votes had been contested in the Congress only twice before. In 1877, the electoral votes of several states were challenged, some by Democrats supporting Samuel Tilden, others by Republicans supporting Rutherford B. Hayes. (Eventually Hayes won, both sides having arduously agreed to put an end to Reconstruction and, literally, get down to business nationwide.) In 1969, Republicans challenged the North Carolina vote after Lloyd W. Bailey, a "faithless elector" pledged to Richard Nixon for that state, voted for George Wallace. (Offended by the President-elect's first cabinet appointments—Henry Kissinger, Daniel Patrick Moynihan—Bailey was protesting Nixon's liberalism.) The recent challenge was not merely an unusual event, however, but also extraordinarily suspenseful because of what had happened—or not happened—four years earlier. On January 6, 2001, House Democrats, galvanized by the electoral larceny in Florida, tried and failed to challenge the results. Their effort was aborted by the failure of a single Democratic senator to join them, as the law requires. Al Gore—still vice president and therefore still the Senate's president—had ordered Democrats to make no such unseemly waves, but to respect Bush's installation for the sake of national unity. Now, it seemed, that partisan disgrace would be redressed, at least symbolically: this new challenge from the House, by Rep. Stephanie Tubbs-Jones of Ohio, would be co-signed by Barbara Boxer, Democratic senator from California. At a noon press conference on January 6, Boxer heightened the suspense by tearfully acknowledging her prior wrong: "Four years ago I didn't intervene. I was asked by Al Gore not to do so and I didn't do so. Frankly, looking back on it, I wish I had."[61]

It was a story perfect for TV—a rare event, like the return of Halley's Comet; a scene of high contention in the nation's Capitol; a heroine resolved to make things right, both for the public and herself. Such big news would highlight Conyers's report, whose findings, having spurred the challenge in the first place, would now inform the great congressional debate on the election in Ohio. This, however, did not happen. The "liberal media" took a giant pass on the whole episode. If the press *had* tried to deal with the significance of Boxer's change of heart, the task would not have been an easy one, because the press itself had not reported that failed challenge in the Congress four years earlier. Although at least as hot, TV-wise, as *The Jerry Springer Show*—with weeping women straining to be heard, and lots of brutal jeering from the audience—that barbaric session went unwitnessed, and unheard of, by Americans until they saw Michael Moore's *Fahrenheit 9/11*, released in June of 2004. With very few exceptions, the press downplayed the challenge and, in so doing, either buried the report or failed to mention it. This bashful reportage had a perverse effect. Whereas the challengers had hoped to halt the process long enough to show that there was something wrong with the official numbers in Ohio, the press dismissed the effort, certified those numbers and suggested that the challengers had something wrong with *them*.

Such was the message of what little news there was about the crisis. On January 6, the *New York Times* negated both the challenge and the document in a brief item headlined "Election Results to Be Certified, with Little Fuss from Kerry," which ran on p. 16, and ended with this quote from Dennis Hastert's office, regarding the Democrats: "They are really just trying to stir up their loony left." (On the other hand, the *Boston Globe*—a newspaper owned by the *New York Times*, Inc.—ran several articles about Ohio on January 6, the only major U.S. media outlet to provide extensive coverage.) That day, the challenge per se resonated in a headline from the Associated Press—"Democrats to

Force Congressional Debate on Ohio Election"—but with no explanation as to *why* the Democrats were using "force." The item neither quotes nor paraphrases the report, although it does include this comment from Ken Blackwell's office: "Blackwell spokesman Carlo LoParo called the report 'ludicrous' and a waste of taxpayer dollars." Also on January 6, the *Los Angeles Times* came up with 60 words (p. 18)—without mentioning the challenge by Boxer and Tubbs-Jones.[62] For its part, on January 7, the *Miami Herald* devoted over 700 words to the affair, concluding with this line from Tom DeLay: "The Democrats have replaced statecraft with stagecraft."[63]

Otherwise, it made no news in the *Washington Post*, the *Wall Street Journal*, *USA Today*, *Newsweek*, *Time* or *U.S. News & World Report*. It made no news on CBS, NBC, ABC or PBS. Nor did NPR report it (although *Talk of the Nation* dealt with it on January 6). Of all the telejournalists, MSNBC's Keith Olbermann highlighted it on *Countdown*, his nightly show (the only mainstream news source to report on the Ohio mess consistently). CNN did not report it, although Donna Brazile pointedly affirmed its copious "evidence" on *Inside Politics* on January 6. (Host Judy Woodruff failed to pause for an elaboration.) Also on that date, the report was mentioned on Fox News Channel, which briefly showed Conyers himself discussing one of the "irregularities" in Franklin County. Then there was Tom DeLay, raging at the Democrats for their "assault against the institutions of our representative democracy."

No matter how carefully its publication was timed, and notwithstanding all the careful research that went into it, *Preserving Democracy* might just as well have been suppressed outright, for all its impact on the general public. The press ignored its contents and allowed the Republican propaganda choir to spin it as an angry fantasy or malicious fraud. As we shall see, that propaganda was itself a fraud and fantasy, based not at all on the report itself but only on Bush/Cheney's need to cast all doubts about their "victory" as groundless. Thus did the U.S. media perform exactly like George Orwell's Ministry of Truth, presenting fiction as reality and vice versa. For while there is almost no evidence that Bush won the election in Ohio,[64] there is a great embarrassment of evidence that he and Cheney stole this race, just as they stole the one before. As Conyers's report makes clear, this is not an allegation but a fact, notwithstanding the establishment refusal to discuss it. Asked for a response to the report in June 2005, Carlo LoParo, Blackwell's spokesman, countered with a jibe that was far more subversive than he realized. "Why wasn't it more than an hour's story?" he sneered. "Everybody can't be wrong, can they?"

2.

Taking Care of
the Counting

Preserving Democracy divides the evidence into three phases of chicanery. First, there was the long preliminary period of legal and logistical maneuvering whose aim was to *pre-empt* as many Democratic votes as possible. A crucial tactic here was the "wide discrepancy between the availability of voting machines in more minority, Democratic and urban areas as compared to more Republican, suburban and exurban areas."[1] Such unequal placement slowed voting to a crawl at Democratic polls while making matters quick and easy in Bush/Cheney country—a most efficient way to cancel out the Democrats' immense success at registering new voters in Ohio, where Kerry/Edwards forces had outdone the Bush machine by as much as 5 to 1.[2] Thus were thousands of black Democrats discouraged from casting ballots, not by the blunt terror tactics of night-riders but systematically, as if invisibly; yet such discrimination was spectacular throughout the state. At Kenyon College in Gambier, there were only two machines for 1,300 would-be voters, even though "a surge of late registrations promised a record vote."[3] Kenyon students had to stand in line for hours, in the rain and "crowded, narrow hallways," with some of them inevitably forced to call it quits. "In contrast, at nearby Mt. Vernon Nazarene University, which is considered more Republican leaning, there were ample waiting machines and no lines," the officials of Knox County having obviously followed orders or their own partisan desire.[4]

Clearly such imbalance was deliberate, and not just your typical Election Day snafu, as countless pundits shouted afterward. The report notes that fully functional machines went unused on that day, despite the crunch at many polls. In Franklin County alone, as voters stood for hours throughout Columbus and elsewhere, there were at least 125 machines in storage. Moreover, the county's "election officials [had] decided to make do with 2,866 machines, even though the analysis showed that the county needs 5,000 machines."[5] Throughout those prior months, as ever more new Democrats were registered statewide, Blackwell kept illegally concocting ways to neutralize them. (Like Florida's secretary of state, Katherine Harris, who co-chaired Bush's state campaign in 2000, Blackwell, Ohio's secretary of state, chaired his state's Bush campaign four years later.[6]) On September 7, he ordered county boards of elections to reject all voter registration forms not "printed on white, uncoated paper of not less than 80 lb. text weight."[7] Under public pressure, he reversed the order three weeks later, but by that time it had served to further lessen the potential Kerry vote. On September 17, Blackwell limited the use of provisional ballots, effectively disenfranchising over 100,000 citizens, according to Bob Taft, Ohio's Republican governor. The report concludes: "While the Help America Vote Act [of 2002] provided that voters whose names do not appear on poll books are to sign affidavits certifying that they are in the correct jurisdiction and to be given provisional ballots, Secretary Blackwell considerably narrowed the definition of 'jurisdiction' to mean 'precinct.'"8 When that move was condemned in federal court, Blackwell ignored the ruling, which he shrugged off as the mischief of "a liberal judge . . . who wants to be co-secretary of state."9 The state's Republican Party tried to disenfranchise still more Democratic voters through a technique known as "'caging,' whereby [the party] sent registered letters to newly registered voters in minority and urban areas, and then sought to challenge 35,000 individuals who refused to sign for the letters or [if] the mail came back undeliverable.10 (This includes voters who were homeless, serving abroad, or simply did not want to sign for something concerning the Republican Party.)" Blackwell also ordered that provisional ballots not be issued to those absentee voters who were sent their ballots late or not at all. That decree was overturned in court, but not until late on Election Day.11

As the report makes clear, those were criminal maneuvers, breaching state and federal law, and Blackwell has refused to answer for them. He did not acknowledge or reply to the committee's letter of inquiry sent him on December 2.

Throughout the state, such lawlessness was rampant on Election Day itself, although Blackwell did not necessarily play a central role in that day's myriad partisan transgressions. Certainly he worked to hide the lawlessness from public view, seeking on November 2 to exclude the press and exit pollsters from Ohio's polling places. "This would have been the first time in thirty years," notes the report, "in which reporters were prevented from monitoring polls."12 Blackwell's directive was at once struck down in federal court as a violation of the First

Amendment and Ohio's constitution, so that reporters were allowed to watch the process (with one significant exception).

Contrary to a prior understanding, Blackwell also kept foreign monitors away from the Ohio polls. Having been formally
invited by the State Department on June 9, observers from the
Organisation for Security and Cooperation in Europe (OSCE),
an international consortium based in Vienna, were here to witness and report on the election. The mission's two-man teams
had been approved to monitor the process in 11 states—but the
observers in Ohio were kept out. "We thought we could be at
the polling places before, during and after" the voting, says
Sören Söndergaard, a Danish member of the team.[13] Denied admission to polls in Columbus, he and his partner went to Blackwell, who refused them letters of approval, on the basis of a very
narrow reading of Ohio law. The two observers therefore had to
"monitor" the voting at a distance of 100 yards from each
polling place. While not illegal, Blackwell's refusal was improper
and, of course, suspicious. (The Conyers Report does not deal
with this episode.) While it did not, of course, directly cut the
Kerry vote, the attempted blackout indicates that Blackwell, and
the Bush/Cheney campaign, had much to hide.

Election Day in Ohio saw lots of weird things happening to
voters, and to the vote, in county after county—a broad range of
electoral anomalies, *not one of which resulted in a loss for Bush.* At
the end of the day, there was a lockdown in Warren County, "a
traditional Republican stronghold," where officials kicked out
the press so they could tally up the votes in secret.[14] They did
so, they explained, because the FBI had warned them of a major
terrorist attack on Warren County (whose entire population, at
181,743, is not quite the size of Akron's). The FBI denied giving
any such warning. Despite the move's dramatic suddenness,

moreover, the lockdown was in the works some nine days earlier. Such long pre-planning would appear to indicate the measure's tactical importance, for the Warren County vote count shifted as the night wore on, and as Bush/Cheney's numbers in Ohio called for just a little more inflation. In any case, the margin of the regime's victory was astounding. According to a mathematician who examined the returns, "Warren County first did a lockdown to count the votes, then apparently did another lockdown to recount the votes later, resulting in an even greater Bush margin and very unusual new patterns."[15] That "big win," the analyst observed, "was due to one of two things—one of the most successful voter registration drives in American history, or stuffing the ballot box." (A manual recount of all the ballots would decide the issue, but Blackwell has prevented it.)

The report notes many other oddities, each fully documented or well attested. Ohio, like the rest of the nation that day, was the site of numerous statistical anomalies—so many that the number is itself statistically anomalous, as every single one of them took votes from Kerry. In Butler County, the Democratic candidate for State Supreme Court won 5,000 more votes than Kerry/Edwards did. (Bush took Butler County with 65.87 percent of the vote, winning 109,866 votes to Kerry's 56,243—or 33.71 percent. The Democratic candidate for the County Supreme Court received 61,559, while the victor received 68,407, beating the Democrat by 52.63 percent to 47.37 percent.)[16] In Cuyahoga County, ten Cleveland precincts "reported an incredibly high number of votes for third party candidates who have historically received only a handful of votes from these urban areas"—mystery votes that would mostly otherwise have gone to Kerry/Edwards.[17] In Franklin County, Bush received 4,000 extra votes from one computer, and, in Miami County, nearly 19,000 votes appeared in Bush's column *after* all precincts had reported.[18] Bush/Cheney did exceptionally well with phantom populations. Throughout Perry County, the number of Bush votes somehow exceeded the number of registered voters, leading to voter turnout rates as high as 124 percent.[19]

Ohio was bizarrely stricken with an epidemic of pro-Bush "machine irregularities." In Mahoning County, "25 electronic machines transferred an unknown number of Kerry votes to the Bush column," while one precinct in largely Democratic Youngstown reported negative 25 million votes (which is 3.3 times the number—7,972,826—of registered voters in Ohio in 2004).[20] In Cuyahoga County and in Franklin County—both Democratic strongholds—the arrows on the absentee ballots were not properly aligned with their respective punch-holes, so that countless votes were miscast, as in West Palm Beach back in 2000.[21] In Mercer County some 4,000 votes for president—representing nearly 7 percent of the electorate—mysteriously dropped out of the final count.[22] The machines in heavily Democratic Lucas County kept going haywire, prompting the county's election director to admit that prior tests of the machines had failed.[23] (One polling place in Lucas County never opened, as the machines were locked up in an office and no one had the key.) In Hamilton County, many absentee voters could not cast a Democratic vote for president because county workers, in taking Ralph Nader's name off many ballots, also happened to remove John Kerry's name.[24]

Meanwhile, Ohio Democrats were also heavily thwarted or impeded the old-fashioned way, through dirty tricks recalling Nixon's reign, or systematic bullying as in Dixie long ago. There were "literally thousands upon thousands" of such incidents, the report notes, cataloguing only certain of the most egregious instances.[25] Voters were told, falsely, that their polling place had changed, the news conveyed by phone calls, flyers, "door-hangers" and even party workers going house to house.[26] There were phone calls and fake "voter bulletins" instructing Democrats that they were not to cast their votes until Wednesday, November 3, the day after Election Day.[27] Unknown "volunteers" in Cleveland showed up at the homes of Democrats, offering kindly to "deliver" completed absentee ballots to the election office.[28] At several polling places black voters in particular were "challenged"—confirming documents demanded—either by election personnel or by hired goons bused in to do the job.[29] "In Franklin County, a worker at a Holiday Inn observed a team of 25 people who called themselves the 'Texas Strike Force' using payphones to make intimidating calls to likely voters, targeting people recently in the prison system. The 'Texas Strike Force' paid their way to Ohio, but their hotel accommodations were paid for by the Ohio Republican Party, whose headquarters is across the street. The hotel worker heard one caller threaten a likely voter with being reported to the FBI and returning to jail if he voted. Another hotel worker called the police, who came but did nothing."[30]

The electoral fraud continued past Election Day, but in a way more complicated and less visible than the blunt threats and dirty tricks that marked the Bush drive on the day itself. The post-election fraud was also less explicit than the strong-arm tactics used to halt the vote count in Miami four years earlier, when a platoon of stout young party animals from Washington, posing as a posse of indignant locals, charged into the counting room and tore the place apart, chanting angrily and punching people out. (John Bolton, Bush's controversial U.N. ambassador, was a vigorous participant in that Republican-sponsored riot: "I'm with the Bush-Cheney team and I'm here to stop the count," he shouted diplomatically.[31]) By 2004, Bush & Co. had learned to block recounts in vastly more sophisticated ways—relying not on thugs bused in for combat but on the evasive actions of more businesslike conspirators: Ohio's election boards, abetted by a network of large private companies that would appear to specialize in computerized vote fraud.

As the Conyers Report demonstrates, the goal of this alliance was to thwart Ohio's recount law by making it impossible to check the numbers in most counties. The statute is quite clear. (Indeed, Blackwell wrote it.) A recount having been approved, each of Ohio's 88 counties must select a number of precincts randomly, so that the total of their ballots comes to (at least) 3 percent of the county's total vote. Those ballots must then be hand-counted. If the hand count reconfirms the original machine count of those precincts, the remaining 97 percent of the county's ballots may be counted by machine. But if the totals vary by even a single vote, all the other votes must be hand-counted and the results, once reconfirmed, accepted as the new official total.

Because of a successful lawsuit by third-party presidential candidates, the Ohio recount officially started on December 13— five days after Conyers's hearings opened—and was scheduled to go on until the 28th. As the recount (such as it was) coincided with the inquiry, Conyers et al. were able to discover, and reveal in their report, some staggering examples of complicity between pro-Bush county bureaucrats and the purveyors of high-tech electoral fraud. On December 13, Sherole Eaton, deputy director of elections for Hocking County, filed an affidavit stating

that the recount there had been subverted by one Michael Barbian, Jr., an employee of Triad GDI, the corporate manufacturer
of Hocking County's voting machinery.

> Ms. Eaton witnessed Mr. Barbian modify the Hocking County
> computer vote tabulator before the announcement of the Ohio re-
> count. She further witnessed Barbian, upon the announcement that
> the Hocking County precinct was planned to be the subject of the
> initial Ohio test recount, make further alterations based on his
> knowledge of the situation. She also has firsthand knowledge that
> Barbian advised election officials how to manipulate voting machin-
> ery to ensure that [the] preliminary hand recount matched the ma-
> chine count.[32]

Following Eaton's lead, the committee learned that Triad
similarly intervened in other counties—"Greene and Monroe,
and perhaps others." (In May 2005, Blackwell retaliated by having Eaton fired.)[33] In a filmed interview, moreover, Barbian
himself confessed to having altered tabulating software not only
in Hocking County but also in Lorain, Muskingum, Clark, Harrison and Guernsey counties.[34] The point of such collaboration
was subversive:

> Based on the above, including actual admissions and statements by
> Triad employees, it strongly appears that Triad and its employees
> engaged in a course of behavior to provide "cheat sheets" to those
> counting the ballots. The cheat sheets told them how many votes
> they should find for each candidate, and how many over and under
> votes they should calculate to match the machine count. In that
> way, they could avoid doing a full county-wide hand recount man-
> dated by state law. If true, this would frustrate the entire purpose of

the recount law—to randomly ascertain if the vote counting apparatus is operating fairly and effectively, and if not to conduct a full hand recount.[35]

The report notes Triad's role in several other cases:

- In Union County, the hard drive on the vote tabulation machine, a Triad machine, had failed after the election and had been replaced. The old hard drive was returned to the Union County Board of Elections in response to a subpoena.
- In Monroe County, the 3% hand-count failed to match the machine count twice. Subsequent runs on the machine did not match each other [or] the hand recount. The Monroe County Board of Elections summoned a repairman from Triad to bring a new machine and the recount was suspended and reconvened for the following day. On the following day, a new machine was present at the Board of Elections office and the old machine was gone. The Board conducted a test run followed by the 3% hand-counted ballots. The results matched this time and the Board conducted the remainder of the recount by machine.[36]

Some evidence suggests a most undemocratic capability to fiddle with election software by remote access:

- The Directors of the Board of Elections in both Fulton and Henry County stated that the Triad Company had reprogrammed the computer by remote dial-up to count only the presidential votes prior to the start of the recount.

Such stealthy operation is especially worrying in light of Triad's partisan connection. The report notes that the company's founder, Brett A. Rapp, "has been a consistent contributor to Republican causes."[37]

And yet throughout Ohio there were many cases of malfeasance in which Triad, which serviced just under half of the state's counties, played no role.[38] In Allen, Clermont, Cuyahoga, Morrow, Hocking, Vinton, Summit and Medina counties, the precincts for the 3 percent hand recount were pre-selected, not picked at random as the law requires. In Monroe and Fairfield counties, the 3 percent hand recounts yielded totals that diverged from the machine counts—but officials did not then perform a hand recount of all the ballots, as the law requires. In Washington and Lucas counties, ballots were marked or altered to ensure that the hand recount would equal the machine count. In Ashland, Portage and Coshocton counties, ballots were improperly unsealed or stored. Belmont County "hired an independent programmer ('at great expense') to reprogram the counting machines so that they would only count votes for President during the recount." Finally, Democratic and Green party observers were denied access to absentee, or provisional, ballots or were not allowed to monitor the recount process in Summit, Huron, Putnam, Allen, Holmes, Mahoning, Licking, Stark, Medina, Warren and Morgan counties. Thus was Ohio's hand recount demonstrably subverted by Bush/Cheney cadres all throughout the state, whether acting on their own or under orders from Columbus or the White House.

I have thus far noted only those transgressions that would make for "good TV"—that is, wrongs so stark that you could get the gist of any of them in seven seconds from Wolf Blitzer or Brit Hume (neither of whom mentioned any of them). The committee also found more complicated crimes and improprieties. For example, Blackwell arranged Ohio's post-election schedule so as to leave no time for proper recounts.[39] He also made the rules on provisional ballots vague enough that Bush/Cheney's poll workers might discard them on a whim.[40] There are also certain troubling issues raised implicitly by the report—such as, most importantly, the *cost* of all that mischief in Ohio. How did Bush & Co. pay for it? (Like Nixon's 1972 campaign, the regime's Ohio victory required immense amounts of laundered cash. This fact has come to light through the "Coingate" scandal that has, understandably, preoccupied Ohio's press since it started breaking in the spring of 2005, while the national press has all but totally ignored it.) Operations like the Texas Strike Force don't come cheap—as Watergate taught many of us once upon a time. In fact, as of this writing, Blackwell has not filed a compliance report with the Government Services Administration, which had given him $41 million to enforce the Help America Vote Act (HAVA) in Ohio. In other words, the secretary of state has not accounted for that funding, which he clearly spent not for the good of the electorate but on wholly partisan devices, tactics, litigators.[41] Beyond its copious evidence of multiple official crimes and improprieties, the report would also help shed further light on certain other wrongs, if any members of the national press would deign to give it an objective reading.

Because the preponderance of evidence is damning on its face and the report presents it lucidly, the press's silence cannot be explained away as simple journalistic laziness or lack of pertinent expertise. There's no arguing, in other words, that the Ohio story is *too complicated* for the news. That rationale has often been deployed to justify the media's insufficient coverage of such whopping scandals as the savings-and-loan meltdown in the eighties, or the current "campaign finance system" (an end-less giant kickback from both parties to the media themselves). Although it is indeed complex, the story here is not so "compli-cated" as to justify the press's all-but-total blackout. One might just as credibly argue that Ohio's presidential race was simply overshadowed by the "more important" news in early January: the tsunami. Such an argument would be ridiculous. Cata-clysmic the tsunami surely was, but in this country there could be no story, foreign or domestic, more momentous than the subversion of a national election. (Even during the tsunami of tsunami news, there was ample coverage of Alberto Gonzales's pending confirmation as attorney general.) The media's post-election non-performance was the stuff of satire, or nightmare. It is, in any case, amazing that the press in the United States went on and on about the vote fraud in Ukraine while saying nothing of the vote fraud here at home.

So pointed was the silence that it seemed to indicate an insti-tutional *refusal* to go near the story. The press displayed not mere indifference but a certain blithe contempt for the subject. This animus came clear soon after November 2, in a spate of caustic articles throughout the press, dismissing all concerns about the honesty of the election as crazed "speculation": "In a campaign year rife with conspiracies, it's no surprise that post-election theories have started popping up. After all, who didn't gossip about Bush's peculiar jacket bulge during the first de-bate?" So chuckled the *Baltimore Sun* on November 5, in a piece headlined "Election paranoia surfaces; Conspiracy theorists call results rigged" (p. C1). Such "theorists" were laughed off as loony-birds indigenous to cyberspace. "Internet Buzz on Vote Fraud Is Dismissed," proclaimed the *Boston Globe* on November 10 (F1).[42] "Latest Conspiracy Theory—Kerry Won—Hits the

Ether," the *Washington Post* laughed on November 11 (p. A2), and that day's *San Francisco Chronicle* also found humor in the din of groundless "Web rants."[43] In Florida, the *Chronicle* assured its readers, things went fine; and in Ohio things went fine, and things were fine all over. "Accusations of widespread organized voting fraud elsewhere in the country similarly wilt under scrutiny" (p. A4). And yet it was the *New York Times* that weighed in with the most derisive coverage, its front-page story—"Vote Fraud Theories, Spread by Blogs, Are Quickly Buried"—making mock not only of the "post-election theorizing" but of cyberspace itself, the *fons et origo*, according to the *Times*, of all such loony tunes. "The e-mail messages and Web postings had all the twitchy cloak-and-dagger thrust of a Hollywood blockbuster," the piece began, and thus went on for 1,300 words about "the online market of dark ideas," "the Web log hysteria" and "the blog-to-e-mail-to-blog continuum" with its "breathless cycle of hey-check-this-out." That mammoth "rumor mill" had let all sorts of wacky amateurs becloud the public sphere with their "conspiracy theories," "faulty analyses" and other wishful fantasies that "experts were soon able to debunk," the *Times* declared—without ever making clear exactly what those "theories" were, how they were debunked or who exactly had debunked them.

Such articles themselves require debunking. For one thing, the experts quoted as apparently refuting all such "theories" were in fact misquoted, their quite specific caveats distorted into seeming blanket dismissals of all charges of electoral fraud. "'There are people on Earth who claim they were abducted by aliens and had surgery performed on them on spaceships,' said Michael I. Shamos, a professor at Carnegie Mellon University who has studied electronic voting systems for more than 20 years."[44] Thus the *Baltimore Sun* used Shamos's words to cast all doubters as irrational, when he had noted only that he had not yet seen evidence of any tampering with the electronic voting machines. As he noted in a later interview, he *had* seen evidence of other forms of fraud. The "deliberate intimidation of poor and Democratic voters" had appalled him.[45] While he saw no *evidence* of any tampering with the machines, moreover, Shamos did not dismiss the notion of such tampering as paranoid delusion. However, such subtleties did not befit the *Sun's* satiric project. The *San Francisco Chronicle* dealt likewise with its expert witnesses. Although quoted as denying that any fraud had taken place, Will Doherty, executive director of verifiedvoting.org, had spoken only of the electronic voting machines—which, he tried to tell the *Chronicle*, posed "very significant problems" on Election Day. His point was that, from what he knew, those problems per se had not thrown the race to Bush; and yet the *Chronicle* appeared to have him saying that there were no problems at all on Election Day. "The context was not as clear as I would have liked," he said later.[46]

The *Chronicle* also skewed the comments of Thomas Patterson, professor at Harvard's Kennedy School of Government. The paper had him saying, with apparent nonchalance, that the problems in Ohio were "par for elections. If we held a contest where we had to start 500,000 automobiles around the country on a cold morning and have them all start . . . it wouldn't happen."[47] By itself, the statement sounds complacent—whereas Patterson had been *deploring* the condition of U.S. electoral democracy, which, he tried to tell the *Chronicle*, had been dysfunctional for quite some time. "That context was lost in the newspaper story," said Patterson.[48]

The falseness of these articles soon became apparent (if only to attentive readers) when the same press that had loudly jeered those "theories" of electoral fraud now quietly confirmed them. On December 7, the *Baltimore Sun* ran "Silencing the Vote," David Lytel's sober op-ed on the many glaring problems in Ohio and the failure of the press (and leading Democrats) to deal with them; on December 10, the same page ran "Ohio Fight Isn't Over," Jules Witcover's op-ed about the Conyers inquiry. On January 2, Witcover followed up with a long article on the electoral problems nationwide.[49] All this after the *Sun* had, on November 4, deemed such probing just as foolish as the "gossip about Bush's peculiar jacket bulge during the first debate." On December 1, the *Boston Globe*—which had played the "Internet buzz" for laughs—ran "Voting Errors Tallied Nationwide," an excellent front-page overview, and, on December 24, "One Person, One Vote," a punchy editorial on the "thousands" of electoral irregularities and the need for full inquiry into every one of them. And the *San Francisco Chronicle* explicitly reversed itself. "If enough of us don't trust the election system, the count starts to lose its meaning—and our democracy is in jeopardy," wrote Dick Rogers, the *Chronicle*'s ombudsman, in an op-ed on December 9, pledging that the paper would henceforth pay close attention to the issue on both the state and national levels.[50] Rogers hailed Wyatt Buchanan's recent coverage of electoral anomalies in Florida; and the *Chronicle* stuck with the story for at least the next few months, covering the peculiar glitches that beset some state referendums, and, on February 27, 2005, the national "spoilage" problem, covered vividly in Vicki Haddock's story, "The Vote You Cast May Not Be Tallied: 1 out of 100 Shown Uncounted in 2004" (C1).[51]

That tardy wave of articles was motivated by the pleas and threats of countless angry readers, as Rogers noted (grumpily) in his op-ed. It was, in other words, *not* driven by a journalistic hunger for the truth, or for a scoop; for if it had been based on such professional initiative, that late coverage surely would have blossomed into an immense, persistent national story. Instead it petered out into a minor spate of local stories. With very few exceptions, the national media played the issue down—even, or especially, at that moment when Ohio's electoral vote was challenged by that knot of diehard Democrats. (The *Sun*, moreover, dropped the subject after the inauguration, running a vituperative op-ed—"Memo to Kerry: The Election Is Over, and You Lost"—against the Democrats' "conspiracy theories," and then consistently ignoring the whole issue of the use of paperless machines in Maryland.)[52] The *Washington Post* was mute throughout the crisis, although it did run William Raspberry's strong op-ed column—"What Happened in Ohio"—on January 10. (The paper *did* "report" that the exit polls used on Election Day were somehow flawed.)[53] The *New York Times*'s non-response was more mysterious. On the one hand, the *Times* continued Adam Cohen's cogent series of unsigned editorials, "Making Votes Count," which has been calling clearly for electoral reform since January 2004. But while the paper's institutional position has been unimpeachable, its *coverage* of the problem has been hard to find. It's as if the *Times* editors don't read what the *Times* reporters write, and vice versa. From mid-November to April 1, the *Times* turned out some twenty pieces that pertained to the election. None of them addressed the crisis, although some of them referred in passing to the qualms of certain Democrats. Throughout those months, the paper did run two brief articles about the furor in Ohio, both from the Associated Press, and neither of them important.

Meanwhile, the story kept unfolding, with further revelations coming from court cases, academic studies, criminal investigations and independent research nationwide: findings that might just as well have been revealed on Mars, for all the news they made here in the onetime greatest of democracies on Planet Earth. Once Bush was re-inaugurated the story was officially kaput. By March it elicited the same knee-jerk ridicule that had prevailed back in November—but only in those rare moments when somebody dared to bring it up. "Also tonight," CNN's Lou Dobbs deadpanned ironically on March 8, "Teresa Heinz Kerry still can't accept certain reality. She suggests the presidential election may have been rigged!"[54] On April 3, a fourth man was indicted in New Hampshire for an Election Day phone-jamming drive that blocked the Democrats' get-out-the-vote campaigns in Manchester, Claremont, Rochester and Nashua. The Associated Press reported the indictment, as did the *Manchester Union Leader*, the *Spokesman-Review* in Spokane, Washington (where the suspect lived) and a website called Boston. com. (Two of the man's associates had been convicted. The fourth—James Tobin, regional director of the National Republican Senatorial Campaign Committee—pleaded innocent. In August of 2005, AP reported that the RNC was paying Tobin's legal bills, which had so far added up to $722,000, for the services of Williams & Connelly, a leading firm in Washington, D.C. The news broke just days after RNC chair Ken Mehlman had announced a "zero-tolerance policy" on dirty tricks of every kind.)[55] And there were other, larger stories that were buried even deeper by the press. While there had been broad coverage of the claim that all these exit polls were somehow wrong, there were almost no reports on the extreme unlikelihood that such a thing could happen. On March 31, 2005, a study came out from U.S. Count Votes computing that the odds against such an enormous error were 959,000 to one. The story was reported in the *Akron Beacon-Journal* on April 1, and that was it. Asked for a response by Stephen Dyer of the *Akron Beacon-Journal*, Carlo LoParo, Kenneth Blackwell's spokesman, answered, "What are you going to do except laugh at it?"[56]

For all the evidence crammed into it, the Conyers Report is still necessarily incomplete, so many and so varied were the wrongs done in Ohio. On the one hand, the regime's operatives, or persons very eager to assist them, committed outright crimes reminiscent of Watergate and the CIA's notorious shenanigans in "hot spots" like Teheran and Guatemala City—black-bag operations pure and simple, and yet the subject of no coverage, or slight and muted coverage, by the press.

Sometime on the night of Friday, July 2, or in the wee hours of that Saturday, persons unknown somehow stole into the offices of Burges and Burges, an Akron consulting firm employed by the Ohio Democratic Party. There were no signs of forced entry. The only items taken were two computers—one belonging to the firm and one belonging to Rep. Sherrod Brown, a Democratic congressman whose district includes Summit County and who rents an office in the company's suite at 520 South Main Street. There was, on both machines, much sensitive campaign-related information. The perpetrators left no fingerprints. The police report was filed on Saturday. No one contacted the press.[57]

Some three months later, there was a very similar break-in at the Lucas County Democratic Headquarters at 1817 Madison Avenue in Toledo. Sometime between 11 P.M. on Monday, October 11 and 7 A.M. on Tuesday, October 12, there was another choosy burglary—this one reported by the *Toledo Blade*. Bypassing several radios, a microwave, a TV and the petty cash box, the thieves made off with only three computers (out of many). "One of the computers belonged to office manager Barbara Koonce, who was responsible for names and addresses of hundreds of party members, volunteers, and candidates, a master schedule for all candidates' events, and financial information" as well as "a list of registered Democrats—information that had been analyzed as part of the Democrats' campaign strategy." ("So for example, if I wanted to target African-American voters in Ward 10 now, I no longer have that list," Koonce said.) "Also taken was a laptop belonging to Roger Sanders, a volunteer attorney from Texas working with the Victory 2004 campaign in space that was leased by the Kerry/Edwards presidential campaign." Sanders was helping to arrange the placement of attorneys at polling sites throughout the county on Election Day. "Mr. Sanders had been matching as many as 212 local and out-of-town attorneys to specific polling stations November 2. That information was stolen, he said, as were e-mails discussing strategies for counter-attacking subtle measures that could turn voters away from the polls." (In the first week of July 2005, there were two more break-ins at Democratic offices).[58]

Although one perpetrator left some fingerprints, the authorities were disinclined to look too deeply into the affair. "'It's probably a burglary, maybe a breaking and entering,' Lucas County Prosecutor Julia Bates said yesterday," the *Toledo Blade* reported on October 14. "Officials of both the FBI and the U.S. Attorneys Office agreed, saying they will monitor the situation but do not believe a federal crime was committed."[59]

On the other hand, there was also further evidence of crimes much less dramatic, but evidently quite effective nonetheless—

and probably not unrelated to the theft of some of those computers. Denise Shull, a New Yorker born and raised in Akron (and, professionally, a neuropsychologist), returned to her hometown to help the Kerry ticket through the final week of the campaign.[60] Shull worked in the phone bank at the Summit County Democratic headquarters, calling likely Kerry voters to determine which of them were most intent on coming out to vote for him on Election Day. She and ten other volunteers combed through their lists repeatedly, crossing off the names of all who might seem even slightly hesitant, or otherwise unlikely, to cast their ballots on November 2. After finishing that process, the team members collectively devised a master list—known as the pink list—of all the diehard Kerry voters in the county.

On Election Day, Shull served as a poll-checker, covering four precincts (6D, 6E, 6F and 7D) in northwest Cuyahoga Falls. Her job was to determine the absolute vote count for her district—a task entailing two careful comparisons of her "pink list" with the precincts' respective lists of all registered voters. Here is how the process was to work. At 11:00 A.M. and 4:00 P.M. on Election Day, the poll judges in each precinct are required by law to post, on the walls of the precinct station, a comprehensive list of all the precinct's registered voters, with a notation by each name, indicating whether or not that citizen has voted. The poll-checker for each party then studies that big list, to see which of their most devoted people have come out and cast their ballots yet, and which ones haven't. The poll-checker then follows up by calling those who have not voted, to remind that person to come out today, ask if that person needs a ride, and then provide whatever help the voter may require.

At 11:00 A.M., Shull cross-referenced the names on her pink list with the names now posted on the wall—and found that a considerable number of them, one or two out of every ten, *were not on the master list of registered voters.* Of all the other names on her list, most did vote as promised, but some 10 percent to 20 percent of them officially did not exist as registered voters, even though they were ardent Democrats, many of them long-time voters in that area.

Shull eagerly awaited the 4:00 update of the precincts' lists, thinking that, perhaps, those missing names might by then have been added. But a few minutes prior to that exercise, the Kerry headquarters in Columbus called off its poll-checkers. Kerry was by now so far ahead of Bush that there seemed to be no need for that second exercise, and now there was apparently a greater need for volunteers at many of those badly over-crowded polling sites in Democratic areas across the state, as it was raining hard, the lines were long and people were inclined to call it quits. Those poll-checkers who were waiting to cross-reference their pink lists a second time were therefore urged to hurry over to the most chaotic sites, to bolster the morale of all those would-be voters who were getting drenched and losing heart.

However, one of Shull's precincts happened to post early: at 3:40, before the call came from Columbus, and so she had a chance to cross-reference the lists in that one place. And there she saw that none of the missing names had been restored to the precinct's now-updated master list. In short, there had been some stealthy means of purging from the rolls the names of every ninth or tenth registered Democrat. On showing up to vote, those thus eliminated would simply have been told that they weren't registered and that they should call this or that phone number (which was busy) or that they should cast a provisional ballot (which was then likely to be thrown away) or that they should go somewhere else instead (where they would then be sent elsewhere or back to the initial precinct).

As she meditated on her strange discovery, Shull thought back to her first experiences earlier that day, when, at 9:20 A.M., she had started out as a pro-Kerry cheerleader, or greeter, standing out in front of a polling site, at a distance of 100 feet (as the law required). As soon as she took up her position, a brawny Bush supporter loomed at her from the doorway of the polling place, screaming at her to remove herself, as, he said, she was not standing far enough away; and then he came at her. Shull approached a passing cop, and the man turned tail and hustled back into his lair.

Shull crossed the street, so as to separate herself still further from the site, and held her Kerry sign high. A young woman, about 30, walked past Shull on her way to vote: "Yay Kerry!" she called to Shull, stepped into the polling place—and then stepped right back out again. Shull asked what had happened. "They said my name wasn't on the list," she said, adding that she had voted with no trouble in the prior two elections and was still living at the same address. They had simply told her that she couldn't vote there and gave her a phone number. Shull told her to go back and ask for a provisional ballot, which the young woman did, and voted that way, for whatever it was worth.

Shull later pondered that episode, and realized that it was more significant than she had thought at first. She was even more convinced that there was something very wrong after she talked it over with some fellow Democratic volunteers: Mary Jo and Chuck Hanlon, both from Akron, and Gary Brown, a lawyer from Washington, D.C. All three had had a very similar experience at 11:00 A.M. on that Election Day. Somehow the system was automatically eliminating something like a tenth or

more of the would-be Kerry voters in that county—a literal dec-
imation of the Kerry vote, which would be noticeable only to
those poll-checkers who did not stray from their initial posts,
and who were paying close attention. (Throughout the day,
Shull noted, the Republicans kept shifting different people in
and out of those positions.)

Finally, the official numbers seemed a bit peculiar—or rather,
they made perfect sense, in light of what Shull and her friends
had seen. (They still have their pink lists intact, if anyone is interested in calling them, to see what they went through that
day.) Kerry won Summit County by 58 percent—a lower figure
than one might expect from a heavily Democratic area where
the turnout had been very high. In Stark County, just south of
Summit, the results were also a surprise. There, Kerry won by
only 51 percent—although Stark (where Canton and North
Canton are located) had lost more jobs than any other county in
Ohio during Bush's first term.[61] Whatever the official tally, it
was clearly rigged against the Democrats, as the Conyers Report
makes eminently clear, and as Denise Shull's experience, and
those late-night burglaries in Democratic offices, would appear
to reconfirm.

Concerning the election of 2004, the press's readiness to
spike all troubling news—or "laugh at it"—has had precisely the
destructive impact that the Framers feared for this republic,
should it ever lose a free and independent press. The media's
consensus that Bush won re-election fair and square has daunted
most of those Americans who have good reason not to buy it,
but who feel defeated by that immense complacent silence. Certainly the leaders of the Democratic Party were intimidated by
the press's rush to call the fight for Bush. It was the press's
eagerness for "closure," John Conyers told me, notwithstanding

the abundance of unanswered questions (and uncounted votes), that inclined the Democrats to hush the matter up. "Kerry has conceded the election, so what is there to pursue?" their thinking went, as they could sense the media's antipathy to any partisan complaint.[62] That animus appears to have been Kerry's major reason for conceding so abruptly on November 3. According to a member of John Edwards's family, who was present when the call came in, Kerry told his running mate—who urged Kerry to delay—that they must wait no longer to concede: "If we don't concede now," he told Edwards, "they'll call us 'sore losers.'" ("*So what?*" Edwards snapped.) "They" meant not only the Republicans, of course, but the Republicans as seconded, their mockery amplified, by the press: as in 2000, when the Bush campaign's "Sore Loserman"—a snide play on "Gore-Lieberman"—had resonated keenly through the din of editorials commanding Al Gore to give in. And so Kerry folded, figuring that otherwise the "liberal media" would staunchly parrot Bush & Co.'s smears, which would drown out whatever he or any other Democrat might say.

For its part, the press apparently believed, or has at least purported to believe, that it was following *Kerry's* lead, and that it would surely have investigated the election without fear or favor, hang the consequences, if the candidate had even hinted at foul play. That rationale is doubly wrong. First of all, for months before Election Day, the media were already either paying no attention to the copious and flagrant evidence of impropriety by the Republicans, or piously pretending to discern transgressions "on both sides." From the evening of Election Day, moreover, there was a startling lack of curiosity or even interest among journalists, despite the sudden, unexpected swerve of slight majorities into the Republican column, at the eleventh hour, and only in key swing states. Bush/Cheney had, moreover, stolen the election of 2000. And the Bushes' close relations with Diebold and ES&S, the largest manufacturers of the electronic voting machines—used throughout Florida and in some 30 other states—had been on the public record for at least two years. The plan to steal the vote had even been admitted openly by top Republicans themselves. In August of 2003, Wally O'Dell, the CEO of Diebold and a major donor to the Bush campaign, sent out an invitation to 100 wealthy fellow partisans, inviting them to a Bush/Cheney fundraiser at his home in suburban Canton, Ohio: "I am committed to helping Ohio deliver its electoral votes to the president next year," he promised his guests.[63] In the summer of 2003, Rep. Peter King (R-NY), seemingly a tad inebriated at some function on the White House lawn, was interviewed by Alexandra Pelosi for her film *Diary of a Political Tourist.* "It's already over. The election's over. We won," King boozily exulted.[64] When asked, by Pelosi, how he knew that Bush would win, he answered. "It's all over but the counting. And we'll take care of the counting." Despite all that and much more, the press seemed not to bat a single eye at the anomalous victory. On TV in particular, there was no evident surprise but a peculiar air of palpable relief, the telejournalists settling back to jabber knowingly for days about the reasons *why* so many voters chose Bush/Cheney.

Aside from its untruth, moreover, the press's blithe assurance that it would surely have investigated the election if only Kerry had complained about it first reveals a serious civic misconception. The First Amendment guarantees the freedom of the press in order to keep the people well informed as to the government's compliance with their will. Ours was conceived, and once upon a time did really function, as an *open* government, with the newspapers—however faulty—serving as the people's primary means of political awareness, and therefore as a necessary brake on tyranny. "If a nation expects to be ignorant and free, in a state of civilization, it expects what never was and never will be." That much-quoted line of Thomas Jefferson's expresses the profound belief in mass enlightenment that motivated him throughout his public life and that the other Framers shared. It was the ideal of an educated citizenry that inspired them not just to guarantee the freedom of the press but also to realize it, by providing newspapers (three in every state) with printing subsidies; by setting up a Post Office equipped to reach the furthest corners of the nation and dedicated mainly to the circulation of newspapers (the cost of postage minimal);[65] and by limiting the term of copyright so as to make all writings generally available as soon as possible.

Such measures should remind us that the press, in this Republic, was conceived as free specifically, and only, to inform the people. The Framers certainly did not require the press to strive for "balance" in its treatment of the major parties—which did not exist, of course, when they wrote the Constitution, and which possess no rights under that document. The shibboleth of "balance"—a rightist imposition on the press, as David Brock explains—has actually absolved reporters from their civic obligation to inform the people, as "balanced" journalists are those who never dare to broach a topic or investigate a problem until "the Democrats" or "the Republicans" have brought it up and thereby *cleared it* for the news. Thus "balance" blinds the press to any problem on which both sides have decided to agree: "free trade," for example, or the U.S. military budget, or, until it was too late, the Bush administration's education policy. And yet "balance" has compelled the press to do far worse than merely to avoid discussion of those policies that have overt bipartisan support. Obligated to ignore whatever the Republicans-and-Democrats won't mention, the press has shied away completely from those even graver problems that both parties' leaders, whether from perfidy or denial, cannot or will not acknowledge or perceive. Such a problem, for example, is the rising theocratic danger to American democracy itself—a threat now posed *by* the Republicans-and-Democrats, and one that we, the people, have a right to know about, but which the press continues to avoid, despite the looming risks both to itself and all the rest of us, Republicans and Democrats included.

The press's silence on the mysteries of the last election is the best possible example of the Fourth Estate's enormous civic failure. Whether Kerry had the right to pack it in before the votes were counted is a question for the people to decide. Even if he did possess that right, he was no more the final arbiter of the election's soundness than was Bush or Cheney, or Tom Brokaw, or Arthur Sulzberger, Jr., or Silvio Berlusconi, or Tom DeLay, or Ahmed Chalabi. Whatever Kerry's handlers thought they knew about the voters of Ohio (or of Florida, Arizona, North Carolina, Texas or Tennessee), by the morning of November 3 it was too soon to make the call that Bush had won. The press was obligated, moreover, to respect neither Kerry's judgment nor Bush & Co.'s mere reassertion of their power. Its mandate is to respect—and even attempt to ascertain—the people's choice; and that could be known only through a free and fair election, which, demonstrably, had not occurred.

3.

The Requisite
Fanaticism

It was not out of their immense respect for Kerry's judgment that U.S. journalists okayed the last election. As he himself could see too well, the press certainly would not have honored his decision to stay in the fight but would have hammered him just as it hammered Al Gore four years earlier, pompously advising him to face "reality" and not precipitate a "crisis." The press surely would have treated his refusal to concede just as negatively as it treated Conyers's efforts, the Democratic challenge to the electoral vote in Ohio and every subsequent attempt to question even the unlikeliest official numbers. In short, the press has treated the whole subject of electoral fraud exactly as the Bush Republicans have treated it. Although it was undoubtedly effective in suppressing frank discussion of Bush/Cheney's "victory," the press's scattered mockery of the "post-election theorizing" on the Web was but an echo, or anticipation, of the mighty propaganda chorus on the right. It was the Republicans who, overtly or directly, pushed the press to ridicule whatever questions had or might come up; and they themselves did a stupendous job at such dismissal, vigilantly shouting down and ruling out and laughing off all inconvenient facts or threatening inferences.

The propagandists of the right are expert at the denigration of unpleasant truths—or rather, at denigrating anyone who tries to tell such truths. This tactic is as old as tyranny itself, nor has it only figured on the right, as any thorough history of communism will make clear. In U.S. history, however, such paranoid *ad hominem* (or *feminam*) denunciation has been, by and large, a right-authoritarian specialty, from the ordeal of Anne Hutchinson through the anti-French hysteria in 1798, to the later crusades against anarchists, communists and, these days, Muslims, "terrorists," gays and liberals. (The absolute distinction between "left" and "right" must baffle any careful analyst of such paranoid extremism, which is in love with, and defines itself by reference to, the very "evil" that it keeps attacking. Thus ultra-rightist luminaries Paul Weyrich and Grover Norquist, for example, laud the Bolsheviks, whom they admire not only for their tactical acuity but for their anti-democratic zeal.)[1] But while it is an ancient reflex in this nation, the impulse to kill the messenger (or just to mutilate him on the green) has now become the right's defining feature, not only in its rhetoric but even in its ideology. The right, in other words, does not answer criticism or reply to arguments. It only seeks to *mute the enemy*—an endless project without which the Bush Republicans could not exist. This repressive bent became dominant just after Reagan/Bush, with the eight-year drive to demonize Bill Clinton, followed by the reign of Bush the Younger. It seems to represent the dark convergence of complementary trends: the corporate consolidation of the media, which brought the destruction of news and the ascendance of hate radio, and the rise of theocratic activism, with its tendency to see all those not firmly on its side as tools of Satan.

The soldiers of the right are dedicated to continual annihilation of all other points of view: a mission that requires a lot of repetitious, fervent lying, half-believed—or at once believed and not believed—by those committed to it. The primary tactic and the major symptom of this paranoid fixation is the vehement portrayal of truth as "lies," fact as "fantasy," solid case as "conspiracy theory." Such vehemence betrays a mind deeply divided between cynicism and fanaticism—the sort of mind that gravitates toward hate propaganda.

This double-mindedness is not called into play in the propagandists' casual one-time derision of specific inconvenient notions. After Bush's first debate with Kerry on October 1, 2004, the Internet was all abuzz with speculation as to what had caused the strange—and unmistakable—rectangular protuberance on the back of Bush's suit jacket. "Bush's aides tried to laugh off the controversy, with one official joking about 'little green men on the grassy knoll,'"[2] Mike Allen reported in the *Washington Post*. The hump, many bloggers speculated, indicated that the president had been fitted with a wireless receiver, allowing his propaganda team to feed him phrases if and when he should fall silent or become more incoherent than usual.

Bush campaign spokesman Scott Stanzel, during a Web chat on washingtonpost.com, was asked if Bush wore "any kind of electronic device on his back during the first debate that allowed him to receive information."

"Senator Kerry? Is that you?," Stanzel typed back. "I think you've been spending a little too much time on conspiracy Web sites. Did you hear the one about Elvis moderating tonight's debate?"[3]

Such comedy was no doubt wholly tactical. Bush *had* been wearing an "electronic device . . . that allowed him to receive information." (The ploy explains that startling moment when, although no one had interrupted him, the president snapped, "Let me finish!") The *New York Times* verified the story, and was set to run it just before November 2, but then abruptly spiked it, in order to *suppress* the controversy prior to Election Day. The decision was especially remarkable, considering that both *Salon* and *Mother Jones* had already reported on the president's "device."[4] The *Times* subsequently mocked the controversy as delusional, just as Bush's flacks had done. Matt Bai invoked the episode derisively, in a column on "political conspiracists": "A rumor that the president somehow cheated in the televised debates—was that a wire under his jacket? was he listening to Karl Rove on a microscopic earpiece?—flies across the Internet and takes hold in dark corners of the public imagination."[5] But it took no special propaganda effort to dismiss the controversy, which barely resonated in the off-line press. The necessary ridicule was therefore brief and business-like, requiring no protracted counter-drive or angry histrionics.

Of course, such wholly cynical derision has long been commonplace in politics, especially at its most corrupt. When he was still vice president, for example, Bush Sr. used it in his efforts to portray himself as "out of the loop" on Iran/contra. "You know this stuff about my running a secret war?" he cracked in 1986. "It's crazy. Absolutely nuts! I hope you all know that."[6] When such labored protests failed to obfuscate the fact of his neck-deep involvement in the plot, he shifted from displays of scoffing incredulity to bursts of outrage, mainly at the press, which he accused of persecution. That pretense at high dudgeon reinvigorated Poppy's faltering presidential run in January 1988, when he attacked Dan Rather for bringing up the scandal in an interview on *CBS Evening News*. (That counter-blast—which was Dubya's idea—had been planned carefully before the fact.)[7] And yet by 1992, his incessant self-defense against the "big witch-hunt" had turned off both the public and the press.[8] "People are tired of this, and I think they know I've told the truth," he claimed, as Clinton's lead kept widening and editorials turned harsh: "The burden has long since shifted to Mr. Bush to prove his difficult-to-believe assertions of ignorance," proclaimed the *New York Times* on October 19, 1992.[9] Bush only fortified the case against himself when, on Christmas Eve, he issued presidential pardons to his co-conspirators in the affair, thereby defying Lawrence Walsh, the independent counsel, and some 59 percent of the American people, who had registered their disapproval of such pardons. (With a straight face, Bush then insisted at a press conference that "no impartial person has seriously suggested that my own role in this matter is legally questionable.")[10]

This long denial was a failure, not just because the evidence was voluminous and Walsh relentless but also because Bush Sr. lacked the requisite fanaticism. He could not muster the paranoid conviction that is crucial to all deadly mass endeavors, from purveying Big Lies to prosecuting unjust wars to stealing national elections. It is a bewildering mentality; for it delights in melodrama—the absolute conflict of total opposites—and yet it is also deeply split against itself. Although awed by that mentality and always quick to serve it (he went all out for Nixon), Bush I does not exemplify it, and so may help us understand it.

Bush the Elder did not see his enemies as demons and himself as innocent—or rather, did not half-believe in his own innocence. He saw his adversaries as inferiors, and therefore as human beings: insolent, impertinent and inconvenient little people, not to be respected, much less feared. Nor, evidently, did he see himself, or need to see himself, as a paragon of moral rectitude. His lies were not impassioned, although he often became exasperated if the questioners would not back off. He did not lie with any special fury, through gritted teeth or with a livid smile, but in the offhand, lightly sneering way that signifies impunity. His lying was so casual or so facile as to be transparent, and was therefore unconvincing, as it was all too redolent of his protective wealth, exclusive breeding and first-class instruction in the ways of the "intelligence community."

Although Bush Sr. was always very good at going for the jugular, he did so not because he wanted to annihilate the Other and so cleanse the world of evil, but because he wanted not to seem to be a wimp. By contrast, the soldiers serving Bush & Co.—and they include the president himself—perceive their enemies as "evil ones": subhuman beings, supernatural agents and/or wicked people working for or through such agents. Their dissidence, or non-cooperation, indicates not reasonable disagreement (there being no such thing) nor even any of the baser motives, such as an appetite for power or wealth or glory. Those who do not look like us, who will not think and act along with us, who cannot or will not believe in us, are evil. Those, in short, who *are not "us"* are evil, and vice versa: evil is what is not "us," for We can only tolerate ourselves.

This is all pretty vague, of course—and necessarily so, for that "evil," finally, is no essence, quality or spirit separate from the soldier looking for it, firing at it, dreaming of it. It is not *out there* at all, an independent cosmic force inhabiting and animating others' minds or bodies. To put it bluntly: "It" is not. Such evil is within the mind—or, as Bush would say, the heart—of the relentless soldier who wants nothing other than to rout it out, and who therefore never can stop hunting for it. That soldier is forever stalking evil, not because it's always out there, somewhere, everywhere around him, but because it's always still inside him, always with him, *is* the rage with which he chases after it. The soldier is not innocent. And because he senses his own culpability, the only way he can regard himself as "good" is to stay on the attack against those "evil ones" alleged to be attacking "us" out of their boundless and gratuitous malevolence. There is probably no place on earth where "they" are not attacking "us," "they" being Muslims, Christians, Jews, Hindus or whatever other Other may apparently personify the rage within.

Although the issue here may seem abstract, that suicidal animus has great political utility and serves a vital propaganda function. It explains the fierce effectiveness with which Bush/ Cheney, and the theocratic movement backing them, stole the White House in 2004. Unless we recognize the nature of that drive and its important place in right-wing religious ideology, we will be powerless to contend with it and thereby to preserve—or one day realize—American democracy.

An explication of the animus may start with a last look back at George Bush, Sr., whose efforts to shut down all talk about his role in Iran/contra failed, in part, because he lacked the necessary raging half-belief in his own innocence. Without that delusory zeal, the Big Lie will soon fall flat; for without that passion the Big Liar will stumble, say too much, contradict himself and otherwise intensify the very furor he's trying to hush. Without that zeal, moreover, his performance will not agitate those need-

ing to believe in his (and their own) innocence, and in the vile-
ness of his (and their) tormentors. In short, his pique won't be
contagious, and his hyper-sympathizers will be few. In denying
his key role in Iran/contra, Bush Sr. came across not as a perse-
cuted patriot—as Oliver North had done so memorably (a passion that Mel Gibson ought to dramatize, playing the righteous
North himself)—but as a noble mightily annoyed that anyone
would dare to call him to account. Bush the Elder could only
become nettled; he was too preppy, through and through, to
flash and smolder as a winning pseudo-populist must do.

While the elder Bush's prissy irritation could not arouse the
multitudes of the resentful, his creature Clarence Thomas
fought the truth about himself with stunning force, and so became a pillar of—and top crusader for—the Christo-fascist
right. (He was, of course, helped immeasurably by the Republicans, who worked wonders in suppressing further evidence
against him.) Charged with lewd behavior toward Anita Hill,
Thomas came out all on fire, and, as of this writing, has never
cooled. He called the hearing "a travesty," "disgusting." "This
hearing should never occur in America."[11] "This is a circus. It is
a national disgrace."[12] Hill's testimony was "sleaze," "dirt," "this
gossip and these lies," "scurrilous, uncorroborated allegations,"
"uncorroborated, scurrilous lies and allegations," "this nonsense, this garbage, trash that you siphoned out of the sewers
against me," etc. "Today is not a day that, in my opinion, is high
among the days in our country [*sic*]. This is a travesty." It was,
indeed, "a sad day."[13]

when the U.S. Senate can be used by interest groups, and hatemon-
gers, and people who are interested in digging up dirt to destroy
other people and who will stop at no tactics, when they can use our

great political institutions for their political ends, we have gone far beyond McCarthyism. This is far more dangerous than McCarthyism. At least McCarthy was elected.[14]

This was not the doing of Anita Hill, the judge suggested, but of a vast left-wing conspiracy that had merely used her as a pawn in their enormous plot against him—the paranoid perception that was stressed repeatedly by all of Thomas's co-propagandists. At first the judge appeared to see the whole proceeding as a racist enterprise, himself as scapegoated for being an independent-minded African-American. "From my standpoint, as a black American," he famously charged in his opening remarks,

> it is a high-tech lynching for uppity blacks who in any way deign [sic] to think for themselves, to do for themselves, to have different ideas, and it is a message that, unless you kowtow to an old order, this is what will happen to you, you will be lynched, destroyed, caricatured by a committee of the US Senate, rather than hung from a tree.[15]

It was a vivid metaphor, no less effective for its staggering hypocrisy. Black men had been strung up, and much worse, for alleged violations of the wives and daughters of their white superiors, not for sexually harassing black subordinates—and not, of course, for holding ultra-rightist views. If anybody at that hearing represented the "old order" of the lynch-mob-friendly South, it was those supporting Clarence Thomas's appointment; ex-Dixiecrat Strom Thurmond was among the judge's champions on the committee. Thomas was, and still is, a hero on the U.S. racist right, not least because of his blunt animus against affirmative action (although that policy had helped make his career). To those who knew his politics, therefore, it was a shock to see him play the race card right off the bat, and in such graphic terms.

Although the stance was certainly improper, we should not write it off as merely cynical, for that pathetic self-portrayal, whatever Thomas's own views on civil rights, was essentially sincere. Throughout his testimony, Thomas cast himself as cruelly victimized by large and vague malignant forces dedicated to his absolute destruction. His invocation of the lynch mob was but one expression of that paranoia. Throughout his public testimony, he assailed "this inquisition" with acerbic indignation and unlimited contempt: "You spent the entire day destroying what it has taken me 43 years to build and providing a forum for that," he told Senator Howell Heflin.[16] "I have been harmed. I have been harmed. My family has been harmed. I have been harmed worse than I have ever been harmed in my life," he said to a warm supporter, Senator Orrin Hatch.[17] "I was harmed by this process, this process which accommodated these attacks on me. . . . I would have preferred an assassin's bullet to this kind of living hell that they have put me and my family through." And his persecution was no isolated wrong but an injury with apocalyptic consequences for the nation. "I think the country has been hurt by this process," he told Hatch. "I think we are destroying our country. We are destroying our institutions. Our institutions are being controlled by people who will stop at nothing."[18]

THOMAS: They went around this country looking for dirt, not information on Clarence Thomas—dirt. Anybody with any dirt, anything, late night calls, calls at work, calls at home, badgering, anything, give us some dirt. I think if our country has reached this point we are in trouble. And you should feel worse for the country than you do for me.

SEN. HATCH: I feel bad for both.

The judge's outrage was unfeigned. In claiming that "the country" had been badly injured by the "harm" done to himself by his perfidious accusers, he spoke in all sincerity; for he perceived himself, and was encouraged by his inner circle to perceive himself, as suffering the Passion of the Christ—His crucifixion also having scarred the world. Such grandiosity is painfully apparent in *Resurrection*, the highly sympathetic memoir of the Hill/Thomas hearings by Senator John Danforth, the judge's foremost champion (and, since then, a vocal critic of the regime's theocratic tendencies).[19] On October 9, 1991, two days before the hearings started, Thomas and his wife, Ginni, met with close friends Steven and Elizabeth Law. (At the time, Steven Law was on the staff of Senator Mitch McConnell, and became a deputy secretary of labor under Bush. Elizabeth Law worked for the Family Research Council.) "In trying to make sense of Clarence's suffering," John Danforth writes, "Elizabeth Law suggested that perhaps God wanted to strip away any notion that Clarence was being put on the Supreme Court by the president or Senate or political handlers. She suggested that if Clarence is on the court, it must be clear that God puts him there."[20] The Laws then gave some "praise tapes" to the Thomases, with the injunction that the latter's home "should be permeated by religious music."[21]

> Both Clarence and Ginni clearly recall that one of the subjects discussed in the meeting was the reality of evil. Evil was discussed as a cosmic force with earthly manifestations. Spiritual warfare was fought between good and evil, and a theater of that war at that moment was the fight over the confirmation of Clarence Thomas.[22]

The nominee's own body was another "theater of that war." Late that night, Ginni Thomas woke to find her husband writhing on the floor beside their bed. It was "like something was inside of him, physically, like there was this battle going on inside of him," she told Danforth later. "What it felt like is that Clarence still had some sin in his life and he had to get that out in order to be open to the Holy Spirit and that he had a vestige of sin, that he was in this furnace and God wasn't going to let him keep going without eliminating this vestige of sin."[23] Of his "agony" that night, Thomas later told the senator that he had experienced "total accountability" to God, and "opened up and asked Him to take charge of my life, and also to connect myself to following His will. And it was in that sense that I became a better person and purged myself of what I had done before and refined myself and became closer to what Jesus was."[24]

On the morning of October 11, the Thomases were driven to the Russell Senate Office Building ("Ginni listened to religious music through ear phones")[25] for an hour of spiritual preparation with Senator Danforth, an Episcopal minister with a doctorate in divinity from Yale. Sally Danforth was there too. The four of them crowded into the senator's bathroom, where they listened to a tape of "Onward Christian Soldiers" sung by the Mormon Tabernacle Choir. "Go forth in the name of Christ, trusting in the power of the Holy Spirit," the reverend senator told Thomas, who left the office with "a mission," "a purpose that was bigger than he was."[26] Thomas "felt pure" that morning, "felt as though God had cleansed me," "felt as though I was armed for battle then."[27]

I was still scared, but I felt that God was with us. That God was going to guide me. That God had given me these words. And that I was going to speak these words. And that if they ran me out of town, I had spoken what I thought God had put on my tongue.

A patriotic Christian might well be offended by the judge's grandiose conception of himself as a holy warrior whose words come straight from God Himself. That heady sense of perfect rectitude, of heavenly assignment, indicates not the requisite "judicial temperament" but the stunted mind of a fanatic. ("I ain't evolving," the newly minted Justice Thomas told his clerks.)[28] A faithful Christian might also be disquieted by Thomas's (and Reverend Danforth's) acquiescence in the view that evil is "a cosmic force with earthly manifestations"—a tenet not of Christianity but of the ancient Manichaean heresy, which now predominates throughout the "Christian" right (and in the apocalyptic variants of Judaism and Islam). And *any* patriotic citizen, regardless of his/her religion, must be flabbergasted by the fact—obvious to close observers at the time, and since then copiously documented—that Thomas's testimony was, for all his "agony" and prayer, a pack of lies. As Jane Mayer and Jill Abramson have fully documented, and despite the judge's strenuous denials, Thomas was an avid consumer of porn and much given to just the sort of crude and bullying dirty talk that he inflicted on Professor Hill. (It was a habit he largely hid from white acquaintances, which may help explain John Danforth's absolute refusal to believe it.) If we are to believe Mayer and Abramson (and David Brock's account in *Blinded by the Right*), Thomas lied throughout those hearings and did it with a most impressive air of staunch conviction, enabled by an animus quite different from commitment to the truth.[29] ("I have given up on the truth," the desperate judge burst out two days before his testimony on the Hill affair. "The truth is not helping me here.")[30]

The animus that drove the judge's lying, and that made it so persuasively attractive to his champions, who lied energetically on his behalf, was the impulse to deny his own aggression and dishonesty, and, as well, his side's aggression and dishonesty, by projecting them onto the very person hurt by that aggression and dishonesty. Repeatedly he and his advocates insinuated that *she* was somehow at the center of a partisan conspiracy to smear *him*, bring *him* down: an accusation that, while bearing no relation whatsoever to the lonely ordeal of Anita Hill, did refer precisely to the judge and his insinuating advocates, all of them performers in a far-right partisan conspiracy to smear and destroy *her*. That this conspiracy established as "the truth" a nightmarish inversion of the truth is well described in Hill's own memoir of the episode. After her nine hours of testimony on October 11, she writes, "I returned to my family and friends in our headquarters." All there were somewhat hopeful, very glad the day was over, and dead-tired. "Absent were the highly paid public relations handlers Senator [Alan] Simpson suggested were supporting me. Absent also were the 'special interest' groups many felt had encouraged me to come forward. Senator Simpson's suggestion that ours was a well-polished machine aimed at nailing Clarence Thomas advanced a gross inaccuracy." On the other hand, the army ranged against her was just such a well-oiled operation:

> One insider's description of the Republican headquarters contrasts with what I witnessed in my own station. He described the atmosphere in the Republican camp as chaotic and resonant—very much like a "political rally." The observer, a veteran of highly contested legal claims, was uncomfortable with what he saw, finding it "not conducive to getting at the truth."[31]

What Hill's source had glimpsed, and what would soon make her life dangerous and miserable, was an extremist propaganda drive of awesome volume and sophistication. It was not, certainly, an exercise in "getting at the truth" about Anita Hill *or* Clarence Thomas, but a deliberate (if unconscious) effort to distort the truth as thoroughly as possible, by charging *her* with all *his* crimes, and thereby casting *him* as *her* defenseless victim. Hill, the propaganda claimed, was not the self-possessed and modest woman she appeared to be, nor the honest witness she had seemed, but sex-obsessed and slightly cracked ("a little bit nutty and a little bit slutty"), a horny fantasist and therefore a colossal hypocrite—that is, exactly like Judge Thomas as she had so convincingly depicted him. According to the propaganda, Hill, moreover, was the beneficiary, and Thomas the unhappy object, of a vast campaign of character assassination. "They went around this country looking for dirt, not information—dirt. Anybody with any dirt, anything, late night calls, calls at work, calls at home, badgering, anything, give us some dirt." As Mayer and Abramson meticulously demonstrate—and as David Brock, a major player in that drive, described so vividly in his memoir—that bitter plaint by Thomas is an apt description of what his supporters were now doing "in defense" against Anita Hill. It was a crusade that absorbed the skills and zeal of Gary Bauer of the Family Research Council, the Reverend Lou Sheldon of the Traditional Values Coalition, Ralph Reed of the Christian Coalition, leading far-right operative Paul Weyrich, veteran mudslinger Floyd Brown and many other fierce projectors on the theocratic right, who would win that fight for Clarence Thomas and then go on to win far more.

Such warriors shared with Thomas that fanatic half-belief which Bush the Elder lacked, and which propelled them through the nineties after the Republican defeat in 1992. Indeed, the campaign for "Judge Thomas" (which is to say, against Anita Hill) was something of a dry run for the more protracted drive against the Clintons, which climaxed in the failed impeachment of that president and culminated, two years later, in the installation of Bush/Cheney. And "the country has been hurt by this process," as Thomas had projectively complained. Just as he put it then, with that deranged acuity so characteristic of malignant narcissism, "Our institutions are being controlled by people who will stop at nothing."

Since the nineties, the most influential of such people has been House Majority Leader Tom DeLay, aka "The Hammer," Bush Jr.'s fiery regent on the Hill, and yet also, as the theocratic movement's top congressional powerbroker, a colossus in his own right, able to blow off Bush and Cheney, or even dictate to them. It was DeLay who, in 1998, forced the issue of impeachment in the House when even anti-Clintonites as livid as Bob Barr would have settled for a compromise involving censure. ("This is going to be the most important thing I do in my political career," he said.)[32] In 2000, it was DeLay who halted the official recount of the ballots in Miami, by sending party goons to tear the place apart.[33] In 2003, with the blessing of Karl Rove, DeLay engineered the gerrymandering of Texas, thereby growing the number of Republicans in Congress while further weakening the Democrats.[34] (His aim has been to make the Texas Democrats a wholly non-white party.) Also in 2003—without Karl Rove's blessing—DeLay flew to Israel to address the legislature there, exhorting the members, literally, to stick to their guns, and *never* to settle with the Palestinians. This was a direct affront to Bush, who was trying (seemingly) to persuade both sides to buy his "road map to peace." "Terrorism cannot be negotiated away or pacified," DeLay told the Knesset in a Manichaean call to arms: "Freedom and terrorism will struggle—good and evil—

until the battle is resolved. These are the terms Providence has put before the United States, Israel, and the rest of the civilized world." The Hammer ended with a still more grandiose rejection of political solutions:

> One day, Israel—with the United States by her side—will live in freedom, security, and peace. And terrorism will perish from the earth. But until Almighty God, in His infinite wisdom, ordains that day to dawn, free men the world over—whether of the cross, the crescent, or the Star of David—will stand with Israel in defiance of evil.[35]

Such iron certainty is based on Tom DeLay's perception that "Almighty God" is his team captain, coach, co-pilot, comrade, co-conspirator—or, as they say in Texas, his "asshole buddy"— as devoted to the congressman's interests as the congressman himself. In this perception he resembles Clarence Thomas, "armed for battle" and well-guarded by the Lord against all worldly accusations. ("Just visualize Jesus standing behind you, Clarence, with his hands on your shoulders," Elizabeth Law said to him just before the crucial hearing.)[36] Thus shielded, DeLay has always spoken out with that same blunt ferocity that shook the huddled senators when Thomas testified. ("I felt a disdain for the committee," he told Danforth. "They looked like petty little thieves sitting up there.")[37] At the excoriation of "big government" and Democrats, the Hammer has no peer. "The EPA—the Gestapo of government—pure and simply has been one of the major claw-hooks that the government maintains on the backs of our constituents," he said, with more heat than clarity, in 1995.[38] "A lot of politicians in this House and in the country are sucking the blood out of their own constituencies," he said in 1991. "I can point to Hispanics and blacks that have become very rich by becoming civil rights activists, and I think it's pitiful."[39] In 1989 he called Washington a "festering liberal hellhole,"[40] and, four years later, "a liberal bastion of corruption and crime."[41] "Howard Dean is a cruel and extremist demagogue," he said in 2003. "If this cruel, loudmouth extremist is the cream of the Democrat crop, next November's going to make the 1984 elections look like a squeaker."[42]

Like Clarence Thomas's "defense," DeLay's long jihad has been an epic exercise in projectivity, his every bilious shot describing himself, or his own intentions, far more aptly than it described the Democrat or federal agency that was its stated target. Exuberant Howard Dean may be, but "cruel, loudmouth extremist" seems the perfect epithet for Tom DeLay—who cracked a joke about Paul Wellstone's memorial service, jeered at "the Nobel *appeasement* prize" when scientists received the honor for their study of ozone depletion and who, having engineered the killing of Bill Clinton's ergonomics rule—a worker-protection measure that had taken ten years of hard work to put in place—gloated for the record, in the far-right *Washington Times*: "I can't get this grin off my face. I go to sleep and wake up with it."[43] DeLay's projective outbursts are particularly flagrant when he stands accused of doing business as he's always done it. He said of Ronnie Earle, the Texas DA seeking to indict him on a range of counts, "the district attorney has a long history of being vindictive and partisan." ("Being called vindictive and partisan by Tom DeLay," answered Earle, "is like being called ugly by a frog."[44]) Earlier, DeLay had all but single-handedly transformed K Street, the mighty bloc of full-time lobbyists ensconced in Washington, into a fundraising machine for the Republicans.[45] To make that revolutionary move, he had overtly strong-armed the lobbying establishment, which henceforth could not hire top people until DeLay at al. had first approved them. (Now major lobbyists all had to be Republicans *and* generous donors to the party, and that party only. Prior donations to the Democrats would count against the would-be employee.) When Rep. Jerrold Nadler called for an investigation, Mike Scanlon, DeLay's spokesman, fired back, straight-faced, with a bald projective shot: "We don't appreciate Nadler's heavy-handed tactics."[46]

However copiously evidenced, the Hammer's many crimes and improprieties are, in his view, wrongs done *to him* by the Democratic Party and "the liberal media." "It's just another seedy attempt by the liberal media to embarrass me," he said, in early April 2005, about the news that his fundraising juggernaut had paid over $500,000 to his wife, Christine, and daughter, Dani DeLay Ferro, in disbursements tagged in the disclosure forms as "fund-raising fees," "campaign management" and "payroll."[47] That was only one of DeLay's many ethical infractions. He had already been "admonished" three times by the House Ethics Committee—the mildest of reproofs, and yet startling testimony to the scale and nakedness of his transgressions, as that committee was already famous for its toothlessness, and his power was unprecedented. He was thus lightly censured for soliciting "donations" from Westar Energy, Inc., "in return for legislative assistance on the energy bill" in 2002; for using his own PAC to funnel corporate funds to Texas state campaigns in 2002 (a violation of the Texas election code); and for trying, in May of 2003, to get federal agencies to track and nab those Democratic members of the Texas legislature who had fled the state to protest his redistricting scheme.[48] (That scheme also was improper, although the House's ethicists were unconcerned.) So glaring were these "lapses" that the House Committee had no choice but to "admonish" the unbending Texan—who then compounded those sins with yet another one, forcing the committee to change its rules to his advantage. In November 2004, DeLay persuaded the committee to revoke its rule that any member in a leadership position must give up that post if he or she should be indicted by a state grand jury.[49] (The "vindictive" DA down in Texas had been studying the Hammer's recent doings there.) In response, the Democrats withdrew from the committee, which then remained inactive for three months, finally forcing the Republicans to reinstate the rule in late April 2005.[50]

Meanwhile, further stories of DeLay's corruption had kept dribbling out. On April 6, 2005, it was reported that a six-day trip to Moscow back in 1997, when he was House majority whip, had been secretly paid for by Chelsea Commercial Enterprises, "a mysterious company registered in the Bahamas." Aside from covering the cost of DeLay's junket, Chelsea had spent $440,000 lobbying the Russian government. "Chelsea was coordinating the effort with a Russian oil and gas company—Naftasib—that has business ties with Russian security institutions," according to the *Washington Post*. "During his six days in Moscow, [DeLay] played golf, met with Russian church leaders and talked to Prime Minister Viktor Chernomyrdin, a friend of Russian oil and gas executives associated with the lobbying effort."[51]

Through all this DeLay was unrepentant, angrily refusing to acknowledge any wrongs, despite the evidence, and blaming all his troubles on a vast fictitious plot of nonexistent leftist entities. On April 14, in an interview with the *Washington Times*, he complained about an op-ed in the *New York Times*, deploring it as "activist journalism." He then shot an arrow toward the heart of the conspiracy:

Somebody ought to . . . ask the *New York Times*, the *Washington Post*, the *L.A. Times*, *Time*, *Newsweek*, AP why they're spending all these resources they are, who they talked to . . . Are they collaborating with all these organizations that are funded by George Soros and his heavy hitters, and do these organizations ever talk to each other? Of course they do, they have people that are on the same boards. I mean, different boards but same people.[52]

Although there was no such conspiracy against him on the left, there was, of course, a similar propaganda network on the right.

It is the *right* that functions through a tight and influential nexus of like-minded "organizations," with the "same people" sitting on a lot of "different boards" and a number of extremist billionaires and large commercial interests funding the whole enterprise. DeLay's chilling evocation of "George Soros and his heavy hitters" was in fact a dark projection of the infinitely larger, more effective mechanism that has long since overwhelmed "the liberal media," with ample funding from the likes of Richard Mellon Scaife, Howard Ahmanson, Pete Coors, Robert Krieble, Philip Anschutz, Robert Hurtt (Container Corporation of America), Richard DeVos (Amway), Tom Monaghan (Domino's Pizza) and many others, with vast material support from Rupert Murdoch, and untold billions from Sun Myung Moon, aka "the Messiah." Next to that colossus—"the Republican noise machine," as David Brock has aptly dubbed it—the efforts of George Soros (the *only* billionaire who has spent substantially against the right) appear quixotic.

Far from bolstering his claim to have been targeted by an enormous leftist propaganda juggernaut, DeLay's shot at George Soros proved that there is no such thing. It showed, on the contrary, that the right wields massive propaganda power, not only through its own organs but through "the liberal media" at large. DeLay's view of Soros as a leftist Croesus pulling strings behind the scenes had been purveyed throughout the presidential race, beginning on June 3, 2004, when Tony Blankley, editorial page director of the Moon-owned *Washington Times*, appeared on Rupert Murdoch's *Hannity & Colmes*, and, associating Soros with John Kerry, called the financier "a Jew who figured out a way to survive the Holocaust," as well as a "left-wing crank," "a robber baron," "a pirate capitalist," "a reckless man," "unscrupulous," "a self-admitted atheist" and "a very bad influence in the world."

With his legal troubles mounting in the spring of 2005, De-Lay et al. sought to distract attention from them by reviving the attack, casting Soros as alone responsible for his ordeal. On March 17, DeLay met with some 30 leading rightists at the Family Research Council, arousing them with this projective call to arms:

> The point is the other side has figured out how to win and defeat the conservative movement. And that is to go after people personally, charge them with frivolous charges and link that up with all of these do-gooder organizations funded by George Soros, and then get the national media on their side.[53]

Here DeLay unconsciously described what he was just then doing *to* George Soros: mobilizing sympathetic advocacy groups with an eye toward helpful coverage by the national press. The drive took shape throughout the rest of March. On the 24th, Richard Mellon Scaife's NewsMax.com ran a long piece asserting that DeLay had been targeted by "a shadowy group of liberal organizations, all backed by one man: George Soros."[54] To one such outfit, Citizens for Responsibility and Ethics in Washington (CREW), the stealthy billionaire had granted "a whopping $7.5 million" to foil DeLay's agenda, NewsMax reported. The anti-Soros drive continued through the week. In response to an anti-DeLay ad from the Campaign for America's Future, the Hammer's office claimed, "These groups are funded by Democratic heavy hitters like George Soros."[55] The statement ran in *USA Today*, the *Washington Times*, the *Houston Chronicle*, the *Austin American-Statesman*, *Congressional Quarterly Weekly* and a story from the Knight Ridder news service, also resonating elsewhere on the right, in cyberspace and on hate radio.

The drive intensified on April 12. DeLay showed up, surprisingly, at a lunch for Senate Republicans to give those boys their marching orders ("He said, 'Tell them that this is all a plot and the Democrats are out to get me,'" an anonymous luncher told the *Chicago Tribune*)[56] and then sat for that seething interview—about "George Soros and all his heavy hitters"—with the *Washington Times*, which spread the word to all the heavy hitters on the right. In a press release, Rep. Joe Wilson (R-SC) decried the "desperate smear campaign" carried out against DeLay by "radical liberals, such as George Soros."[57] In Wilson's view, the Hammer was as innocent as Soros was malevolent: "His critics are inspired by bitterness, hatred and partisanship." On CNN's *Crossfire*, veteran propagandist Barbara Comstock—formerly John Ashcroft's flack, now a major player in the anti-Soros drive— argued that those torturing DeLay were doing it for "George Soros money."[58] On Rupert Murdoch's Fox News Channel, William Kristol, editor of Rupert Murdoch's *Weekly Standard*, asserted "a George Soros–financed attack on Tom De-Lay," the accusation deftly freighted with a hint at Jewish perfidy: "He gives a speech in the Sunday school—a church—and they sneak somebody in to tape it."[59] "The hysterical Democratic attacks on House Majority Leader Tom DeLay," wrote Richard Lessner, head of the American Conservative Union, in Philip Anschutz's *Washington Examiner*, "are part of a coordinated effort to strike down conservative leaders in and out of Congress"—a drive "lavishly funded by George Soros."[60] "Multi-billionaire George Soros," warned Phyllis Schlafly's Eagle Forum, "is bankrolling this attack on Tom DeLay!"[61] "Atheist billionaire George Soros is funding a number of the organizations that are attacking DeLay," cried the website of the Traditional Values Coalition, headed by the Reverend Lou Sheldon. "Soros is a one-world socialist who hates Christians and seeks a one-world government and legalized drugs."[62] Of all such coded pot-shots at the financier, the one most clearly redolent of Nazi propaganda came from Richard Poe, a contributing editor for Richard Mellon Scaife's *NewsMax Magazine*. On David Horowitz's website FrontPageMag.com (a venture partly subsidized by Richard Mellon Scaife), Poe offered this Goebbelsian speculation:

> The pattern of the attack suggests that DeLay may be confronting a political machine far wealthier, more ruthless and better skilled at media manipulation than the Democratic Party itself. When the hysteria subsides and the facts are examined, we may learn that DeLay's foe all along has been the Shadow Party—a murky and inscrutable entity controlled by leftwing billionaire George Soros.[63]

As planned, such material also leached into the mainstream. As early as March 31, in an editorial on the "embattled House Majority Leader Tom DeLay," the *Rocky Mountain News* observed that "the campaign, according to some reports, may be bankrolled by George Soros' Open Society Institute."[64] On April 8, Juan Williams helpfully restated the main talking point on National Public Radio, casting it as "gossip" on the right:

> The Republicans feel there's a concerted effort, the gossip being that they believe that George Soros, the multibillionaire who has been supportive of so many Democratic causes, is one of the people who's in charge of a concerted effort to unseat a very effective and powerful Republican leader.[65]

"Billionaire George Soros's Open Society Institute," wrote Gail Russell Chaddock in the *Christian Science Monitor* on April 12, "has contributed some $2.5 million to ethics coalition groups" set up to "target DeLay."[66] And three times on CNN— on April 21, 23 and 27—Robert Novak scathingly referred to "leftist billionaire George Soros" and "the poison" administered by MoveOn.org, Soros's "left-wing organization." Meanwhile, on Rupert Murdoch's Fox News Channel, Bill O'Reilly took only one shot at Soros, on April 23: "I don't want George Soros in charge of this country. I think he's a rank socialist and a hypocrite."

Thus did DeLay et al., in their ostensible attack on Soros, actually portray themselves; for while Soros certainly did subsidize MoveOn and otherwise attempt to sway the electorate against Bush/Cheney, he played little if any role in DeLay's troubles. The drive against him was a pack of lies. Contrary to News-Max.com, for instance, CREW did not receive "a whopping $7.5 million" from the billionaire to do the Hammer in.[67] In fact, Soros paid CREW not one dime for that or any other purpose (as Raw Story reported on its website, forcing NewsMax to revise its story, slightly).[68] The constant whine of partisan complaint—the endless fury over "Democratic heavy hitters"—was also a deception, as the hue and cry over the Texan's ethics was bipartisan. The Congressional Ethics Coalition—an umbrella group that criticized DeLay—included such conservative outfits as Judicial Watch and the Campaign Legal Center.[69] And yet that drive—like all such rightist drives—depended less on bald concoction than on wild projection, as no endeavor of George Soros's or by the Democrats resembled even slightly the immense, malevolent conspiracy evoked so passionately by DeLay et al. *Theirs*—"inspired by bitterness, hatred and partisanship"— was the only such conspiracy in evidence. As in the prior drive against Anita Hill, the evil lay entirely in the hearts and minds of those decrying it.[70]

Those "defensive" drives for Thomas and DeLay anticipated the Republican campaign to deny the party's theft of the 2004 election—in its vast subversion of American democracy, the culmination of the party's prior paranoid campaigns. The central players in these drives have figured prominently in the theocrats' assault on our democracy. It was Clarence Thomas's appointment that enabled Bush the Younger to steal the presidency in 2000 (even though, as a federal appellate judge noted, Thomas ought to have recused himself from *Bush v. Gore* because Mrs. Thomas, an ardent party activist, would have excellent employment prospects under Bush and Co.).[71] As noted earlier, DeLay did all he could to force Bill Clinton out of office, going further even than his staunchest colleagues in rejecting any compromise, so desperate was he to negate the people's choice. Since Bush's installation, the Hammer has worked night and day to clinch his party's permanent control of all three branches of the U.S. government. He engineered and subsidized the GOP's decisive gerrymandering of Texas in 2003, oversaw the party's seizure of the lobbying establishment in Washington and transformed the House into a rubber stamp assembly, where Democrats have now become extraneous. More generally, both Thomas and DeLay have taken every opportunity to force their Biblical worldview onto American democracy—the primary motive of the countless grass-roots operatives who helped to steal the last election.

4.

Do Unto Others
Before They
Do Unto You

It is not "conservatism" that impelled the theft of the election, nor was it merely greed or the desire for power per se—although many of the perpetrators are insanely greedy and crave power as avidly as the troops of any other movement bent on total domination. The movement now in power is not entirely explicable in such familiar terms. Lyndon Johnson had a monstrous appetite for power, yet he would never have been part of a crusade like this one. The project here is ultimately pathological and essentially anti-political, albeit Machiavellian on a scale, and to a degree, that would have staggered Machiavelli. The aim is not to master politics but to annihilate it. Bush, Rove, DeLay, Ralph Reed et al. believe in "politics" in the same way that they and their corporate beneficiaries believe in "competition." In both cases the intention is not to play the game but to end it—because the game requires some tolerance of the Other, and tolerance is precisely what these bitter-enders most despise. They can abide no players other than themselves—and need no others, as they are already fighting with themselves, and to the death. In their every adversary they see, or purport to see, an absolute oppressor. DeLay has called the EPA "the Gestapo of government," the International Criminal Court "Kofi Annan's kangaroo court," the House Democrats intoxicated by "the arrogance of power."[1] But who, really, are those swaggering, jackbooted martinets goose-stepping through the congressman's vituperation? Of all the little Hitlers in the House (or Senate), surely none of them has trampled on due process, or threatens U.S. democratic governance, as brazenly and gleefully as Tom DeLay—who once roared at a man who had the gall to ask him not to smoke a cigar on federal premises, "I *am* the government!"[2]

Forever locked in mortal combat with his inner devil, the Bush Republican—or Bushevik—sees every deviation from the party line as evidence of further devilishness. "If you oppose Karl on anything, you're on the enemy's list," a Texas Republican once said about Karl Rove. "You become the enemy even if you're not really one."[3] The Bushevik's jihad takes all his concentration, all his energy, as that struggle is the only thing that keeps him moving forward in one piece. Without endlessly demanding more reconfirmation, from himself and everybody else, he fears he would break down or fly apart—surrender absolutely to whatever urge he keeps on working (often unsuccessfully) to stifle. Hence his hatred of the very mode of democratic politics: the necessary endless talk, among groups or persons necessarily in disagreement, and necessarily inclined to compromise. To honor someone else's viewpoint is effeminate, a sign of *politesse* that is far better-suited for the parlor—or the *salon*—

than the battlefield. And yet the Bushevik's deep hatred of political deliberation is far more passionate than mere machismo. He loathes such talk not just because he sees it as a feeble substitute for violence against the enemy, but because he sees those talkers *as* the enemy, perceives such talk itself as evil: a permissible exchange of different views—as if different views should be permissible! Such civil discourse fosters heresy, or even welcomes it, or rather is itself heretical. It honors notions that one shouldn't even hold, much less promote. It is inhospitable to holy zeal, inducing the believer to restrain himself, capitulate, fall short. It is therefore an abomination (and temptation). The righteous must engage it not by taking part in it, but by taking arms against it. The Bushevik would load his guns and saddle up, and lead his posse not away from the assembly hall, with its humanistic denizens irrelevantly nattering, but straight into the hall itself, where all of them had better shut their mouths and start to read from the same page, or face the consequences.

The Bushevik, so full of hate, hates politics, and would get rid of it; and yet he is himself expert at dirty politics: an expertise that he regards as purely imitative and defensive. Because his enemies, he thinks, are all "political"—dishonest, ruthless, cynical, unprincipled—he is thereby forced to be "political" as well, in order to "fight fire with fire." As we have seen, this paranoid conviction of the Other's perfidy suffuses and impels the propaganda campaigns of the right, and it was especially important in Bush/Cheney's drive to steal the last election. Indeed, it was their firm conviction that they *had* to steal the race, in order to frustrate the Democrats' attempt to do it first.

Thus was the theft of the election largely carried out by officers and troops who deemed it a pre-emptive strike: the rationale (or delusion) that armed paranoids have always used to justify their exterminationist campaigns. As, say, Roman Catholics used to slaughter Protestants and vice versa, and as countless Christian champions have slaughtered Jews and Muslims (and are now slaughtering Muslims once again, although this time with Jewish allies), and as Islamists have lately slaughtered Jews and Christians, each such army wiping out those evildoers who would otherwise wipe out that army first—so has the Bush regime believed (or purported to believe) that it must act "before things happen," as the president incessantly put it in his propaganda for the "toppling" of Saddam Hussein. Such propaganda was ubiquitous and unrelenting (and seldom contradicted by the U.S. media) throughout the months before the war—a deft logistical and psychological accomplishment that certainly suggests deliberate mass deception. "We don't want the smoking gun to be a mushroom cloud," said Condoleezza Rice, although she knew or had to know that there was not a shred of evidence for an Iraqi nuclear capability.[4]

And yet their stridency and passion suggest that those cool liars were also hotly lying to themselves, in their inevitable tendency to see themselves as the long-suffering victims, and their victims as ruthless persecutors. In January of 2003, Bush told a friend of party propagandist Peggy Noonan's that he was having "some trouble sleeping, and that when he awakes the first thing he often thinks is: I wonder if this is the day Saddam will do it"— by which Noonan's friend took him to mean, "he wonders if this will be the day Saddam launches a terror attack here, on American soil."[5] ("We're facing something we've never faced before," Laura Bush told Barbara Walters on December 11, 2003. "There are moments when you wake up at night and say a little prayer." "You comfort each other?" "You bet," said the president.)[6]

There was the same maniacal sincerity in Cheney's war propaganda. "Cheney, say those who know him, is in no way cynically manipulative," *Newsweek* reported in November of 2003.[7] "By all accounts, he is genuinely convinced that the threat is imminent and menacing." Only such conviction could explain the futile doggedness of Cheney's line that there *was—is—*a vast reserve of taboo weapons hidden somewhere in Iraq: a charge that the vice president maintained for months after it had been disproved by chief U.S. weapons inspector David Kay, among many others.[8]

Meanwhile, those fearful perpetrators were themselves preparing a greater terror—a huge campaign to "shock and awe" the masses through apocalyptic violence—on *Iraqi* soil. That such inversion of the truth is more a matter of projectivity than of deliberate deceit is evident in the compulsiveness with which they tell the lie. In every case they cast themselves as victimized because they *see* themselves as victimized, actually or potentially; and therefore always justified in striking first. As this has been their m.o. on the global level, so has it been on the domestic front, where they feel wholly justified in "taking out" their enemies pre-emptively. On March 21, 2005, for instance, three local residents were forcibly removed from a museum in Denver, where Bush had come to give a speech on Social Security.[9] This was a White House event, funded by the taxpayers, and therefore open to the public. Although the three were quiet and presentable, and claimed that they had only come to hear the president, they were thrown out because there was an antiwar bumper sticker ("No More Blood for Oil") on the car that they had parked outside. They were ousted, in short, entirely on suspicion that they *might* disrupt the speech—a rationale complacently explained by White House press secretary Scott McClellan: "If we think people are coming to the event to disrupt it, obviously, they're going to be asked to leave."[10]

Exactly what might make the White House "think" that a particular visitor was "coming to disrupt" the day's event McCellan did not say, nor would his office clarify the matter. "The White House press office did not return calls seeking elaboration on McClellan's remarks, which were made during the daily press briefing." The fracas was especially notable because the man who ousted the three citizens was posing as a member of the Secret Service. He was apparently a party operative, affiliated with the White House, although the White House and the Secret Service afterward would not identify him—even though the three had filed a lawsuit for infringement of their First Amendment rights.[11] (On July 29, 2005, U.S. Attorney William Leone announced that federal prosecutors would not press charges against the "White House volunteer" who had posed as a Secret Service agent. Leone did not give any reason for this decision).[12]

Throughout the six months leading up to the election, such preventive expulsion by the Bush/Cheney campaign machine was almost completely unreported by the national media. As improper as it was in a democracy, the practice was appropriate for that campaign, which was itself a grand pre-emptive strike. That the Democrats were planning an immense electoral theft in 2004 was not only a major talking point among the Bush Republicans but apparently a crucial motivating factor. Although Republicans have long accused the Democrats of rank electoral corruption (a charge that, in certain times and places, has been wholly justified),* the specter of a national Democratic coup did

---

*As one who came of age in Cook County, Illinois, where the first Mayor Richard J. Daley ruled the roost, I suffer no illusions about Democratic practice at the polls. Moreover, it was, of course, the Southern Democrats who invented and perfected the machinery of disenfranchisement throughout the Jim Crow era. However, between the parties there is an enormous difference in the scale, boldness, cynicism and sophistication of their respective efforts to meddle with

not preoccupy the rightist mind until the evening of Election Day 2000, when Fox News Channel suddenly—and ground-lessly—called the race in Florida for Bush, other networks, in-cluding CBS, having called the race for Gore. (It was John Ellis, a cousin of George W. Bush, who had made that bold decision, in constant contact with his cousins George and Jeb and his boss Rupert Murdoch.)[13] NBC News then seconded Fox's call (at the spirited insistence of parent company General Electric's CEO, Jack Welch, who personally marched into the network's news-room to demand that NBC "confirm" the word from Fox).[14] Within minutes, the other networks followed suit—and that consensus, although mistaken, made it impossible to shift once more and call the state for Gore without arousing the suspicious fury of the right, regardless of the vote itself. Whether that ef-fect was deliberately intended by the Bush/Fox combination we may never know for sure. In any case, the right, stoked by the Bush campaign, immediately figured, and wrathfully pro-claimed, that the Democrats were trying to steal Florida, and therefore the national electoral vote, from the rightful heir to the American throne.

That charge resonated loudly coast to coast throughout the frantic interim between Election Day and the Supreme Court's move to halt the Florida vote count on December 12. It was chiefly Rupert Murdoch's sturdy propaganda apparatus (Fox

elections. While Democrats have certainly filched races in the past, Bush/ Cheney's second effort was a systematic national and local enterprise, involv-ing not just the traditional methods for *suppression* of the vote but the subver-sion of the very infrastructure used to *count* the vote. In any case, the Gore and Kerry campaigns were both extraordinarily scrupulous, as opposed to the ex-traordinary perfidy of the Bush/Cheney machine, which has returned the South, and forced the entire nation, back toward the bad old days of poll taxes and literacy tests, among other anti-democratic methods once unique to Dixie.

News Channel, the *New York Post*, the *Weekly Standard*, etc.) that purveyed the claim that the Republicans, who were just then engaged in stealing the election, were at risk of having it actually snatched *from them* by the Democrats. On Fox's *Hannity & Colmes* on November 12, as the votes in Florida were still being arduously counted, Sean Hannity and Peggy Noonan sang a bellicose duet that lasted quite a while, including this exchange:

HANNITY: There are no standards here. The people that are deciding are Democratic operatives with connections to the Gore camp, and they start with one standard, it's not working out! In the middle of it they change to another—

NOONAN: They go to another standard.

HANNITY: And then they charge a third one!

NOONAN: I know! And they will keep going. They'll find *new* standards! One of the problems with this story, it seems to me only four or five [unintelligible], whatever we are, is that we see this tape of what's happening in Florida, we see the people talking and everybody's sound bites and we think this is a farce. Well, farces make you laugh. But we shouldn't be laughing—!

HANNITY: It's not funny!

NOONAN: It seems more like an attempted coup in some respects than it does like a farce.

HANNITY: Well, I think they're trying to steal the election, as the *New York Post* pointed out!

"I'll tell you this," CNN's Bob Novak railed about the Democrats, "almost every Republican I talk to thinks they're trying to steal the election!"[15] "The Gore campaign is attempting to steal the election," claimed a November 13 press release from Rep.

Nick Smith (who would go on to co-sponsor President Bush's Faith-Based Initiative in Michigan, and later run afoul of Tom DeLay).[16] "I am increasingly alarmed at what appears to be a blatant attempt by Vice President Gore to steal this election," claimed a November 14 press release from Rep. Dave Weldon (later the co-author of the Incapacitated Person's Legal Protection Act, aka "Terri's Law II," and a vehement supporter of Principle Approach International, which bills itself as "grounded in a biblical worldview and dedicated to strengthening the Body of Christ and reforming the culture").[17] On CNN's *Crossfire* on November 17, Mary Matalin joined in, not to be deterred by her debating partner, David Corn:

MATALIN: Manufacturing votes, bribing electors, intimidating local officials, investigating electors. This is the only way Gore can win: lie, cheat and steal! It's your bumper sticker: "Lie, cheat and steal! Vote Gore!"

CORN: So you don't trust the Florida courts? You have a secretary of state—

MATALIN: Did I say that? I didn't say that—

CORN: —that's done her decision, will you still claim—

MATALIN: I said lying, cheating, stealing!

CORN: Will you still claim that the election was stolen if the Florida courts say that it's OK for the recounts to go ahead?

MATALIN: Not unless they include looking at all these irregularities of stolen, manufactured ballots [*sic*]!

CORN: You know, I say put the spin aside—

MATALIN: I'm not spinning!

"It should be obvious to all by now that Mr. Gore is trying to steal a victory in Florida by means of legal machinations,"

charged Richard Lessner, executive director of American Renewal, "the legislative action arm of Family Research Council,"
in a November 28 press release. "I think Al Gore is trying to
steal the election," William Bennett said to Bill O'Reilly—who
thought so too—on that same day (and, Bennett added, with a
telling slip, "I think a lot of people don't care in the media because they want Bush to win").[18]

The voices of sanity were few, and even fewer those sane
voices that spoke with the requisite bluntness. "In fact," Novak
said (again) on *Crossfire* on December 12, the day that *Bush v.
Gore* came down, "it's the Gore people who are trying to steal
votes in this election." "No," replied Bill Press, "I think you have
it backwards, my friend." Such voices being rare, or rarely heard,
the press largely refraining, in the name of "balance," from distinguishing what was true from what was false, the charge of
widespread Democratic "mischief"—as James Baker put it
apoplectically in his TV appearances—aroused that same plurality of fiery minds that had conceived the Clintons as pure Evil.

Many such Americans converged on Florida between Election Day and December 12, prepared to fight the scheming
Democrats unto the death. "I'm out here because if Gore is allowed to prevail, we will no longer live in a country with the rule
of law," said one such Minuteman, who had arrived with high-
power semiautomatic weapons in the trunk of his Grand Mar-
quis, and some seventy rounds of ammunition.[19] "Today the
Democratic Party is an un-American party with an alien
agenda," said another demonstrator, a retired naval aviator.
"Otherwise, it wouldn't be doing what it's doing."[20]

Such was the logic that, in spite of the electorate, prevailed in
the election, once the fiction of Bush/Cheney's victory had been
certified as real by Clarence Thomas and his four associates.

The myth that Gore had illegitimately tried to seize the White House did not fade away after Bush/Cheney's triumph. A week after the Supreme Court's termination of the race, Sean Hannity was still going at it: "He did try and steal the election," he asserted about Gore, referring to the latter's effort as "a coup"; and, seconds later, having thus denied that the Republicans had stolen the election, Hannity denied that he, or anybody on the right, had ever accused Gore of stealing it. Opposing Hannity and rightist Niger Innis,[21] the strikingly uncharismatic Alan Colmes tried valiantly to challenge the Republicans for having charged *ad nauseam* that Gore was trying to steal the race:

COLMES: Republicans were saying things like: "Al Gore's going to steal this election!" "If he wins, he'll never be my president!" There are many Republicans—
HANNITY: Who?!
COLMES: —and many conservatives who said that: "He'll never be my president" and "He's trying to steal the election."
INNIS: All right. It wasn't Sean. It wasn't me. I don't know what you're talking about.[22]

Regardless of that eerie disavowal, the myth of Gore's attempted "mischief" quickly hardened into rightist gospel, thanks in large part to Bill Sammon, a *Washington Times* reporter whose apparent exposé, *At Any Cost: How Al Gore Tried to Steal the Election*, was published by Regnery in May of 2001. The book is a farrago of half-truths, selective evidence and dark insinuations, making an absurd but by-and-large coherent case— and one rendered dramatically enough to garner a broad readership and arm the propagandists for the endless fight.[23] The book's argument was further propagated, and its sales no doubt

increased, by Sammon's numerous promotional appearances on
Rupert Murdoch's Fox News Channel, including stints on *The
O'Reilly Factor, Hannity & Colmes* and *The Edge with Paula Zahn*
(which show included a long, cuddly interview with Katherine
Harris, Florida's infamous secretary of state and co-chair of the
Bush campaign in Florida). Well beyond the pitch for Sammon's
book, however, the whole rightist propaganda mechanism kept
the cauldron boiling: "Al Gore, as far as I'm concerned, tried to
steal an election," snapped Hannity, apropos of nothing in particular, on September 30, 2002. "Democrats steal 2 percent to 3
percent of the vote in a typical election," David Horowitz told
Richard Mellon Scaife's NewsMax.com, in a piece posted on
November 7, 2002.[24]

Even as they went on damning Gore and warning that the
Democrats would steal elections in the future, the Republicans
themselves were evidently planning to steal votes, or were already stealing votes, or had just stolen votes, in the midterm
elections of 2002. Having captured one branch of the federal
government by non-elective means, the Bush Republicans
moved on to gain a comfy margin in the Senate, which, thanks
to the defection of Vermont Senator "Jumping Jim" Jeffords (as
Sean Hannity called him), had been in Democratic hands by just
one vote for eighteen months. In the 2002 elections, there were
extraordinary "upsets" in Minnesota, Georgia, Colorado and
New Hampshire—all statistically remarkable, all effected by
the Christian right (with heavy input from the White House)
and all, of course, decisively advantaging the GOP, which enjoyed a sudden four-seat margin in the Senate: 52 Republicans
to 47 Democrats, with Jeffords making a de facto 48th. (After
2004, the Bush Republicans enjoyed a ten-seat margin: 55–44 +
Jeffords.) Although it ought to be the subject of another book

entirely—or of several books, or at least a spate of journalistic exposés[25]—the likely heist of the Senate in 2002 was in certain ways so similar to the theft of the election in 2004, with the same corporate entities involved in both, that some mention of the oddities is here appropriate, especially as the *Republicans* were making so much noise about the *Democratic* danger of election fraud (while the Democrats, who had every reason to pursue the subject, said not one word about it).

In Colorado, Republican Wayne Allard, a born-again with a 100 percent approval rating from the Christian Coalition, beat Democrat Tom Strickland by nearly five percentage points, although the polls had shown the Democrat ahead by several points.[26] (Diebold touch-screen machines were used in Saguache, Weld and El Paso Counties, collectively accounting for over 750,000 votes. Strickland lost by 70,000 votes.)[27] Allard went on to play a leading role in the radicalization of the Senate, authoring the Marriage Protection Amendment, which would make gay marriage unconstitutional, and co-sponsoring the apocalyptic Constitution Restoration Act of 2004, which would make God—that is, the Bible—the sovereign basis of American law: a stroke that would enable federal judges to pass sentence as prescribed in, say, Leviticus, without risk of reversal by some higher court.[28]

In Minnesota, Zogby had Walter Mondale at 50 percent or slightly more before Election Day, with born-again Norm Coleman (formerly a Democrat, and Jewish) at a consistent 45 percent.[29] Coleman, who hailed from Brooklyn, had a 100 percent approval rating from the Christian Coalition.[30] Mondale was a favorite son and a last-minute substitute for the popular Paul Wellstone, who had been leading Coleman by four points when he died in a small plane crash on October 25.[31] Coleman defeated Mondale with nearly 50 percent of the vote, winning by a 2.2 percent margin. (Of all four suspicious races in 2002, only Minnesota did not use Diebold equipment.)[32] Coleman went on to lead the senatorial attack on Kofi Annan and the U.N. generally—a drive irrelevant to national security in the middle of the "war on terrorism," but pure catnip to Coleman's feral backers on the right.[33] (Coleman is also a good soldier for the pharmaceutical cartel.)[34]

The most dramatic upset was in Georgia, where Democratic Senator Max Cleland, a severely disabled veteran of the war in Vietnam (he is a triple amputee), lost by seven percentage points to Saxby Chambliss, who had a 100 percent approval rating from the Christian Coalition (and 0 percent from the Sierra Club) and whose campaign was managed by Ralph Reed.[35] This was a great surprise, as Cleland had been narrowly ahead of Chambliss in the polls. "The Hotline, a political news service, recalled a series of polls Wednesday showing that Chambliss had been ahead in none of them," reported the Atlanta-based Cox News Service.[36] With his record as a soldier, Cleland was immensely popular in military-minded Georgia. Chambliss was a chickenhawk, who backed the war in Vietnam but elected not to fight in it because of a "bad knee."[37] The Chambliss campaign was pure Reed/Rove, with Cleland's patriotism noisily impugned by the unwounded Chambliss, who played up Cleland's opposition to Bush/Cheney's program for "homeland security." The Chambliss campaign ran a TV spot depicting Cleland with Osama bin Laden and Saddam Hussein: "Max Cleland says he has the courage to lead, but the record proves he's just misleading," sneered the voiceover.[38] And it was all downhill from there, with Chambliss ultimately charging treason, flaying the Democrat in a press release for "breaking his oath to protect and defend the Constitution."[39] (Cleland had lost his arm and legs when he had moved toward a live grenade that had rolled off a supply truck. He had intended to throw it away.)[40]

After the apparent rout, all agreed that Chambliss's amazing "come-from-behind victory" had resulted from expert character assassination and, at the end, from three exciting joint appearances with Bush.[41] In Minnesota too, Coleman's startling win was tidily ascribed to the well-orchestrated statewide outcry over Paul Wellstone's memorial service; the liberal horde's barbaric "booing of Trent Lott" and other infamies that actually had not occurred.[42] (As usual, the Republicans politicized the issue by ferociously complaining that the Democrats politicized the issue.) Such is the state of most "political analysis" in the culture of TV, where every victory or defeat is knowingly explained as wholly consequent on how the winning side pitched itself and begrimed the losers. Such childish reasoning, based on the fallacy of *post hoc ergo propter hoc*, ignores the possibility of more complex responses, and, more importantly, of other factors—those, in particular, that were invisible (as most factors tend to be). Such reasoning also begs the question of whether what we saw was in fact a victory, or just a seeming one. By overfocusing on Chambliss's slanderous theatrics and overlooking the statistical unlikelihood of Chambliss's "win," the press ignored the more material fact that the election had been run *not* by the sovereign state of Georgia but—literally—by Diebold and its executives and programmers.

On May 3, 2002, Diebold signed a contract with Cathy Cox, Georgia's secretary of state—a Democrat of the Zell Miller type, wildly popular with Republicans, and a most ambitious politician. The $54 million deal, to install 19,000 touch-screen machines throughout the state, had been negotiated by a 12-

member committee and was duly noted in the press. Three months later, Cox and Diebold secretly invalidated the agreement by co-signing a "First Amendment" that wholly privatized the electoral system in the state of Georgia. This accord—unknown to the legislature, unreported in the press—gave Diebold full authority to train poll workers, build election databases and prepare all ballots in 106 of Georgia's 159 counties. In those counties Diebold's employees would henceforth supervise electoral proceedings, program the machines and render technical assistance—all without the oversight of any state officials. It was a secret deal, fraught with improprieties; and the machines performed abysmally in 2002, requiring various furtive technical expedients by Diebold's employees.[43]

Throughout the campaign in 2004, talking heads warned heatedly and often that the Democrats were going to steal the election. "I think there are plans underway by the Democrats to steal this election in Florida," announced Bob Novak on July 31, on *CNN Capital Gang*. "I have some factual material which will come out in due course,[44] because the plans are being laid, have been laid for four years." "Why are they trying to steal the election by cheating?" cried Alan Keyes on CNN on August 30, referring to his hopeless senatorial bid in Illinois.[45] (A week later, on the radio in Chicago, Keyes said that "Christ would not vote for Barack Obama"—who, nevertheless, went on to win with 71 percent.)[46] "Your dirty tricks make me suspicious of all you Democrats," said Sean Hannity to Bob Beckel on September 17. And on September 27, Rush Limbaugh descanted on the danger with his usual good humor and precision:

When I grew up, I mean—I—I thought once you were a felon, you lost your voting rights forever. It's only recently, when the Democrats noticed their shrinking dominance, needing every vote they could get, they started importing Haitians the day before elections. Remember that in 2000? A Haitian boat that went—went aground down there in Florida?

They started importing Haitians the day before elections, and now—and now—and now the—they got to go out and scour the country for felons. Is it not enough that they're registering dead people in Ohio and Illinois? Is it not enough?

That riff was not an honest exposé of Democratic dirty tricks but a dirty trick itself, its purpose being to link the Democrats with criminals and Haitians—that is, black people, as "felons" is Rushspeak for that community. In any case, no Haitians "went aground down there in Florida" on "the day before elections" in 2000: Limbaugh was thinking of October 30, 2002, when a freighter ran aground off Key Biscayne, and 200 starving Haitians leapt off the boat and made a desperate run for it.[47] State troopers tracked them down, and six men were arrested for organizing the illicit trip. The detention of the would-be immigrants roused protests and complaints. Limbaugh's reaction at the time:

I can't help but think of DNC head Terry McAuliffe saying that he would do whatever it took to defeat Jeb Bush in next week's election—not because he's a bad governor, but just to embarrass the Bush family! I can't help but wonder if this isn't an "October Surprise," designed to put the screws to Jeb and energize the African-American voters. I would keep a close eye out for facts on this.

It's important to point out that I think people who go in for conspiracy theories are fools, but this is suspicious! The early reports said they spent 18 days at sea and the people were disheveled. But then the *New York Times* said the trip took *eight* days, and you can see that the people do not look like they've been at sea for this length of time. I have no proof of this. This is just my intelligence guided by experience—especially in light of last night's Wellstone exploitation rally.[48]

Of course, the Democrats had no connection with the Haitian crossing, which had been in the works in Haiti for nearly a year.[49] The effort could have done the Democrats no good in any case, as the Coast Guard does not naturalize illegal immigrants but of course repatriates them. Although it was pure hooey, Limbaugh cast his Haitian tale as fact ("intelligence"); and, two years later, he *recalled*, as if it really had occurred, that "they started importing Haitians the day before elections"—and on that airy basis he accused the Democrats of "registering dead people in Ohio and Illinois."[50] The rant continued, Limbaugh hammering at the "evidence" in his imagination, or at stray rumors floated by the Bush machine itself:

> The unlikely voter is the fraudulent voter, the—but—so they—if—if you—if you add in all the potential fraud that the Democrats may be gearing up in this election, and you look at—we've already got evidence in Ohio [*sic*]. They had two stories last week about the—they're registering people that have been dead for 25 years.[51]

In Lake County, Ohio, Republicans had charged the Democrats with trying to register a dead voter—and that charge was all the "evidence" of fraud that Limbaugh had.[52] (There were *no* such reports from Illinois.)

While the right's on-air propagandists ranted and insinuated and connected invisible dots throughout the 2004 campaign, the ticket's propagandists in the world of print, with somewhat more (ostensible) propriety, re-echoed the ever-growing charge of Democratic perfidy. The far-right press began this work in early summer, warning that the Democrats had plans to steal the race—a threat asserted vividly and often in Sun Myung Moon's *Washington Times*, which cast the accusations by Bush/Cheney operatives as news. "Liberal groups supporting Democratic Sen. John Kerry for president," the *Times* reported on June 29, "have been accused of fraud and of sending felons into people's homes in their efforts to register new voters in Missouri."[53] Dire predictions of a Democratic theft were also common on the Web throughout the months before Election Day. "Despite Kerry's lagging polls, the Democrats still plan to win this November. How? Perhaps by the old-fashioned way: stealing the election."[54] Thus began an "Insider's Report" on Richard Mellon Scaife's NewsMax.com on September 27—followed up, the next day, with "Democrats Trying to Steal Iowa, Too?" ("More evidence the Democrats are planning an Election Day surprise for George Bush.")[55] Such faux-news abounded in the final weeks of the campaign. In Colorado, the *Washington Times* reported on October 14, there was an effort by the legislature to "ease concerns about the integrity of the state election process," which was evidently jeopardized by "voter-registration groups [that] tilt politically to the left."[56]

> Republican Gov. Bill Owens said yesterday, "I am extremely concerned about the widespread allegations of serious and sustained criminal activity surrounding voter registration in Colorado."[57]

And on October 21, Moon's daily reported that Marc Racicot, chairman of the Bush/Cheney campaign, had "called on the Democrats to put an end to efforts to intimidate and confuse voters."[58] Meanwhile, the party's flacks were out in force, spinning the uncomprehending press. The Republicans, the *Washington Post* reported, planned to keep a close eye on Ohio's

Democratic neighborhoods. "Those are the places most likely for the Democrats," said GOP spokesperson Mindy Tucker Fletcher, "to try to steal the election."[59] On November 1, Mark Weaver, a diligent Bush/Cheney lawyer, said on MSNBC: "The Democrats want to steal this election. We're not going to let them."[60] On CNN that day he made the same dramatic point more vividly: "Piles and piles and piles of fictitious, fraudulent and erroneous voter registration cards! Someone out there is trying to steal this Ohio election! The Ohio Republican Party feels strongly that we should not stand by and let that happen!"[61]

Subtler propaganda was also at work. On September 5, Encounter Books came out with John Fund's *Stealing Elections: How Voter Fraud Threatens Our Democracy*.[62] Ostensibly an even-handed survey of the danger posed by voter fraud among both parties, the book is in fact a thinly veiled broadside against the Democrats—which should come as no surprise given the record of both publisher and author. Encounter Books is a non-profit house relying heavily on grants from the Lynde and Harry Bradley Foundation, a rightist funding institution in Milwaukee.[63] Encounter's publisher is Peter Collier, longtime literary partner to David Horowitz, whose work is in Encounter's catalogue along with titles like *Vile France: Fear, Duplicity, Cowardice and Cheese*, *The People v. Harvard Law* and *Red Star over Hollywood*. Fund himself is an accomplished far-right propagandist who, having started out as an assistant to Robert Novak, became an editorial writer for the *Wall Street Journal* (he played a role in that newspaper's lethal smear campaign against Vince Foster) and also ghost-wrote *The Way Things Ought to Be*, Rush Limbaugh's first best-seller.[64]

Any rational reader unacquainted with these facts, however, will quickly spot the propaganda function of Fund's pseudo-analysis, which deals only glancingly with rightist fraud—a rarity, according to the author. Mostly there are only Democratic claims that the Republicans have broken laws—mere propaganda by "the left," in other words. "Why do liberals persist in propagating the Myth of the Stolen Election?" Fund asks plaintively about Bush/Cheney's "victory" in 2000.[65] His pretension to the high ground is at times hilarious. While Democrats, he writes, think that "the most important value is empowering people to exercise their democratic rights," the other party is concerned primarily to do what's *right*: "Republicans tend to pay more attention to the rule of law and the standards and procedures that govern elections."[66] The book is filled with such outrageous guff, but then its purpose is not to illuminate but obfuscate: explicitly, through its fake balance bolstering the convenient myth that "both sides" do it and "both sides" complain about it; and, implicitly, to seize the issue of electoral fraud for those engaging in that crime themselves. (The book was actually commissioned by Karl Rove, early in Bush's first term.)* Certainly Fund's research is worth nothing, as his sources, by and large, are other party op-

---

*This, at any rate, was Fund's claim, according to his ex-fiancee Morgan Pillsbury; and he told her also that the book was to be published by the Family Research Council, which would have meant a much higher profile for the project (a claim that Fund denies). In early 2002, however, Fund's high hopes were dashed by the scandal following his arrest in New York City on February 23 for allegedly assaulting Pillsbury. (According to Cynthia Cotts' account in the *Village Voice*, the police found Fund hiding in a bathroom at the Manhattan Institute, a neoconservative think tank.) In the wake of his arrest, Pillsbury claimed that Fund had been pressuring Pillsbury to get an abortion and that, a few years before, he had been romantically involved with Pillsbury's mother. Although Fund took a leave of absence from the *Journal* after this episode and apparently had violated the ideal of "family values" that he had long promoted, there was little mainstream press coverage of the scandal. Fund continued working as a eratives much like himself. (In his acknowledgments he thanks, along with far-right kingpin Grover Norquist and the late Robert Bartley, longtime overseer of the *Wall Street Journal* editorial page, "John Samples of the Cato Institute, Ed Feulner of the Heritage Foundation, John Raisian at the Hoover Institution and Jim Piereson of the John M. Olin Foundation.")

The evidence for all those rightist charges was so thin as to suggest that it was made up out of nothing, just to give Bush/Cheney's soldiers a way to pique suspicions of the Democrats. Far more important, however, is that even if this or that charge was true, Democratic fraud would still be trivial by contrast with the massive fraud by the Republicans—prodigious and innumerable frauds, disabling Democratic voters by the hundreds of thousands at least; unprecedented fraud, ongoing even as the

---

"commentator" for the right, moving on to Pat Robertson's Christian Broadcasting Network. Cynthia Cotts, "Press Clips: John Fund, Come Clean," *Village Voice*, 2/27-3/5/02 (http://www.villagevoice.com/news/0209,cotts,32638,6.html); interview with Morgan Pillsbury, 5/20/03.

(In a letter sent to this book's publisher on August 4, 2005, Fund denied that he had ever beaten Pillsbury or left the *Journal*, and denied also that Karl Rove had "anything to do with the book." The police reports of Fund's assaults on Pillsbury, and the restraining orders that she filed against him, are available online at http://apj.us/20020116fund1.jpg, http://apj.us/20020116fund2.jpg, http://apj.us/20020221nypd072.jpg, http://apj.us/20020223order072.jpg, and http://apj.us/20020225order072.jpg. As of this writing, Fund's name is unlisted in the Wall Street Journal's automatic employee directory.)

This story, and many others like it, are highly pertinent to this analysis. First of all, they further demonstrate the startling projectivity of the theocratic movement and its propagandists. (It was Fund who had devised the slander, circulated by Matt Drudge, that Clinton adviser Sidney Blumenthal had beaten up his wife. Fund also charges that Pillsbury "has difficulty in distinguishing fact from fiction.") Secondly, such stories further clarify the rightist double standard of "the liberal media," which has overlooked the sexual excesses of the moralizing right (while over-focusing on the amours of Democrats) just as it has carefully looked away from the Republicans' electoral misdeeds.

fraudsters tore into the Enemy for, say, having fabricated 18 voters in Ohio. Certainly that fabrication, if it occurred, was criminal. The point here is not to exculpate those Democrats who crossed the line. The point is to suggest that the Republican attacks were not intended mainly to expose the evils of the Democrats but to obscure the many more, far more enormous sins of the Republicans themselves. Under the barrage of Limbaugh's accusations, the ill-read listener would assume that Bush and all his people were campaigning honestly; the more knowing listener—like the cowed reporter—would retreat into the comfy fiction that "both sides" had been playing dirty tricks, and now "both sides" were "attacking each other." Thus did the Republicans obscure the crucial fact that it was only they who had been playing dirty tricks immense enough to tip the election, and only they who were attacking anyone for playing dirty tricks; and yet the wide dissemination of their propaganda made it seem partisan, irrational or naïve to lay the blame where it belonged.

And yet, again, that propaganda was not just a tactical device, its users secretly aware of the truth and venting lies with a deliberate perverseness. The propaganda "took"—aroused those spreading it, and convinced, or cowed, those hearing it—because it was sincere as well as cynical. The wrath of Limbaugh or Hannity, Mark Weaver or Mindy Tucker Fletcher, enabled each to argue their preposterous case with the ingeniousness and volubility that only fear and hatred can call forth; and it was mainly their own "evil" that they feared and hated, having unconsciously projected it onto those warped, fanatical, duplicitous, election-stealing Democrats. This was particularly evident in their belligerent delusion that the Democrats were endlessly and groundlessly accusing *them* of fraud. In fact, on this subject the Democrats were largely mute—a silence as bewildering as the indignant fury of Bush/Cheney's troops, since there was every evidence of Republican mischief, and yet the Democrats refused to talk about it.* Throughout the race, while the Republicans were loudly and unanimously bellyaching over the impending Democratic fraud, the Democrats made no responses, either to those charges or, still more perplexing, to the fraudulent maneuvers by Bush/Cheney's forces all across the nation (see Chapter 5). In short, despite the right's propaganda, and the comfy journalistic commonplace that "charges have been flying on both sides," charges were flying only on one side.

This imbalance partly reflects the extreme rightist bias of the U.S. media, there being no liberal or Democratic counterpart to the propaganda juggernaut of Fox/Clear Channel and "the liberal media," from the *New York Times* and *Newsweek* to CBS and PBS. There simply is no dissident equivalent to Hannity, O'Reilly, Limbaugh, Michael Savage, Ann Coulter ("We have the

---

*In February of 2003, with the Democratic contest for the party's presidential nomination underway, I got myself invited to a fundraiser for John Kerry in Manhattan. I wanted to alert him to the danger posed—not to his chances only, but to American democracy itself—by Diebold and ES&S. When I finally had my chance to talk to him, I told him that those companies are owned and run by right-wing interests, that they had contracts in some thirty states (the number has gone up), that their programming codes are deemed proprietary information, that their machines are highly insecure and, most important, that they leave no paper trail. Kerry listened with an air of grave concern, and then apparently forgot about it, as he did not address the subject publicly until January 11, 2004, when he made a passing reference to it at a Democratic candidates' debate in Iowa. (Howard Dean had been the first contender to make mention of the problem, on November 11, 2003, and Dennis Kucinich issued a strong press release—"Private Voting Machines; Private Interests"—on November 20.) "We are going to prechallenge some of these automatic machines—the Diebold machines—where there have already been problems," Kerry vowed. In fact, he did no such thing; and the rest, sad to say, is history. (For what it's worth, Teresa Heinz Kerry was, at least at that fundraiser, passionately interested in the Diebold problem.)

media," she said to Hannity on July 26, 2005) and their comrades
throughout the "liberal" and "centrist" press, like George Will
and Charles Krauthammer at the *Washington Post*, David Brooks
and John Tierney at the *New York Times*, Joe Scarborough on
MSNBC, Robert Novak all over CNN, Robert Novak on PBS,
Tucker Carlson on PBS *and* MSNBC, Kate O'Beirne and on and
on. Blunt and lucid liberals and independents are so few that they
stand out as bold exceptions: Keith Olbermann on MSNBC
(Deborah Norville having been replaced by Tucker Carlson),
David Brancaccio on PBS, the op-ed all-stars at the *New York
Times* (Paul Krugman, Bob Herbert, Frank Rich and, when she
forgets Bill Clinton's sex life, Maureen Dowd), and the struggling
Air America, whose very novelty as a dissentient network demonstrates the inordinate sway of the far right throughout the Fourth
Estate. And the punditocracy is a model of political diversity by
contrast with the guests on shows like *Meet the Press* and *Hardball*,
or with the experts routinely quoted in the news, such voices always representing, or defending, the interests of the White
House and the Pentagon. Thus the U.S. press is just *not built* to
accommodate both sides although it is forever claiming to do so;
and so any liberals and Democrats who would decry the fraud by
the Republicans had little opportunity to do so.

This explanation is inadequate, however, for the press's imbalance was not only a result of its systemic rightist bias. Even if
it had been receptive to the Democrats' complaints, the Democrats themselves, with very few exceptions, simply didn't have it
in them to address the issue with the proper clarity and force.
Although they *were* being robbed, they seemed to be afraid to
say so, or afraid to face it; while the Republicans, who were not
being robbed, asserted that they *were*, and that the *Democrats*
were making lots of groundless charges—and that Big Lie,

which the Republicans repeated and repeated with passionate intensity, certainly had less to do with propaganda training than with paranoid conviction. On the fact of the Republicans' attempts at fraud, there was, of course, a lot of talk among the Democratic rank-and-file, and by some state and city legislators; but the top Democrats themselves, and most liberal commentators, were largely silent. Robert Kuttner, co-founder of the *American Prospect*, wrote some honest op-ed pieces for the *Boston Globe* ("The Art of Stealing Elections," on October 19, was extraordinary for its bluntness), and Joshuah Bearman of *L.A. Weekly* wrote about the contest with refreshing candor.[67] The Democrats' official comments, on the other hand, were very few, and not too rousing. On October 20, on CNBC's *Capitol Report*, Terry McAuliffe, chairman of the Democratic National Committee, had this to say:

> When [RNC chairman] Ed Gillespie's on your show, ask him why he spent a half a million dollars of the Republican National Committee money to hire a company called Sproul & Associates, where two employees, one in Nevada and one in Oregon, specifically said that they were ordered to rip up voter registration cards for only the Democrats and not the Republicans. So we are very concerned.

Between that feeble, over-complicated one-shot and the punchy unanimity of Bush/Cheney's propaganda chorus, there was all the difference in the world; nor did Kuttner's single piece, however strong, a winning propaganda campaign make. In order to accuse the Democrats of running such a drive, the tribunes of the right were forced to make it up.

On those very few occasions when a Democrat would hark back to the mess in Florida four years before, the rightists went bananas. On July 16, Sean Hannity reported that Rep. Corrine Brown (D-FL) had "had a virtual meltdown" in the House, "while debating a bill that would allow international monitoring of the presidential election in November."[68] They showed a clip of Brown's remarks:

> I come from Florida, where you and others participated in what I call the United States coup d'etat. We need to make sure that it doesn't happen again.
>
> Over and over again, after the election, when you stole the election, you came back here and said, "Get over it." No, we're not going to get over it. And we want verification from the world.

"'Coup d'état'! 'Stole the election'!" sneered Hannity in livid disbelief. "Will Democrats ever get over the 2000 election?" Rightist shock jock Mike Gallagher, introduced as Sean's "good friend," then made the crucial link between the congresswoman and the Democrats in general:

> It's like her medicine didn't kick in. I mean, I'm really not sure if they *will* get over it—but the real question, Sean, is: Is she just a loose cannon or does she represent the heart and soul of the Democratic Party? I'm convinced she represents what they're thinking.[69]

In fact, if Brown had spoken what was really in the minds of all the Democrats, they had a funny way of showing it. Her remarks were stricken from the record on a vote of 219 to 187, with 28 abstaining (18 of them Democrats, including Henry Waxman and Dick Gephardt).[70] The debacle in Florida came up again, in more restrained language, on September 27, when the *Washington Post* ran "Still Seeking a Fair Florida Vote," an admonitory op-ed by Jimmy Carter. Having co-chaired, with Gerald Ford, the bipartisan commission that had led to Congress's passage of the Help America Vote Act (HAVA) in 2002, Carter noted that "the Act's key provisions have not been implemented" and expressed his fear that "a repetition of the problems of 2000 now seems likely," as Governor Jeb Bush had done nothing to prevent it. While carefully refraining from a categorical indictment, Carter ended with a bang:

> It is unconscionable to perpetuate fraudulent or biased electoral practices in any nation. It is especially objectionable among us Americans, who have prided ourselves on setting a global example for pure democracy. With reforms unlikely at this late stage of the election, perhaps the only recourse will be to focus maximum public scrutiny on the suspicious process in Florida.

Carter's piece was wholly accurate in every point—and the Republicans did not refute a one of them. Indeed, they tacitly confirmed them all by pounding on the table in an orgy of suspicious fury, singling Carter out for repetitious personal abuse. "The former president," snarled John Gibson on Fox News Channel, "is now warning U.S. voters that Team Bush is preparing to steal the Florida election this year!"[71] That warning was *outrageous!* Why? Well, Jimmy Carter "was a calamity as president," Jimmy Carter's term "shall live in infamy," Jimmy Carter's "presidency created the worst and most bitter years of my life and the lives of every American I knew," etc. "I think the Democrats are hysterical! The president *won* the election in Florida!" Rep. Mark Foley (R-FL) said on CNN.[72] "It's amazing! They can't get over this! Four years later!" The congressman then took his shot at that day's major talking point, although the effort seemed to tax his eloquence: "And now they have *Jimmy Carter*, who I'm glad they are reminding us of the Carter administration's handling of events during the '76 through '80!" (That day, CNN's Judy Woodruff thus "reported" on the controversy: "Carter cites what he calls highly partisan election officials and a lack of uniform voting procedures. A spokeswoman for Florida's secretary of state responded by saying that the agency is run in a, quote, 'nonpartisan manner.'") The next day, Jeb Bush himself sashayed into the protest, also steamed, but with a whole new talking point (as yesterday's *ad hominem* assault had evidently backfired):

"If I see a conspiracy," said the governor, referring to a charge Carter never made, "it is an organized effort by varying different groups, including MoveOn.org, you know, that has said that the hurricanes happened because of global warming, or something like that."[73] From that incisive stroke (as everybody knows that hurricanes and global warming are completely unrelated), Jeb went quasi-statesmanlike: "There's this constant haranguing of nonsense, including President Carter, which is a huge surprise to me, because I've admired his compassionate actions in his post-presidency period."

Thus the Republicans, in straining to depict the Democrats as morbidly obsessed with voter fraud, used as their examples two atypical pronouncements. At least those instances were public. The only other case the Republicans could find was buried in a party manual for campaign workers, which made big news three weeks before Election Day thanks to Matt Drudge's propaganda website.

The manual included a detailed advisement on "How to Organize to Prevent and Combat Voter Intimidation," which began with this entirely rational observation: "The best way to combat minority voter intimidation tactics is to prevent them from occurring in the first place and prepare in advance to deal with them should they take place on Election Day."[74] This was followed by a number of specific recommendations as to how one might most powerfully publicize and thereby eliminate, or at least modify, the threat. At one point the manual suggests, "If no signs of intimidation tactics have emerged yet, launch a 'pre-emptive strike' (particularly well-suited to states in which these techniques have been tried in the past)." This is best done by first "issuing a press release" which pointedly and vividly "review[s] Republican tactics used in the past in your area or state," and then by condemning it and getting ready for its happening again.[75]

This very sound advice—based squarely, it must be reemphasized, on the GOP's long use of such intimidation tactics—was angrily denounced, and thoroughly distorted, by the regime's propaganda chorus, whose members all expressed their boundless indignation at those Democrats for *making charges based on nothing*. "The guide instructs Kerry operators to accuse Republicans of trying to prevent minority groups from voting even if there's no evidence that the charge is actually true, no evidence at all!" sputtered Tucker Carlson on CNN.[76] "They want to rile up the minorities to denounce tactics that do not exist," Ted Halaby, chair of the Colorado GOP, fumed in the *Rocky Mountain News* and, in the *Denver Post*, deplored this use of "false allegations."[77] John Kerry "is working to scare those voters with lies and wholesale fabrications," RNC chair Ed Gillespie bristled in the *Washington Times*.[78] "A Colorado Election Day manual, and it's a voter intimidation drive, and they say that none exists!" Sean Hannity ranted surrealistically on Fox, with Dick Cheney facing him. "In other words, if you don't find any voter intimidation, launch a pre-emptive strike!"

CHENEY: Claim that there is intimidation anyway.

HANNITY: Claim that there is!

CHENEY: Well, it's—it's unfortunate. I really think that the American people are not all served by those kinds of tactics.[79]

And so it went for days, with hearty condemnation of "these lies" (as William Bennett put it) pouring forth, it seemed, from everybody and his brother (Jeb Bush called it "disgusting").[80]

Here was Republican projection at its purest—for, as we have seen, the disingenuous "pre-emptive strike" was, is, and will always remain the central tactic of the regime's military policy and domestic politics, the two being therefore often difficult to tell apart. In thus flaying the Democrats for their own habitual sin, the Busheviks were also noisily denying history. "He's *lying*, saying Republicans have an effort to suppress the black vote!"[81] raged Hannity about John Kerry—the same defensive pitch that Bush & Co. had been making since its theft of the election in 2000. "No black voter," smirked Rich Lowry, editor of the *National Review*, on CNN on March 3, 2001, "could point to any actual instance when he or she was disenfranchised. . . . It's ridiculous. It's an urban myth and it's a poisonous one."[82] "There was no disenfranchisement," blinked Fox's Fred Barnes in August of that year.[83] It is the same line that we keep hearing now, and on all sides.

The long Republican projection came to an enormous climax on January 6, 2005, in the House "debate" over the Democratic challenge to the electoral vote in Ohio—that is, over the Conyers Report.[84] One could not call it a debate without quotation marks, since a debate, as the Oxford English Dictionary puts it, is "a discussion of questions of public interest in Parliament or in any assembly," and what took place on January 6 was not a discussion. Rather than exchange opinions on the Conyers findings, the Republicans and Democrats merely took turns at the podium, the latter duly quoting the report, the former luridly maligning it. While, clearly, none of the Republicans had read it, all of them had obviously memorized the talking points against it, and vented them with zeal. The two parties might have been representing different planets; and yet their clashing testimonies made it very clear, to anybody who was paying attention, that the report was fundamentally correct. There were few findings in it that Bush/Cheney's soldiers even bothered to contest, much less refute; and what rebuttal they gave was as weak as it was vehement. Their speeches were of interest partly for that reason, and partly as tremendous specimens of propaganda at its crudest: speaker after speaker trumpeting the same catchphrases, shouting the same "arguments," their rants all based entirely on the same talking points.

"Mr. Speaker, this is a sad day," began Rep. Bob Ney (R-FL). "It saddens all of us that we have to be here debating this issue." It is "a sad day in the history of this nation," he added later. "It is a sad day," said Rep. Thomas Reynolds (R-NY). (In a press release that morning, Sen. Mike DeWine, R-OH, had opined, "If Ohio's electors are challenged, I think it will be a sad day for the United States Congress.") "I rise with a heavy heart today on this issue," began David Hobson (R-OH). "It is also with a heavy heart that I address this House," said Rep. Bobby Jindal (R-LA). And Tom DeLay (R-TX), as ever, pushed the mournful rhetoric into a more inflammatory key: "Mr. Speaker, what we are witnessing today is a shame. A shame." ("It was a sad day for Congress," Rep. Rob Portman, R-OH, told Judy Woodruff on

CNN's *Inside Politics* that night.) "This petition is beneath us," said DeLay. "I am glad that my daughter and father are no longer here to watch this debate taking place in this House," said Jindal, adding that "this is not a good day for our country, not a good day for democracy."[85]

What was sad and shameful was not that tens of thousands of Americans had been disenfranchised in Ohio, but that "we are spending time on debating the challenge to the validity of the Presidential election," said Rep. Candice Miller (R-MI). It was sad, and "shameful and reprehensible" (Rep. Tom Price, R-GA), that "this frivolous debate" (Deborah Pryce, R-OH)—"a publicity stunt" (Hayworth)—"political grandstanding" (Price)—"a cynical political ploy" (Portman)—should "waste Congress's time and taxpayer dollars" (Rep. Thelma Drake, R-VA), as it "is not the proper use of the people's time" (Rep. J. D. Hayworth, R-AZ). For those behind "this exercise" (Oxley) were *not* the people, but "certain extreme elements of Sen. Kerry's own party," who "have cast themselves in the role of Michael Moore, concocting wild conspiracy theories" (Pryce). The problem is "the Michael Moore wing of the Democratic Party," that is, "the Michael Moore side that defines 'democracy' as Democrats going to the polls, and 'conspiracy' as *Republicans* going to the polls!" (Rep. Ric Keller, R-FL). "Everybody in the world has accepted" Bush's victory, Rep. Mario Diaz-Balart, R-FL, said that night on Fox News Channel, "except a small group of radicals in the U.S. Congress and a couple of anti-American activists around the country, such as Michael Moore."

These "radicals" deliberately played up some very minor glitches on Election Day. "Now, it is true that no election is perfect. We have seen this since the beginning of our democracy" (Rep. David Dreier, R-CA). "No election is ever perfect. They never are" (Portman). "There is no such thing as a perfect election. There has not been. There never will be a perfect election" (Ney). "But small imperfections here and there do not a mass conspiracy make" (Dreier). In fact, "there is absolutely no credible basis to question the outcome of the election" (Portman). These "activists" had long since wasted too much of "the people's time" (Hayworth), demanding recounts that have only reconfirmed what everybody else already knew. "The request for an Ohio recount has been fulfilled, and it verified what we already knew" (Pryce). "The Ohio recount requested by the other party has been completed and has been verified" (Rep. Ralph Regula, R-OH). "The votes were counted and then recounted" (Portman). In short, their "so-called evidence" (Ney) has "no basis of fact" [*sic*] (Miller). "The bottom line is those bringing this challenge today simply cannot accept the fact that George Bush has been elected President of the United States" (Ney). Bush won Ohio by "an overwhelming and comfortable margin" (Pryce). He won Ohio by "an overwhelmingly comfortable margin" (Keller). "The president's margin is significant" (Rep. Roy Blunt, R-MO).

These radicals could not, or would not, face reality. It is a "*fact* that their candidate lost this election," a "*fact* that . . . their vision for America has been rejected by the majority of Americans," a "*fact* that George W. Bush simply received more votes than Sen. John Kerry" (Miller). Hating that reality, those diehards are "a band of conspiracy theorists" (Ney), their "righteous indignation based on fantasies" (Miller), "advancing wild-eyed conspiracy theories" (Reynolds), "irresponsible conspiracy theories" (Portman), "Hollywood inspired conspiracy theories" (Keller). Or perhaps those "fantasies" are not real delusions but mere pretexts for obstructionism, compelled sheerly by resentment. "Apparently some Democrats only want to gripe about counts, recounts, and recounts of recounts" (Pryce). "In the blue states, they call it a recount. In the red states, we call it what it is: sour grapes" (Keller). "Mr. Speaker, it is called sour grapes" (Hayworth). Whatever impulse drove them, those "extremist elements" within the Democratic Party finally stood revealed as dangerous subversives, who, if things didn't go their way, were willing to tear the system down.

Their short-term purpose was to "try to somehow delegitimize the President of the United States and his election" (Portman). It was "an attempt to sow doubt on the legitimacy of this President" (Rep. Steve Chabot, R-OH), by "sowing seeds of doubt about a legitimately decided election" (Dreier). Their larger goal, however, was "to plant the insidious seeds of doubt in the electoral process" itself (Hayworth)—and to do so is to "undermine the prospect of democracy" (Dreier). "Every time we attack the process, we cast that doubt on that fabric of democracy that is so important" (Rep. Dave Hobson, R-OH). Therefore, the Republicans could not "allow the conspiracy theorists to undermine the public confidence in the electoral system itself" (Keller). Tom DeLay summed up the threat: "Many observers will discard today's petition as a partisan waste of time, but it is much worse than that."

> It is an assault against the institutions of our representative democracy. It is a threat to the very ideals it ostensibly defends. . . . It is a crime against the dignity of American democracy, and that crime is not victimless. . . .
>
> This is not a normal debate. This is a direct attack to undermine our democracy by using a procedure to undermine the constitutional election that was just held. . . .

Democrat leaders are not just hurting themselves. By their irre-sponsible tactics, they hurt the House, they hurt the Nation, and they hurt rank-and-file Democrats at kitchen tables all around this country.

In short the Democrats, like the Devil, were acting out of sheer malevolence, and thereby carrying out "the party's primary strategy: to obstruct, to divide and to destroy" (Pryce). The Hammer hit the nail right on the head: "They have turned to what might be called the 'X-Files Wing' of the Democrat Party to make their first impression. Rather than substantive debate, Democrat leaders are still adhering to a failed strategy of spite, obstruction, and conspiracy theories!"

For *there was no evidence of fraud* (by the Republicans). The Democrats were using "baseless and meritless tactics" (Pryce) to present their "so-called evidence" (Ney), "making allegations that have no basis of fact" (Miller), making claims for which "there is no evidence whatsoever, no evidence whatsoever" (Dreier). "No proven allegations of fraud. No reports of wide-spread wrongdoing. It was, at the end of the day, an honest elec-tion" (Bill Shuster, R-PA). "Mr. Speaker, the challenges to those votes in Ohio are turkeys!" (Miller). The challenge is "without merit" (Boehner), "without any merit whatsoever" (Dreier), the alleged perps committing all that fraud "without leaving a shred of evidence" (Drake). "We are told, without any evidence, that unknown Republican agents stole the Ohio election," said DeLay. "No such voter disenfranchisement occurred in this election of 2004, and for that matter the election of 2000. Everybody knows it. The voters know it, the candidates know it, the courts know it, and the evidence proves it."

"Everybody knows it." Bush's victory in Ohio was "unques-tioned by the Democratic nominee" (Blunt) and reconfirmed by

Kerry aides Joe Lockhart and David Wade (Hayworth), and by Jeff Ruppert, a Kerry/Edwards lawyer (Portman). "Not one board member has objected to the process in Ohio, not one" (Rep. Pat Tiberi, R-OH). Bush's victory was "unquestioned by anybody involved in this process who certified the election" (Blunt). "I have not heard one election official in any of the 88 counties, Democrat or Republican, raise any concern about the outcome or fairness of the election that occurred in their counties" (Boehner). The election boards, moreover, are "bipartisan teams" (Blunt) conducting "a very bipartisan process" (Boehner) in a "bipartisan system" (Tiberi)—that is, a system that is "totally bipartisan" (Portman)—with "bipartisan county boards . . . in every area in Ohio" (Keller). "You have a system of 88 separate bipartisan county election boards" (Regula). "Every single thing that is done by a Republican—it is also done at the same time by a Democrat" (Blunt). And they were not the only ones who found no fault with the election in Ohio. "Even those foreign officials who many of our colleagues invited to the United States as election observers have come to the conclusion that George Bush won the election" (Dreier).

And so the gracious, the responsible, the right thing for the Democrats to do would have been to face reality, admit defeat, halt their obstructionism and start doing the people's business, in friendly partnership with the cooperative Republicans, who are only looking out for everyone's best interests. "Mr. Speaker, there is a saying we have used in Florida over the past four years that the other side would be wise to learn: 'Get over it'" (Keller). "Is it not ironic that the very people who refuse to move on are the people from Moveon.org and their hero Michael Moore?" (Keller). "It is time for those who refuse to accept the American people's decision, if you will pardon the expression, to move on" (Reynolds). "The election is over. Let us get on with it" (Tiberi).

"We need to move on . . . to move forward" (Portman). "I say let's move on to do what we were elected to do, make positive change in this country. It's time we put partisan politics behind us" (Shuster).

And yet the Republicans, of course, being only human, also had to mention the gigantic fraud and countless dirty tricks played by the Democrats—who, it must not be forgotten, had been trying to rig Kerry's victory as shamelessly as they had tried to rig Al Gore's election four years earlier. While the Conyers people had a lot to say against Ohio's Bush campaign, they said nothing about the many shocking crimes by their own party. For example, "fraudulent voter registration forms were being submitted and the worker who collected them was paid in crack cocaine" (Miller). That sordid crime, which reportedly involved over 100 forms, was not a party operation but a case of personal corruption, as is always likely when you pay strangers to register new voters. (The culprit, who had been recruited by a woman hired by someone in Toledo, was busted two weeks prior to Election Day.)[86] In any case, it was a rare occurrence in Ohio—as the Republicans themselves made clear, their lurid stories of electoral chicanery referring mostly to misdeeds, or allegations of misdeeds, in other states. Rep. Jack Kingston (R-GA) reeled off several criminal episodes, or suspected episodes (at least suspected by Jack Kingston) that the House Committee *should* have mentioned:

> Why not Minnesota, where Kerry *won*, where there were discrepancies and Democrat groups working inside polling places at polling booths [*sic*]? Why not New Hampshire, where Kerry *won*, where Democrat operatives allegedly slashed wheels of vehicles intended to take Republicans to the polls? Why not Wisconsin, which Kerry *won*, where Democrat operatives physically intimidated Republican

voters? Or why not even Colorado, where a Democrat worker with ACORN [Association of Community Organizations for Reform Now] signed herself up to vote 25 different times? Or why not New Mexico where a 13-year-old was registered to vote by the same Democrat front group?

In Minnesota, MoveOn.org had been accused, reportedly by several thousand citizens, of stationing activists too close to— that is, within 100 feet of—polling places. Neither they nor any "Democrat groups" had been charged with "working inside polling places," in Minnesota or anywhere else. (The several thousand charges seemed to represent a propaganda drive by the Republicans, who tried, and failed, to sideline MoveOn with a temporary restraining order.) On Election Day, MoveOn's Eli Pariser responded to the charges with a statement, which concluded thus:

> Make no mistake—this is clearly a pre-meditated, planned, orchestrated attempt by the Republican Party. They have now made these charges today from state parties in at least 5 states, including New Hampshire, Iowa, Minnesota, Colorado and Michigan.
>
> Of course MoveOn volunteers went to civics class and know that you can't electioneer near the polls. And of course MoveOn knows such a move would totally backfire against us. We categorically deny these charges. Our instructions to our volunteers were vetted by our lawyers. And we don't believe in such tactics. This is a smear campaign against us. It's the Swift Boat veterans smear story of November 2nd. Its purpose is clear and false. The public won't be fooled.[87]

In New Hampshire there were *no* reports of "Democrat operatives" slashing tires, and in Wisconsin, *no* reports of Democrats bullying Republicans.[88] (Tires *were* slashed in Wisconsin, and the perpetrators caught and punished.)[89] And those wrongs in Colorado and New Mexico were merely further instances of maverick opportunism at ACORN. The girlfriend of an ACORN worker did indeed sign herself up to vote 25 times, and also signed up three friends to vote another 40 times—a scam that made $130 for her boyfriend, who was paid two bucks per vote. ("I was just helping out downtown," she said. "Everybody needs an extra dollar here now and then to make their quota for the day.")[90] ACORN disavowed the scam and cooperated fully with investigators. The ACORN worker who had registered the 13-year-old in New Mexico had actually been fired *before* the incident.[91]

From that underwhelming catalogue of minor or fictitious crimes, Kingston shifted his remorseless gaze to the key state:

> And why not some of the other problems that were going on in Ohio, why do we not talk about them? For example, in Franklin County in Ohio where a dead person was registered to vote, or 25 addresses were submitted for the same man, why are they not concerned about that? Or why not raise a question about Lake County where a man who had been dead for 20 years was registered to vote?

These tales too were dubious. The "case" in Franklin County was entirely based on the assertions of Republican officials there and in Kenneth Blackwell's office; and, as ever, ACORN was the villain of the piece, with 62 "suspicious forms" ascribed to it (and six more from the Columbus Urban League).[92] The single case of "fraud" in Lake County also was impossible to verify, as it was based entirely on the say-so of Charles Coulson, the Republican county prosecutor there; and he, as of this writing, has ignored requests for further information.

Although ACORN claims to be nonpartisan, it certainly supports the Democratic Party and had clear partisan connections all throughout the 2004 campaign. (On the other hand, ACORN received no funding from the DNC.) Its "fraud," however, was neither systemic not collective, but merely the predictable result of using needy volunteers to register new voters, and paying them for every one that they find, or, as in some desperate cases, fabricate.[93]

Even if such tales are true, the totality of ACORN doings throughout the country pales to insignificance before the Republican Party's massive and diverse vote-stealing apparatus in Ohio alone. For Bush/Cheney's apparatchiks to decry the registration of dead voters by pro-Democratic groups—or, rather, by *one* such group—was rather like the Mafia deploring petty crime among the blacks. And yet Kingston's brief was either groundless or hyperbolically exaggerated—like the Republicans' whole contribution to the House "debate." Here again Bush/Cheney's soldiers were themselves the guiltiest and crudest perpetrators of the very crimes that they appeared to be denouncing, as, in falsehood after falsehood after falsehood, they charged the Democrats with telling lies.

First of all, those who had charged fraud by the Republicans were no "small group of radicals" but many thousands of Ohioans from every walk of life. Those citizens, moreover, were entirely unaffiliated with "the Michael Moore wing of the Democratic Party," whatever that may be. (The filmmaker has always been a gadfly on the party's heavy hide, his buzzing sometimes welcome, sometimes not.) Moore, in fact, was not "concocting wild conspiracy theories" about Bush's victory. As he made clear on his website on January 4, he backed the challenge purely out of democratic principle—"the right of the people to vote AND have ALL their votes counted." As for the "theories" of electoral fraud, Moore did not subscribe to any of them:

> Now, I know a lot of you wish this little problem of Ohio would just go away. And many of you who wish this are Democrats. You just want to move on (no pun intended!). I can't say I blame you. It's rough to lose two elections in a row when the first one you actually won and the second one you should have won. And it seems this time around, about 3 million more Americans preferred to continue the war in Iraq and give the rich more tax breaks than those who didn't. No sense living in denial about that.[94]

Bush/Cheney's soldiers lied repeatedly about the recount: "The Ohio recount requested by the other party has been completed and has been verified." In fact, as we have seen, the recount had not been completed (nor, therefore, verified), but rather was successfully subverted by the state Republican machine. (That talking point was a revival of one used just as cynically by Bush & Co. back in 2000.)[95] They also lied about the unanimity of Ohio's election officials—not one of whom, "in any of the 88 counties, Democrat or Republican, raise[d] any concern about the outcome or fairness of the election," the troops proclaimed. In fact, Sherole Eaton, a Democratic election official in Hocking County, spoke out loud and clear about the fraud involving Triad—and was fired because of it. As her case demonstrates, the fact that the election boards were all "bipartisan," a fact belabored heavily by Bush's troops in the "debate," meant very little in Ohio, where all served at the pleasure of the vigilant and micro-managerial Republican Ken Blackwell. The same soldiers also lied about "those foreign officials" (from OSCE—see above, p. 29) who came to the United States to monitor the race. As *Ohio* was the point at issue, it was at best misleading to assert that those officials "have [concluded] that George Bush won the election," since, as we have seen, the two would-be observers posted to that state were not allowed to enter, or even to approach, a single polling place. (Moreover, while OSCE did, in its executive report, approve the contest overall, its individual members were less sanguine. "Monitoring elections in Serbia a few months ago was much simpler," noted Konrad Olszewski, an OSCE observer stationed in Miami, in a post-election interview with the *International Herald Tribune*.[96])

To nail every single lie by the Republicans in that "debate" may threaten to obscure the more important fact that the entire drive was itself a lie. Its whole purpose, first of all, was to propagate the staggering canard that there were "no reports of widespread wrongdoing"—as if John Conyers and his peers had not reported what they had in fact reported. In other words, that drive was a particularly brazen exercise in faith-based propaganda, a counter-factual effort as egregious as the regime's war campaign against Iraq, its drive against the truth of natural selection, its crusade to define this secular republic as "a Christian nation," its global jihad against condom use, and all its other pious efforts to deny reality.

> We are told, without any evidence, that unknown Republican agents stole the Ohio election. No such voter disenfranchisement occurred in this election of 2004, and for that matter the election of 2000. Everybody knows it. The voters know it, the candidates know it, the courts know it, and the evidence proves it.

And yet the untruth of the campaign's central talking point does not itself account entirely for the deep and total wrongness of that drive—which was fundamentally directed not at its apparent targets, but at the very people who had mounted it. *They* were the "extreme elements" in their own party, the "small group of radicals in the U.S. Congress." Perceiving all who disagreed with them as plotting to destroy them, they were the ones "advancing wild-eyed conspiracy theories," their "righteous indignation based on fantasies." Moreover, they are the ones who "cannot accept the fact that their agenda, that their vision for America, has been rejected by the majority of Americans." Today that blindness is more dangerous even than when Clinton was in power (and the Republican extremists were doing all they could to "try to somehow delegitimize the President of the United States and his election"). Now that they *are* the government (although, of course, they hate "the government"), and they now dominate the media (although, of course, they hate "the media"), they have successfully propounded an idea—that "President Bush won Ohio by an overwhelming and comfortable margin"—for which there was, and is, "no evidence whatsoever." Thus these extremists now "undermine the prospect of democracy," which calls for pluralism, tolerance and compromise, whereas they are in power only "to obstruct, to divide, and to destroy." In short, they hate democracy, for they "do not like the result"—and so they won, although they did not win, and could not win.

To the Bush Republicans it was quite clear that they could not beat Kerry/Edwards honestly. Some of them believed that they were *forced* to act illegally or unethically because the Democrats were so much slyer and more cynical. Such was the paranoid subtext of much Republican war planning, especially on the theocratic right. In July of 2004, Nelson Books came out with *If It's Not Close, They Can't Cheat: Crushing the Democrats in Every Election and Why Your Life Depends On It*, by *Weekly Standard* columnist Hugh Hewitt (also author of *The Embarrassed Believer: Reviving Christian Witness in an Age of Unbelief*). A work more frankly partisan than John Fund's pseudo-neutral *Stealing Elections*, Hewitt's diatribe is rich with variations on the propaganda theme of the Democrats' habitual lawlessness. "A party with a tradition of cheating as rich as the Democrats' finds it easy to bend the rules or to celebrate those who do," notes Hewitt, who quotes Al Gore to make his point: "'I'm not like George Bush,' Al Gore said during Campaign 2000. 'If he wins or loses, life goes on. I'll do anything to win.'"[97]

> This general attitude among Democrats, articulated so perfectly by Gore, is the reason that it is important for Republicans not merely to win election. Republicans must win by comfortable margins. If it is close, you can count on the Democrats cheating. You can count on dirty tricks. Putting a close election in front of the Democratic Party is like putting a beautiful woman in a bikini on a kickboard in the *Jaws* movies. Cue the music.[98]

The Democrats play dirty tricks because of their extremism, Hewitt claims without a hint of irony. "The bile of the Left has poisoned a significant slice of the Democratic Party. These fanatics positively hate President Bush," he writes, and then adds hilariously that "they make no effort to embrace the traditional tone of debate and the courtesies of campaigns."[99]

That take on "the Democrats" is not based on induction from experience or history, but is itself a very old religious trope—at least as old as Christianity itself, although its implications would have troubled Jesus. To say that "they" are *naturally* dishonest, predatory and insatiable, as prone to fraud as sharks are to attacking women, is tacitly to call for a pre-emptive strike against them—or for continual strikes, inasmuch as "your life depends" on "crushing the Democrats." Such inflammatory riffs, wholly based on a projective fantasy about the Other, have been commonplace among crusaders ever since the knights of Western Christendom set out to murder Muslims (and many Jews along the way, and, ultimately, countless Christians in Constantinople). "It would indeed be forbidden to kill pagans if one could oppose in any other way their violence and hatred and oppression of the faithful," preached Bernard of Clairvaux to the Templars, the monastic warriors who policed the conquered Holy Land, in 1146. "But as it is, it is better to massacre them so that their sword is no longer suspended over the heads of the just."[100] With such fiends one does not bandy words or adopt half-hearted measures. ("No one who is not a learned clerk should argue with Jews," warned the great crusader Louis IX— "St. Louis"—about a century later. "A layman, as soon as he hears the Christian faith maligned should defend it by the sword, with a good thrust in the belly as far as the sword will go.")[101]

The pious call for a pre-emptive strike resounds throughout our nation's history—which often has itself been understood as a crusade, to forge, through violence, the New Jerusalem. Thus were the Indians wiped out, by settlers certain that there was no other way to deal with them except through "savage war." After 1700, no tribes threatened or attempted to exterminate the whites or drive them away; yet it remained a given in this country that the natives were intent on killing all of "us," and not the other way around. According to historian Richard Slotkin:

The accusation [that the Indians were bent on genocide] is better understood as an act of psychological projection that made the Indians scapegoats for the morally troubling side of American expansion: the myth of "savage war" became a basic ideological convention of a culture that was itself increasingly devoted to the extermination or expropriation of the Indians and the kidnapping and enslavement of black Africans.[102]

"History scarcely presents an example of a civilized nation carrying on a war with barbarians, without adopting the mode of warfare of the barbarous nation," wrote Dr. Joseph Doddridge of Virginia, an eminent physician and Episcopalian minister, in 1824.[103] "The original settlers of the Western regions"—that is, the west of Pennsylvania and Virginia—"adopted the Indian mode of warfare from necessity, and a motive of revenge." The civilized, in other words, had no choice but to answer fire with fire. General Custer wrote, in his memoirs, on the Indian's incorrigible savagery:

> We see him as he is, and, so far as all knowledge goes, as he ever has been, a savage in every sense of the word; not worse, perhaps, than his white brother would be similarly born and bred, but one whose cruel and ferocious nature far exceeds that of any wild beast of the desert. That this is true no one who had been brought into intimate contact with the wild tribes will deny.[104]

Many whites familiar with "the wild tribes" *did* deny that charge; but Custer was a staunch crusader, fighting not existent human beings but a bogey partly of his own imagination. (Knowing his record, the Indians were very pleased to massacre him and his men at Little Bighorn.) Our history is rich with such phantasmal hordes, and with crusaders going after them—making enemies where there were none, or making latent enemies more numerous, ferocious and resolved. The working class, the slaves, the abolitionists, the black freedmen, the urban poor and the new immigrants from Europe's South and East (Jews, Sicilians, Slavs, etc.) were all perceived as posing drastic threats to civilized society, so that the preservation of our very lives and way of life required that, in responding to the danger, we dispense with ethical and moral niceties.

The Cold War was the culmination (to date) of America's history of paranoid projection. That conflict was itself, among other things, a global face-off brought about, and sustained, by mutual projection, each side obdurate in its conviction that the other was "implacable, insatiable, unceasing in its drive for world domination," as Senator John Kennedy proclaimed in 1960.[105] Each side, even at its most aggressive, saw itself as making even its most lethal moves from a defensive crouch; and on our side were those who saw it as essential, if regrettable, that We learn to be as brutal as They are by nature. (This was as true of China as it was of the Soviet Union and the United States. In Mao's eyes, the Chinese invasion of Korea was *defensive*.)[106]

It is now clear that we are facing an implacable enemy whose avowed objective is world domination by whatever means and at whatever loss. There are no rules in such a game. Hitherto acceptable longstanding American concepts of "fair play" must be reconsidered. We must develop effective espionage and counterespionage services and must learn to subvert, sabotage, and destroy our enemies by more clever, more sophisticated and more effective methods than those used against us.[107]

This advisement was included in a classified assessment of the CIA, written by General James Doolittle at the request of President Eisenhower in 1954. Ike wanted guidance in his supervision of the agency, which, after its orchestration of "regime change" in Iran and Guatemala, was poised for bigger budgets and still more grandiose designs. While Doolittle did suggest a bit of bureaucratic tightening and noted some deficiencies in Allen Dulles's management, his main point was to urge the moral emulation of the enemy—an adaptation that would not have seemed bizarre to Eisenhower, as the National Security Council had been making the same argument since 1947. Ike did balk, however, at Doolittle's proposition that the immoralist worldview—the infamous conviction that the ends justify the means—be clearly propagated nationwide: "It may become necessary that the American people be made acquainted with, understand and support this fundamentally repugnant philosophy."[108] That step Eisenhower would not take, as the United States would thereby sacrifice the high ground, which would have posed a giant propaganda problem; but he agreed entirely with Doolittle's central point that the contest with global communism was a "savage war," wherein We must fight the Enemy with his own tactics. However sensible that strategy may have seemed, it too was nothing more than a crusade; and it doomed us *and* our enemies to ever further misery, in Southeast Asia, Central and South America, Africa and—most disastrously—Arabia and the Middle East, where the Cold War's repercussions, aggravated by a toxic blend of Christian eschatology, Islamist jihad and religious Zionism, threaten all of us.

That sort of zeal is now particularly threatening here at home—as Bush's second "win" and his regime's agenda have made clear. The Cold War, despite its soothing name, was

atrocious; and yet it enabled a rare stability—only in the First
and Second Worlds—that appears especially valuable in retrospect (although that war in fact begat the forces of Islamist terror, and the movement that is now the Christian right). While
nuclear parity between the United States and Soviet Union
forestalled a nuclear catastrophe, there were also certain short-
term social benefits to either side, as the fiercest energies in
both states were absorbed in opposition to the national enemy—a vast sideshow that could not last. If the Soviet threat
was dangerous to this country, so too were the consequences of
its disappearance. When that occurred, surprisingly, in 1991,
that old crusading animus, all stoked up but with no place to
go, exploded *here*, afflicting U.S. politics and culture with a
kind of blowback not envisioned by the CIA. The disaster
started with the evangelical crusade against Bill Clinton and
continues with the full complicity of Bush & Co., whose soldiers now crusade against their fellow citizens, and against democracy itself.

> The Florida elections have taught us that the Democrats with their
> liberal/socialistic worldview will stop at nothing to seize control of
> the government. For the government is the instrument whereby the
> legislator and the courts shape man into what they want.
>
> Instead of half-hearted and compromising responses from so-
> called conservatives, we need an explicitly Christian response in
> politics that has its own worldview, an agenda, and courageous men
> to implement it confrontationally.[109]

This call-to-arms comes from an essay entitled "Slash and
Burn Politics," by Dr. Val Finnell, a major in the Army Medical
Corps and the Chief of Clinical Pathology at the William Beau-

mont Army Medical Center in El Paso, Texas.[110] From February 2001 until November 2003, the essay was highlighted on the website of the Chalcedon Foundation, a "Christian education organization" founded in 1965 and dedicated to the spread of Christian Reconstructionism (sometimes known as dominionism). This is a pre-millennialist doctrine holding that the End Times, as envisioned in the Book of Revelation, must take place *before* Christ will return. According to the Reconstructionists, this means that every Christian must work *now* toward the establishment of "Biblical law"—as specified in the Old Testament—throughout the world.

> We believe that the whole Word of God must be applied to all of life. It is not only our duty as individuals, families and churches to be Christian, but it is also the duty of the state, the school, the arts and sciences, law, economics, and every other sphere to be under Christ the King. Nothing is exempt from His dominion. We must live by His Word, not our own.[111]

This theocratic vision is explicit also in Finnell's homily against the Democrats:

> The Christian worldview is the answer. We need Christian statesmen who press for the Crown Rights of Jesus Christ in all areas of life. This isn't political salvation or an overnight fix. It will take decades of mobilization and confrontation to undo a century of godless socialism. It must be a grassroots movement that starts in individual families and churches and then moves outward to take dominion. It must encompass every area of life and not just the political arena. Finally, it must start soon, for there isn't much time left.[112]

As we shall see, the Republicans had countless zealots on the ground from coast to coast, doing everything they could to steal the race lest Kerry and his henchmen steal it. Such activists were fired up with the merciless crusading spirit that impels all Christianists (and all Islamists, and all extreme religious Zionists) to do anything and everything it takes to vanquish the unholy ones. "It's going to be a spiritual battle," cried Pat Robertson, founder of the Christian Coalition, at the Christian Coalition's Road to Victory gathering in 1991. "There will be Satanic forces. . . . We are not going to be coming up just against human beings, to beat them in elections. We're going to be coming up against spiritual warfare."[113] That attitude suffused Bush/Cheney's GOP throughout the campaign of 2004. Such were the cadre that proclaimed themselves the Texas Strike Force, traveling the nation, all expenses paid by the Republicans, to do in all the swing states what they did for Bush & Co. in Ohio: bully and harass the Evil Ones. Travis Fell, a rightist blogger known as Texas Tommy, thus described his motivation for enlisting:

> On a personal note, reigning in out of control courts was a big part of the reason I joined the "Mighty Texas Strike Force" and ventured from warm, cozy Texas to cold, rainy Iowa last November to campaign for President Bush. I'm expecting the GOP to use the political advantage I helped win them to combat evil, both in the War on Islamic Fascism and the War on Judicial Activism![114]

Such were many of Bush/Cheney's polling personnel—such as the folks at precinct 324 in Pima County, Arizona, where John Brakey, Cluster Captain of the Democrats' local get-out-the-vote effort, was menaced when he tried to monitor the vote-

counting on Election Night, the true believers in command re-
viling him, in unison, as a "pagan" and "liberal scum."[115]

And such are the young Christianists at Patrick Henry College, a dominionist academy set up in Purcellsville, Va., in 2000
by Michael Farris, a protégé of Tim LaHaye. With most of its
students home-schooled in the "biblical world-view," Patrick
Henry seeks "the transformation of American society" by readying its Christian cadre for "careers of public service and cultural
influence."[116] More specifically, the school serves as a training
ground for theocratic service in the firm of Bush & Co.—and, in
2004, fed its young idealists directly into the political campaign.
In October, the RNC came to campus to recruit them into various theaters of that war, "where races were tight," as the *Washington Post* reported.[117] There were some plum positions—Elisa
Muench, a junior, interned in Karl Rove's Office of Strategic In-
tiatives—while others hit the road to knock on doors throughout the land.[118] After one recruitment session, having volun-
teered for various assignments, the operatives-to-be took turns
praying aloud: "Heavenly father," said Leeann Walker, 20, "I
hope you prepare the hearts and minds of the people we encounter so that we can be ministers for your word. Even more
than representing a campaign or an idea, we represent you."[119]
(According to its filings with the Federal Election Commission,
the RNC paid Walker $10,751 for her missionary labor in the
Bush campaign.)[120]

Of course, other Republicans were more cynical, and knew
that they could not win honestly for the simple reason that their
candidate and his agenda turned off a clear majority of the electorate. Such realism was at times expressed with startling candor
by politicians motivated more by allegiance to their party than
by fear of Satan. On July 16, the *Detroit Free Press* quoted Rep.

John Pappageorge (R-MI) as speaking very frankly of his party's prospects in his state: "If we do not suppress the Detroit vote, we're going to have a tough time in this election."[121] A week before Election Day, Pennsylvania House Speaker John Perzel, representative for Northeast Philadelphia (and the most powerful Republican in Harrisburg), described his electoral assignment in an interview with *U.S. News & World Report*: "The Kerry campaign needs to come out with humongous numbers here in Philadelphia. It's important for me to keep that number down."[122]

5.

The Most Uncontrollable
Form of Cancer

Whether they were doing God's business or just working for the party, the Bush Republicans were well aware that they could not win without miracles. To produce them, as Fawn Hall once famously said, "sometimes you have to go above the written law." Well before Election Day, Bush/Cheney's soldiers pulled so many fast ones nationwide—mischief seemingly intended to thwart mischief by the Democrats—that several of them were exposed and even (locally) reported. In Clark County, Nevada, on October 10, Dan Burdish, former executive director of the state Republican Party, tried to have 17,000 voters, mostly Democrats, disqualified from voting.[1] So flagrant was this stroke ("I am looking to take Democrats off the voter rolls," Burdish told the press), and so weak the reasons given, that the county's registrar of voters (a nonpartisan position) disallowed it.[2] A week later, Bush's campaign operatives in Pennsylvania tried to slash the Democratic vote in Philadelphia by attempting to relocate 63 polling places, most of them in black precincts. They used the names of local politicians, who insisted that the move was not about "denying anyone the right to vote," as the black minister and Republican Congressional candidate Deborah Williams put it.[3] "We're more concerned about people's comfort." (Matt Robb, GOP ward leader for South Philadelphia, was more frankly racist in defense of the petition: "It's predominantly, 100 percent black," he said about one polling place. "I'm just not going in there to get a knife in my back.") The petition was denied. And there was something fishy going on in South Dakota until mid-October, when six Republican operatives were forced to step down for suspicious handling of 1,400 absentee ballots—a crime that Bill Janklow, the state's Republican ex-governor and a former congressman,[4] blamed loudly on the national party's Victory Program, which oversees the states' get-out-the-vote drives. "These people are cheating," Janklow said. "When you tamper with it, you cheat the system. And cheating in elections is the worst form of cancer because it's uncontrollable."[5] (One of the operatives, Larry Russell, was quickly shuffled to Ohio, to "lead the ground operations" there for Bush.[6] He brought three of the others with him. A fourth went right to work as a party lobbyist in Pierre, S.D.)[7]

For each such story of a fraud aborted there were many stories of apparent fraud that went unchecked or unexamined—that even went unmentioned after the initial article or post. In every case, the evidence was covered with crusaders' fingerprints.

In Georgia, on September 29, it was reported in the *Atlanta Journal-Constitution* that a new initiative allowing early voting also made it possible for Georgians to vote twice—a felony under state law.[8] And yet the program had an even bigger flaw. It was not reported, then or ever, that all of those who voted early had unknowingly waived their right to cast a secret ballot.[9] The Diebold machines used by Georgia's early voters made it possible for the state's election boards to see who voted how—and to change the vote at will. (367,777 Georgians voted early, accounting for some 10 percent of the 3 million ballots cast.)[10] This convenient defect seems especially significant when we recall Max Cleland's startling loss to Saxby Chambliss in 2002, and it is still more worrying in light of the enormous theocratic presence in the Peach State.[11] Ralph Reed runs the Georgia GOP, using it, as well as many other instruments, to win at what he calls "guerilla warfare." ("I paint my face and travel by night. You don't know it's over until you're in a body bag. You don't know until election night," he told *The Norfolk Virginia-Pilot* in 1991.)[12] For years a kingmaker in his home state, Reed now plans to run for lieutenant governor of Georgia—a great advance for one committed to religious rule. In 1990, Reed spelled out his political agenda:

> What Christians have got to do is take back this country, one precinct at a time, one neighborhood at a time and one state at a time. I honestly believe that in my lifetime, we will see a country once again governed by Christians and Christian values.[13]

Minnesota, throughout the month before Election Day, was already an electoral disaster because of a new statewide voter registration system that had been put in place before many of the bugs had been worked out. Those glitches slowed the process to a crawl—a particularly troubling handicap given that Minnesota had the nation's second-highest registration rate (80 percent of eligible voters). It was imperative, if everyone was to cast a ballot, that things run smoothly. But in October 2004 things were running bumpily or not at all, with two-thirds of Minnesota's 74 counties reporting "problems with errors or being knocked off the system," and a survey of 27 county auditors showing that most of them had found the system "slow and, at times for some, very slow."[14] Somehow, that system was especially hard on non-Republicans—as was Mary Kiffmeyer, Minnesota's (Republican) secretary of state, who had insisted on its hasty installation, and who had otherwise betrayed a party bias more appropriate to an apparatchik than a civil servant. In 2003, Kiffmeyer had sacked her own director of elections, because, he claimed, he had asked both Democratic and Republican lawmakers to attend a presentation on new voting machines, while Kiffmeyer wanted only the Republicans.[15] (ES&S makes most of the machines deployed in Minnesota, while some come from Diebold.)[16]

Kiffmeyer also refused to give voter registration forms to grassroots anti-Bush or pro-Kerry groups that wanted to go door-to-door to register new voters. (Her office had run out of forms, she said.) She attempted to disqualify the Independence Party candidate for governor—an effort that she undertook with the attorney general, a Democrat—and tried as well to stop a maverick (that is, secular) Republican from running for the House by keeping his name off the ballot. (In both those cases she was eventually overruled by the Minnesota Supreme Court.) She also did whatever she could do to lower voter turnout—trying to over-complicate the voter identification process, and adorning polling places with alarmist posters warning of the likelihood of terrorist attack.[17] In short, Kiffmeyer's aim, like Reed's, is not to foster democratic governance but to hinder it.

The fewer unbelievers get to vote, the likelier it is that the minority of true believers can force their New Jerusalem on everybody else.[18] Kiffmeyer has not been shy about her views. According to a Minneapolis weekly, she had often "raised eyebrows with public remarks complaining about the separation of church and state."[19]

Of course, Bush/Cheney's troops were not all theocrats; or rather, they were not all primarily driven by the wish to intermingle church and state. Among the countless other moves to disenfranchise Democrats before November 2, many were compelled less by religious zeal than by mere racism—as, of course, has generally been the case all too often since Reconstruction. Weeks before Election Day, civil rights activists throughout the nation were estimating that "millions of U.S. citizens, including a disproportionate number of black voters, will be blocked from voting in the Nov. 2 presidential election because of legal barriers, faulty procedures or dirty tricks," reported Reuters's Alan Elsner on September 27.[20] "I think it will be worse than in 2000," long-time civil rights advocate Julian Bond told *Salon* a month later, noting the GOP's long reliance—since the sixties—on "underhanded, tricky, illegal and immoral tactics."[21]

By November 1, reported Greg Palast of the BBC, Kerry/Edwards were way down already, thanks to an array of furtive anti-democratic measures: ballots "spoiled" mechanically, minority voters illegally stricken from the rolls; absentee ballots sent out just before Election Day or never mailed at all. "Through a combination of sophisticated vote rustling," Palast wrote, "John Kerry begins with a nationwide deficit that could easily exceed one million votes." Thus, before November 2nd, Kerry illegitimately lost support in Florida and New Mexico, as well as in Ohio and elsewhere.

Despite its national importance, this news was almost wholly absent from the U.S. media, but it was prominently covered by two British outlets, Reuters and the BBC (with Palast's findings also noted in an essay that he posted on the website Common-Dreams.org). Likewise, egregious cases of disenfranchisement were covered only locally, or just online, or in left-of-center publications, or by the doughty independent commentators on the *New York Times* op-ed page. On August 17, 2004, six black civil servants in Waller County, Texas, filed suit in federal court charging their white colleagues, and Governor Rick Perry, with conducting "an extensive [and] illegal reign of terror against African-American" officials.[22] The defendants' aim, according to the suit, was "to intimidate, harass, oppress, malign, beleaguer and torment plaintiffs in order that they might become discouraged from participating in any aspect of the political process in Waller County." The man driving much of that animosity, the suit alleged, was Oliver Kitzman, the county DA, who had a long history of such enterprise—which, in Waller County, could make all the difference, as the population is 29.2 percent black, 19.4 percent Hispanic and 57.8 percent white.[23]

In November of 2003, Kitzman had arbitrarily decreed that the students at Prairie View A&M University (PVAMU), a largely African-American institution, had no "lawful right to a special definition of 'domicile' for voting purposes,"[24] which meant that they could not vote where they attended school. The diktat was universally denounced (even by Republican Rick Perry, governor of Texas) and was eventually refuted by Texas's Attorney General Greg Abbott, who, on February 4, 2004, reconfirmed that PVAMU students—just like students at all other Texas campuses—may vote locally if they claim to be residing at their school addresses.[25] The next day, four PVAMU students filed a lawsuit to ensure that Kitzman's office would not try to keep such residents from voting.[26] On February 18, Robin Willis, an alderman in the town of Brookshire, formally requested that the attorney general launch an investigation into Kitzman's record of indicting black officials in the county.[27] One week later, Kitzman published an elaborate apology for his "actions and statements" in the PVAMU matter. "I want the PVAMU community to know that I apologize, and I welcome them as participants in the democratic institutions in Waller County,"[28] he wrote, apparently to get those people off his back (the entire episode was reported only by the *Houston Chronicle* and the Associated Press). By the summer, however, he was up to his old tricks.

In the final week before Election Day, there were countless other racist ploys, some of which were covered, albeit only locally or by AP. A bogus letter circulated throughout South Carolina, ostensibly from the NAACP, warning people not to vote if they had outstanding parking tickets or were behind in their child support payments. Anyone who tried to vote with such a record would be hustled off to jail. "This is old South Carolina politics," observed the Reverend Joe Darby of the NAACP.[29] It was indeed, although the same thing happened in Milwaukee, where a flier from the "Milwaukee Black Voters League" warned people to avoid the polls if they had cast a vote in any other race that year, or if they or *any family member* had ever been convicted of a crime, however minor. It was too late to register, the flyer added. "If you violate any of these laws you can get 10 years in prison and your children will be taken from you," it asserted.[30] (Everyone was outraged by the flyer: "We will not tolerate any effort to suppress or intimidate voters," said Merrill Smith of the Bush campaign.)[31] White hatred of black citizens drove endless pro-Bush crimes and improprieties, especially in the South, as we shall see.

Under Bush & Co.'s spell, Hispanic voters also seemed to vanish on Election Day, particularly in those states—Nevada, Arizona and New Mexico—where they were numerous, and apt to vote for Kerry. (In Florida, of course, there is a large Hispanic bloc, which, with its many Cuban and Nicaraguan emigrés, has long tended toward the GOP.) From the summer it was clear that those Hispanics favored Kerry by 2 to 1 among registered voters.[32] Bush was floundering with that Southwestern population—which would have been a problem for him, if the contest had been honest, as his pollsters claimed that he would have to strengthen his appeal, increasing his percentage of that vote by 5 percent. In 2000, he had (allegedly) won 35 percent of the national Hispanic vote, and now needed 40 percent, said Team Bush's Matthew Dowd in May.[33] Moreover, the support of Florida's Republican Hispanics was beginning to go soft, an inevitable upshot of the aging of the anti-Castro generation. "'The embargo made sense 40 years ago, but it's time to open things up like we did with China,' said Frank Chinea, a 52-year-old artist who normally votes Republican but is now on the fence. 'Let the families get together,'" AP reported from Miami on June 7.[34] Whereas Bush (allegedly) had beaten Gore among Hispanics there by 61 percent to 39 percent, his advantage over Kerry—55 percent to 35 percent in May—was a little less impressive. Kerry's goal in Florida, according to New Mexico's Gov. Bill Richardson, was to seize 5 percent of Bush's Cuban vote, while hanging on to Gore's 2000 majority among the state's non-Cuban Hispanic voters.[35]

Nationwide—that is, in all 11 states with the largest Hispanic populations—those citizens thought even less of Bush and his accomplishments than other voters did. According to a survey by *The Washington Post*, the Hispanic TV network Univision and the Tomas Rivera Policy Institute at USC, released in late July, the economy was, among Hispanics, the most urgent issue, leading all the others for a third—33 percent—of all those polled.[36] Education was the second most important issue, mattering most to 18 percent, while terrorism most concerned 15 percent, and the war in Iraq 13 percent. (Priorities were different for the general electorate, for which the war and terrorism mattered significantly more than education, which nationwide was noted first by only 12 percent.)

Moreover, with the "war on terrorism" and the real war in Iraq—i.e., the defining struggle of Bush/Cheney's term—Hispanics were obviously not on board: 63 percent perceived the war as not worth fighting, while that view was held, or admitted, by just over half of the electorate at large; 40 percent of the Hispanics said that the U.S. was losing the "war on terrorism" (with only 36% discerning victory). In fact, 43 percent deemed *Kerry* the more promising commander in that war, while only 35 percent preferred to have the president conduct it. Among Latino voters Bush had a 36 percent approval rating, and a disapproval rating of 54 percent. Many of those surveyed strongly disapproved of the president's adventure in Iraq, where young Hispanic soldiers have been disproportionately represented.

"'Bush is wrong on Iraq,' said Maria Cerda, 42, of the Bronx, who is from the Dominican Republic and cleans offices for a living," *The Washington Post* reported on July 22.

"There are a lot of young people dying over there. Education and better jobs is what we need. Not war." Cerda sees Bush as a "weak leader—people are always telling him what to do." Her opinion of

Kerry is only slightly better. "He doesn't seem that strong to me, either, but he's better than Bush.[37]

Bush was especially unpopular throughout Latin America—where most of our Hispanic citizens have family, and other cultural connections. "Since Bush took office in 2001, the proportion of people with negative opinions towards the United States in Latin America and the Caribbean has doubled, according to surveys carried out by Latinobarometro, a Chile-based firm," reported Diego Cevallos for Inter Press Service on Sept. 16. Also in September, an international poll by GlobeScan of Toronto and the University of Maryland, conducted in nine Latin American countries, revealed that 42.5 percent of those surveyed were hoping for a Kerry victory in November, while just 19 percent supported Bush's "re-election." Such findings tally clearly with the many packed and noisy anti-Bush protests that had been taking place throughout the region for some months. Such ardent foreign disapproval surely bears connection with the president's unpopularity among U.S. Hispanics, whose notions are inevitably influenced by those at home (and vice versa).

By mid-October it was clear that, even in Florida, Bush's hold on the Hispanic bloc was looking weaker than expected—as it was *not* a "bloc," in fact, but as diverse as any other cosmopolitan community. "A huge influx of Puerto Ricans, Mexicans and people from Central and South America has diluted the political clout of Cubans, loosening the Republican lock on the Hispanic vote," the *New York Times* reported on Oct. 17.[38] Not only were the state's Colombians, Puerto Ricans and Dominicans favoring Kerry, but even the far more conservative Nicaraguans and Cubans "may throw some support to the Democrats for a change." Not even Florida, then, was in the bag, or so it seemed:

Little wonder, then, that Florida's 3.2 million Hispanic residents—the state's largest minority group, tens of thousands of whom will be first-time voters next month—are among the most coveted voters in the nation this year.

"The message for both parties is, these people can go either way and you've got to work it," said Jorge Mursuli, national director of Mi Familia Vota, a voter registration group that signed up 73,000 Hispanic voters here this year, 40 percent as independents.[39]

Meanwhile, the Democrats were wooing the Hispanic vote aggressively, and not just in the swing states. The New Democrat Network, a Hispanic outreach operation, spent $6 million on that effort, with the Democratic Party and the Kerry campaign throwing in $5 million more. (By contrast, Bush/Cheney's effort seemed half-hearted, as that campaign did not appreciably increase its spending over what it had disbursed against Al Gore, although there were 6.9 million Hispanic voters—one million more than there had been four years earlier.)[40] Whether that barrage of propaganda did the trick, or whether it was disapproval of the president that made the difference, by Election Day John Kerry stood out as the very likely victor in the contest for U.S. Hispanic votes. According to a Zogby poll for the *Miami Herald*, conducted in the final week of the campaign, 61 percent of Hispanic voters nationwide were claiming to support the Democrat, while roughly 33 percent supported Bush.[41]

And the turnout was impressive on November 2. In California, for example, the turnout of new voters—both Anglo and Hispanic—was particularly high, according to the *Sacramento Bee*. "First-time and younger voters turned out Tuesday in larger-than-usual numbers, boosting Democrat John Kerry's margin of victory in California, according to a survey of those leaving the polls. Latino voters also represented a larger share of the electorate and supported Kerry by a substantial margin, the survey found."[42]

And so it was a bit of a surprise when Bush apparently outdid all expectations by winning 44 percent of the Hispanic vote, while Kerry's victory margin was a mere 9 points, the Democrat attracting only 53 percent of that constituency (according to CNN's exit polls).[43] In 2000, Gore had taken 62 percent of the Hispanic vote, while Bush, as noted earlier, had taken 35 percent—and Kerry now did worse, although Ralph Nader was no factor in this race, and Bush was obviously *less* appealing to Hispanics than he had been as the governor of Texas, with Kerry generally outpolling him, as we have seen, by 2 to 1.

What happened to the Democrat's wide lead among Hispanic voters? No exit poll could help to solve that mystery, as many of those votes were disappeared before Nov. 2. New Mexico provides us with a good example of the regime's practice with Hispanic Democrats. Prior to the Election, Greg Palast had already noted that "John Kerry is down by several thousand votes, though not one ballot has yet been counted."[44] He attributed that loss to, first, the inordinate rate of "spoilage"—ballots deemed illegible or incorrect or otherwise improper—that magically afflicted only Democratic votes. "New Mexico reported in the last race a spoilage rate of 2.68 percent, votes lost almost entirely in Hispanic, Native American and poor precincts—Democratic turf," wrote Palast for TomPaine.com. "From Tuesday's vote, assuming the same ballot-loss rate, we can expect to see 18,000 ballots in the spoilage bin."

Spoilage has a very Democratic look in New Mexico. Hispanic voters in the Enchanted State, who voted more than two to one for

Kerry, are five times as likely to have their vote spoil as a white voter. Counting these uncounted votes would easily overtake the Bush 'plurality.'

Already, the election-bending effects of spoilage are popping up in the election stats, exactly where we'd expect them: in heavily Hispanic areas controlled by Republican elections officials. Chaves County, in the "Little Texas" area of New Mexico, has a 44 percent Hispanic population, plus African Americans and Native Americans, yet George Bush "won" there 68 percent to 31 percent.[45]

Hispanic voters in New Mexico were also disenfranchised, Palast found, through the strategic distribution of provisional ballots, which were clearly headed for the trash. "They were handing them out like candy," reported Renee Blake of NPR in Albuquerque.[46] Some 20,000 provisional ballots were distributed—primarily to Hispanics, Palast found.

Santiago Juarez who ran the "Faithful Citizenship" program for the Catholic Archdiocese in New Mexico, told me that "his" voters, poor Hispanics, whom he identified as solid Kerry supporters, were handed the iffy provisional ballots. Hispanics were given provisional ballots, rather than the countable kind "almost religiously," he said, at polling stations when there was the least question about a voter's identification. Some voters, Santiago said, were simply turned away.[47]

The national press all but refused even to notice, much less talk about, such extra-legal means of cutting down the Kerry vote.

"Political analysts are still scratching their heads over what share of the crucial Hispanic vote President Bush won last month," *The Washington Post* quizzically reported in December, floating various demographic theories as to how Bush pulled it off: Hispanic *men*, and/or Hispanic *protestants*, came out for him in force.[48] The overall fishiness of Bush & Co.'s success among Hispanics was noted just in passing. "News media exit polls on election night reported Bush winning 44 percent of Hispanics this year, a startling nine percentage-point jump from 2000. Some skeptics weren't buying it, saying the data were flawed. Antonio Gonzalez, president of the William C. Velasquez Institute, said his exit poll showed Bush taking 33 percent."[49] From there the *Post* rushed on to entertain less troubling "explanations."

In New Mexico there were some cases of bald fraud, committed rather clumsily by fervent party men. In Bernalillo County, for example, a Republican judge in one precinct discarded hundreds of provisional ballots—all of them for Kerry, while all those he accepted were for Bush. (Bernalillo County, which has Albuquerque as its county seat, is 42 percent Hispanic, and went to Kerry by about 9,000 votes.)[50] That little crime was noted in the *Albuquerque Tribune*, while no news outlet has reported a far more disturbing study of the vote throughout New Mexico.[51] Weeks after the election, the numbers in that state, for every precinct, were scrutinized by statistician Robert Plotner (under the cyber-handle "ignatzmouse"). His meticulous analysis, which he posted on the Internet, provides clear evidence of a sophisticated program for the erasure, or rejection, of Democratic votes. Simply put, Plotner noted a strong correlation between the rate of undervotes—no vote cast for president on the ballot—on touch screen machines (DRE's) and countywide party affiliation. There was a direct correlation of high under-votes to strong Kerry support while under-votes dramatically decrease with strong Bush support.[52] The state's Hispanic voters were especially hard-hit by this phenomenon. For instance,

> the case can be made with small, minority, low-income communities like Guadalupe County with a per capita income of under $15,000 and an 81% Hispanic majority who under-voted at rates of 0.51% in early voting and 0.33% in absentee voting, both via pen and paper optical scan, and yet had an inexplicable increase to a 6.09% under-vote on election day via DRE.[53]

New Mexico recorded nearly 19,000 undervotes in the presidential race—"and a whopping 17,147 [of them] came from all forms of DRE and touchscreen voting."[54] This is especially remarkable, since Bush "won" New Mexico by 7,047 votes.

Not surprisingly, the RNC also campaigned against American Indians—playing on white animosity against them, and trying to suppress their votes. This was an electoral necessity in those wide-open spaces where the demographics called for it, as Native Americans vote mostly Democratic. In New Mexico, Indians account for 9.5 percent of the population, and are therefore a pivotal community, as Hispanics make up 42 percent of the state's residents, which means that there may be a potent red/brown coalition.[55] The threat of such a Democratic combination would explain the Bush regime's tough efforts to suppress the Indian franchise in New Mexico.

Throughout the state, Bush/Cheney's soldiers tried, in the final weeks of the campaign, to halt an on-site, nonpartisan voter registration program managed by the staffs at Indian Health Service (IHS) hospitals and clinics. (The soldiers were officials at the Department of Health and Human Services, of which IHS is part.) Such drives are not allowed on federal property, the white men said—a notion hard to square with all those voter registration drives on U.S. military bases. The regime finally "clarified" its stance with a decree that only outside groups could mount such drives at IHS facilities, but that "no IHS employee will be registering voters as part of his or her official duties."[56] Asked, by the *Washington Post,* for further explanation, the enforcers would say only that IHS's staffers must observe the Hatch Act, whereby federal employees may not engage in partisan activity while on the job. As the drives at IHS were ostentatiously nonpartisan, the government's position was absurd. When, therefore, a few days later, Senator Jeff Bingaman (D-NM) publicly urged HHS to drop the ban, Secretary Tommy Thompson promptly did so. ("Bingaman said the victory was bittersweet," reported *Native Times* on October 11. "Several states with large Indian populations have already seen their voter registration deadlines come and go.")[57]

The anti-Indian pitch was far more virulent in South Dakota, where Native Americans comprise just under 5 percent of the population—an important bloc in a close race; and, while Bush held a wide lead there over Kerry, South Dakota's senatorial race was very close, and mattered greatly to the GOP for reasons both political and psychological.[58] As the party's overall aim in the election was to strengthen its domain in Washington, which meant bolstering its hold on Congress while prolonging Bush & Co.'s executive control, that extra Senate seat would be a boon indeed; and to pick off Tom Daschle, who had been Senate majority leader since 2001, would add immeasurably to the perception of the GOP's invulnerability, and so would be demoralizing to the Democrats, and super-sweet to the Republicans, who hated the innocuous Daschle for no clear reason. Thus the White House and the RNC put everything they had into the

South Dakota race, on behalf of Christianist extremist John Thune—who became, in Hannah Rosin's words, the theocratic movement's "new David" after overthrowing "el Diablo," as Rush Limbaugh commonly called Daschle on the air.[59] The Republican crusade to unseat Daschle (a drive that entailed a lot of propaganda work by White House operative Jeff Gannon) necessitated several dirty tricks against the Indians of South Dakota, as they might make the difference between Thune and the incumbent senator.[60] (Thune won by only 4,508 votes.) In Lake Andes, a town in Charles Mix County—whose population is over 28 percent Native American—Thune's men harassed the Yankton Sioux who voted early by following them out of polling places and writing down the license numbers of their cars and trucks. "They did it pretty much every time" an Indian voted, testified David Jordan, a Daschle poll watcher. (A judge enjoined the Thune men from all such activity.)[61]

The drive got uglier in the state's Western counties. Aside from photographing early voters on the Rosebud reservation, the Thune campaign sent area whites an anti-Daschle flyer with a vicious subtext: "The dogs are lining up to vote for Tom Daschle," read the copy, over an image of a pack of furtive-looking prairie dogs.[62] To outsiders this would seem to be a reference only to the problematic rodents: the state's white farmers wanted to exterminate them, while Daschle—like the Indians—proposed less drastic ways to deal with them. However, any local would at once perceive the flyer's racist message: "No dogs or Indians allowed," posted at the entrances of white establishments, had once been an exclusionary legend commonplace in South Dakota, and the flyer belabored the association. "No wonder the varmints are heading to the polls to vote for him!" it ended with a wink, as 1,300 Sioux from Rosebud, and another thousand from the reservation at Pine Ridge, had indeed already "headed to the polls" to vote for Daschle. (Certainly no prairie dogs had voted for him.)[63]

Bush/Cheney's soldiers also mounted further drives to disenfranchise students. On August 31, Fox 11 News in Tucson—home of the University of Arizona—interviewed Chris Roads, Pima County Voter Registrar, who claimed that it would be a felony for students from outside the state to register (or to be registered) to vote unless they planned to stay "indefinitely" after the election. The Fox reporter, Natalie Tejeda, treated this as fact:

TEJEDA: What many don't realize is that legally, students from out of state aren't eligible to vote in Arizona because they're considered temporary residents.

ROADS: If they are only here to attend school and their intention is to immediately return to where they came from when school is over then they are not residents of the state of Arizona for voting purposes and they cannot register to vote here.

TEJEDA: . . . Those caught misrepresenting their residency can face a severe punishment.

ROADS: The form in Arizona is an affidavit; it is a felony offense if you are lying on that form.

TEJEDA: So how easy is it to get caught? Well, starting this past January all voter applications are cross-checked with the Motor Vehicles Department and Social Security Administration. If they find that you are falsifying your residency you could be prosecuted. At this time we don't know if anybody has yet been indicted, but Roads says one of the easiest things you can do to avoid all that is simply go online or pick up the phone, call your home state's elections office and ask for an absentee ballot.

ANCHOR: Better to be safe on that one! Thanks, Natalie.[64]

Although the whole report was false, and created a big stir at AU, Fox reran the segment on September 9—the same day that Roads's boss, County Recorder Ann Rodriguez, made a statement vaguely modifying Roads's claim, which neither Roads nor Rodriguez would retract outright. Not until September 24 did Fox 11 bother to report Rodriguez's statement, although it may not have helped much: "If they see themselves as residents of the state in their mind," she said, "they can register to vote here."[65]

In many states, the Bush campaign also used the automated phone bank as a highly cost-effective method of black propaganda—a most sophisticated use of digital technology, extraordinarily precise and untraceable as well as cheap, and yet the subject of no national story. In pro-choice Wisconsin, many households got repeated robo-calls, ostensibly from the National Abortion Rights Action League (NARAL), urging votes for *Bush* (whom NARAL had been working to defeat).[66] The system was so sly that, when you got the call, you would see "NARAL," and the group's phone number, on your caller I.D. (This news was reported by NARAL itself and ended up on DailyKos.com.) In Michigan, black residents of Detroit, Flint and Pontiac, all heavily Democratic areas, and Grand Rapids, a Democratic-leaning district, got robo-calls throughout the campaign's final weekend, telling them that their polling places had been changed, or thus pink-baiting Kerry: "When you vote this Tuesday, remember to legalize gay marriage by supporting John Kerry. It's what we all want. It's a basic Democratic principle."[67] (Kerry opposed gay marriage.) The Republicans knew nothing of it. "I checked with both the party and campaign and nobody knows anything about it," said John Truscott, a spokesman for the Bush campaign in Michigan. (The story ran in the *Detroit Free Press*.) Such slick disinformation drives apparently went on for days throughout the swing states, and got no coverage. It seemed impossible to the find the source of, or anyone responsible for, those automatic calls. On October 21, Lynne Orengia, an outspoken Democrat in Erie, Pa., came home to find *five* GOP calls on her answering machine, all slandering Kerry. Furious, she tried to call the callers, only to find no listing for the Republican headquarters in Erie County (which did maintain an office in a local shopping mall), nor any listing for the Bush campaign. The only number listed for the GOP was in the tiny town of Meadville south of Erie, and there was no answer there.[68]

SPROUL & ASSOCIATES

The boldest effort to suppress the national Democratic vote involved the services of Nathan Sproul, an industrious young theocrat whose company, Sproul & Associates, was active in the swing states and elsewhere from September through Election Day, ostensibly to register new voters. That furtive enterprise—involving fraud, deception, copyright infringement, the systematic disenfranchisement of untold thousands of Democrats and Independents, and the secretive reregistration of still further thousands as Republicans without their full consent—played a far larger role in Bush's victory than anyone has thus far understood. For Sproul's peculiar expertise, the Republican National Committee paid millions, and, moreover, paid his firm for two months *past* Election Day; and then the RNC apparently "revised" its numbers to convey the misimpression that the firm did far less work for Bush & Co. than it had actually performed.

Nathan Sproul's biography is pertinent here, as it will help illuminate the blend of zeal and avarice that largely drives Bush/ Cheney's juggernaut. Born and raised in Tempe, Arizona, and a graduate of Pillsbury Bible Baptist College ("[It] is the mission of Pillsbury Baptist Bible College to glorify God through a Christian higher education program which imparts a biblical worldview, preparing students for Christian ministries in and through local Baptist churches"),[69] Sproul started his career in far-right politics as an intern in the office of Rep. Jon Kyl (R-AZ), who was among the rightmost members of the House, with a 100 percent approval rating from the Christian Coalition, 0 percent from NARAL and warm relations with the nation's defense contractors.[70] Sproul was working in Kyl's office when the congressman parlayed those assets into his successful senatorial bid in 1994, beating Democrat Sam Coppersmith by a substantial margin. After that campaign, Sproul was hired as Executive Director of the Arizona Christian Coalition, where he fought to stop sex education in the public schools. ("There's no way you can do contraception education without saying we know you're going to have sex," he said in 1997, noting that he himself had not had sex until his marriage, in the summer of 1996.)[71] While preaching abstinence to teens, Sproul was also surreptitiously exhorting fellow evangelicals to infiltrate the GOP. At the Christian Coalition's 1995 "Road to Victory" Conference, Sproul urged attendees at the Arizona Caucus meeting to become precinct committee chairs in order to elect delegates to the 1996 Republican National Convention. He also warned his listeners not to mention, ever, that the Coalition was involved. Throughout that meeting, Coalition guards were posted at the door, prepared to throw out anyone unknown to Sproul himself. (This incident was noted in a 1998 Senate inquiry into crimes and improprieties pertaining to the 1996 elections.)[72]

In 1999, Sproul abruptly left the Christian Coalition (along with scores of others, mostly from the Texas chapter) and started serving as executive director of the Arizona Republican Party, a post he held until 2002.[73] He then became regional president of Voyager Learning, which had lately set up shop in Arizona land in Texas.

The tale of this boondoggle says so much about Bush/Cheney and their apparatchiks—Sproul among them—that it calls for a digression here. Although not demonstrably effective as an educational concern, Voyager is very well-connected. Senior Vice President Jim Nelson has been Governor George W. Bush's pick to head the Texas Education Agency, and the corporation's president, Randy Best, had served with Donald Rumsfeld on the board of Westmark Systems, "an Austin-based holding company specializing in acquiring military electronics companies," according to the *Syracuse Post Standard*. Voyager had also greased the wheels of Texas government by generously contributing to Governor Bush's run for re-election, donating over $45,000 to him and over $20,000 to his running mate, the state's lieutenant governor. Bush repaid the gesture with a $25 million state bequest for after-school programs, with Voyager enjoying a big slice.

In 2003, when the New York City Department of Education awarded Voyager a $50 million contract to strengthen the city's phonics curriculum, Public Advocate Betsy Gotbaum investigated the contractor, and she had this to say:

Voyager has produced little results. Research on Voyager programs is rare. When it is done at all, it is almost never conducted by evaluators with not connections to, or financial interest in, the company. The research and claims made by Voyager have been cited [as] flimsy and unscientific by several university scholars who specialize in reading curriculum.

Despite this record—and even though the No Child Left Behind Act stipulates that only scientifically tested teaching methods and curricula will be federally funded—Voyager has been clearly favored by Bush and Co.'s Department of Education, which has suggested that its grants for reading programs will be likelier to go to applicants who indicate a preference for particular commercial entities, Voyager among them.[74]

Having wet his beak at Voyager, Sproul returned to politics in 2004, leading No Taxpayer Money for Politicians (NTMP), an abortive rightist drive to scuttle Arizona's Clean Elections Law. (The measure, heavily backed by "a who's who of industry," as the *Arizona Republic* put it, would have eliminated public funding for elections.)[75] The petition drive for NTMP was supervised by Aaron "A. J." James, president of Voters' Outreach of America (VOA). In June, Sproul had paid VOA to collect signatures for Ralph Nader's presidential candidacy in Arizona.

Sproul helped keep Bush & Co. in the White House by deploying an exclusive form of "voter registration" that would have made Chicago's first Mayor Daley blush (if that were possible). It first made the papers in Las Vegas on July 31, although Sproul's involvement in the scam was not yet known. Outside the Department of Motor Vehicles in Vegas, Aaron Johnson-

Hall and his wife, Christine, were asked to sign two petitions, one to get Nader on the ballot in Nevada, and the other to raise the minimum wage.[76] The couple were Democrats, and therefore quite surprised to learn, a few weeks later, that they had voluntarily switched parties. Several weeks would pass before such stealth registration was connected to Sproul's operation in Nevada. In an interview with KLAS-TV, the CBS affiliate in Las Vegas, on October 13, Eric Russell, who had worked for Sproul, charged that he had seen his supervisor shred eight to ten registration forms filled out by Democrats. "We caught her taking Democrats out of my pile, hand them to her assistant and he ripped them up right in front of us. I grabbed some of them out of the garbage and she tells her assistant to get those from me."[77] According to the local GOP, Russell's story was not credible because he was "a disgruntled employee"—a charge that Russell readily verified, as Sproul had docked his pay for registering Democrats.[78] "They held our paychecks," he told the Associated Press. "Who wouldn't be disgruntled if some lady told you she wasn't going to pay you? That doesn't take away from the fact that I saw them rip up the forms."[79]

In response, Sproul told the *Arizona Republic* that he was suing Russell for defamation: "That lawsuit claims that after Russell was fired, he returned to the office holding what appeared to be voter registration forms and told workers he would claim that he saw a supervisor tear up the forms unless he was paid what he wanted." Sproul's charge appears to have been false, as Russell never was served with a lawsuit, his lawyer, Michael Mushkin, told *Salon*.[80]

More reports emerged that month. On October 21, the *Las Vegas Mercury* ran an op-ed by George Knapp, the KLAS reporter who had broken Russell's story. "Jeannie Morgan, the manager [of VOA], was given at least 4,050 forms by the Clark County Election Department," Knapp wrote.[81]

Of those, she returned about 2,400. No one knows what happened to the other 1,600-plus forms since there is no requirement that unused forms be turned back in. Of the 2,400 registration forms that were turned in, 1,900 were from Republicans, with 300 or so from Democrats. . . .

Two Logandale women who spoke to [me] say they were at VOA headquarters and were bothered when they saw the registration forms separated into piles, one pile of Republican forms that were placed in a box on the table, while all other forms were tossed into a box on the floor.

On the day after his report on KLAS, Knapp wrote in his op-ed piece, Jeannie Morgan had "issued a sworn statement in which she denied trashing any forms and further that she had no knowledge of any forms being destroyed. The following day, she told me in an interview that Eric Russell had torn up the forms himself. So which is it?" All this evidence of crime and cover-up induced the FBI to claim an interest in the case, prompted the Nevada Democratic Party to file suit to extend the state's voter registration deadline, and provoked a few lawsuits from Nevadans disenfranchised by Sproul & Associates. The lawsuits came and went, and the FBI was still "investigating" on Election Day.

Meanwhile, the story had progressed much further. In Charleston, West Virginia, a woman named Lisa Bragg, who had almost gone to work for Sproul, told all. The enterprise was cloaked in secrecy right from the start—or from before the start: Bragg went to Kelly Services, the national temp agency, to apply for the "customer service job" it had advertised, and found the agency strikingly tight-lipped about it.[82] They showed the applicants a workplace-safety video, then admitted that their "customer service job" had nothing to do with customer service but would involve conducting a "political survey."[83] Some applicants, annoyed by the charade, walked out. The rest were told to attend an "orientation session" at the Charleston Civic Center the next day. Questions were deliberately unanswered, the Kelly staffers saying that "the less you know about the company, the better off you are, especially if the media would come asking questions."

The next day's "orientation session" was another exercise in paranoia. Applicants were given sheets of paper with instructions on evading members of the press. Should they be approached by any prying media types, they were to clam up, hurry over to a pay phone and call the number printed on the sheet. Then the applicants were finally told the truth: "They said we were working for the Republicans."[84] (At this point, Bragg, a Democrat, resolved to quit, but not before collecting all the evidence she could.) The group were told that they would start by working in the parking lots of West Virginia's One Stop stores (whose pro-Bush owners had approved the action).[85] They were also told to congregate outside convenience stores. Wherever they gathered, they were to pose as nonpartisan pollsters, interested, for purely scientific reasons, in what local folks were thinking. Bragg had a copy of the script, which said: "If anyone asks what kind of poll, it is a simple field poll to see what neighborhood support is."[86] Respondents claiming to be Bush supporters were to be signed up for voter registration on the spot, while those supporting Kerry were to be thanked politely, and ignored.

Bragg provided *Salon*'s Farhad Manjoo with a copy of the script, which the website duly published (and which was published nowhere else). "Hello, we are doing a simple survey. If the election were held today, would you vote for President Bush or Senator Kerry?" According to the letterhead, the survey was a joint endeavor by Sproul & Associates and America Votes—a large, authentic coalition of Democratic groups intent on registering new voters, and not, of course, allied with Sproul.[87] (Elsewhere, Sproul has used the name "Voters Outreach of America.") For the purpose of deniability, the script had stamped across the top, in giant bold-face letters: "ALL CITIZENS WILL BE PROVIDED THE SAME OPPORTUNITY TO REGISTER." The fine print made it clear, however, that that claim was accurate only in the narrowest sense. The goal was to ensure the registration of *only* Republicans. "If a person is angry, it is important to listen to them, but not argue back."

If a person is agitated, they might complain to the store manager, risking the loss of this location to register voters at. Please be sensitive toward others of different political affiliations who do not want to support President Bush. The Goal is to Register Republicans, and to remain positive.

The script implied that Democrats were not to be registered. If any Democrat should ask for help in registration—what the script termed the "Kerry Scenario"—the Sprouler's bright and courteous reply should be, "Thank you very much for your time, I will record this." Bush supporters, on the other hand, were to be welcomed warmly—"Great, well this is a very important election. Are you registered to vote at your current residence?"—and then, if need be, assisted in filling out a registration form.

For undecided voters, the script included questions meant to separate the sinners from the saved, and to recruit the saved—a version of "push polling." According to the *Pittsburgh Post-Gazette*, the undecided were to be asked, "Do you consider yourself pro-choice or pro-life?" and "Are you worried about the Democrats raising taxes?" If voters answered rightly (so to speak), they would be urged to register Republican. "If they are pro-choice," on the other hand, "say thank you and walk away."[88]

At the orientation session, Bragg recalled, some of the aspiring Sproulers murmured their intent to register Democrats despite the rule against it, but the folks in charge made clear that there would be Sproul agents in the field, keeping a close watch on the workers. In any case, there was a very powerful disincentive for those workers who might try to sign up Democrats: Sproul paid nothing for such registrations and sometimes even docked its workers for submitting them, while paying readily for each Republican added to the rolls. It therefore *paid* to find Republicans—or to trick people into registering as Republicans, notwithstanding the disclaimer about "OPPORTU-NITY." On the other hand, it was downright risky to go after Democrats. "I was told, 'Your job is to bring in Republican cards. If you don't, then you won't be working here for very long,'" said Adam Banse, who worked for Sproul in Minneapolis for two hours.[89]

Thus were Bush voters recruited (or created), and Democrats passed over, in many states. (We do not know how many.) The initial come-on varied according to locale and population but always bore the same misleading whiff of liberal/leftist altruism or populism. On campuses in Pennsylvania, Sproulers bore petitions for the legalization of marijuana for medical purposes. On campuses in Oregon, there were petitions against child abuse and violence against women. Outside a Department of Motor Vehicles office in Las Vegas, there were petitions for raising the minimum wage and putting Ralph Nader on the ballot. (That last cause was a pro-Bush venture nationwide, largely funded by Republicans, and one served vigorously by Sproul at least since June.)

The fakery did not stop there but often blossomed into outright fraud, as Democrats and Independents by the thousands were registered as Republicans without their knowledge, or fooled into re-registering themselves. In Pennsylvania—where some Sproulers claimed to be doing "some market analysis in the area," and others claimed to be affiliated with a *different* America Votes, not the "partisan" one—hundreds of students at Indiana University of Pennsylvania and Montgomery County Community College were conned into filling out blank registration forms, which Sproulers then completed.[90] In Oregon, where Sproul routinely used America Votes to get permission to do canvassing in front of public libraries, students at the University of Oregon, Western Oregon University, Mt. Hood Community College and Chemetka Community College were similarly scammed, signing petitions to halt violence against women and children or for lower auto insurance rates for students, and then being asked to sign a second form, or just initial it, supposedly (and inexplicably) to improve the petition's chances. Some Democratic students had misgivings about changing their affiliation but were assured it was only temporary. In Eugene, Stephanie Erickson, a junior at the University of Oregon, signed a petition protesting violence against women and children, and then the Sproulers told her that it would be more effective if she registered as a Republican just for the moment. "I wasn't sure what to do, but felt becoming a Republican for a week was worth it if my signature would count."[91]

And in Florida—which was again ground zero, sharing that unfortunate distinction with Ohio even if the national press was silent on the countless civic horrors in the Sunshine State— thousands of students at the University of Florida (in Gaines-ville), the University of South Florida (in Tampa), Florida State University and Florida A&M University (Tallahassee) and Hillsborough Community College ("The Community College of Tampa Bay"), as well as various schools in Orange County (in and around Orlando), were deceived by Sproulers into sign-ing up as Bush supporters.[92] So heavy was the Florida traffic in young faux-Republicans that Sproul evidently had to share the job with another anti-democratic goon squad. Asked what group they represented, some Sproulers named "YPM," which refers to Young Political Majors LLC, a wee firm owned and managed by one Mark Jacoby (who, one summer's day, turned up at the Board of Elections office in Gainesville with 1,200 voter registration cards, of which 510 were from Floridians who had switched to the GOP). While Jacoby could not be reached for comment by the *St. Petersburg Times*, YPM turned out to be employed by something called JSM Inc., which was in turn employed by Arno Political Associates, a rightist propa-ganda powerhouse whose clients have included Reagan/Bush, Bush/Quayle, Phillip Morris, R. J. Reynolds, Occidental Petro-leum, Mobil Oil, waste management colossus Browning-Ferris Industries, the California Timber Association, "Save Our State (Immigration Reform)," the Florida and California "Civil Rights Initiatives" (against affirmative action) and Wal-Mart.[93] "Since our founding in 1979, APC has collected more than 75 million signatures to qualify nearly 300 ballot initiatives in twenty states," proclaims the website for the outfit, whose motto is "Democracy in Action".[94] According to owner Bill Arno, the firm was registering voters in Florida as well as Oregon, Nevada and Ohio—all states where Sproul was also operating.[95]

Of Sproul's activities there was very little news in the United States before Election Day, and none afterward. Aside from local stories in the *Charlotte Gazette*, the *Oregonian*, the *Pittsburgh Post-Gazette*, the *Minneapolis Star-Tribune* and the *St. Petersburg Times*, there was near-total silence on Sproul's and Arno's national wipe-out-the-vote campaign. There was a paragraph about it in the *Washington Post*, and the *San Francisco Chronicle* devoted a few hundred words to it.[96] The *New York Times* referred to it in passing, in a brief article on something else ("Judge Rules for Democrats in Dispute Over Ohio Voting," 10/15/04). Otherwise, the *Times* did not report on Sproul's endeavor—although the paper did deplore it in a modest editorial (460 words),[97] and columnist Paul Krugman mentioned it in his powerful October 15 column, "Block the Vote." On October 21, *Salon* ran Farhad Manjoo's "Sproul Play," the most comprehensive treatment of the matter yet (until now). To those few who had read such articles, the tale of Sproul's activities seemed, once Bush had been "re-elected," like a half-baked theory or an ancient rumor, now seemingly exposed as false; while the majority who had not even heard of Sproul before the race were none the worse for not remembering him now.

Thus was that extensive criminal campaign, which disenfranchised thousands of Americans, transformed into a crackpot Democratic fantasy—which is precisely what Republicans, including Sproul himself, had counter-charged back when the scandal got what little press it did. The GOP responded to the charges over Sproul much as the House Republicans "debated" the Conyers Report on January 6. "This is clearly the Democratic plan to make these baseless allegations," RNC spokeswoman Heather Layman told the *Pittsburgh Post-Gazette*.[98] ("She said no Sproul workers were involved in such tactics in Oregon or Pennsylvania.") "This is nothing more than a thinly veiled politically motivated effort to draw media attention away from the real issues just days prior to early voting," said Brian Scroggins, chairman of the GOP in Clark County, Nevada.[99] "This is all about making accusations. They allege fraud where none exists and get the media to cover it," Sproul told the Associated Press.[100] "If no sign of voter fraud exists, make it up, manipulate the media into covering baseless charges and spread fear," Layman told the Associated Press.[101] "Democrats' tactics are shameful," Chris Carr, executive director of Nevada's GOP, told the Associated Press.[102] "The Democrats continue to follow the Kerry campaign/DNC playbook. They allege fraud where none exists and get the media to cover it. They have now broadened their attack to include alleging fraud by Sproul & Associates where no work was even done," Sproul's office told the *Minnesota Star-Tribune*.[103] In fact, a temp at Sproul weeks before the scandal broke, had told an Oregon newspaper that "the company already has set up registration drives in Pennsylvania, Minnesota, Michigan, Ohio, Florida and Nevada."[104]

In fact, Sproul served the Bush campaign far *more* extensively than this brief overview suggests. Indeed, that stealthy operation did much more for Bush & Co. than Nixon's plumbers ever did for that stiff, sneaky president. Exactly what Sproul did in that campaign (and after it) should be the subject of a full investigation, as the record indicates that the Republicans paid an immense amount for Sproul's activities, and also tried to hide that great expense, which, if reported honestly, would make it very clear that the Republicans were up to something foul.

Between December 3, 2004 and June 17, 2005, the RNC filed a number of reports with the Federal Election Commission, ostensibly divulging their campaign expenditures. The payments cited for Sproul's services—an alleged total of $4.5 million for the period Oct. 14/Nov. 22—were especially vague (of the six payments reported, three were unenlighteningly ascribed to "Voter Registration Costs"), and so the FEC persistently requested to know more. Finally, after receiving a stern letter, dated May 18, from the Commission, asking, finally, for a comprehensive reckoning, the RNC responded with one more revised report (their third) on June 17. In it, those three suspicious Sproul expenditures for "Voter Registration Costs" were now defined as payments for "Political Consulting." (Although that change cleared nothing up, the FEC seems to have let the matter drop, as its database contains no letters asking for some further explanation.) With that report the RNC included several thousand pages of campaign expenses—in addition to the thousands they had already submitted. There were several startling revelations in the body of reports, and in that cumulative mass of paperwork.

It turned out, first of all, that the RNC paid Sproul not only for their pre-election work, but also paid them for work *after* the election. According to their Year-End Report, filed on Jan. 28, 2005, the RNC paid Sproul for "Political Consulting" in December—long after all the voter registration drives had ended.

And two months later, when the RNC filed their amended Year-End Report on May 3, the dates of those December expenditures mysteriously changed. A payment of $210,176, once made on Dec. 20, was changed to Dec. 22. A payment of

$344,214, initially recorded on Dec. 22, was changed to Dec. 9. (The payments in December, and the changes in those dates, may pertain to the abortive recount in Ohio, which was scheduled to take place from Dec. 13 through Dec. 28. It surely took tremendous effort to subvert the recount in all 88 Ohio counties, and so Sproul may have helped do that job.)

Most remarkable, however, was the new evidence of what would seem to be deliberate fraud by the Republicans. In going through the latest pile of documents in June 2005, the Center for Responsive Politics discovered nine expenditures from the *future*: Sproul somehow received a total of $1,323,154 between Sept. 2 and Sept. 29, *2005*. Another $472,642 was hidden elsewhere in the 2005 cycle. Four of those prospective items were for "Generic Media Buys" or "Lodging, Transportation." The other four were for "Voter Registration Efforts"—surely an expense incurred in September of 2004, not 2005. Larry Noble, executive director of CRP, considered such future expenditures for, say, "Lodging, Transportation" rather odd, but gave the RNC the benefit of the doubt. "My guess is that it's an error," he suggested. "It's possible that they're cleaning up voter registration lists in September, but it's also possible they made a mistake." However, even if that mistaken date is just a typo, it is, to say the least, not likely that they made the same mistake in nine uniquely dated items for 2004.[105] In any case, all the payments by the RNC to Sproul add up to a whopping $8,359,161—making it the RNC's eighth-largest expenditure of the 2004 campaign, and a major piece of evidence suggesting that the party broke the bank to fix the national vote for president.[106]

What Sproul did for all that money, and where that money came from, are, ideally, questions for the FEC, Congress and the press. There has been silence on those fronts, however, although the Oregon Attorney General is, as of this writing, now investigating Sproul, and other state authorities, such as in West Virginia, Pennsylvania and Nevada, would certainly be interested in knowing more about his firm's activities and compensation.[107] At the top, meanwhile, there is clearly no concern about Sproul's lawlessness, other than to see that it remain concealed. Indeed, Nathan Sproul was grandly entertained by Bush himself soon after the Ohio "recount." "Several of Arizona's leading GOP muckety-mucks secured treasured invitations to Bush's swanky Christmas party Thursday," reported the *Arizona Republic* on December 5, 2004. "Also spotted [was] petition gatherer to the stars Nathan Sproul. Bush, it seems, doesn't have much of a problem with the allegations in several states that Sproul's employees misrepresented themselves as nonpartisan during a Republican National Committee voter registration drive and were accused of tossing out registrations from Democrats."

What with Sproul's costly national operation; the legal or bureaucratic roadblocks arbitrarily set up by Kenneth Blackwell, Mary Kiffmeyer and other influential party operatives across the nation; the countless Democrats erased from countless voter rolls; the deliberate misinformation and confusion propagated from on high or spread by bogus flyers, misleading robo-calls and other methods of black propaganda; the men with clipboards showing up at people's doors or calling on the telephone to threaten and intimidate those who would vote, and who had the right to vote; the polling places changed or closed without explanation or announcement; the untold thousands of absentee ballots never sent to those who had requested them, or sent too late, or sent with Bush & Co. pre-chosen by some patriotic state official with a ready pen; and—not least—with electronic touch screen voting machines and central tabulators, manufactured and maintained by highly partisan Republicans, used in over thirty states—and, in those states, the pro-Bush districts well-supplied with functional machines, while Democratic polling places often had one-third or half the number that they should have had, and of the few they did have, many were defective; and with the polls too often staffed and managed not by civil servants but by theocratic true believers glad to break whatever rule might hinder Bush and Cheney's Second Coming: with all of this, and more, accomplished by Election Day—and with the U.S. press ignoring it, and the Democrats not saying much about it—the Bush regime was in an unassailable position. This despite the many signs, statistical and anecdotal, that the American majority did not like, admire, respect or trust it, and strongly disapproved of its policies.

And yet power never feels secure, and never can, but always must take more draconian measures, more elaborate precautions, to perfect and preserve its stranglehold. On Friday, October 29, as reported in the *Los Angeles Times*, lawyers from the Department of Justice were in court in Florida, Ohio and Michigan, arguing the novel view that only the Department, and not voters themselves, may sue to enforce their voting rights under the Help America Vote Act. Thus Attorney General John Ashcroft would enjoy sole power to contest the states' electoral policies or actions, which meant that he would have the power *not* to prosecute the states for noncompliance with the law. In Ohio not long before, the Sandusky County Democratic Party had sued Secretary Blackwell over his refusal to allow the county's voters to file provisional ballots even if they had gone to the wrong polling place; Ashcroft's department filed an amicus brief on Blackwell's behalf. The Bush regime's position was unprecedented, as several legal scholars noted. "This is the first time in history the Justice Department has gone to court to side against voters who are trying to enforce their right to vote," said J. Gerald Hebert, former chief of the department's voting rights division, where he had worked from 1973 to 1994.[108] "I think this law will mean very little if the rights of American voters have to depend on this Justice Department." "Before this administration," said Pamela Karlin, a law professor at Stanford University, "I would say that almost uniformly, the Department of Justice would argue in favor of private rights of action . . . to enforce statutes that regulate state and local government." Although the courts in all three states rejected the department's case, the effort made clear that the Bush regime would go as far as possible to give the citizens whom they had disenfranchised, or whom they planned to disenfranchise, no recourse.

6.

An Orderly Election

On the Thursday before Election Day, the Bush campaign sought to promote a national illusion of widespread support among the young by offering college students $75 each per day to do electioneering for the ticket, primarily in liberal areas. Run in the swing states by the College Republicans, this last-minute drive-for-hire, involving some 200 students nationwide, was not illegal or improper, but it was a clear sign of the party's hearty appetite for images of victory—and, of course, the short supply of young people out there campaigning for Bush/Cheney voluntarily. It was also another good example of the Bush Republicans themselves doing just the sort of thing that they indignantly condemned the Democrats for doing—the major difference being that the Democrats, through groups like ACORN, paid needy people a very modest sum to register new voters in poor neighborhoods, while the Republicans were paying handsomely to foster the positive impression, in more affluent neighborhoods, that the kids were out there working for the president.

The Democrats were quick to emphasize the latter point: "John Kerry and John Edwards and Democrats across New Hampshire have inspired thousands of volunteers to flood New Hampshire, and we don't need to pay them," said Kathleen Strand of the New Hampshire Democratic Party. Defending the program, Aaron Graham, Dartmouth's College Republicans field representative, tried to argue that it *would* increase the Bush vote. "If they're still working for Bush, then they're not hardcore Kerry fans and are probably undecided. I wouldn't work for Kerry for $75." He also intimated that the money was intended to reward the president's supporters. "They're trying to entice students who already support Bush. It's just an incentive to go out and support a candidate they're already behind." The weakness of those arguments was tacit confirmation of the program's basic purpose as a propaganda exercise.[1]

Elsewhere there were similar pro-Bush strokes of propaganda just before Election Day. According to the *Rocky Mountain News*, which had endorsed the president, Bush beat Kerry by 41 to 34 percent in Colorado and, in the senatorial race, Democrat Ken Salazar was beaten handily by theocratic beer mogul Peter Coors. The main problem with this news—billed as the paper's "final" election results—was that it hit the web on Monday, November 1, the day before the voting started.[2] (While Bush did seemingly win Colorado, Salazar beat Coors by four points.) Whether this was a pre-emptive strike against the Kerry vote, intended to discourage his supporters in the state, or merely a strange case of wishful thinking, that fake news report suggests a certain over-eagerness to see Bush win, regardless of what Colorado's voters wanted.

But it was the swing states where, on the eve of the election, Republicans took every opportunity, broke or bent all rules that could be bent or broken and used every trick in the book (and invented new ones) to fool, frighten or confuse the Democrats into not registering or voting. Take Pennsylvania. There, Team Bush sent out leaflets on fake county stationery asking Republicans to vote on November 2 and Democrats on November 3—a point they also made in phone calls from "Bill Clinton" or progressive groups like America Coming Together (ACT). (The November 3 ploy was used nationwide.)[3] They circulated flyers, "quoting" an article (doctored) from the *Chicago Sun-Times* that warned students registering to vote in Pennsylvania that they would lose grants from their home states.[4] The day before Election Day, the party sent official letters to the men and women charged with running Philadelphia's 1,681 polling places, instructing them to check voters' signatures "at will"—a violation of the local election law, as such a step would slow the process down. (This also was apparently the first time in the city's history that any party had attempted to instruct the polling personnel.)[5] Such monkeyshines continued right up through the early morning of November 2, when various county and municipal officials had to make public assurances that Pennsylvania's voting machines were not preprogrammed with phantom Kerry votes, a charge flying from the lips of many rightist operatives statewide—and elsewhere, thanks to Matt Drudge, who globalized the falsehood through his "Drudge Report."[6] In any case, it was the Republicans themselves who had already messed with the machines in over thirty states, as would become increasingly apparent through the day, and afterward.

Election Day itself was a national catastrophe, with foul-ups and transgressions of all kinds occurring coast to coast, most of

them advantaging the Bush ticket. Early in the campaign, all
eyes had been on Florida—to the extent that the disaster of
2000, and the likelihood of its happening again, made news at
all. Then the spotlight shifted to Ohio, where it stayed right
through Election Day, as that state apparently gave Bush his
winning margin. The mysteries there, as we have seen, were legion. That focus was surely understandable, given that the media juggernaut can only flatten one thing at a time. The press's
vague fixation on Ohio was unfortunate, not just because the
coverage of that mess was mostly cursory, as we have seen, but
because it served as a distraction from the enormous mess that
littered nearly every state, the signs of civic perfidy defacing our
democracy like a continental oil spill. In their over-eagerness to
call Election Day a great success, the media tacitly portrayed
Ohio as the *only* state where there were problems, thereby suggesting that, if there were actually no major problems in Ohio,
then there had been no major problems anywhere. In short, to
repeat the words of Rep. Bill Shuster (R-PA): "It was, at the end
of the day, an honest election."

By the end of that day, in fact, the Republicans had made it
clear that, in their eyes, "an honest election" would have meant
an ignominious defeat comparable to Appomattox or the Bay of
Pigs. Unless Rep. Shuster spent Election Day up in Vermont
and not in his home state, "at the end of the day" he must have
been exhausted by the strain of not perceiving the abundant evidence that Pennsylvania was, in civic terms, a shambles.
Statewide, voters in Bush-unfriendly precincts had to stand in
line for up to five hours, while their Bush-friendly fellow citizens had an easy time of it. "'A lot of people got disgusted during the day and decided not to vote because of the long wait,'
said Laurie Durante, 45, who waited more than two hours to

vote in a tiny guard shack at a housing development in the Poconos," reported the Associated Press.[7] Polling places in several counties, including Chester, Berks and Lehigh, had to stay open late into the night so everyone could vote. In about a dozen precincts, Mercer County's touch-screen machines repeatedly malfunctioned, some of them requiring voters to vote *backwards*—starting on the system's final page and working their way forward to page one—so that their votes would (apparently) count.[8] There was also lots of outright human interference, especially in urban and/or academic areas. On the campus of the University of Pittsburgh, 800 student voters were held up for hours by GOP "challengers," and in the city, according to William Peduto, a Democratic city councilman, "a number of Republican attorneys are fighting every single person."[9]

"Many students headed to Pittsburgh's City-County Building to vote by provisional ballot, and an Allegheny County judge extended the deadline for voting in that manner until 9:30 P.M. But attorneys for the county said they anticipated that those votes would be challenged."[10] About 150 precincts in Allegheny County ran out of provisional ballots. "Many of the ballots were in areas with large populations of minorities and college students."[11]

In Philadelphia, the district attorney's office received 138 complaints of problems at the polls. (Four years before, the office had received just 48.)[12] Meanwhile, the Philadelphia Republican Committee halted the absentee ballot count by filing suit in federal court, claiming that the GOP had not been given advance copies of the ballots.[13] All such mischief helped keep Kerry's winning margin down to just two points, or 128,869 votes, despite a massive Democratic turnout and local polls predicting a Kerry win.

Like Ohio, Pennsylvania was a major swing state, meaning that suppression of the urban vote there was all-important. But there were bad signs everywhere—in every region, "blue" and "red." It was the regime's strategy to do whatever must be done to lower the Kerry vote and exaggerate the Bush vote coast to coast, so that the president could say, in his victory speech, "America has spoken." And so Kerry votes were stolen not just in the swing states but in Democratic *and* GOP strongholds. Under Bush, in other words, the sort of anti-democratic practices once thought peculiar to the South have gone national; and, more troubling still, this new national "Southern strategy" appears to have become acceptable to the Establishment, just as the racism predominant down South has long been tolerated, albeit reflexively condemned, by knowing Northerners.

It must be noted that, in this last presidential race, the South was an electoral mare's nest, regardless of how deeply "red" most southern states might be. On November 5, an organization called Count Every Vote 2004, having monitored the goings-on in 700 precincts in Alabama, Florida, Louisiana, Georgia, Mississippi and the Carolinas on Election Day, reported "hundreds of voting irregularities" in all seven states.[14] Certainly the anti-Democratic drive down there was not atrocious, nor, often, was the racist effort ostentatious: Bush/Cheney's "Southern strategy," in short, was not a simple case of "Dixie rising," with 2004 recalling the bloodbath of 1876. As Julian Bond noted, speaking *not* just of the South but of the entire nation, the old Redeemer project, to wipe out any trace of Reconstruction, was again (or still) in force, only this time with "subtler and more creative tactics" than in the epoch of Jim Crow.[15] Down South this time there were no lynchings, no poll taxes charged or literacy tests imposed. The time—in the South and in the North and West—the anti-democratic enterprise was by and large systemic, bureau-cratic, quasi-automatic and therefore far too undramatic to be quite perceptible, much less attract camera crews.

Not that Election Day was peaceful in the erstwhile Land of Cotton (although any casual reader or viewer of the news would think it was). Voting was in fact disrupted or prevented by many instances of racist bullying. In South Carolina, a posse of Republicans converged on Benedict College, a black institution in Columbia, demanding to see drivers' licenses and challenging the right of several dozen people, mostly students, to cast votes. "Students from Benedict College being turned away," one witness reported from the scene, "[and] being told they don't have 'proper ID' even though they have their voter registration card and student ID. People are also outside the polls telling voters that Bush is already going to win and their vote won't count." Some of the students left in tears, according to David Swinton, the college president, who also noted that the operation slowed things down so much—there was a four-hour wait at one point—that would-be voters had to call it quits.[16]

There were reports of similar tactics used at Morris College, another all-black institution in Columbia. That day there was also an attempt to disenfranchise students at Stillman College, a largely African-American school in Huntsville, Alabama, through the same tactic used a year before to discourage the would-be student voters at Prairie View A&M University in Waller County, Texas. "Many students registered to vote on [the Stillman] campus before October 22. . . . When they showed up at the polling site on campus, students originally from other counties in Alabama were told that they could not vote on campus, and that they had to go back to their original county and file a provisional ballot there. The polling site officials told students from other states that as students, they could not vote in Alabama, and had to go back to their original state to vote."[17]

While such overtly militant group actions were comparatively rare, the southern climate was by no means easygoing for those trying to vote against the party. For every bit of outright thuggery like the attack on Benedict College, there were countless cases of deliberate unhelpfulness, feigned helplessness or frank hostility by poll workers and poll watchers. Witnesses throughout South Carolina were at times astonished by the open partiality of the state's poll workers, who favored the Republicans with a boldness that suggested frank encouragement from their superiors, which is to say, a culture sympathetic to "family values." "In several Greenville precincts," poll monitor Ian Whatley observed, "the Republican representative was allowed to look over the voter roll as it was signed, but the Democratic representative was not allowed within ten feet." When challenged on this, Whatley added, "a poll manager produced the classically impartial statement that there was no way he was going to let some Democratic attorney intimidate him!"[18]

"Driving by another location and saw Republican party signs at entrance," another monitor reported from the town of Easley. One need not be a monitor to spot such flagrant bias, which was quite obvious to countless voters. From Pendleton in Anderson County:

Went to vote, was turned away because wanted to vote Democratic. Told he was not listed and to go to main office to get new paperwork. Then went to second polling place in his county and was told to go back to first polling place and fill out a provisional ballot. Went back to first polling place and was told he could not have a provisional ballot. Filed complaint with NAACP.[19]

From Malden in Greenville County:

Computer system down all over Greenville; not set up this morning; sites shut down all over Greenville. Broke out paper ballots
@8:30, wouldn't give before people had to go to work and left.
Won't stay open later.[20]

From Greer in Greenville County:

Electronic voting—many people were having difficulty with it and
wanted to bring someone into the booth with them to help them
figure it out, but the poll worker was not allowing that, as to black
voters, but was allowing white voters to bring in a helper.[21]

Most of the interference in the South was not so confronta-
tional but had been built into the system. On Election Day,
would-be Democratic voters were inordinately hobbled by what
seemed to be mere mishaps. Registration forms had not arrived,
absentee ballots had not arrived, machines were breaking down,
the lines were just too long. In South Carolina many voters who
had registered when applying for their drivers' licenses—taking
advantage of the so-called Motor Voter law (the National Voter
Registration Act was passed in 1993, much to the resistance of
several states)—found that, somehow, they had not registered.[22]
This was the experience of Meka Ramsey when she tried to vote
in Anderson County on November 2. Having stood in line for
quite some time, she was told there was no record of her registration. As she *had* registered, she was inclined to make a fuss,
and so was promptly given the phone number of a state "problem desk." She called, and started to describe her situation to
the person at the other end, who cut her off: "Don't tell me! You

registered to vote at the DMV," he said wearily. "Well, we've had a problem with them not sending in registrations, and so you may well *not* be registered."[23]

In surveying South Carolina, I have thus far cited cases mainly from a region of the state that is regressive even by local standards—Greenville and Anderson counties, which comprise "the Upstate," an area heavily influenced by two far-right voting blocs: Christianists—Bob Jones University is in Greenville—and neo-Confederates. It was primarily the virulence of those two factions that defeated John McCain in the state's GOP primary in 2000 (in July 2005, the Upstate would become the destination Christian Exodus, a movement of End-Times secessionists).[24] And yet Election Day was much the same throughout the rest of South Carolina, with numerous reports of mechanical collapse, logistical disinformation, bureaucratic interference and/or blunt partisan harassment pouring in from every corner of the state, from Aiken to Beaufort, from Columbia to Myrtle Beach. "Caller was told she had to go into restroom and put her Kerry t-shirt on inside out before they would allow her to vote."[25] "Elderly parents unable to wait in long lines."[26] "Only republican candidates for several offices including U.S. Senate. Only room for write-ins and Republicans."[27]

Long lines out front of polling place; voters being required to sign in AFTER standing on line and told to go to back of line; no one advising voters they need to sign in first. Many discouraged and leaving rather than wait on line a second time.

Called local county election and they said she wasn't registered—they hung up on her. Black men in her area are receiving fliers that they can't vote if they don't pay child support. Men are scared to call us because they owe child support.[28]

GOP poll monitors and inside the polling location . . . telling predomin[ant]ly African-American voters that they cannot vote for various reasons, including a misspelled name or a driver's license with another ID.[29]

Overall, the cumulative cost of such glitches, crimes and improprieties would ensure the largest victory possible for Bush/Cheney in that deep-red state. (On Election Night, the South Carolina Progressive Network reported that its voter hotline had received 350 complaints, many from counties with new installed electronic voting machines; and the Voter Protection Hotline reported over 160 calls, mostly about the voting machines, voter identification and registration complaints).[30] But such attempts to cut the Democratic vote, it must be reemphasized, were not restricted to South Carolina. The subversion of the Motor Voter Law was evident throughout the nation—even in some states that had not seemed to resist the law when it was passed. What happened to Meka Ramsey and countless other South Carolinians also happened in Indiana and California, where it was reported in the press. According to the Election Incident Reporting System (EIRS), it also happened in North Carolina, Arizona, Maryland, Louisiana, Colorado, Georgia, Illinois, Louisiana, Maryland, Nevada, Texas, New Jersey and New York—as well as in, predictably, Ohio, Florida and Pennsylvania.

Returning to the Carolinas, the problems on Election Day were more explicit and more numerous in more liberal North Carolina, whose Democratic precincts had the worst mechanical problems of any state. In Gaston County, a bastion of exurban Republicans (with a black population of 14 percent), 13,200 votes went missing, while in tiny Carteret County, another GOP stronghold on the state's southeasternmost Atlantic coast (with a black population of 7 percent), another 4,438 votes were "irretrievably lost."[31] In both counties Bush won by especially large margins: 36 percentage points in Gaston (68 percent to 32 percent), and 39 in Carteret (69 percent to 30 percent). Thus Bush did even better in those counties than he had four years before. In 2000, he had won by 34 percentage points in Gaston County, and, in Carteret, by 32. Thus his victory margin grew by two and seven points respectively. There was a different kind of pro-Bush computer glitch in Craven County, another small Republican domain just north of Carteret (with a black population of 25 percent).[32] There, Bush/Cheney got 11,283 more votes than the entire number of votes cast for president. However, as that particular snafu kept the GOP from taking control of the county's board of commissioners, a number of concerned Republicans resolved to fix it with the guidance of Tiffiney Miller, director of the county Board of Elections, and Owen Andrews, the local representative of ES&S, the maker of the errant machines. "Andrews will work with the manufacturer, Miller and the elections board to correct the problem to ensure it will not happen again, but said 'it really has nothing to do with the integrity of the vote as cast or counted,'" reported the *Sun Journal*, the daily paper in New Bern, the county seat.[33]

Meanwhile, in the far more populous and liberal Mecklenburg County (Charlotte, North Carolina's largest city, is its seat), there were many instances when the machines themselves insisted on a vote for Bush. These miscarriages were often not reported, but informally recounted among friends. "Here in

Mecklenburg County, we voted on Sequoia machines," recalled Lisa Sarinelli, a voting rights activist from Charlotte.

> Many voters I've talked to since E-Day told me that when they used the option to check their vote on the machine before pressing the "red button" to cast the vote, their choices had been flipped to the opponent (in all cases, a Kerry vote became a Bush vote). When the voter went back through the selections to correct it and checked the vote again, the same thing happened. In some cases, with some help from the poll workers, it was fixed—but not all cases. Some voters just didn't cast a vote rather than have their vote go to Bush.[34]

All those uppity machines and disappearing votes no doubt pertain to the extraordinary aberration in the state's electoral results: "a clear, obvious, and unaccounted diversion from the norm in both the Senate and Presidential races," first noticed, and punctiliously demonstrated, by Robert Glenn Plotner on the website Democratic Underground ten days after the election.[35] Briefly, Plotner found that North Carolina's absentee and early votes were copious, comprising a full third of the electorate; and that this bloc of ballots would enable him to measure "an unadulterated voting pattern against the strange results of Election Day." (Those "strange results" included the discrepancy between the exit polls and the official vote count as well as Erskine Bowles's surprising loss to Richard Burr in the Senate race.) Plotner went painstakingly through all the precinct data for the state, and found a tight consistency between the overall vote, the early/ absentee vote, and the poll-only vote in every single local and state race—*except* the senatorial and presidential races.

In the former, the poll-only vote was startlingly askew, with "a sudden shift of 6.4%" toward the Republican, assuring Burr's election. "There is absolutely nothing to account for the bizarre drop of support in the electorate by 6.4% between the early voting (mostly the week prior) and election day," writes Plotner. "But when we compare it to the Presidential race, it is dwarfed by absurdity." Plotner gives the figures for that race:

PRESIDENT (early/absentee vote):
Bush: 529,755 52.9%
Kerry: 469,522 46.9% –6.0
Others: 2,749 0.2%

PRESIDENT (overall vote):
Bush: 1,961,188 56.0%
Kerry: 1,525,821 43.6% –12.4
Others: 13,989 0.4%

PRESIDENT (poll only):
Bush: 1,431,433 57.3%
Kerry: 1,056,299 42.3% –15.0
Others: 11,240 0.4%

Plotner sums up:

Kerry was behind by 6 points in the absentee/early voting. The result is consistent with the pre-election polls and most importantly with the exit polls of November 2nd. THE EXIT POLLS TELL US THAT PEOPLE VOTED IDENTICALLY TO THE OTHER THIRD OF THE ELECTORATE. By all standards of reason, the other two-thirds of the vote should be very close to the same result. But look at what happens— a sudden and unexplained plummet in the very same electorate of NINE POINTS at the . . . polls, more than doubling Kerry's overall margin of defeat. A 15-point edge for Bush in North Carolina on election day??? Come on—I'm not that gullible.

The only feasible explanation for the odd results in those two races, Plotner reasons, is some sort of default setting programmed into the machines.

Throughout Bush Country, the Democrats were similarly plagued by statistically impossible bad luck. There was "a city-wide problem of malfunctioning voting machines" in New Orleans—the largest Democratic city in Republican Louisiana—with 30 percent of the precincts reporting technical breakdowns.[36] "I know of at least two precincts that didn't have their machines operating until well into the afternoon," said Alaina Beverly, assistant counsel with the NAACP Legal Defense Fund.[37] Such epidemic dysfunction—and certain of the city's polling personnel disastrously confused, and therefore over-stingy with provisional ballots or prone to garble the instructions for their use—disenfranchised several thousand Democrats. The glut of voters was so acute, with so many forced to quit, that voting activists filed for an emergency order to keep the city's polls open for an extra two hours, until 10:00 P.M., but the petition was summarily denied by Civil Court Judge Sidney Cates (a Democrat).[38] There was similar chaos leading to a similar request (also denied) in Little Rock, where the technical setbacks included a protracted power failure—from November 1 through November 3—that shut down two precincts in "West Little Rock," a largely Jewish neighborhood.[39] The machines were breaking down—freezing, turning off, changing Kerry votes to Bush votes—and the poll workers screwing up (or worse) in the Democratic precincts of Kentucky, Tennessee, Missouri, Texas and Nebraska, and in a lot of places to the north and east and west.[40]

Nationwide, the anti-democratic point of such apparently random accidents and errors was frequently confirmed by the overt obstructionism of Republicans too partisan to try to hide what they were doing. In Iowa, for instance, there were several seeming inadvertent moves to cut the Kerry vote, both before and on Election Day: hundreds of registered voters were rejected in mid-October, when the computer system used by county auditors could not access the Social Security database; many registration forms were thrown out for missing checkmarks on the little boxes indicating that the voter was a U.S. citizen at least 18 years old—even though such certification was included in the signed, sworn voter affidavits that accompanied the forms; as in Florida 2000 (and 2004), voters were wrongly purged from the state rolls because they had been misidentified as felons.[41] On the other hand, some attempts to block the vote were patently non-accidental. Ten days before Election Day, the Iowa GOP—following Secretary Blackwell's example in Ohio—tried to suppress provisional ballots cast in the right county but the wrong precinct;[42] and on October 21, a day of early voting, Mary Mosiman, auditor of Story County, interfered illegally with the process at Iowa State University by dispersing would-be student voters still on line at closing time. The secretary of state then ordered Mosiman to organize a second day of early voting on November 1 to compensate those who had been dismissed—and she refused (because, she claimed, she lacked sufficient time to post a notice).[43] All such maneuvers were significant and should have been investigated rigorously, as Bush won Iowa by just over 10,000 votes.

Wisconsin also was the site of multiple and disparate strikes against democracy. It was a brilliant drive. Although the president did not prevail, Kerry took that very liberal state by fewer than 12,000 votes. (In 2000, Ralph Nader picked up over 94,000 votes in Wisconsin, while Gore beat Bush by over 5,700 votes.)

By Election Day, the Republicans had already done quite a number on that state—or rather, on its cities, with their many blacks and student-types and other infidels. Voters in Kenosha and Racine were told, wrongly, that they could not register to vote on Election Day.[44] In Milwaukee, late in the campaign, the local GOP abruptly dumped over 5,600 voters' addresses onto the desk of the city attorney, claiming they were fraudulent; and by the time City Hall had found them to be genuine, Team Bush came up with many more, finally naming over 37,000 Democrats whom the GOP wished to disenfranchise. The Republicans, insisting that the voters on their list be asked for proof of their identity, threatened to besiege the polls with challengers. (After much expostulation by the party, the city turned them down.)[45] In Madison, the College Republicans and local GOP congressional candidates misdirected unwary would-be voters by urging them to "vote at the polling place of your choice."[46] All such activity, the bogus calls from "NARAL," the flyers from the "Milwaukee Black Voters League" and God knows what else, contributed immensely to the climate of confusion and exasperation on Election Day—which, there as in so many other places, was all long lines and warped machines for Democrats, while voting was a snap for most Bush supporters; and in Republican precincts too, countless Democrats were turned away. The zealots on the ground did all they could to baffle and intimidate the opposition. In one polling place in Madison, a Republican poll-watcher ordered a young woman to take a Kerry button off her jacket—a double violation, as he had no authority to dictate anything, and she had every right to wear the button.[47]

This overview could, and maybe should, be much longer and far more detailed. It could go on to catalogue the most egregious strokes of vote suppression in the East Coast's bluest states. In New Jersey, for example, thousands were denied the right to vote, the state having failed enormously to register the many new voters who turned out, presumably to vote for Kerry, as those disenfranchised were largely Democrats. Students were especially hard hit in the Garden State. "Hundreds, perhaps thousands, of new voters at Rutgers University reluctantly filled out paper provisional ballots or walked away from the polls when their names could not be found at polling locations," reported the *Newark Star-Ledger* in a November 7th article entitled "Rutgers Not Only Campus to Report Voting Problems." Thus Bush lost the state by only seven points (or 218,752 votes), whereas on October 31, Rasmussen's polls had foretold a Kerry victory by 12 points (53 percent to 41 percent).[48] And all across New York there were thousands of reports—many of them logged at 1-866-MY-VOTE—of voters turned away, machines malfunctioning, registration cards or polling information or, above all, absentee ballots not received. Such was the scene throughout Erie County (whose seat is Buffalo, where a voter, having registered as Independent, found that he was registered as a Republican);[49] Albany, the state's capital city (where a voter who had lately moved within the city was told "that it would be a felony" if she tried to vote at her old precinct);[50] Westchester County, a Democratic stronghold with many civic horror stories: "At noon on election day it was discovered that the information in one voting booth was 2 years old (voting for Pataki for governor, not voting for president). Election officials found out about it at noon and stopped the use of machine."[51] (That caller noted that his parents, who had used other machines, had encountered the same problem.) "Poll workers impatient, bad attitude"[52]—an experience shared by many others: "Tried to read the sample ballot while waiting in line to vote but was told that he MUST go in the voting booth immediately and had 3 min-utes to vote."[53] And here is what befell someone who almost voted for Ralph Nader in Westchester:

> Individual went to write in a ballot for the non-mainstream Party. Changed her mind and wanted to vote for mainstream candidate. She tried to pull a lever for the mainstream candidate and it wouldn't work. In the end, she wasn't able to vote for the main-stream candidate (as she wanted). She did not change her write in ballot to mainstream candidate's name, but was not instructed by poll workers of this option. Poll workers hurried her out and did not address her issues.[54]

This sort of thing was epidemic throughout New York City—site of 9/11 and the president's apotheosis on September 13, 2001, and therefore the place that he relentlessly invoked in fur-therance of his re-election. (Once re-installed, he kept relent-lessly invoking it in furtherance of the U.S. occupation of Iraq.) Machines were few and often stumbling, or just unresponsive, all over the Bronx, Queens, Brooklyn and Manhattan, so that the lines were very long and very slow, as in Ohio and so many other places. Thousands of the city's would-be voters did not re-ceive the absentee ballots that they had ordered. At the polls, more would-be voters were summarily dismissed, often without any guidance. "At the polling site on Bennett Street in Wash-ington Heights, two people (in five minutes) came in to vote while I was there and were turned away," recalls Megan De-markis. "When they showed their state IDs, the addresses didn't match the site [i.e., their addresses were not listed at the polling place]. They were dismissed rudely and were given no informa-tion as to where they could cast their votes. I doubt they voted

. . . I called the 'my vote' 800 number to report the situation, and was told by a recorded voice to call later—all day."[55] Thus Kerry's winning margin in New York—an impressive 17 points, the Democrat apparently receiving some 1,800,000 more votes than the president—should clearly have been larger still, as was the case throughout the nation.

FLORIDA

Although it was Ohio that gave Bush his (seeming) victory in the Electoral College, the race in Florida—where Bush reportedly prevailed by 5 points (52 percent to 47 percent), or 381,147 votes, although by Election Day, the polls predicted a close race with Kerry as the winner[56]—was actually the most significant. While Ohio clinched the horse race for the president and was indeed a site of numerous and massive frauds and other crimes by the Republicans, the theft in Florida was even more sophisticated. The very fact that Florida's vote has not been controversial is an indication of just how advanced the art or science of election stealing has become in Brother Jeb's domain. (It also reconfirms the general civic failure of our national press, which has continued to ignore the mischief there just as it has ignored the Bush campaign's mischief nationwide—although the felonies, anomalies and improprieties in Florida were more numerous and flagrant than in any other state.) In fact, an overview of what went on in Florida is now especially important, as voting there appears to be the regime's paradigm for voting everywhere. Florida, in other words, is what the whole United States is fast becoming in the civic sphere. There—unless we act as soon as possible to reclaim the republic—lies our future as

American subjects: a system built specifically to disenfranchise an aroused and even militant majority, and to do so without leaving many traces. At its heart it was a hidden play of light, as tightly managed as it was ephemeral. In many cases, there was no vote to audit.

Bush & Co.'s first coup in Florida left their shattered opposition understandably incensed, and dead set on reversing it in 2004. "We're coming for revenge," William McCormick, president of the Fort Lauderdale NAACP, told *Salon*'s Farhad Manjoo a few weeks before November 2.[57] "They're going to see the greatest turnout they've ever seen. And I guarantee that every ballot cast in Broward County is going to be counted—over my dead body they won't. I'm not going to be intimidated, swayed, threatened away from voting. I guarantee you they're going to be fired." Kerry's Florida campaign was manned abundantly by dozens of attorneys likewise "coming for revenge." "I'll tell you an interesting story about lawyer recruitment," Steven Zack, who led Kerry's legal forces in the state, told Manjoo in October.[58] "When I first started to do this a few months ago, I sent out an e-mail to 50 lawyers I'd worked with around the state asking for help. I got 65 yes answers, from 50 e-mails. They'd sent it on to friends saying, 'I got this e-mail. You ought to get involved.'" Whereas, in Zack's experience, the usual reply rate for pro-bono calls-to-arms was 10 percent, his summons to the Democrats in Florida brought some 2,000 attorneys to the pre-election battlefield. "There isn't a day that I don't walk down the street here in downtown Miami that I don't have a lawyer come up to me and volunteer."

In retrospect, such Democratic pluck seems at once tragic and a bit ridiculous, like the Charge of the Light Brigade or the conviction that, thanks to the Maginot Line, "France shall not again be invaded," as a *March of Time* newsreel put it in 1938. Those partisans apparently had no idea what they were up against, as neither firm resolve nor legal vigilance, nor resolved and vigilant voters, could possibly prevail against the Bush machine in Florida—which was, if anything, *more* resolute and vigilant than any of its keenest adversaries, and also wealthier, more ruthless and far more sophisticated. The Democrats in Florida may have been "coming for revenge" as soon as Bush began his term as president, but the Republicans were also quick to start preparing for the fire next time. Their plans to burn the Florida (and national) electorate were in the works soon after the regime was first installed. In early 2003, Jeb Bush started trying to eliminate the paper trail of Florida's 2000 contest by defunding the state agency responsible for warehousing the actual ballots.[59]

Indeed, it was the memory of Florida—the hanging chads, the dimpled chads, the punch cards held aloft and arduously scrutinized by squinting bureaucrats as if those ballots were so many fragments of the Talmud—that was the pretext for "electoral reform," by which Bush & Co. meant obviating any further human interference with their plans. "Once this is over and the passion subsides, we will look at all our election laws," Jeb Bush vowed ominously a few days after the election.[60]

"Electoral reform" was of particular importance to the Democrats, who, by the time Bush was inaugurated, had come to use it as a tacit—some might say timid—way to keep the (stolen) election on the national radar. The Republicans quite deftly used this to their own advantage. At a press conference on January 24, 2001, after having met with Bush, the leaders of the House laid out their concerns, "electoral reform" being chief among them for the Democrats. David Bonior spoke about it

pointedly, as did Richard Gephardt and Tom Daschle. A reporter then asked Bonior: "Was there any discussion about who
actually won the election or should have won the election, any
assertion brought on the president's part?" Trent Lott jumped
in: "Well, I'll respond to that—*no*. I think the feeling was that
the time for that is over. The election is over. We're moving forward. And I think the president made that point."

That day, Ari Fleischer emphasized Lott's point—clearly a
top talking point—and in so doing seized "electoral reform" for
the new president. "In this meeting today," he was asked, "a
couple of the members said that there was a bit of discussion
about electoral reform after the Florida recount. Did the president convey to the leaders what he thinks should be done to—?"
"The president does believe we can have electoral reform,"
Fleischer interrupted, "and the president made clear in the
meeting that he thinks that we need to do that looking forward,
that we need to take a look at what's happened, but do so with an
eye on solving problems and not reliving past experiences for
the purpose of casting any type of aspersion or blame, that we
can learn from what's happened. And the president is very interested in electoral reform."

Bush & Co.'s agenda dovetailed neatly with the interests of
another corporate entity concerned with national "electoral reform": Election Systems & Software, Inc. (ES&S), the nation's
largest manufacturer of touch-screen voting machines, which
was already doing business in Nebraska (ES&S is headquartered
in Omaha), Arizona, Michigan and Illinois. The corporation
had a certain party bias. As American Information Industries
(AIS), it had been variously chaired, co-owned and directed by
Chuck Hagel for several years before he quit in 1995 to run for
senator from Nebraska the next year. (In 1997, AIS became

ES&S, after merging with Business Records Corp.—a part of Cronus Industries, a holding company controlled by several wealthy hard-right activists, including Caroline Rose Hunt of the Hunt oil dynasty and other figures evidently interested in wielding quiet influence on government.)[61] Hagel's long association with ES&S was notable for several reasons. On Election Day, 1996—the climax of his long-shot run against Ben Nelson for the Senate—ES&S machines were the only ones used in Nebraska, counting at least 80 percent of the vote. That fact may or may not be germane to Hagel's upset victory over Nelson, the novice candidate winning by 57 percent to 42 percent, or 96,054 votes, despite a predicted dead heat.[62] Once elected, furthermore, Hagel kept his shares in the McCarthy Group, a private merchant banking company in Omaha and the parent company of AIS/ES&S—an investment worth up to $5 million. Not only did the senator retain those holdings, but he also failed to disclose his interest in ES&S, asserting that the McCarthy Group was not a private company but a publicly traded corporation. ("He did not report the company's underlying assets," *The Hill* reported in January 2003, "choosing instead to cite his holdings as an 'excepted investment fund,' and therefore exempt from detailed disclosure rules.")[63] Hagel also kept a close political affiliation with ES&S: Mike McCarthy, an owner and director of the company, was also Hagel's campaign finance director.

Such was the outfit pushing for "electoral reform" in Florida. ("Better elections every day" is its unreassuring motto.) In mid-November of 2000, with the parties in the middle of their strident (and unequal) post-electoral propaganda war, ES&S was smoothly lobbying the folks in Florida, offering to help them to avoid all such unpleasantness in future races. They showed off the PBC 2100, a great new punch card tabulator that would catch all overvotes (that is, more than one vote cast for a single office). "The voter would be alerted that they spoiled their ballot" and get the chance to try again, said ES&S's Todd Urosevich on November 15.[64] They also pitched touch-screen voting machines, which were far costlier than the optical scanners, but which stood to make elections even *better*, as the machines were paperless, and, from the incumbents' point of view, it is of course far better not to have a paper trail at all than to let voters rectify their faulty ballots.

ES&S's lobbying eventually paid off. At first the state considered, or purported to consider, merely leasing optical scanners until the new touch-screen technology was up to speed. "I think it would be wrong-headed and precipitous to purchase any equipment now. If you buy now, you're buying antiquated technology," Katherine Harris argued on February 22, 2001.[65] Despite that recommendation, on May 9 the governor, as promised, signed a new election law including a disbursement of $24 million to help the counties *buy* optical scanners; although there seemed to be a sort of groundswell for the more advanced technology: "Elections supervisors in Clearwater and Dade City said Tuesday they want the even-more-advanced paperless, touch-screen voting machines in time for the 2002 election," reported the *Tampa Tribune*.[66] That view prevailed. After months of lavish lobbying by ES&S, Harris formally approved the use of ES&S in the state of Florida.[67] Two months later, Pasco County was the first to sign a contract with ES&S, pledging $4.6 million for the civic overhaul. (Whether or not ES&S had anything to do with it, Bush beat Kerry with amazing ease in Pasco County—a huge improvement over his performance there four years earlier.)[68]

The new system was first put to the test on September 10,

2002, when it was used in Florida's largest county, Miami-Dade, in the primary election. That Election Day was a colossal failure there, in part because ES&S's machines would not start up on time, so that the opening of several precincts was delayed for hours. The machines were slow because ES&S had had to mess around with them to make them work as advertised. In May 2003, Miami-Dade's inspector general released a highly critical report both on the contract with ES&S and that corporation's sleazy conduct. "The report points out many instances in which the super slick sales pitch of company reps didn't match up to what they actually delivered. For instance, the county needed to have ballot items appear in three languages, and the company promised that its system could do that with no problem. Yet, according to the IG report, ES&S knew that this would require a bit of jury-rigging of the slug-brained machines. In this case, it meant that the machines took much longer to boot up on election day and required the county to buy more equipment for them to work properly." [69]

The biggest loser in the race was Janet Reno, U.S. attorney general under Clinton—and, prior to that, Florida's state attorney, to which post Floridians had re-elected her four times. Facing Bill McBride for the Democratic gubernatorial nomination (which would have meant that she, not he, would challenge Jeb Bush in November), Reno seemed to lose by over 8,000 votes, and conceded. Over the next few weeks, however, officials kept "finding" thousands of new Reno votes until she had enough to file a challenge—but not before it was too late to file.[70] (McBride, of course, went on to lose big-time—56 percent to 43 percent—to Governor Bush. "The victory made Bush the only Republican governor ever to capture re-election in Florida," CBS News exulted.)[71]

To the evidence that there was something wrong with the machines, Jeb and his henchpersons responded, then and forever afterward, that there was nothing wrong with the machines. The problems in 2002 were due to "human error," Jacob DiPietre, a spokesman for the governor, told *Salon*'s Manjoo in 2004 (without divulging what that error was, or who the humans were).[72] Likewise, Glenda Hood, Katherine Harris's replacement as Florida's secretary of state, told CNN a few weeks prior to November 2, 2004: "The track record shows that, since 2002, when electronic voting equipment's been used in Florida, . . . we've delivered successful elections. There have not been problems with the equipment that's been used."[73]

Such bald denial of inconvenient facts—from global warming (*not* a "human error") to the "war on terrorism" (going beautifully) to the wars in Iraq and Afghanistan (both going beautifully) to Dick Cheney's financial ties to Halliburton (he has no financial ties to Halliburton), and on and on—is, of course, the daily m.o. of the Bush regime, which seems incapable of saying anything that does not contradict the truth. Yet, the routine denial of its own illegitimate ascent is Bush/Cheney's central and definitive falsehood, or delusion; for this regime is essentially anti-secular, anti-rational, anti-republican and anti-democratic, ironically posing as a champion of "freedom" and "democracy" throughout this world. The extinction of democracy and freedom would appear to be the regime's mission; and yet its soldiers have insisted all along that they revere our democratic institutions (and the press has never called them on it). "Have any black voters in the state been disenfranchised, to your knowledge?" Larry King asked Katherine Harris on January 16, 2001. "To our knowledge, *no*," she answered firmly, and yet also kindly, gently, through her light cosmetic mask (she had learned to tone it down); and she went on her voice all honeyed earnestness:

Let me just say this: Florida's always been a very *progressive* state, and we have a *zero tolerance policy* towards discrimination, whether it be for *race*, or *creed*, or *gender*, or *age*. And so, of *course*, we'll *look into* these allegations, and we'll *thoroughly* follow up on them, and *thoroughly investigate* them.

"Will you get to the root of it?" King asked. "We *absolutely will* get to the root of it!" she vowed. "Because," King continued, "it should concern any citizen, Secretary of State, if any person is denied the right to vote." "You're *absolutely right!*" she replied with quiet passion, and a melting gaze. "I *couldn't agree with you more!* And we will *vigorously* pursue this!"

From then on, Harris's office, like all other stations of the Bush machine in Florida, continued not just to ignore the "allegations" of election fraud but newly dedicated its resources to disenfranchising still more Floridians. Certainly there did not seem to be a whole lot of investigating going on inside the office of the secretary of state. Some nine months after Harris made goo-goo eyes at Larry King, state officers produced some harsh assessments of the civic spirit in that office: "State Auditor General William O. Monroe reported that Harris' employees sometimes traveled first-class air to foreign cities, failed to monitor personal use of 55 cellular telephones assigned to her office and routinely misreported some expenditures," the *St. Petersburg Times* reported on September 29, 2001.[74] Around the same time, Dwight Chastain, who had lately been the secretary of state's inspector general, reported that the office had for two years been in violation of state law, which required that he report to her directly. His post had been created, and the requirement that the secretary regularly meet with him had been imposed, in order to "promote accountability, integrity and efficiency in government," as the statute puts it. In the two years that he spent in his position, Chastain met only once with Harris, who made him deal with her through a subordinate. The two years ended just before Chastain came out with his report—for which, he maintained, Harris had fired him. All in all, the spirit of democratic governance, or even professional collegiality, appeared to be conspicuously absent from the clique surrounding Katherine Harris. "It was either do what they want, be fired or resign," Chastain observed. (For some months there was no inspector general in the Office of the Secretary of State.)[75] Such is the attitude atop Jeb Bush's Florida no matter who has been appointed as its managers.

Harris lingered at her post into mid-2002, until she suddenly announced on August 1 that she had just tendered her resignation—effective on July 15, she said belatedly. She claimed that she had been "de facto Secretary of State" since then, although Florida allows no such position.[76] On August 2, the governor obligingly (and only temporarily) replaced her, and she started running for Congress in Florida's 13th district; or rather, started running openly, as she had already raised over $2 million in campaign contributions by mid-July. (In fact, she had raised $1.7 million by April.) On September 10, having spent eight times as much as all the other candidates—four Democrats and one Republican—combined, she defeated John C. Hill, a former TV anchorman, by an awesome margin: 68.3 percent to 31.7 percent. There was some outcry on September 28, when Candice Brown McElyea, a Sarasota TV reporter and seemingly one of Harris's erstwhile Democratic rivals (who, in the primary, had come in third, losing to Jan Schneider), showed up at a joint press conference to endorse Harris. "After their joint announcement, they hugged and acted all girly together, smiling and touching in mutual admiration like reunited sorority roommates, as the press conference cameras rolled," observed an op-ed in the *Sarasota Herald-Tribune* (which, for the first time in Harris's political career, had editorialized against her election).[77] McElyea, whose slogan had been "Anyone but Katherine," turned out to be a recent ex-Republican whose entire candidacy had evidently been a covert operation. (Other Busheviks have posed as Democrats— Theresa LePore, the infamous designer of the Palm Beach County "butterfly ballot," among them—a ruse that is, of course, especially effective when it is *not* exposed or even noted.)[78] On Election Day, Harris beat Schneider by ten points, 55 percent to 45 percent, or 24,323 votes.

On her introduction to the House on December 6, the freshman was appointed an assistant majority whip, among a handful of newcomers tapped for the position.[79] (Tom Feeney, Republican from Seminole County, and another freshman honored thus, would later be accused of having helped steal votes for Bush/Cheney in 2000.)[80] Harris went on to a largely unremarkable congressional career.[81] On December 21, Governor Bush finally named her permanent replacement: Glenda Hood, exmayor of Orlando and a seasoned veteran of the campaigns— 1994, 1998, 2000, and 2002—for both Bush brothers. (In 1998, when he first ran for governor, Bush considered having Hood run with him for lieutenant governor.)[82] Bush—having made her post appointive, not elective—formally anointed her on January 7.

Although lacking Harris's flamboyance, Hood has more than

compensated with the steely fervor of a born crusader. (She had helped to turn Orlando into what the Associated Press, in 1999, called "one of the major centers for Christian ministries and organizations in the United States.")[83] Throughout the nearly two years of her readying Florida for Bush & Co.'s second presidential race, she nailed the Democrats with a consistency, rigidity and blatancy that would have done her proud if she were slaughtering Muslims in medieval Palestine. In late September of 2004, Democrat Jim Stork, who had been set to challenge Rep. Clay Shaw (R-Ft. Lauderdale), was forced out of the race because of a severe heart condition—and Hood denied the invalid's request to stop campaigning, ostensibly because he made it after the official deadline, but actually because she did not want his party to replace him with a healthy candidate. When a circuit court judge in Tallahassee ruled that the secretary of state had erred by forbidding Stork to quit, Hood appealed the ruling; and the appeals court also found that she had erred. By now, however, it was just a week before Election Day, and so Stork's name was on the ballot anyway; Robin Rorapaugh was the replacement candidate whom the court belatedly allowed the Democrats to pick, but there was literally no way to vote for him. "It's rather bizarre," Shaw commented five days before Election Day.[84] (He beat Stork, who wasn't running, 63 percent to 35 percent, by 84,000 votes.)

Hood suppressed the Democratic vote in every way she could. (Like the GOP nationwide, Hood used Ralph Nader, whenever possible, to whittle down the Kerry vote a little further).[85] Sometimes, as in the Stork case, she did it through an overzealous application of the letter of the law, using trivial slips as grounds for disenfranchisement. Her policy on voter registration forms, for instance, was simply to reject all those submitted with the little box marked "U.S. citizen" unchecked.[86] This was a gratuitous requirement, as all those who had filled out the forms but overlooked that little box had duly signed Line 17, confirming that "I am a citizen of the U.S." In short, the little box was redundant, and its exclusionary use by Hood et al. a form of disenfranchisement by technicality. It was thus used in Broward County, and wherever else there was a strong disinclinaton to let Democrats and black citizens cast ballots. ("More than a third of the incomplete forms in Broward and Miami-Dade counties came from African-American registrants, even though African-Americans make up only 17 percent of the electorate in Broward and 20 percent in Miami-Dade," the *San Francisco Chronicle* reported on October 14.)[87] In Duval County—where sprawling, racially explosive Jacksonville (see p. 221) is the county seat—31,155 black voters had been added to the rolls by early October. As of October 13, however, 1,448 of those new would-be voters had had their forms tagged as "incomplete," with another 11,500 still to be "processed" by the county. There were "nearly three times the number of flagged Democratic registrations as Republican," the *Washington Post* reported.[88] "Broken down by race, no group had more flagged registrations than blacks."

For this and other restrictive practices, some illegal (requiring a Florida driver's license number or a Florida Identification Card number) and some just niggling (registration blocked for failure to check a little box affirming that the applicant is of sound mind and has not been convicted of a felony), on October 13 Florida was sued in federal court for disenfranchising over 10,000 eligible voters.[89] On October 20, the Florida GOP asked to intervene in the case. The court agreed. On the 22nd—ten days before Election Day—Hood et al. requested that the court hold off on its decision, and the court agreed. On October 28, the court dismissed the lawsuit on procedural grounds (which, of course, was what the Florida GOP had wanted). And so an unknown number of Floridians could not register to vote, as hundreds complained on Election Day.

The state of Florida also used provisional ballots to suppress the vote, by so narrowly restricting their acceptability as to make them all but useless. With the Election Reform Act of 2001, the Florida legislature first allowed provisional ballots for those voters whose names are absent from the rolls in their assigned precincts. Implicitly, such ballots cannot be provided, or accepted, at any polling site outside the voter's precinct—a limitation made explicit in 2003, when the legislature passed the Provisional Ballot Statute, which dictates that provisional ballots *must* be cast in the voter's precinct, *and nowhere else*—just as in Ohio, where Secretary Blackwell clearly followed Florida's example. There is no such limitation stipulated in the Help America Vote Act (HAVA), passed by the U.S. Congress in 2002, which claims only that the voter must be registered "in the jurisdiction" where he wants to vote:

> If an individual declares that such individual is a registered voter in the jurisdiction in which the individual desires to vote and that the individual is eligible to vote in an election for Federal office, but the name of the individual does not appear on the official list of eligible voters for the polling place or an election official asserts that the individual is not eligible to vote, such individual shall be permitted to cast a provisional ballot as follows. . . .[90]

Several courts around the nation were just then studying the question of whether "jurisdiction" meant "precinct" or "county."

On August 17, in a bid to outlaw Florida's restriction, the AFL-CIO filed suit in the State Supreme Court. On August 26, that court transferred the case to the Second Judicial Circuit Court, which then dismissed it on September 8. On September 28, the AFL filed an amended complaint with the Second JCC, which at once "dismissed the case with prejudice." The AFL then filed a notice of appeal, which, on October 1, was certified by the First District Court of Appeals, so that the Supreme Court was now obliged to hear the AFL's case after all. On October 18, that court ruled against the plaintiffs, finding that provisional ballots may *not* be cast outside the voter's precinct. Thus had the Bush machine in Florida succeeded in weakening that crucial section of the HAVA. Their success was reconfirmed again on October 21, when U.S. District Judge Robert L. Hinkle ruled against the Florida Democratic Party, finding for the Florida Bush machine. "Florida law has long required voting at the proper polling place," Hinkle wrote, "and nothing in HAVA invalidates that approach."[91]

Hood and her posse were, of course, quite happy with Judge Hinkle's ruling. It was "a victory for all Floridians who want an orderly election," said Alia Faraj, a spokesperson for the secretary.[92] While the election was by no means orderly in Florida, it surely was a victory for Hood, not least because the state was not obliged to let its voters cast provisional ballots—although the impact of the Florida courts' decisions on that issue should not be exaggerated. As things turned out, it probably would not have made much difference if the state had been required to let Floridians cast provisional ballots anywhere they wanted, because the state trashed as many of those ballots as it could. "I think we threw out a ton," Broward County Mayor Ilene Lieberman said after Election Day.[93] On January 3, 2005, AP reported that two-thirds of Florida's provisional ballots had been tossed.[94] "Of 27,742 provisional ballots cast, 9,915 were counted and 17,827 were rejected." (This news was not reported anywhere off-line in the United States, nor on the Website of a single mainstream news organization.) If the party had been forced to hand out more of them, they only would have had to throw that many more of them away. That so much paper did not have to be discarded was, perhaps, a tiny victory for conservationists.

Hood's hardball tactics and demeanor worked wonders for the Florida machine. There was Bush & Co.'s pre-emption of a proper recount in the state. Hood stood firm throughout the dauntless one-man drive by Rep. Robert Wexler (D-DelRay Beach) to force the state to use voting machines with paper trails: a wholly rational and patriotic innovation, one would think—"as American as apple pie," said Wexler—and yet one that the Republicans have fervently opposed, in Florida and elsewhere.[95] Wexler wrote to Hood, and to Theresa LePore, the infamous Palm Beach County Supervisor of Elections, for months over the issue. His point was that, as the touch-screen systems were in only 15 counties (including the big Democratic counties in South Florida), the current recount system was unfair to the voters there, whose ballots, if a race was close, would not be recounted manually, while those cast in the other counties would.

Such fears were not unfounded. They had already been confirmed by a special election on Jan. 6, a tight race for a state House seat in Broward and Palm Beach counties, which had resulted in a 12-vote victory. It turned out that 137 came out to vote on the touch screen machines—and did not participate in a single race. There was no way to investigate those numbers, or even to recount them—notwithstanding a state law that requires a recount in just such a case—for those machines had left no paper trail. The results were finally certified by the Palm Beach County Board of Elections, once its members had determined that there were no actual "ballots" to recount.

After his correspondence with the state officials got him nowhere, Wexler filed suit against them on January 7, 2004. On February 11, Circuit Court Judge Karen Miller ruled against him, upholding the defendants' arguments that this was a legislative not judicial matter and that the plaintiff lacked standing, as the lack of paper trails had not done Wexler per se any injury. The next day, Hood took advantage of her legal victory by informing all the state's election supervisors that touch-screen ballots need not be included in any manual recount. (On March 8, Wexler sued Hood et al. in federal court, this time arguing that paperless voting violates the Constitution's Equal Protection Clause and contradicts the spirit of *Bush v. Gore*, which mandates a consistent voting standard in all counties.)

In thus exempting touch-screen ballots from the manual recounts, Hood was not just stubbornly resisting the demand for paper trails, but going even further in her drive to make the vote unverifiable, and therefore that much easier to suppress. For no good reason, she was urging that, in conducting manual recounts after close elections, state officials *not* consult the touch-screen machines' internal logs.[96] Fully detailed and extraordinarily precise, those logs document the day's electoral traffic with the sort of specificity and clarity that would appear to justify the use of electronic voting systems in the first place; indeed, the logs are advertised by the marketers of touch-screen systems as an excellent means for measuring the vote's integrity on each machine. So intent was Hood on nullifying that protective feature that she engineered the proposition of a law to set her policy in stone. And so in March a strange new bill—filed in the name of one Rivers Bufford III, a state elections department lobbyist—was getting muscled through the legislature, dictating that manual recounts in close elections need not include the ballots cast on paperless machines. The ploy touched off a noisy public drive against Hood's law, organized by the Miami-Dade Election Reform Coalition, a feisty group of voting activists formed in response to the electoral disaster on September 10. Wexler was the Coalition's vigorous ally. So intrusive was the public pressure on the legislation's sponsors that they gave up after just two days, and took out all of Hood's offending language.

Having lost in the state legislature, Hood simply made up an administrative rule that did what her law would have done. Suddenly it was a standard practice of the state elections division: manual recounts in close elections do not apply to ballots cast on paperless machines. That new rule could, and did, go right into effect without consideration by the legislature. Nevertheless, on March 31, 2004, it was endorsed, 8 to 1, by Florida's Senate Ethics and Elections Committee, and by a like committee in the House. Thus the recount statute—which states clearly that a ballot must be counted after an election, if there is "a clear indication on the ballot that the voter has made a definite choice"—had been voided by mere fiat.[97] Hood read the statute differently, of course, although she would have liked to have the legislature draft a new one. Hood's rule read:

> When a manual recount is ordered and touchscreen ballots are
> used, no manual recount of undervotes and overvotes cast on a

touchscreen system shall be conducted since a review of undervotes cannot result in a determination of voter intent as required by Section 102.166(5), F.S. In this case, the results of the machine recount conducted pursuant to paragraph (5)(C) shall be the official totals for the touchscreen machines.[98]

"Although the division contends existing law rules out a manual recount of paperless ballots," the *Palm Beach Post* reported on April 1, "Secretary of State Glenda Hood endorses changing the language of the statute.[99] Said Hood spokeswoman Jenny Nash: 'This way it's in black and white and there's no question about it.'"

Hood's victory, and the defeat of Wexler and the voting activists, appeared to be judicially confirmed on May 24, when U.S. District Judge James Cohn rejected Wexler's suit because the issue was still before state courts, as Wexler had appealed; and then, on August 6, Wexler lost that fight too, when state appeals court judges Martha C. Warner, George A. Shahood and Melanie G. May all upheld Hood's exemption. (Later, Judge May was the sole dissenter in the ruling to disclose Rush Limbaugh's medical records.)[100] After all those setbacks, then, it was a great relief when things apparently began to turn around. On August 27, responding to a challenge by the ACLU, Common Cause and other advocacy groups, Judge Susan Kirkland ruled that Hood had overstepped her bounds by ruling out the manual recounts of the ballots cast on paperless machines. The judge also ordered her to write a new directive that would clarify, once and for all, the proper way to do a manual recount in a precinct with touch screen machines. Legally, these were auspicious weeks for voting activists. One month later, in response to Wexler's litigation, the federal appeals court in Atlanta struck down Judge Cohn's decision and ordered that the case go back to him in Fort Lauderdale.

Hood then trumped all opposition with a bureaucratic diktat straight from Wonderland. On October 15, just eighteen days before Election Day, she came out with the new rule that Judge Kirkland had directed her to write on August 27. Here is her revised procedure for the state's election supervisors doing manual recounts: First, they are to see how many undervotes—i.e., ballots with no candidate selected—the machine itself has tallied up. Then they are to check each electronic ballot image, and count the undervotes, if any, one by one. If the total thus determined matches the machine's tally, then the vote for that precinct will be certified. On the other hand:

> If there is a discrepancy between the number of undervotes in the manual recount and the machine recount, then the counting teams shall re-tabulate the number of undervotes for such precinct up to two additional times to resolve such discrepancy. If, after retabulating the number of undervotes for each such precinct, the discrepancy remains, then the canvassing board shall investigate and resolve the discrepancy with respect only to such precinct. In resolving the discrepancy, the canvassing board shall review the records produced by the voting system and may request the verification of the tabulation software as provided in section 102.141(5)(b), F.S.[101]

Such "verification" is defined:

> [102.141(5)(b), F.S. Request that the Department of State verify the tabulation software. When the Department of State verifies such software, the department shall compare the software used to tabu-

late the votes with the software filed with the department pursuant to s. 101.5607 and check the election parameters.[102]

Once the software has been "verified" by Glenda Hood's office, the supervisors are to "conduct any necessary diagnostic examinations."

And that's all she wrote. The new rule does not mention the machines' internal logs. Basically, the supervisors are instructed to go down a number of dead ends, and thereby end up where they started. If "the discrepancy remains," they will somehow "resolve" it, which evidently means that they will bow to the machine, and trust the tally that it gave them in the first place. As Rep. Wexler's lawyer, Jeffrey Riggio, observed: "You don't have any way of telling with the way these machines are configured whether an undervote is a situation where a voter intended not to vote or if it was a mistake by the machine."[103] Hood's "new rule," in short, was but another stroke of partisan suppression, feebly represented as a bureaucratic compromise. "They are still playing games with words to try to get by," commented Riggio.

And that was that, except for the collapse of Wexler's legal effort. On October 25, a week before Election Day, Judge Cohn ruled that the state was not obliged to leave, or even to concern itself about, a paper trail, and yet apparently could see the sense in Wexler's case. "Based upon record evidence," he concluded in his memorandum:

the court notes the preferable voting system would include a paper printout reviewed by the voter to ensure that it contains his or her selections, which the vote then places in a ballot box to be counted in the event a manual recount is required. However, this Court's authority in this case is not to choose the preferable method of casting a ballot, but to determine whether the current procedures and standards comport with equal protection.[104]

And, finally, on Oct. 28 Hood's rule was upheld also by the 1st District Court of Appeals—although that court certified a question to the State Supreme Court, as to whether Hood had sufficiently justified her new rule in the first place. Belatedly certifying the congressman's defeat, on Nov. 10 that higher court declined to exercise its jurisdiction, and denied the future possibility of a rehearing.[105] Thus was the groundwork finally laid for the erasure of (literally) countless Democratic votes throughout Florida.

Nor, of course, was that the only way in which the Bush regime—not just in Florida, moreover, but throughout the nation—took advantage of the defects in the touch-screen voting system. That the system "counts the vote" without a paper trail serves merely to conceal the system's many more-complex, less obvious miscarriages. All over Florida, as nationwide, countless would-be voters told of the machines they used, or tried to use, malfunctioning in Bush's favor. Machines would not take Kerry votes, or turned them into Bush votes. However, while the system was demonstrably exploited to Bush/Cheney's great advantage, it was also highly unreliable. The glitches that undid the vote primarily in Democratic precincts also might undo some votes for Bush. Some in the Florida Republican machine were clearly conscious of that possibility, and so they actually warned party members *not to use the system*. In late July, flyers were sent out to party members in Miami, urging them to vote by absentee ballot—because the touch-screen machines would leave no paper trail, and therefore could not "verify your vote." "That's the same argument Democrats have made but which Bush, his elections director and Republican legislators have repeatedly rejected," the *St. Petersburg Times* reported on July 29.[106] The warning was a classic case of tactical duplicity, or paranoid projection, or both at once:

> "The liberal Democrats have already begun their attacks and the new electronic voting machines do not have a paper ballot to verify your vote in case of a recount," says [the] glossy mailer, paid for by the Republican Party of Florida and prominently featuring two pictures of President Bush. "Make sure your vote counts. Order your absentee ballot today.[107]

That the Republicans would tell their troops to shun, as insecure, the very apparatus that they had themselves been forcing on the rest of the electorate, while loudly hailing its security looks to be, to say the least, suspicious. Indeed it was so suspicious that the party instantly renounced the flyers: "The Florida GOP has apologized for sending out a flier contradicting the views of Republican Gov. Jeb Bush on the upcoming elections," UPI reported the next day.[108] That apology included no explanation, only this "reassurance" by party spokesman Joseph Agostini:

> "The recent absentee request ballot flier is in no way meant to shake the confidence of voters in Florida's electoral process," Agostini said. "The Republican Party of Florida encourages all Floridians to exercise their right to vote, whether by absentee ballot or in person."

It was a most revealing gaffe, and yet the party had no need to worry, since the news remained as good as secret. The story was reported by the *Palm Beach Post* and the *Miami Herald*, and, nationally, by the Associated Press.[109] At the time, the U.S. press was all but totally absorbed in the Democratic National Convention, which would have been a worthy forum for any party member brave enough to make an issue of the flyer. From then until Election Day there was no reference to it in the news.

Of all the stratagems deployed in Florida throughout Bush/Cheney's first campaign, the most notorious was the systematic use of overly inclusive "scrub lists," ostensibly to purge ex-felons from the voter rolls but actually to disfranchise as many Democrats—in particular, African-Americans—as possible.[110] As Greg Palast first reported, the lists had been compiled for Katherine Harris's office by DBT/Choicepoint,[111] an Atlanta-based data aggregator, which named as felons tens of thousands of Floridians with clean records, just because they shared a name or an address, or seemed to share it, with someone who had done hard time. Harris's office then purged the rolls of all those names: over 90,000 citizens, most of them entirely innocent. Nearly 1 percent of Florida's electorate—and 3 percent of Florida's black eligible voters—were listed. DBT/Choicepoint's error rate was 97 percent. The Bush machine also illegally disenfranchised over 2,800 Floridians who had done time in other states, even though the state's Supreme Court had twice ordered the government not to do so (the second time nine months before those names were stricken from the rolls). While the purges did incalculable damage to the civic sphere in Florida, they were very good for the Republicans—and for Choicepoint, which, not long after the campaign, the regime handsomely rewarded with a range of contracts relating to the "war on terror." Among the many goodies handed Choicepoint, the Department of Home-

land Security signed a $1 million contract giving it full access to
the corporation's database on foreign nationals. (According to
AP, the information may have been illegally acquired from "sub-
contractors"—that is, government employees—in Mexico,
Colombia, Venezuela, Costa Rica, Nicaragua, Honduras, El Sal-
vador and Guatemala.)[112]

As with the issue of "electoral reform" in general, so here the
Bush machine at first purported to agree to clean up the whole
felon-purging operation, which, a few months after Bush and
Cheney were inaugurated, prompted Florida's legislature to attempt to shut that operation down. In May 2001, it approved,
and Jeb Bush signed, a $32 million electoral reform package,
voiding Florida's contracts with Choicepoint and forbidding
Harris to hire any outside companies to review the voter rolls.
Henceforth the vivacious civil servant was required to collabo-
rate on all such business with the Florida Association of County
Clerks (FACC), which presumably would check her autocratic
tendencies. There were also calls for an investigation of the
state's contract with DBT. "By most accounts, this contract was
an unmitigated disaster, which led to Floridians being denied
the right to vote, and millions of taxpayer dollars wasted or mis-
spent," charged Democratic Leader Tom Rossin of West Palm
Beach.[113]

All such reformist hubbub came to naught. No investigation
was mounted, and the arrangement with the County Clerks dis-
integrated in July, when FACC asked the state to pay $300,000
for a study of the data on the purge lists used by Secretary Harris, and the state refused. Clay Roberts, Florida's Elections Director, said that "the Legislature did not require the study and
provided no money for it," the *St. Petersburg Times* reported
later.[114] And so, on October 15, 2001, the state announced that

it had signed a $1.6 million contract with Accenture—an outside company by any definition, even though it has three offices in Florida (and 107 other offices in 48 countries). Accenture was hired to design a "turnkey" system that would, presumably with more precision than had marked DBT/Choicepoint's work, identify all would-be voters with criminal histories in Florida. Known formerly as Andersen Consulting, which had been spun off from Arthur Andersen after the Enron scandal, Accenture got the contract, it was said, because of its alliance with Election.com, a Garden City, New York–based startup that had helped devise the voter registration database in Arkansas.

Whatever had gone down in Arkansas, Accenture was certainly no stranger to Bush/Cheney and their friends. The company was represented by Poole, McKinley and Blosser, a bigfoot lobbying firm closely connected to Jeb Bush. James Blosser, who had started his career as H. Wayne Huizenga's top lobbyist, expert at securing public funds to help build private stadiums, was the local finance chair for Jeb's 1998 gubernatorial campaign. Justin Sayfie, another major player at Poole, McKinley, was Jeb's political assistant in the early nineties, when the governor-to-be was a Miami developer. Once at the helm of state, Jeb hired Sayfie back as his speechwriter and media director, and eventually promoted him to deputy policy director. Sayfie moved from Bush's office to Poole, McKinley in 2001. Van Poole came to the consulting world from Exxon, where he was a marketing manager. He ended up in the state legislature, and chaired the Florida GOP from 1989 to 1993. As governor, Jeb appointed Poole's wife, Donna, another lobbyist, to chair Florida's Public Employees Relations Commission, and in 2001 appointed Poole himself to the Florida Federal Judicial Nominating Commission.[115]

"But the company said the database contract involved no lobbying," according to the press reports.[116] The firm has also done extensive business with Dick Cheney, both during and since his stint as CEO of Halliburton. In 1996, Accenture found a most appreciative client in Halliburton, seeing to its multiplicitous and mammoth information needs. ("Accenture's consulting and outsourcing services enabled Halliburton to focus on strategic work and its core business while going through major changes, including a multi-billion-dollar merger with oilfield services provider Dresser Industries.")[117] The two eventually became close partners. In early 2001, with Cheney in the White House, Halliburton "signed a five-year master service agreement that encompasses much more than information technology. The agreement establishes Accenture as a preferred provider across every division of Halliburton."

Election.com is similarly well-connected. In February 2003, *Newsday* reported, the company "quietly sold controlling power to an investment group with ties to unnamed Saudi nationals, according to company correspondence."[118]

In a letter sent to a select group of well-heeled Election.com investors Jan. 21, the online voting and voter registration company disclosed that the investment group Osan Ltd. paid $1.2 million to acquire 20 million preferred shares to control 51.6 percent of the voting power.

Election.com had several jobs pertaining to the presidential contest in 2004. Aside from safeguarding the integrity of the voters rolls in Florida, the company was competing for the contract to provide 100,000 US military personnel, living overseas, with online absentee ballots.

This enterprise fell through at the end of March 2004, when the Pentagon, persuaded that the Internet was far too insecure for any such electoral purpose, decided to abolish it, even canceling the $22 million experimental pilot program that it had planned with Accenture.[119]

Not long after partnering with those Saudis, Accenture went global as a purveyor of election services: "Accenture has launched a new business called Accenture eDemocracy Services that is focused on delivering comprehensive services to election agencies around the world. Accenture eDemocracy Services will provide strategy and planning, program management, election systems management, voter registration systems development, and transformational outsourcing services and solutions."[120]

Despite its many glittering connections, or because of them, Accenture's work in Florida discomfited some sticklers in the Florida bureaucracy, who argued that the governor should dump the felon-listing program at his earliest convenience. On May 4, 2004, Jeff Long, a computer expert with the Florida Department of Law Enforcement, wrote his boss an e-mail reporting that election officials had urged Bush to bail out fast. "Paul Craft called today and told me that yesterday they recommended to the Gov that they 'pull the plug,'" Long wrote, adding that the officials "weren't comfortable with the felon matching program they've got."[121] Bush refused, and the next day the latest list, with over 47,000 names, went out to Florida's 67 counties with instructions that they be purged from the rolls. Jenny Nash, a spokesperson for Glenda Hood, assured the public that this list was dead accurate—culled exclusively from records of arrests in Florida, the information coming from the Florida Department of Law Enforcement, the circuit courts and the clemency board tasked with reinstating felons' civil rights. "Election supervisors will retrieve the data on a secure site over the Internet, compare names with voter rolls and the clerk of court before they send a registered letter to the voter notifying them they are about to be purged," the *St. Petersburg Times* reported on May 7.[122] "Nash said the new list has the approval of the U.S. Department of Justice and the NAACP." Certainly, that list had Glenda Hood's approval. "'The new data is owned and operated by the Division of Elections,' Nash said. 'We're pretty confident the margin of error is very minimal.'" And yet despite her sky-high confidence as to the thoroughness, precision and correctness of this list, Hood refused to publicize it.

The fact that Florida had once again devised a felons list, and a secret one at that, provoked loud outrage from many quarters (except, of course, the governor's). "Some [election] supervisors question why the administration is making the move this close to the election. Florida's primary is Aug. 31 and the general election Nov. 2," AP reported on May 6.[123] "'Why is the state doing this now?' said Ion Sancho, the election supervisor in Leon County.[124] 'Within three minutes we identified an individual who should not be on the list. Right off the bat,' he added. 'How do you make somebody prove on election day that they're not a felon?' asked Kay Clem, Indian River County supervisor and president of the Florida Association of Supervisors of Election. 'I'd rather err on the side of letting them vote than not vote.'"[125] Civil libertarians were also angrily incredulous. "I'm sorry, but that list is suspect," said Barbara Petersen, president of the First Amendment Foundation. "I just can't understand, considering all of the trouble we went through four years ago, why they wouldn't want anyone else to help them verify it."[126]

"Frankly, the state should first fix the problems with people who were erroneously thrown off in 2000 before they start on another purge," said Elliot Mincberg, legal director of People for the American Way.[127]

For withholding the list, meanwhile, Florida was sued on First Amendment grounds by CNN along with ABC News, several Florida newspaper publishers, the ACLU and other entities. Circuit Court Judge Nikki Ann Clark ruled for the plaintiffs. When she released the list on July 1, one reason for the secrecy came clear at once. There were almost no Hispanics on that list of over 47,000 names. Although Hispanics make up one-fifth of the population of the Sunshine State, they comprised only one-tenth of 1 percent of Florida's "felons"—who were disproportionately black and tended to be Democrats, whereas Florida's Hispanics tend to vote Republican.[128] It was a huge embarrassment. "We are deeply concerned and disappointed that this has occurred," Hood said ambiguously,[129] while Jeb seemed more forthright in his apologies. It was "an oversight and a mistake," he said, and pledged to scrap the list entirely.[130] "We accept responsibility," he said, "and that's why we're pulling it back." He also said (falsely, as we have seen) that he had never been warned of any problems with the list. And so, on July 11, the county supervisors of elections were instructed not to use it.

However, once that infamous list had been withdrawn, or at least retired from view, Jeb Bush continued his crusade for Democratic disenfranchisement. On July 15, Florida's 1st District Court of Appeals ruled that the Department of Corrections must ensure that felons are prepared, when they leave prison, to apply for the reinstatement of their voting rights. In Florida as in six other states, such rights are not automatically restored to felons who have done their time. Those would-be voters must petition a clemency board headed by the governor. The court found that most prisoners did not know the process was required, much less how to go about it; and so the court ordered that each prisoner be informed about the process, provided with the proper forms, and given any help that might be needed in completing them. This law was already on the books, but the state had not enforced it; and so the purpose of this ruling was to make it stick. Jeb responded to the danger with his customary bravado. On July 23, he simply disappeared the application form, ordering instead that the department just send "electronic notice" to the Office of Executive Clemency once each prisoner is set free, whereupon the Office will decide whether to restore the ex-offender's right to vote. The court had already deemed that plan unsatisfactory—and for good reason, as the *St. Petersburg Times* reported: "Critics say felons are often transient and it's unlikely clemency officials will be able to reach them by mail for months or years after release"—which was, of course, the very reason the governor preferred to do it his way.[131]

The Bush machine also intensified its war on "felons" by generating "caging lists," as in Ohio—that is, lists of black Democratic voters to be challenged on Election Day. As Greg Palast reported for the BBC, an e-mail with a 15-page list of names was sent both to Brett Doster, the executive director of the Bush campaign in Florida, and to Tim Griffin, the campaign's national research director in Washington. The list contained the names and addresses of 1,886 voters in Jacksonville—the most populous city in the state (and, geographically, the biggest in the country), with a long history of bloody racial conflict, and, therefore, a restive and politically attuned black population.

(Jacksonville is roughly 29 percent black, 64 percent white.)[132] Those listed were mostly African Americans. When asked by Palast to explain the list, party spokespersons said that it "merely records returned mail from either fundraising solicitations or returned letters sent to newly registered voters to verify their addresses for purposes of mailing campaign literature."[133] The list was *not* compiled "in order to create a challenge list," said Mindy Tucker Fletcher very carefully, and yet she would not say simply that it would not be thus used. An election supervisor in Tallahassee spoke more frankly: "The only possible reason why they would keep such a thing is to challenge voters on Election Day." Although widely circulated on the Internet (including washingtonpost.com), Palast's scoop made news nowhere off-line in the United States.

And as the Bush machine thus prepared to bully would-be voters throughout Florida, its troops, as usual, were vehemently charging that the *Democrats* had plans to bully would-be voters throughout Florida. "A group of 50 Republicans in the House led by Representative Tom Feeney of Florida sent a letter on Oct. 7 to Attorney General John Ashcroft suggesting the existence of 'a plan to intimidate volunteers who were supporting their candidate' and requesting an investigation," the *New York Times* reported on October 26.[134] Thus Rep. Feeney—a veteran anti-democratic operative, alleged to have helped steal votes in Florida—was warning, in a tone of righteous anger, that the very people he and his associates were planning to intimidate had actually been planning to intimidate the troops that he and his associates had mobilized and were now enflaming with that very lie (or delusion). Two days later, the party went on the attack again, now charging that 921 felons had already cast votes illegally or requested absentee ballots, and that the party had, moreover, just identified another 13,568 felons who were scheming to vote (Democratic) on Election Day. "We believe this is simply the tip of the iceberg and there could be potentially additional felons who have registered," said the tireless Mindy Tucker Fletcher.[135] These new lists were, to put it mildly, dubious. Scanning the list of 921 felons, reporters at the *St. Petersburg Times* quickly found two Floridians who had had their rights restored: Neil D. Bolinger, a St. Petersburg ex-con who had done two years for grand larceny back in the early seventies, had had his voting restored in 1974 (and had just voted straight Republican by absentee ballot); and Jeffrey Arnold of Tampa said that he had been re-enfranchised some 12 years earlier, and had had no problems voting since. No one, in short, had any evidence that these lists were authentic; but in the end they worked precisely as intended.

That the party of Tom Feeney had "a plan to intimidate" the Democrats will soon be wholly clear. Here it is appropriate that we conclude this modest history of the felons list by noting that Floridians were finally disenfranchised on Election Day, allegedly because they had committed felonies when in fact their records were entirely clear or they had had their voting rights officially restored. According to the Election Incident Reporting System, eleven Floridians—ten of them in Miami-Dade—showed up to cast their ballots on November 2 and found that they could not, as they were guilty of fictitious crimes, or were confused with someone who had committed real ones. "He is on the felony list at the polls, but he claims that he has never been arrested," says the incident report for one Miami man (whose address was different from the one on the arrest form, and who had cast his vote in previous elections).[136]

Many a Miami resident was similarly disenfranchised:

Keshia was told that she was ineligible to vote, even provisionally, due to a felony conviction. She said she was tried, but not convicted, and had paperwork to prove this.

Has been denied right to vote in past because family member with similar name was convicted of crime.[137]

A voter was denied the right to vote by the poll workers because the voter's name was status [*sic*] as a convicted felon. The voter claims that he was not a convicted felon. The poll worker refused to provide a provisional ballot to the voter.[138]

Voter was told [he] could not vote at all because according to the computer he is a convicted felon. Voter says he has no convictions.[139]

"Brother is felon, he is not," reads a report from Broward County.[140] "Was told she was no longer registered [and] couldn't vote because she had a felony. Says it's false asked for a provisional ballot, was denied," reads a report from Palm Beach County; and so on.[141]

Thus did the state successfully repeat the crime that it had already controversially committed. All that fuss about the latest list meant nothing whatsoever, as the Bush machine, once more needing to disenfranchise countless "felons," struck again—the major difference being that this time there was no uproar over it.

As elsewhere throughout the nation—most controversially in Ohio—in Florida the Democratic vote had been logistically disabled by the tens of thousands, through deliberate scarcities and inequities that could be, and that have been, comfortably explained away as mere incompetence. This strategy was obvious throughout Florida's early-voting season—a pattern that, despite its flagrancy, received no general coverage, but that one has to piece together from a smattering of stories, mostly local, on specific counties.

In Duval County, for example, the enormous size of Jacksonville—a city of 840 square miles—enabled the Republicans to slash the early vote by setting up just *one* early-polling place, conveniently located miles away from Jacksonville's black neighborhoods, in the hospitable offices of Dick Carlberg, Duval County's assistant election supervisor. There are half a million registered voters in Duval County—the same number as in Orange County, which had nine early-polling places. (Not that Orange County, whose county seat is heavily Christianist Orlando, was an electoral Eden on November 2. The machines in certain Democratic precincts kept on breaking down, or never started up.)[142] Carlberg's civic temperament may best be captured by this episode, described by Jo Becker for the *Washington Post* on October 12:

JACKSONVILLE, Fla. — Nearly a dozen African American ministers and civil rights leaders walked into the Duval County election office here, television cameras in tow, with a list of questions: How come there were not more early voting sites closer to black neighborhoods? How come so many blacks were not being allowed to redo incomplete voter registrations? Who was deciding all this?

Standing across the office counter under a banner that read "Partners in Democracy" was the man who made those decisions, election chief Dick Carlberg. Visibly angry, the Republican explained why he decided the way he had: "We call it the law."[143]

Asked repeatedly to open up new early polling places, Carlberg just kept saying no. After Florida got several bits of such unflattering publicity, the governor appointed a new interim election supervisor, who announced the opening of four new early-voting sites in Duval County, "including one on the city's northwest side, a predominantly black area," the AP reported on Tuesday, October 19.[144] The four new sites were set to open on Saturday, October 23.

The situation was quite similar in Volusia County (where, on Election Night 2000, a sudden and precipitous—and momentary—downswing in the Gore vote gave Fox News Channel, and then NBC, and then all the other corporate media, the opportunity to claim that Gore did *not* appear to be front-runner after all, and that Bush was evidently going to win). With over 340,000 registered voters, Volusia County had also just one early-polling place—in Deland, an administrative capital just southwest of the county's center, whereas the county's African Americans live mostly in the east, along the coast. (Volusia is 86 percent white, 9 percent black and 6 percent Hispanic.)[145] The election supervisor not only refused to open any other sites but also kept the office closed on Sundays throughout the early voting period. Confronted with a lawsuit, the county finally added four new sites, which opened on Monday, October 18. (In the end, officially, Kerry won Volusia County by 3,874 votes—garnering 115,319 to Bush's 111,544. In 2000, Gore beat Bush by nearly 15,000 votes, with over 2,900 going to Nader.)

In Palm Beach County, with nearly three quarters of a million registered voters, there were only eight locations—and the longest early voting lines in Florida. By November 1, only 30,000 residents had voted. "'These long lines are ridiculous,' said Omar Khan, whose father, a diabetic who was fasting for Ramadan, was forced to abandon his attempt to vote after hours of standing in the hot sun.[146] 'Either it is tremendous incompetence or deliberate voter suppression. In either case, the supervisor is not doing her job.'" That negligent or mischievous official was the ever-controversial Theresa LePore. Benjamin and James also reported that Liz Grisaru, a lawyer with the Kerry team, had lengthily negotiated with LePore for more early voting sites, more machines, more poll workers and longer hours, but LePore refused, for no clear reason. "The supervisor has failed miserably in her duty to the public by not responding to the large volume of voters," Grisaru said.[147] (In the end, Kerry won Palm Beach County by 115,804 votes, with 327,698 to Bush's 211,894. In 2000, Gore won there by 143,781 votes, with 296,732 to Bush's 152,951, and Nader took 5,565 votes.)

Throughout the early voting period, similar inequities occurred in other counties with obstreperous minorities. Clay County—87 percent white, 6.7 percent black, 4.3 percent Hispanic—had just one site for its 140,000 voters, leading to the usual logjam: "Many Clay Early Voters Face Long Drive to Polls," reported the *Florida Times-Union* on October 29.[148] Election Supervisor Barbara Kirkman claimed that her office had considered opening three extra sites for early voting. "But because the buildings weren't open year-round, the state prohibited the office from using the sites to operate touch-screen voting machines," Kirkman said.

Bush won a staggering victory in Clay County. Four years earlier, Bush had defeated Gore by over 27,000 votes (41,736 to

14,362, with 562 votes going to Nader). In 2004, Bush won by 42,976 votes (61,881 to 18,905)—an increase of 57 percent. Thus early voting, which became a statewide practice in the wake of the electoral chaos of 2000, as a way to make it easier for Floridians to do their civic duty, had itself become yet one more way to slash the Democratic vote.

If Florida Democrats could register, and find their polling places, and get there on the proper date; and if those polling places happened to be open, and the machines were functioning, and the voters were allowed to vote, there was a good chance that their votes would vanish anyway. Even so, the "if" in that last sentence was a giant one. The Republicans were especially active in South Florida, doing all they could to frighten Kerry voters into going home, or staying home. This sort of intimidation was already going on throughout the early-voting period. The early voters at that lately added polling site in Jacksonville (that is, the one "on the city's northwest side, a predominantly black area") found themselves under surveillance as they came to cast their ballots, a private detective *filming* every one from behind a car with blacked-out windows.[149] Before and on November 2, moreover, there were throughout South Florida, as elsewhere, countless dirty tricks: disinformation as to the true date of Election Day, the true location of the polling places, the risks of going to vote without your Social Security card or if you had an unpaid parking ticket, and so on. "People posing as election officials are visiting residents of several counties and offering to take absentee ballots," the *St. Petersburg Times* reported on October 22.[150] Reports of such chicanery in Pasco County drove officials to warn absentee voters away from all such "helpful" types. Complaints were legion in some counties. "We've had a bunch of them—100 at least," said the elections supervisor for Manatee County. "It's probably going on all over the state of Florida."[151]

By Election Day, the climate was especially tense in heavily Democratic Broward County,[152] where Kerry's victory margin was slightly less than Gore's had been four years before, although, this time, Ralph Nader was not on the ballot. Early voting had already been a long nightmare for Democrats in Florida's second most populous county. From the moment early voting started, the complaints came pouring in—the EIRS hotline racking up more calls from Broward than from any other county in the state.[153]

Caller . . . reported a problem in Coral Springs at the N.W. Regional Library polling place.

She indicated that the clerk requested two additional intake terminals, but has not received them. Only two intake terminals are currently on site, and lines for voting are very long—she estimated a wait time of at least one hour, with limited places for people to sit. She indicated that voters are getting frustrated and leaving the polling place without voting (10/19).

1) Caller spent 2-1/2 hours in line to vote. Approximately 250 people were in line, starting at 11 A.M. During this time, approximately 7 people walked out. 2) There were 9 machines, but two of them went down. 2 or 3 were reserved for Spanish speakers. 3) Employee tending to the machines was an elderly woman who appeared to be untrained in voting machine technology. When first machine went down, someone was voting on it. Employee moved voter to another machine but could not explain to them what happened to their vote (if it went through or not). Employee waved a computer "wand" to

re-activate the machine, could not get it started. Second machine went down, and employee still did not know what to do. 4) When second machine went down, caller made comment to a poll watcher. Another poll worker came over and shouted at caller, telling her that she had no right to question the actions of employees. Caller stated that she felt intimidated by his words but responded in kind to him (Coconut Creek, 10/29).

As November 2 neared, there was an upsurge of suspicious incidents throughout the county (as elsewhere):

Voter reported a woman going around Broward County neighborhood requesting absentee ballots from residents so that she may turn ballots in from residents. Voter said that woman requesting ballots was not from the board of elections, rather woman said that she simply wanted to save residents on postage. Voter did not give absentee ballot to woman, notified police, took license plate # (Broward County, 10/30).

Individuals canvassing the community apparently giving incorrect information out on polling locations. Woman and her husband called to verify her location and report the incident (Tamarac, 10/30).

Several Haitians (according to the caller) came by their house and told them their polling place had changed. They gave them a paper that looked unofficial telling them to go to a polling place a long way away. They were going house to house (Fort Lauderdale 10/30).

"America Coming Together" distributed flyer with incorrect polling place (North Lauderdale, 10/30).

Caller saw two women distributing flyers in the neighborhood which said "Are you sure where you're supposed to vote?" The flyers had an address in Margate (9200 NW 70 Street) but that's not where the residents receiving the flyers are supposed to vote. The flyers say "Paid for by America Coming Together" (Margate 10/31).

Caller received an ACT pamphlet in mailbox on 11/1 that listed incorrect precinct information. The pamphlet told him to go to 37M when the correct precinct was 37N. Voter found correct precinct but worries about others (Plantation, 11/2).

Such use of "America Coming Together," or "ACT," is a good example of black propaganda, as ACT is a progressive group with ties to labor, and one that was quite active at the grass-roots level nationwide, *opposing* Bush.[154]

Most of the complaints concerned systemic defects—promised absentee ballots not arriving, polling places closed or secretly located, endless waiting and poll workers unhelpful or even hostile. Scores of reports in Broward County (and thousands throughout Florida) attest to such problems. If this was "an orderly election," the mind reels at the thought of a disorderly one.

At the early voting site at 3151 N. University Dr., Coral Springs, FL (the northwest regional library), the caller went to vote at early voting today at noon, one hour before the site opened, and the line was, by her estimate, 4 hours long. There was no parking, so that voters were walking a mile from where they could park across the street. She went and waited 2 hours Tuesday, 2 hours Thursday, and again today (Coral Springs, 10/31).

The voters were turned away from the polls after standing in a four hour line because they were out of provisional ballots. The election official told them to come back the next day. He wouldn't put it in writing, and ripped the voter's early voting voter's certificate in half (Coconut Creek 10/31).

Father disabled and 89 years old. Has requested absentee ballot 3x and not received. She was supposed to get a ballot by overnight FedEx but has not received. The 954 831 4000 number is not answered—the recording says it is after business hours and does not answer (Broward County, 10/30).

And there was this report from Palm Beach City, included in the log of Broward incident reports:

Voter was videotaping lines in P[alm] B[each] City early voting place on W. Atlantic Blvd. She was more than 50 feet away and was not intimidating voters. She wants to capture the fact that voters are being good citizens and waiting in lines for hours to get their vote counted. A security officer and then poll worker threatened to arrest her.

"Did not mention voter intimidation," the account concludes irrelevantly.

Election Day itself was a catastrophe in Broward County, in many places reminiscent less of democratic process than of martial law. "Heavy police presence," complained one woman. "Never seen so many police in one place before in this town," a man from Hallandale reported. A woman called from Lauderhill Mall, where she went to vote. (Her workplace was behind the mall.) "There are a lot of people voting so parking lot is congested," she reported. "Cars are being towed." The fearful climate was maintained not only by police, but, more often, by Republican poll workers, poll watchers and GOP "challengers"—partisan harassers of apparent Democratic voters, like the "Texas Strike Force" in Ohio. (Indeed, they may themselves have been more soldiers from the "Strike Force.")

The hordes of "challengers" in Florida roused much anxiety, and so the state took propaganda steps to calm it, or to foster the illusion that they wanted people to be calm. "Hoping to ease rising concern over voter challenges, state elections officials on Friday released new guidelines for handling such challenges without delaying other voters.

> The four-page memo from state Elections Director Dawn Roberts was an attempt to clarify a 109-year-old election law that in recent days has generated widespread anxiety about whether it would be used to deter voters.
>
> The memo emphasizes that voter challenges must be resolved without delaying other voters. . . . As recently as Wednesday, Gov. Jeb Bush said he didn't expect poll watcher challenges to be a problem.[155]

After voting at Faith Christian Church in Hollywood, one citizen reported: "Bush supporters harassing before the voter went in, too close to the polling place, 10 ft. from door charging $1 for water." "Voter voted early, received a call this morning that his vote would not be counted because he owes child support." The racial animus was often clear, determining where the Florida party placed its troops throughout the voting period. "In Miami-Dade County, Democrats said, 59 percent of predominantly black precincts have at least one Republican poll watcher, while 24 percent of predominantly white precincts have them," reported the *St. Petersburgh Times*.[156] "In Leon County, 64 percent of black precincts have at least one Republican poll watcher, compared with 24 percent of majority white precincts. In Alachua, 71 percent of black precincts have a Republican poll watcher assigned, while 24 percent of white precincts do.

"Bush-Cheney adviser Mindy Tucker Fletcher dismissed the complaint, saying Republican poll watchers are being concentrated where Bush performed best and worst in 2000, because those are where 'we thought the Democrats are most likely to cheat.'"

That animus was reported by a resident of Miramar:

Arrived at 7 AM. Had to show several forms of i.d. and voted in same place since 2000. Lived in same co. since 1989. Even though [he] had registration card, he had to go through several verifications. Felt all black people were being questioned but whites were not.

One entry synthesizes several other such reports from Miramar:

All people with these challenges were Hispanic or black. A number of voters throughout the day (15–20) complained about 1. Not receiving information regarding change of polling place to Sea Castle Elementary (from local church?) or 2. Being redirected to polling places other than what their co-resident (husband, wife, roommate, etc) was assigned and what their cards said or 3. Being redirected to two different polling places 4. Also, poll workers enforcing ID verification of non-first time voters. When Mayor of Miramar came to visit polls around 6:30 PM, I mentioned some of these challenges

(when asked) and she mentioned possibility of providing poll workers with computer access (laptops) to check/verify voters' polling
places.

Not even the infirm were spared harassment, if they apparently intended to vote Democratic. "Voter on crutches with
voter registration card was sent home to get photo i.d." "Voter
told by deputy that she must get out of car, even though she is
wheelchair bound. Deputy said that precinct clerk said that if at
all possible [she] must come in. Voter said that in the past, she
has voted here and has not had to get out of car."

> Voter handed a [sample ballot] in to her cousin, a recent stroke vic-
> tim, who was voting in his car. As she did so, the Republican poll-
> watcher snatched it from him on the premise that the car was within
> the 50' limit. Much tension ensued. Voter finished voting after his
> wife rolled up the window.

The caller claimed to have handed her cousin a "palm card,"
which would seem to mean a sample ballot—which was entirely
legal, as such ballots are permitted in the polling booths in
Florida. Voting in one's car—"curbside voting"—is also legal if
the voter is disabled. The law requires that one worker from
each party go out and observe the curbside vote, which may or
may not be what finally happened in this case.[157]

The party's poll workers were often nasty, answering voters'
questions with abuse. "Voting machine problem. Pushed Kerry
got Bush—pushed Castro got Martinez[158]—[same with] all others," reported a caller from Fort Lauderdale. "Accused of not
being able to read." "Voter's registration card lists 5T as [her]
polling place," claims a complaint from Pompano Beach. "At 5T

she did not appear on the roster. Poll worker started to give her a provisional ballot but then sent her to 37T. A poll worker at 37T threw a map in her face and told her she was in the wrong place." "Voter does not know where to go," concluded the report. Whether there was open animosity or not, the polls in Broward County were suffused with that malevolent surreality which is common to all bureaucratic tyrannies.

> Voter appeared in person to vote on Nov 2. Poll worker told her that she had already voted via absentee ballot. Voter insisted she had not submitted any absentee ballot. Poll worker called "downtown" and they confirmed they had in their possession a completed, signed absentee ballot. Poll worker offered voter a provisional ballot. Voter refused to cast the prov. ballot. Voter knows of 2 other people who faced the same problem in same county (Fort Lauderdale).

And there was this absurdity, reported by a man in Miramar: "Was told at precinct that he is registered in Collier County. Voter has never been to Collier County."

Meanwhile, absentee ballots were especially scarce in Broward County—and sometimes not so easy to submit. "Absentee ballot said postage was 60 cents," complained one caller. "Actual postage required was 80 cents. This might have been [a] pattern. Person did what envelope requested, but post office rejected it due to lack of postage." Often those who voted absentee discovered that there was no record of their having cast a vote at all. "Kerry volunteer called to report problem with absentee voters appearing on 'did not vote' list. At least 8 of these voters are elderly residents of Crystal Tower (322 Buchanan St). . . . All voters in Broward City." These voters had at least received their ballots. Tens of thousands of the folks in Broward County (like countless other citizens from coast to coast) did not get to that point, as the state had failed to send the ballots out, or sent them out too late. "In Massachusetts, [caller] was told on Thursday that ballot was going to be overnighted. Was told it was sent on the 28th and would be there by the 30th. Still [has] not received it," according to an entry for Pompano Beach. "Called Broward County Board of Elections about getting an absentee ballot a couple of months ago because she's living in Pittsburgh right now. She mailed in her request but never received her absentee ballot and now she can't vote," according to a call from Margate. The frequency of such complaints in Broward County surely has to do with the peculiar disappearance of 58,000 absentee ballots, said to have been mailed on October 7 and 8. There was evidence that such ballots were not handled properly by Post Office personnel in Florida's Southern District. On the other hand, there seemed to be no reason to believe that they were ever sent at all. "It's highly unlikely that 58,000 pieces of mail just disappeared," said U.S. Postal Inspector Del Alvarez on October 27. "We're looking for it, we're trying to find it if in fact it was ever delivered to the postal service."[159] However it occurred, the vanishing of all those ballots did not seem much to trouble Brenda Snipes, Broward County's supervisor of elections, who "estimated she would resend no more than 20,000 ballots," although "about 76,000 ballots sent by her office have not been returned."[160]

Thus John Kerry, officially, did less well in Broward County than Al Gore had done four years before. In 2000, Gore beat Bush by 209,801 votes (387,703 to 177,209). Ralph Nader garnered 7,105 votes in that contest. In 2004, Kerry beat the president by 208,671 votes (452,360 to 243,699). In short, he won by 827 *fewer* votes than Gore received—notwithstanding Nader's absence from the ballot, the massively successful Democratic voter registration, the record turnout and—most poignantly—the fierce resolve of all those people who were robbed before not to be robbed again. And yet the full results in Broward County were not just surprising but downright bizarre.

The Democrats had registered 77,000 new voters for this election, and realized 66,170 new votes. The Republicans registered far fewer new voters—only 17,000—and yet somehow realized 66,772 new votes: about six hundred *more* than Kerry/Edwards did. Thus the Democrats were weirdly cursed, as their success at voter registration seemed to hurt them badly at the polls. In 2000, they had registered 39.5 percent of all new voters, and garnered nearly 67,000 new votes to the GOP's 35,000. In 2004, the Democrats *increased* their share of newly registered voters to 45.3 percent—and yet the GOP outdid them anyway. Perhaps new hordes of old Republicans came out to vote for the first time since 1980. That would seem to be impossible, however, as overall voter turnout in the county had risen only 0.85 percent, compared to the statewide increase of 4 percent.[161]

Finally, Bush did very well with Broward County's absentee voters, 40 percent of whom supported him—a figure six points higher than his victory margin among the voters on Election Day. Absentees made up 14 percent of the total vote. This was, to say the least, remarkable, considering how well the *Democrats* had done in polls of absentee and early voters. Bush's numbers in the county were indeed miraculous. And as Broward County went in 2004, so went the state of Florida, which, officially, Bush won by five points, even though the polls had Kerry leading.

On October 31, the *Palm Beach Post*/Reuters/Zogby International poll had Kerry leading Bush by just one point (48 percent to 47 percent).[162] The next day, a *USA Today*/CNN/Gallup poll had Kerry with a three-point lead (50 percent to 47 percent).[163] He had an even bigger lead among the multitudes of early voters. "In Florida," *USA Today* reported on October 31, "30% of registered voters said they already had cast their ballots, using early voting sites and absentee ballots. They supported Kerry 51%–43%."[164]

Then Bush "won" in Florida and Kerry "lost." And as that state went in 2004, so did the United States—and so did the enormous U.S. vote beyond our borders.

7.

One Last Scandal

The great domestic effort to cut down the Kerry vote, and pad the Bush vote, could have been subverted by the votes of U.S. citizens abroad if the members of that very large constituency had been allowed to cast their ballots. Expatriate America—a global bloc some have called "the 51st State"—includes up to seven million voters.[1] Of course both parties' various efforts to attract those votes go largely unreported to the rest of us. Nevertheless that huge bloc constitutes the Great Unknown in our national contests, as it has ever since all U.S. expatriates, civilian and military alike, were enfranchised by an act of Congress signed by Gerald Ford in 1975.

This far-flung extra-territorial vote is largely Democratic, as expats tend toward a worldview more cosmopolitan and pluralistic than seems decent to the Christianist "conservatism" that defines the GOP. A majority of those several million dispersed citizens are young professionals, college-educated or multilingual progressives, as well as retired GIs who have chosen, for whatever reasons, not to live in the United States. The "liberal bias" natural to such a worldly population has, predictably, steepened since Bush & Co. came to power, as many who have lived abroad can well remember times when the United States was *not* detested the world over, and have seen up close the global damage that this regime has inflicted on our image and our interests.

The Democratic sympathies of the expatriate majority were also hardened by Bush/Cheney's installation in 2000. To that majority, the coup was especially outrageous. In the hands of Katherine Harris and her crew, the absentee ballots—the votes of the expatriates—were mishandled with particular abandon. They were the last to be counted, when Bush was seemingly ahead of Gore by only a few hundred votes. There was no scientific method to their tabulation. On the contrary, until the process was aborted, ballots from Republicans were "counted" while those from Democrats were tossed as spoiled or incomplete. Harris ordered that all ballots from the military abroad—which tends Republican—be "counted," even if they were unstamped or late, while those that were missing certain necessary information were obligingly completed by party operatives in county governments statewide.[2]

The Florida debacle reconfirmed the judgment that, ironically enough, had been rendered by the state's Department of Law Enforcement back in 1998, after a mayoral election in Miami had been nullified because "vote brokers" had signed bogus absentee ballots by the hundreds: "The lack of in-person, at-the-polls accountability makes absentee ballots the tool of choice for those inclined to commit fraud."[3] In 2000 this was again proven true throughout the state. "Canvassing boards in counties carried by Mr. Gore," the *New York Times* reported later, invalidated ballots at a far higher rate than those in counties carried by Mr. Bush, in part because Republican-dominated counties accepted ballots postmarked after the election or with no postmarks, while Democratic counties rejected them. Among counties with large numbers of overseas votes, for instance, Broward, Miami-Dade and Orange, which voted for Mr. Gore, threw out more than 80 percent of the ballots, while Escambia, Clay and Okaloosa, which went for Mr. Bush, threw out about 40 percent.[4]

And yet, true to form, while thus disenfranchising countless Democrats, the Bush campaign charged loudly that the *Democrats* were trying to steal the vote by disenfranchising "our troops."

Such doings were neither lost on nor forgotten by the expatriate Democrats, who, like their fellow partisans in Florida, were on their guard the second time around. Democrats Abroad—a group recognized by the DNC as an official party committee—knuckled down in 2004, sending 22 delegates to the Democratic National Convention and holding party caucuses throughout the world, from Belgium to Hong Kong. They were keen supporters of the ticket, vigorously fundraising as much as possible. On the other hand, Bush & Co.'s outreach efforts on the foreign stump notwithstanding, expatriate Republicans were not exactly blazing with enthusiasm. George P. Bush, Jeb's sultry son, toured France, Germany and Switzerland for his uncle, and Dan Quayle worked a roomful of Republicans in Belgium: "It was the absentee votes that turned the tide in Florida," he cried. "Every vote counts! We need to get the word out!"[5] Such oratory had no magical effect. Like the U.S. party, the GOP abroad was split, with moderates and others choosing Kerry. Christian D. de Fouloy, former head of Republicans Abroad Belgium, started up Republicans for Kerry Europe, because, he said, he "could no longer stand up for what this administration was standing for." Like so many of his fellow partisans at home, de Fouloy found Bush & Co. *de trop*, and said so. "I've always been a moderate Republican, but this administration has shown there's no room for us in the party."[6]

Of course, the regime did have high hopes for one bloc of U.S. citizens abroad: the military (although Kerry had made inroads there as well, necessitating further measures to suppress the Democratic vote within the armed forces, as we shall see). Thus each party had its own constituency overseas—but one bloc was far larger. Within the global multitude of 7 million eligible voters, civilians outnumber military personnel by 15 to 1.[7] Although there was no comprehensive poll of voting trends abroad, there is evidence that Kerry was the choice of the American diaspora. A Zogby poll of active passport holders, released in August 2004, found Kerry favored over Bush by 58 percent to 35 percent.[8] And there is, of course, some partisan corroboration of the Democrat's advantage. In a letter to the *Boston Globe* published on June 6, Connie Borde, chair of Democrats Abroad France, claimed that her group's mailing list was ten times longer than the GOP's—a claim not audibly disputed by Republicans.[9]

And so the global vote, as we might call it, was a plus for Kerry, and a potentially decisive one. Predictably, many Democrats abroad found it just as hard to vote as did so many Democrats at home. Those foreign dissidents were often thwarted by two levels of state interference. At the top, there was the Pentagon—which, oddly enough, is the bureaucracy responsible for administering the U.S. vote worldwide, military *and* civilian.*

*Some prior history of the U.S. vote abroad would be appropriate here. U.S. military personnel posted abroad were first allowed to vote during World War II. (They simply mailed their ballots in.) From 1945 to 1955, it was left to the states to decide exactly how a serviceman might cast his ballot. In 1955,

The State Department would appear to be the more appropriate medium for civilian votes, but Ronald Reagan made the choice on June 8, 1988, with Executive Order 12,642, which created the Federal Voting Assistance Program (FVAP). FVAP's website—fvap.gov—went up in 1996. In 2002, in order to make ballots more accessible to citizens abroad, the Help America Vote Act instructed the Department of Defense to amplify the site so that it might serve as a comprehensive nonpartisan clearinghouse of voting information coast to coast.

This electronic system certainly appeared to be a great improvement over the archaic methods of the recent past. The FVAP, first of all, now made it infinitely easier to begin the voting registration process, as one might simply use it to request an absentee ballot from one's home state. The system also served as an unprecedented clearinghouse for electoral requirements in all 50 states, the District of Columbia and wherever else the residents can vote as U.S. citizens. Formerly, expatriates had to make their way to local embassies or consulates, to skim through bulky and confusing handbooks cataloguing all the different rules for every state. One could not register to vote in, say, California or Kentucky without a fair grasp of its Byzantine electoral requirements. The handbooks were in short supply (many embassies and consulates did not have copies), and so FVAP

Congress passed the Federal Voting Assistance Act, permitting members of the Armed Forces, Merchant Marine, and their families to cast votes from abroad. (It also urged the states to accept votes for federal offices from federal employees whose work has temporarily taken them outside the country.) The Voting Rights Act of 1975 then permitted expatriate civilians *and* military personnel to cast ballots from their countries of current residence. Although the Pentagon was formally assigned the job of overseeing the global vote in 1988, it had already been playing a significant role in that process since 1975, as, at first, most Americans voting from abroad were military personnel.

seemed to be a godsend. For a year before November 2, 2004, the site was heavily advertised throughout the foreign press as indispensable to all those citizens abroad who wanted to take part in the election.

The site was an immense success, attracting tens of thousands of requests to register from U.S. citizens the world over. The volume of requests had been growing steadily when, on August 23, the website suddenly shut down. To be more precise, it abruptly became inaccessible to those civilians using any one of several foreign Internet service providers from some 25 countries.[10] Now you could not get to FVAP via Yahoo Broadband in Japan, Wanadoo in France, BT Yahoo Broadband in Britain or Telefonica in Spain, among other digital dead ends. Why had this happened? In an e-mail to a riled American who had hoped to register from France, Susan Leader, FVAP's Web manager, endeavored to explain: "We are sorry you cannot access www.fvap.gov. Unfortunately, Wanadoo France has had its access blocked to U.S. government Web sites due to Wanadoo users constantly attempting to hack these sites. We do not expect the block to be lifted." That claim was vaguely echoed by Lt. Col. Ellen Krenke, spokeswoman at Defense, who told the *International Herald Tribune* that the Pentagon had had to blacklist several foreign Internet service providers in order to thwart hackers.[11]

That claim is "patently ridiculous," asserts an army officer who was involved in the administration of the U.S. vote in Germany (and who has requested anonymity). The Department of Defense maintains a broad array of highly sensitive websites and has never had to shut them down to keep them or their data safe from hackers. There is a DoD site called MyPay, for example, which allows military personnel to do online transactions that involve their salaries—a potential goldmine for the cunning hacker, and yet somehow it is always up, while FVAP stayed inaccessible from August 23 to September 22. Thus the site went down just when the requests to register were at their height; and it stayed down until six weeks before Election Day, making it that much likelier that absentee ballots mailed from overseas would arrive too late to count in the election. In fact the FVAP's recommended deadline for mailing absentee ballots overseas is 45 days before the election, which would have been September 18th.

In September, Reps. Henry Waxman (D-CA) and Carolyn Maloney (D-NY) sent a letter to Defense Secretary Rumsfeld urging him to find another means to protect the security of the site—and the block was abruptly lifted on the 22nd.[12] While it did not explain exactly how the service was resumed, the Pentagon did offer a few different explanations as to why the service had been halted. The site had simply been closed for remodeling. According to one statement: "Access to the FVAP website . . . has been modified to further increase the number of Internet service providers able to access the site."[13] DoD spokesman Tim Madden came up with a wholly different reason. No block had been "imposed," he said. Rather, a security block implanted years ago had inadvertently been left in place.[14] Not only did these explanations contradict each other, but the second one was patently absurd, as that residual "security block" had not been blocking anything before August 23. If it had been implanted inadvertently, it was somehow inactive for years, then active for 30 days, then just as inexplicably removed.

Whatever tales the Pentagon was telling, the shutdown of that website had a powerful disenfranchising effect on U.S. citizens abroad. During the shutdown, thousands of complaints poured in from angry would-be voters. And, again, the block was timed so as to disenfranchise voters even after its removal. The site itself warns that citizens intent on taking part in the election must "remember to register and request your ballot in a timely manner—not later than September."[15] By shutting down the site for the first three weeks of that final month, the Pentagon disenfranchised thousands of voters, most of whom were likely to have voted Democratic. According to a poll conducted by the Overseas Vote Foundation, 17 percent of expatriates who failed to vote gave a missed deadline as the reason.[16] (It was the reason given most often for expatriate failure to cast ballots.)

The states too were complicit. While countless would-be voters were thwarted at the national bureaucratic level, countless others were shot down by state election boards. Over a dozen states—including Ohio and, of course, Florida—missed the recommended deadline for mailing ballots overseas. (Often the process was delayed by legal squabbling over Ralph Nader's presence on the ballot.) Although most expatriates used, or tried to use, the website, as many had been born overseas or had lived abroad for years,* it still was often necessary to (try to) contact the election board near one's official U.S. residence (if any). For example, the states' requirements posted on fvap.org were, to put it mildly, not always self-explanatory, or easy to meet, with some requiring proof of employment, photos and a witness to the signing of the ballot application. According to the army officer in Germany, applications for absentee ballots from the southern states are excessively complicated, making it difficult for expatriate black veterans and their offspring in Germany to vote.

---

*According to a post-election poll by the Overseas Vote Foundation, 52 percent of respondents were "first time overseas voters," while 27 percent were "first time voters."

And if it was exasperating to try to register in person here at home, trying to register from overseas was a bureaucratic nightmare specially designed for Democrats who don't know how to quit. Don Farthing, a U.S. citizen who has run a business in Hong Kong for the last ten years, was troubled by the silence from Pinellas County, Florida, as he had received no confirmation of his application for an absentee ballot (and was concerned that it had been delayed because his Chinese zip code was too long for the space on the application form). So, very late, Hong Kong time, one night in May, he called the Pinellas County Board of Elections and was told that his request had not yet been received. Farthing reapplied in June, and once again received no confirmation (and no ballot), so he reapplied again in July, this time by downloading and printing out a request form from the Internet, and signing it before a witness. To that submission he got no reply of any kind.

Farthing started making what turned out to be an epic series of followup calls to the Pinellas County Supervisor of Elections. In the course of the first two calls, he was told that he was not listed in their office and that they had received no mailings from him. He was also told that he was not qualified to vote, because the registration deadline had passed (although registration was to last until one month prior to Election Day). There was, moreover, no record of his registration from the years before his move to China, although he had taken pains to vote in every state and federal election (as a registered Democrat). Finally, when he made those early calls, Farthing was consistently provided with the wrong addresses for his further mailings. For instance, he was told to send his application form to Tallahassee (which is in Leon County; Clearwater is Pinellas's county seat), and, in order to contact the GOP headquarters in Tampa, to address the envelope to "Friends for a Better Tomorrow."

In mid-September—two weeks before the registration dead-line—Farthing called back several times. Twice he was told, again, that his name was unknown to the office, and that it was too late to register to vote absentee. "You're going to waste your vote on Kerry," the clerk told him, "because votes for Bush are outnumbering his by ten to one." Politely Farthing asked the clerk her name and volunteer I.D. number. "Mary," she replied, and then emended that to "Suzy." She would not give Farthing her I.D. number.

At the start of every conversation with the people in Pinellas County, Farthing had been asked which party he belonged to. Thus far he had always answered truthfully. Desperate times, however, call for desperate measures; so Farthing waited forty-five minutes, called back, and told the clerk now on the line (it was not Mary/Suzy) that he was a Republican. He also poignantly recited all his difficulties from the outset—but now was treated in a very different way. "Immediately," Farthing re-calls, this clerk "assured me it *wasn't* too late—and that, if I thought I'd have any difficulty downloading, printing out and filling in the proper forms, they would overnight them to me, with a return pre-paid envelope inside, to ensure that my vote reached them in time." He then received his ballot quickly, used it to vote for Kerry, and mailed it in. (That it finally counted as a Kerry vote is, of course, not likely.)[17]

Certainly not every would-be Democratic voter living over-seas had such a rich experience with state bureaucracy (or demonstrated such persistence in the face of party enmity). The incidence of deliberate non-cooperation was quite high, how-ever. Forty-three percent of expatriate voters, or would-be voters, never received their ballots or received them too late, ac-cording to the Overseas Voting Foundation. HAVA provides a recourse for certain of such citizens, who, having not secured a

ballot by one month (30 days) before Election Day, may then
ask for a Federal Write-In Absentee Ballot (FWAB), and use
that form instead. (To qualify for such a substitute, the voter has
to have received confirmation from the state that he or she is
duly registered. The FWAB would not have done Don Farthing
any good.)

And yet that fallback measure also was subverted. Although
the State Department ordered embassies and consulates to
stockpile copies of the FWAB, the backup ballots were in short
supply worldwide, according both to representatives of Democrats Abroad and to the army officer who has requested
anonymity. Direct requests by voters to the FVAP also went ignored or unfulfilled. On the other hand, *Salon* reports, a million
hard copies of the backup ballot were sent to military bases in
Europe and in Asia, and to the troops in Iraq and Afghanistan.[18]
While thousands of expatriates had no way to vote for president,
the military had a great surplus of write-in ballots—enough to
give each service member *two*. According to the army officer involved in FVAP's efforts, U.S. citizens employed by Daimler-
Chrysler showed up at the U.S. military base in Stuttgart, beg-
ging for the soldiers' unused ballots.

This high-ranking officer was one of thousands working in
the FVAP effort to assist Americans abroad with voting. According to this witness, the Pentagon is uninterested in helping
"non-propagandized people"—expatriates, retirees and new
voters—to cast votes. Indeed, the FVAP is systemically constructed to ignore civilian voters. Within the program there is
one Voting Assistance Officer (VAO) for every 50 uniformed
servicemen and -women, but no such ratio for assistance to
civilians. (One expatriate estimates that there is one VAO for
every 268,000 civilians.) This seemingly fraternal bias—the mil-

itary helping only its own people—was actually an indication of a sharp ideological divide, between the military and civilian populations, and also within the military. The army officer in Germany put the case succinctly: "The government bent over backwards to let right-wingers vote."

The assumption there, of course, was that the military is a monolithic rightist bloc, pro-Bush all the way. But as with "the blue states" and "the red states," so with "the military" and "civilians": there are not such stark divisions as the press (and propagandists of the right) would have us think. There were several reasons why enlisted men and women would vote Democratic in 2004: the losing wars in Iraq and Afghanistan; the Democrat's heroic military record, as opposed to Bush's privileged absenteeism; the Democrat's impressive record on veterans' issues, as opposed to Bush's consistent efforts to cut way, way back on veterans' benefits; and Bush's failure to provide the necessary weaponry and armor for the soldiers in the field. The president's indifference to the military casualties sustained by his own people (not to mention the Iraqi and Afghani people) was very clear to many in the military by Election Day. In order to ensure the highest number possible of Bush votes, the Pentagon resorted to additional measures.

According to a poll released on October 15, 2004 by the Annenberg School at the University of Pennsylvania, at least one-third of uniformed servicemen abroad admitted to a favorable view of Kerry—a plurality especially remarkable in light of the extensive and relentless rightist propaganda blasted at our troops day after day.[19] (The U.S. military's airwaves are athunder with the voices of Rush Limbaugh, Dr. Laura, televangelist James Dobson and the like, while some "subversive" websites have been blocked in the Iraqi theater of the war.) The well-concealed political divide within the military expressed a class or caste divide, according to the army officer in Germany. While the lower-ranking service members leaned toward Kerry, by and large, the officers leaned more toward Bush. Such stubborn dissidence among the ranks may help explain the Pentagon's keen interest in deploying, for the use of military personnel abroad, the most serviceable touch-screen voting system on the market.

Such a silent technical expedient would certainly be preferable to the far more obtrusive—and at times embarrassing—strong-arm tactics used by the Department of Defense against dissenting soldiers in the field. On July 15, 2003, a group of disenchanted fighters in the 2nd Brigade, the 3rd Infantry Division, stationed in Baghdad, spoke out against the regime's conduct of the war on ABC's *World News Tonight*.[20] "If Donald Rumsfeld was here, I'd ask him for his resignation," said one. The regime's ever-changing orders, said Army Sgt. Felipe Vega, made him feel as if he'd been "kicked in the gut, slapped in the face." Sgt. Terry Gilmore said that when he called his wife to tell her she would have to wait a few months more for his return, "she started crying. I mean, *I* almost started crying. I just felt like my heart was broken." "These men will continue to do their job," concluded ABC's Jeffrey Kogman, "but their heart is no longer in it."[21]

"The retaliation from Washington was swift," reported Robert Collier in the *San Francisco Chronicle*.[22] "It was the end of the world," one officer told him. "It went all the way up to President Bush and back down again on top of us. At least six of us here will lose our careers." All service members were instructed firmly not to bitch out loud again. The government's response was so repressive that the coverage proved unflattering, and so the Pentagon backed off; and yet the crackdown on dissent continued, or intensified, especially as Election Day approached. In May 2004, AP reported that Sgt. Samuel Provance, who had spoken out honestly about the doings at Abu Ghraib, had lost his security clearance and "had been disciplined." On July 26, the *Army Times* reported that Capt. Oscar R. Estrada, for having written a dissentient letter to the *Washington Post* ("Are we winning their hearts and minds?" he asked, and cited some appalling incidents under the U.S. occupation), "was accused of 'aiding the enemy,' lost his job, lost a planned two-week rest and recuperation, lost his wedding date as a result and was reassigned to a remote, less important duty station."[23] Three days later, *USA Today* reported that Marine Lance Corporal Abdul Henderson, who had appeared in Michael Moore's *Fahrenheit 9/11* saying that he would not return to Iraq, was now under investigation. "He made it very clear that he would not follow orders," said Marine spokesman Captain Patrick Kerr. "We're trying to determine what, if anything, he said or did wrong."[24]

Such reports of outright punishment could not have pleased the propagandists in the White House or the Pentagon, any more than, say, the news about the felons list redux in Florida or the news of Secretary Blackwell's effort to cut back on voter registration in Ohio could have pleased the regime's busy army of "perception managers." Rather than try openly to crush dissent by landing hard on those who dare engage in it, Bush & Co. would do much better to *negate* such dissidence entirely, by faking an electoral "victory" that appears to make moot all prior disagreement. Thus it was, as we have seen, throughout America's civilian realm—and thus it surely was among "our troops" as well.

In July 2003, the Pentagon contracted with New Jersey–based Accenture eDemocracy Services to undertake the Secure

Electronic Registration and Voting Experiment (SERVE), so as to implement an electronic voting system that included absentee e-ballots for all soldiers serving overseas. Accenture is the company hired by Florida to make up the new "scrub lists" of "felons" who might try to vote. Accenture eDemocracy Services, it will also be remembered, included Election.com, which was the corporate wing responsible for designing and administering the electronic absentee ballots for our troops. As noted earlier, in January 2003, Election.com had quietly sold a majority share—51.6 percent of voting power—to Osan Ltd., an investment group with ties to unnamed Saudi nationals. According to *Newsday*, an Osan representative, Charles Smith, "declined to name the Saudi Arabian investors with a stake in the company, other than to say they were 'passive' and part of a larger group that included Americans and Europeans. Smith didn't return phone calls Wednesday."[25]

Whatever was going on behind the curtain, SERVE was ultimately terminated, without explanation. In January 2004, an advisory group with FVAP found that Election.com's voting program had serious computer and network security problems, and urged the Pentagon to drop it. The Pentagon's self-contradictory response is noted in a letter to the GAO sent by Henry Waxman and Carolyn Maloney of the House Committee on Government Reform, on October 19, 2004. The DoD "dismissed this criticism in strong terms, stating, 'we think the thing will be secure, and security will continue to be enhanced. We're not going to stop it.' Then, less than two weeks later, the Department halted implementation of SERVE with little public explanation."[26]

The Pentagon persisted in its quest for an effective electronic method of delivering absentee ballots from our soldiers fighting overseas. In August 2004, the DoD made arrangements with the secretaries of state—all of them Republicans—of Missouri,* North Dakota and Utah, permitting military service members from those states to e-mail their absentee ballots, in partnership with Omega Technologies, a private company that had been under contract to the Pentagon since 1999. Omega was not a stellar candidate for any enterprise, except maybe covert party operations. In 2003, the company had been sued by Adams National Bank for defaulting on a loan of over $500,000. According to court records, the bank also charged that Omega had gained illicit access to a Pentagon computer in order to reroute its payments to the company's new lender.[27] With access to Pentagon computers, Omega could tamper with military records— and with ballots. Omega was also sued in 2002 by Gaylord Opryland, a Nashville resort where Omega had run an army symposium, because Omega was $136,187 in arrears and otherwise at fault: "In its lawsuit," the *New York Times* reported on September 16, 2004, "Gaylord said the Omega president, Patricia A. Williams, falsely said the payment had been sent and on one occasion provided a fictitious Federal Express package tracking number. Gaylord also said Ms. Williams sent a $50,000 check that bounced." The dubious Omega had certain party ties. President Williams, it was reported, had lately donated $6,600 to the National Republican Congressional Committee and sits on the NRCC's business advisory council.[28]

*Missouri was the first state to sign on. "Missouri Secretary of State Matt Blunt, a Republican running for governor, announced the plan Wednesday, saying that 'simplifying the voting process for these heroes is the least we can do.' The move surprised some computer security experts and voting watchdog groups, who said yesterday that the new rules could lead to Election Day fraud." Jo Becker, "MO Plan to Let Military Cast Votes by E-Mail Draws Crit," *Washington Post*, 8/27/04.

And there was still another initiative to get our soldiers voting right. In an arrangement with 20 states (with 20 more soon signing on), the DoD enabled military personnel to *fax* their absentee ballots to their home states—a method of transmission that struck some troops as potentially intimidating, as it meant, in effect, the end of secret ballots. In their letter to the GAO, Reps. Waxman and Maloney quote "an Army sergeant in Germany, who asked not to be identified for fear of retribution."

"Some places you have to hand it off to get it faxed because the machine is behind the counter, at the finance office or personnel support battalion," the sergeant said. "They should come up with a better, more surefire system."[29] Thus did Bush's Pentagon pressure soldiers into backing the regime, deciding not to vote at all or forcing themselves to cast their votes in anguish.

As a safeguard against tampering with the U.S. global vote, HAVA stipulates that the Election Assistance Commission (EAC), so as to figure out how many absentee ballots have been validated, must quickly contact every state in order to collect and analyze all data on the overseas vote, and to report its findings within ninety days of the election. The EAC's 2004 report was due on February 2, 2005. As of this writing—nine months after Election Day—the EAC has not received such information from the states, and so it is still unknown how many of the several million U.S. citizens abroad were finally able to cast their ballots. Nor can we ever know how many of those votes were finally counted, or counted as intended. In March 2005, the EAC's chairman, Reverend DeForest B. Soaries Jr.,* resigned in

---

*A staunch Republican, Soaries is Senior Pastor of the First Baptist Church of Lincoln Gardens in Somerset, N.J. Since taking over at First Baptist in November, 1990, Soaries has increased church membership from 1,500 to 6,000 members—and has, under Bush and Co., been a very fortunate recipient of government largesse. "A pioneer of faith-based community development,

protest over the regime's unwillingness to fund and otherwise support the Commission's work.

According to a comprehensive post-election survey by the Overseas Voting Foundation, over half of U.S. expatriates suspected that their ballots had not been handled properly. Forty-three percent of those who planned to vote had failed to do so. Of those who did receive their ballots, 20 percent claim not to have been sent the proper ballot. (Some received ballots for Republican primaries.) Many voters reported oddities of various kinds. Some claim to have received two ballots, or a crumpled ballot, or a ballot meant for someone else, or an official envelope without a ballot in it, or a photocopy of a ballot, or a ballot already completed, the phantom voter having voted straight Republican.[30] Thus was the largest of all of Kerry/Edwards's constituencies cut down to size.

And while that theft was in the works, the far right's propaganda was asserting that the U.S. global vote might go to Bush, and that *both parties* were fiercely going after it. "U.S. Voters in Foreign Nations Could Decide the Election," ran an item on Richard Mellon Scaife's NewsMax.com on August 16—just one week before fvap.gov was suddenly and inexplicably blocked for millions of Americans abroad. "When decision time comes this fall, the real swing votes in the 2004 presidential election might not come from Pennsylvania, Ohio or even the notorious

Rev. Soaries has led First Baptist in the construction of a new $17 million church complex." In short, the reverend has been very close to the regime, and so his resignation is significant. (Soaries created something of a stir in mid-July, when he proposed consideration of the cancellation or postponement of the upcoming election, in the event of terrorist attacks. Soaries's official bio available at http://www.eac.gov/soaries.asp; "Counterrorism Officials Look to Postpone Elections," posted 7/12/04 at USAToday.com,http://www.usatoday.com/news/politicselections/nation/president/2004-07-12-postpone-elections_x.htm.)

Florida. The ultimate Bush-Kerry battleground could turn out to be somewhere more far-flung and unexpected: Israel, Britain, even Indonesia."[31]

In fact there was no contest on that global battleground. Through determined and sustained effort, it too was delivered to the Bush regime against the will of the electorate.

Epilogue

"Four more years. That's the verdict from the voters. President George W. Bush gets a second term. Conservatives get stronger majorities in Congress. And we get an unprecedented opportunity to shape America's future for generations to come."[1]

Thus began an email from Edward J. Feulner, president of the Heritage Foundation, sent to the group's 200,000 members on the morning of November 3. The message was itself predictable—a morning-after pitch for one more "generous contribution" to help Heritage do "what we have to do right now" (i.e., help "President Bush and his allies in Congress" to "keep cutting taxes," "modernize Social Security," "weed out terrorists and perfect the military," and so on). Predictably, the tone was at once jubilant and urgent:

> We must serve as a check on the angry liberals who are humiliated by the stinging defeats they suffered yesterday. They'll be more desperate than ever, and thus more ruthless than ever in their attacks on our conservative policies. The liberals will twist the facts about tax relief, the war against terrorism, Social Security—you name it. Every time Heritage must push back with the facts.[2]

The message was remarkable not for its style or substance but for the evident clairvoyance of its author(s), who had somehow ascertained "the verdict of the voters" while the candidates were still officially at odds. Feulner's e-mail went out at 10:22 A.M. EST—over three and a half hours before John Kerry conceded (at 1:57 P.M.).

It made sense, propaganda-wise, for the Republicans to jump the gun, in order to define Bush/Cheney's "victory" as a *fait ac-compli*. Once Heritage (and others) had proclaimed that it was over—or, that is, once the media and even certain Democrats had started echoing that view—John Kerry would be under that much greater pressure to give up. Thus had Bush & Co. prematurely seized the White House in November of 2000, rushing their "transition" into power several weeks before the count in Florida was halted by the Supreme Court on December 12. (As early as November 10, Bush started to discuss his cabinet appointments. "First Lady Bush will be arriving here soon," he said in passing on November 11.[3]) In a democracy, the only way to foil that tactic would be for the press not just to point it out but to insist that the pretenders hold their horses and allow the counting process to determine who the winner is and when he might start acting as the President-elect. Here the press did nothing of the kind. They merely bowed to the pretenders in 2000, and nagged at Gore to pack it in. Four years later, there was no need for such collaboration, as Kerry mooted the whole issue by conceding faster than a dog can trot.

A functioning democracy requires a skeptical and independent press, whose job is to inform the people, so that they will know enough to rule themselves accordingly and keep their government in line. At that crucial task our press has largely failed.

Throughout the race—as it had been, by and large, since 1999—the national press was a consistent advocate for Bush &

Co. Its partiality went far beyond suppressing or downplaying nearly every indication of the regime's rampant fraud, and far beyond the propagation of the comfy line that "each side accuses the other of improprieties," as a subhead from the Cox News Service put it on October 15.[4] The national press also tuned out the many signs of Bush's actual unpopularity. There was no mainstream coverage of the president's true standing in his party, with numerous well-known Republicans opposing him and often backing Kerry; nor, beyond the pithy *Editor & Publisher*, edited by tough investigative journalist Greg Mitchell, was there any national news of all those U.S. dailies that, having gone for Bush against Al Gore, would not support him now. (Both trends have been elaborated here in Chapter One.) The mainstream press ignored many other signs of the president's unpopularity among Republicans. On June 27, AP reported that a poll conducted for it by Ipsos-Public Affairs had found the president admired far less than Ronald Reagan, whose showy funeral had taken place the week before the survey. "By a margin of 6-to-1," the item noted, "those surveyed said they thought Reagan would be remembered as a better president than Bush." (The story ran only in the *The Salt Lake Tribune*.)[5]

The press sat on all evidence of Bush's low repute not just among Republicans, but nationwide, and its silence grew only more anomalous as Election Day approached. (The press was also silent on the president's international unpopularity—not reporting, for example, that Tony Blair refused to travel to the White House for a campaign photo op, so badly would such posturing have hurt him back at home.)[6] Throughout those last suspenseful weeks, a free and independent press—and one commercially inclined to go for scoops—would surely have played up all startling revelations. In the 2004 campaign, on the other hand, our national press ignored or minimized whatever stories might diverge too sharply from the picture of a well-liked president neck-and-neck with, or out ahead of, his plodding challenger. For instance, the press ignored new voters, who favored Kerry overwhelmingly. On October 21, Sidney Blumenthal reported on a Democratic poll of newly registered voters: "Four months ago, [pollster Stanley] Greenberg told me, the newly registered made up only 1 percent of the sample. One month ago, they comprised 4 percent. Now, in the poll completed on Oct. 18, they are at 7 percent and rising. And they will vote for Kerry over Bush by 61 to 37 percent."[7] A few days later, another poll, although non-partisan, reconfirmed the trend: "A new Ipsos-AP analysis of their poll data shows new voters leaning very heavily toward Kerry," reported Ruy Teixeira on October 25. "Among [likely voters] who are new voters, Kerry is favored over Bush by a smashing 25 points, 60–35."[8] The trend was reconfirmed in yet another poll released the day before Election Day: "Zogby International and partner Rock the Vote found Kerry leading Bush 55 percent to 40 percent among 18–29-year-old likely voters in their first joint Rock the Vote Mobile political poll, conducted exclusively on mobile phones October 27 through 30, 2004."[9]

These polls (and others) went wholly unreported in this country, other than in cyber-space. (Blumenthal's column ran in the British *Guardian*; Teixeira wrote about the Ipsos-AP poll on his own blog; and Zogby's findings were reported in a press release from Rock the Vote.) In its quiet crusade to magnify the president's appeal, the national press not only buried problematic poll numbers, exactly as Team Bush was doing, but also kept completely mum about the regime's frequent and egregious efforts to police the spectacle out on the campaign trail. The White House was routinely barring people from campaign events, denying them admission, or having them arrested, in order to project the king as basking in unanimous mass adulation. The national press assisted in that effort by refraining from reporting on it, or, if they mentioned it at all, by playing it down. Such collaboration, which was no doubt unconscious, started well before the coverage (or, to coin a term, the "coverage-up") of the Republican convention in New York. There hundreds were arrested, only some of them protestors, and were held illegally, and often in deplorable conditions—a mass abuse of civil rights that only made the news in driblets, and belatedly. On the convention floor, meanwhile, the campaign's cops were also playing hardball as they forced all non-enthusiasm out of sight. At one point journalist Irene Dische, covering the convention for the German magazine *Die Zeit*, was hustled into temporary custody when, chancing out onto the floor before the president's appearance, she refused to take and wave a tiny U.S. flag—a story that, in these United States, ran only in *Salon*.[10]

Such strong-arm tactics had been used on Bush & Co.'s behalf throughout the summer. On June 28, Lani Frank, a Chester County Democratic committeewoman from Berwyn, Pa., was arrested for "disorderly conduct" for handing out voter registration forms outside a multiplex in East Cain, just after a screening of *Fahrenheit 911*.* She was arrested by state troopers. (On Sept. 5, Frank was found guilty, and fined $230, by District Judge Rita Arnold, who, after passing sentence, immediately left

---

*Moore's film, and Moore himself, were variously censored in October. On Oct. 1, it was reported that the TV networks had refused to air ads for the movie—which, on Oct. 16, was itself pulled from Time-Warner's In Demand pay-per-view service "for legal reasons." On Oct. 4, George Mason University abruptly cancelled a personal appearance by the filmmaker that had been scheduled for Oct. 29.

the bench without further comment.)[11] On Independence Day, Nicole and Jeff Rank of Corpus Christi, Texas, were led away in handcuffs for "trespassing" when they showed up wearing anti-Bush t-shirts at a presidential speech in Charleston, West Virginia. (Forced later by the city council to express "regret" for the arrest, Republican Mayor Danny Jones claimed that the police had acted on the orders of the Service Service, whose spokesman then denied the claim.)

The Ranks were not a feral pair of teen-aged anarchists, but a peaceful married couple, he an oceanographer, she a deputy environmental liaison officer for the Federal Emergency Management Agency, posted to Charleston after the Memorial Day floods. After the arrest, Nicole was told by FEMA that she was no longer needed in West Virginia. "I have not been fired per se," she said. "But I was released from this job. And when they release you from a job, you no longer get paid."[12]

On August 17, it was reported in the *Traverse City Record-Eagle* (serving Northern Michigan) that Kathryn Mead, a 55-year-old high school social studies teacher who had planned to hear Bush speak, had her ticket ripped up at the door and was refused admission, because of the small Kerry/Edwards sticker on her blouse. ("We were told," said Ralph Soffredine, who was in charge of security, "that anyone with stickers on shirts would not be let in if they would not take them off.")[13] On August 25, Walter Brasch, an award-winning syndicated columnist and, for 25 years, a professor of journalism at Bloomsburg University in northeastern Pennsylvania, was denied access to a speech that the vice president was delivering at the university, although Brasch had a media credential from the Bush/Cheney campaign and was a tenured member of the Bloomsburg faculty.

Brasch said he was approached by a group of men who refused to identify themselves, including who they worked for and why Brasch was suddenly no longer allowed to attend the event.

"I repeatedly said I was there as a reporter, not a protestor or anything else," Brasch, 59, said. "I had my notepad, and they could see that I was taking notes on what they were saying.

"Every time I asked who they were, they said, 'We don't have to tell you that,'" he added.[14]

The incident was noted only in a press release for the Reporters Committee for Freedom of the Press; and those other incidents, in West Virginia, Michigan and Pennsylvania, were reported only locally or on-line. Such incidents continued, and seemed to get more violent, as Election Day approached, yet there never was a national story on Bush & Co.'s fascistic practices on our own soil. One story did get ample coverage, when, on September 16, Laura Bush, speaking in a firehouse in Hamilton, N.J., was interrupted by Sue Niederer, the 56-year-old mother of Army 2nd Lt. Seth Dvorin, 24, who had been killed in Iraq on February 3 while trying to defuse a roadside bomb. "If this war is so justified, why aren't *your* children serving?" shouted Niederer, whose T-shirt bore a photo of Sean's face, over the legend, "PRESIDENT BUSH, You Killed my Son." Although she had a ticket to the speech, Niederer was hauled away and charged with "defiant trespass." (The charges were soon dropped.)[15]

While Niederer's experience was widely televised and otherwise recounted by the major media, less dramatic cases of repression were ignored, except by activists and other close observers of the race or of the press. That Bush and Cheney played only to preselected groups of partisans was an important and revealing aspect of their drive for re-election, and yet it had to be inferred from what little detailed coverage the Republican campaign received. "President George Bush will be making another campaign stop in our area," reported WNEP-TV, a station serving northern and central Pennsylvania, on October 4.

> He will be speaking to a select group about national security and medical liability. The event will be held at the F.M. Kirby Center on Public Square in Wilkes-Barre Wednesday morning and will be invitation only.

Later in October, it emerged—again in Wilkes-Barre—that the regime would not allow any "known Democrat" into its campaign events. This became apparent on October 23, when a 27-year-old registered Republican and Army soldier (who would not give the press his name) got himself in trouble when, waiting outside Bush's venue, he generously let a stranger share his place in line.

"Individuals from the Bush campaign spotted the individual with the soldier," a local daily reported, "and identified the person as a Democratic supporter."

> The spotters, and eventually police, asked the Democratic supporter to remove a jacket, a sweater and some other articles of clothing in what was described as basically a police search.
>
> The soldier said the Democratic supporter did what was asked without any complaint. The person also provided a ticket to the event.
>
> The soldier said that when he asked why the person was being hassled, the spotters said the Democrat's name wasn't on their "master list."
>
> "So I asked if we could see the master list? They said they didn't have it," he said.

The soldier said he stood up for the supporter, but was in no way hostile, because he was there to see the president and hoped to justify voting for him.

Not long after showing his own ticket and being told he wasn't part of the "master list" either, the police asked the soldier to leave. He was told the event was for Bush supporters or undecided voters only.[16]

Such pre-emptive strikes were commonplace throughout the race. On October 15, three schoolteachers were threatened with arrest and then ejected from a Bush rally in Medford, Oregon, because their T-shirts said "Protect Our Civil Liberties." (The piece ran only in *The Oregonian*.)[17] Back in Pennsylvania, on October 28, the *Bucks County Courier Times* reported that Simi Nischal, an undecided voter from Lower Makefield, had been denied admittance to a presidential speech—along with her husband and two children, the older one a Bush supporter—because the co-worker who drove the family to the campaign site had a Kerry/Edwards bumper sticker on her car. "I deny you the right to attend this rally," the party bouncer told her. "'He was so rude, he made me feel like a criminal,' Nischal said. 'I said, "That's not fair, you are losing a supporter." [And he said] 'We don't care about your support.'" As she left, the paper reported, "Nischal said onlookers cheered and laughed at her."[18] Far uglier incidents received no formal coverage whatsoever. On October 16, in the tiny town of Jacksonville, Oregon, state police and Secret Service agents, without any provocation, charged a peaceful crowd of 70 with gunshots and pepper spray—an armed assault reported only in some anguished emails from a number of its victims.*

*See Appendix.

By ignoring such repression, our media abetted it—while foreign journalists in the U.S. were well aware of it, as they too were repressed. (*They*, of course, reported it to *their* respective publics.) "Journalists from England, Sweden, Holland and other friendly countries are being detained at U.S. airports, strip-searched and deported," *Salon* reported on June 16.[19] Here too the regime turned up the heat as the campaign approached its climax. On October 24, the Inter-American Press Association formally criticized the U.S. government for restricting foreign journalists' travels, and for using courts to order journalists to name their sources. (The statement was reported by AP, and the *Miami Herald* ran it.)[20] As members of the U.S. press were silent on the treatment of their foreign colleagues, so did they air or publish nothing of the regime's censorship of U.S. news outlets on foreign soil. On October 8, FBI agents in the UK seized the global servers for the Independent Media Center (IndyMedia. org), and kept them shut down for six days. The bureau gave no explanation for the seizure, nor was there ever any mainstream news about it here in the United States; and so Americans not only didn't know about it at the time, to this day they don't know about it.[21]

Nor did our national press report on any incident or issue, whether foreign or domestic, that might not have reflected well on the regime. The FBI's appropriation of those British servers was the least of it. Our press's rosy vision, especially throughout the 2004 campaign, of the losing wars in both Iraq and Afghanistan could be the subject of a shelf of other books. Here we must make do with only one example of our press's marked distaste for painful truths about the war. On June 29—the first day of the new Iraq's alleged sovereignty—a squad of national guardsmen from Oregon, on patrol in East Baghdad, happened on a grisly scene of torture in a courtyard of Saddam Hussein's Interior Ministry, where a man in plainclothes was beating a prostrate. handcuffed and blindfolded prisoner with a metal rod. The soldiers quickly burst into the complex, where they found scores of miserable prisoners who had been brutalized by the Iraqi agents there. The victims had been picked up for "crimes" like lacking proper identification, and had been starved and beaten for days. Having separated the abusers from their prey, the men radioed for instruction from the Army's First Cavalry Division. They were ordered to stand down—to yield the prisoners back to their custodians, and leave the premises. Outraged by this order, the guardsmen took their story to the U.S. press.

It was reported by Mike Francis in *The Sunday Oregonian* on July 8.[22] Picked up by AP, the piece also ran in *The Seattle Times*. And that was it, despite the manifest heroism of those soldiers, which stood in vivid contrast to the hearty sadism of the U.S. military personnel (and others) at Abu Ghraib—another story that, although not even close to fully told, had disappeared by mid-October. On the 14th, the *New York Times* ran "U.S. Considers Reopening Inquiry Into Possible Abuse Before Iraq Prison Scandal," then dropped the subject, as if out of deference to the White House as Election Day approached. Indeed, throughout the last few months of the campaign a sort of magic spell appeared to have been cast upon the Fourth Estate, which suddenly could see no evil whatsoever in the Bush administration. Such deference, of course, was nothing new; but our press seemed positively resolute in its desire not to discomfit the regime at the very moment when such discomfiture was most appropriate and necessary. As with Bush & Co,'s electoral highjinks and its catastrophic war abroad, so was it with the many other scandals, great and small, that were just lying in the open all around, and in, the White House.

Some dared call it "Teflon," as if Bush & Co.'s protective coating somehow inhered in the regime itself and was not carefully applied, on a daily basis, by "the liberal media." The press's treatment of Bush/Cheney in the last campaign was something of a radical departure from the (already deplorable) standard practices of U.S. mainstream journalism. Now a story would be spiked before Election Day *because* it might be "controversial," as editors atop the *New York Times* did with William Broad's strong piece* about the probability that Bush really was wired for secret audio reception at his first debate with Kerry (see p. 57). Asked about this precedent, Ben Bagdikian, former dean of the journalism school at the University of California at Berkeley, noted that it was extraordinary, and indefensible:

> I cannot imagine a paper I worked for turning down a story like this before an election. This was credible photographic evidence not about breaking the rules, but of a total lack of integrity on the part of the president, evidence that he'd cheated in the debate, and also of a lack of confidence in his ability on the part of his campaign. I'm shocked to hear top management decided not to run such a story.[23]

Many sensitive inquiries were aborted or suppressed by the regime, particularly in October. On the 19th, it came out that the White House would withhold the long-awaited CIA report on 9/11 until "after the election"—a dodge decried by Robert Scheer in both the *Los Angeles Times* and *Salon* but otherwise acknowledged with a yawn, or not at all.[24] This postponement was

---

*Reporters John Schwartz and Andrew Revkin also worked on the story.

especially outrageous, inasmuch as 9/11 was the Bush regime's entire platform. The U.S. press had already dropped the ball on 9/11, in its acquiescent treatment of the report by the 9/11 Commission—an evasive masterpiece, which raised more questions than it answered.[25] On October 8, the U.S. Commission on Civil Rights, at the insistence of its Bush appointees, voted "to wait until after next month's election to discuss a report critical of the Bush administration's civil rights record,"[26] as the AP put it. That move too roused little interest in the national press, although its purpose, to minimize the damage among African-Americans, was obvious—and especially outrageous considering what the party was already doing to that population's votes. (In February, 2005, Bush dumped Mary Frances Berry, the bumptious chair of the commisson, replacing her with Gerald Reynolds, a staunch opponent of affirmative action.)[27] Bush & Co. even deferred the president's annual physical examination until "after the election," for reasons unknown then and now. Prior to the election, some whistle-blowers found themselves unable to attract the interest of a single journalist. In her efforts to alert the public to the dangerous condition of our national parks, U.S. Park Police Chief Teresa Chambers—who had herself been disciplined for speaking out—had to rely on the resources of the Public Employees for Environmental Responsibility (PEER) to try to tell the people that a "culture of fear" had taken over the Interior Department, making it extremely risky to go public with unhappy news, such as the glaring vulnerability of all the nation's public icons to terrorist attack.[28]

The press's fealty to Bush & Co. was most apparent in the skimpy coverage of the president's military service. On the one hand, there were many column inches and much airtime dedicated to the "Swift Boat Veterans for Truth," a costly propaganda venture hatched in furtherance of Karl Rove's main anti-Kerry strategy, which was to hit the Democrat precisely at his strongest point. Although the "Swift Boat Veterans" were exposed as fraudulent in several thorough stories, both on-line and in print, those few debunking exercises made no difference in the long run, as the lie was so well-funded that no one-shot refutation, however solid or complete, could slow its rise to authenticity in countless minds. (Kerry's troops, meanwhile, were AWOL in that crucial fight, his campaign dithering for three weeks after the Swift Boat Veterans started up.) While largely acquiescing in that lie, the press ignored the president's own military record, although the White House kept flaunting its deceptive version of that history. In August, for example, Bush postured as a veteran—a fact that outraged certain genuine veterans, who attempted fruitlessly, and off the record, to get reporters to look into it. "As a combat veteran and member of The American Legion, I blew a damn gasket this evening when my September edition of 'The American Legion' magazine arrived," wrote one such source to several journalists.

> Inside, on page 32, The Legion reports that Bush is a member of American Legion Post 77 in Texas. Well, Bush isn't a veteran, so Bush can't be a member of The American Legion. This issue is timely because Bush is set to speak before the Legion convention this weekend in Nashville, Tennessee.
>
> Here's the bottom line: Either Bush has a discharge from active duty or he doesn't. Unless Bush can cough up a valid and complete DD214 as evidence of active duty, then Bush is a fraud, and he can't be a member of The Legion, either.[29]

Four days later, the Kerry campaign raised a similar issue—and finally struck back on the military front—when the Democrat assailed the president for wearing medals he had not earned. (In a 1970 photo in his father's presidential library, Bush stands grinning in his uniform, with an Air Force Outstanding Unit Award pinned on his chest—an honor that had not been given to his unit, the 111th Fighter Intercept Squadron, and would not be until 1975.) This counter-thrust received no U.S. coverage (although the British *Daily Telegraph* reported it).[30] Even though much was known already, and had already been ignored, about Bush's days in the Texas Air National Guard, much new dirt came pouring forth, all of it fastidiously overlooked by U.S. mainstream journalists. In September it emerged that Bush had been dispatched to Alabama not just to help out in the senatorial campaign of Bush Sr.'s buddy, Winton Blount, but because Bush Sr. wanted badly to get the troubled Junior—a "drunken liability," according to the *Guardian*—out of town.[31] Also that month, Russ Baker reported in *The Nation* that the young Bush had been desperate *not* to take his mandatory yearly physical exam in 1972, which would explain his failure to show up for it.[32] New records appeared reconfirming Bush's failures to report for service as required.[33] On September 5, AP reported that several mandatory and crucial documents were missing from the president's official service file. (AP seemed not to want to spill those beans, as it posted the report on the Sunday during Memorial Day weekend.)[34] Also that month, Janet Linke, the widow of Jan Peter Linke, who had served along with Bush in that unit of the Texas Air National Guard, recalled that "Bush's flying career was permanently disabled by a crippling fear of flying," and that Jan Peter Linke had therefore had to take his place in 1972. This tidbit was reported by Citizens for Legitimate Government and ended up on lots of Web sites.[35] All of that the press ignored as Election Day approached. On September 11, *U.S. News & World Report* came out with a hard-hitting story challenging the president's honorable discharge;[36] the rest was silence—or, to be precise, the rest concerned CBS News and Dan Rather, both of them condemned and shamed for having had the moxie to report those "controversial" memos that comprised still further proof of Bush's total military failure. As if with a collective sigh of relief, the press obligingly diverted its attention to that pseudo-scandal, thereby helping Bush & Co. punish Rather for the president's misdeeds.

The press, in other words, was serving not the public interest, as the Framers had intended, but the livid movement that had partly seized the U.S. government four years before and was now about to try to grab it all. Far more troubling than the journalistic silence on the problems of one addled and addicted airman (although directly linked to that peculiar blackout) was the press's utter failure to report on the regime's extremist tendencies—its theocratic aims and hatred of democracy; its love of punishment and force; its proud irrationality; its endless wrathful projectivity. The members of the press looked stalwartly away from every evidence of Bush & Co.'s *character*. Upon Bush's victory, Grover Norquist told *El Mundo* on September 12, "the Democratic party will be forever doomed."[37] The press chose not to hear such candid statements, which were as common on the theocratic right as that movement's efforts to transform this nation's culture and society—efforts that the press also ignored.

When, three days before Election Day, a Pennsylvania school board voted to include "intelligent design" in its curriculum, the news came forth in press releases from the Center for Inquiry (CFI) and the Committee for the Scientific Investigation of Claims of the Paranormal (CSICOP).[38] As with such local symptoms, so the press ignored the far more dangerous national drive toward theocracy. When, on September 23, the House passed legislation to prevent the Supreme Court from ruling on the question as to whether "under God" should be deleted from the Pledge of Allegiance, the motion was, for once, reported widely. The purpose of that legislation, however, was to pave the way for passage of the Constitution Restoration Act (HR 3799, S. 2082), which would establish God, not the Constitution, as the sovereign basis of all law in the United States—a step that would enable any judge to base his rulings on the tribal strictures in Leviticus and Deuteronomy. When this bill was introduced into both houses of Congress, on February 11, 2004, it was not covered anywhere; and in the months to come, the only journalists to write about it were Katherine Yurica on her excellent Web site (yuricareport.com) and Chris Floyd in the *Moscow Times* (in Russia).[39]

When, in October, the White House announced its approval of a book claiming that the Grand Canyon was formed by Noah's flood—a book therefore available at bookstores in our national parks—the news was broken by a press release from Public Employees for Environmental Responsibility (PEER).[40] When the White House distributed, free to churches, 300,000 DVDs of a film entitled "GWB: Faith in the White House"—in which Bush appears at one point in a split-screen tableau with Jesus—that stroke of propaganda was reported by Frank Rich in his weekend column in the *Sunday New York Times*.[41] When, at the 2004 Republican convention in New York, there were crosses clearly visible in the design of both the podium and a small table next to it, that blasphemous display was either laughed off by the press (the RNC denied that they were crosses), or reported only as a grievance by non-Christians, as in the Reuters story on September 1, "Jewish groups irked by Cross on Republican platform." When the Republican attacked George Soros as the secret Croesus of the Democratic Party, the far more grandiose and expensive theocratic works of South Korean billionaire Sun Myung Moon—a major donor to the movement, honored with a coronation ceremony in the Senate Office Building in the spring of 2004—got no mainstream coverage whatsoever, although independent journalist Robert Parry did report it on his first-rate Web site consortiumnews.org.[42] And when, in September, the Republicans purveyed the rumor that the Democrats would ban the Bible if they won the White House, NBC's Tom Brokaw thus reported the canard:

> One more note on politics tonight. The Republican National Committee now has acknowledged sending mass mailings to two states that say liberals want to ban the Bible.
>
> Republican Party officials say the mailings in Arkansas and West Virginia are aimed at mobilizing Christian voters for President Bush. Some Christian commentators say liberal support for same-sex marriage could lead to laws that punish sermons denouncing homosexuality as sinful.
>
> Up next—getting ready for a fourth strike. Hurricane Jeanne heading for Florida and another direct hit![43]

All this should concern us as Americans not just because it really happened here but because it is still happening at this moment, and therefore is likely to keep happening until there's little left of our democracy—or, for that matter, any other democratic system. The theft of the 2004 election will recur unless we—not the Democratic Party, and not the media, but we, the people—take the actions necessary to prevent it. Since their victory, the Bush Republicans have made still further progress in their drive to undermine the Constitution. Needless to say, the national press has by and large ignored these further steps toward a more perfect tyranny, requiring us to be that much more vigilant from this moment on.

As of this writing, Diebold has failed in its second bid to privatize the vote in California, but the corporation will not cease to struggle for that contract, nor will the GOP relent in its campaign to neutralize that mammoth Democratic stronghold. Meanwhile, Diebold has been working, more successfully it seems, to have its product used in New York, Maryland and Illinois—three more major "blue" states, where touch screen voting systems must not ever be adopted. More generally, the Help America Vote Act must be modified, if not repealed, so that this nation will stop using touch screen systems and find some simpler, less expensive, more secure and more transparent mode of balloting. The shady civic reign of Diebold, ES&S, Sequoia and other private vendors must be ended, as one part of a comprehensive program of U.S. electoral reform. (Other nations too should be discouraged from signing contracts with those companies.) Such emancipation must begin with grass-roots organizing drives from state to state, until this nation's long-corrupted patchwork of state, county and municipal arrangements is supplanted by a unitary public system well beyond the reach of party politics.

Meanwhile, the landmark Voting Rights Act of 1965, and its addenda passed a decade later (mainly concerning the provision of foreign-language ballots), must now be protected from the right's drive to "re-authorize" it. As they seek to "improve" Social Security out of existence, so do the Bush Republicans intend to make the Voting Rights Act "permanent," by which they mean completely ineffectual, and eventually dispensable. Basically, it is their strategy to re-authorize only certain sections of the act, so that it ends up likely to be deemed invalid by the Supreme Court. Once the Voting Rights Act has been nullified, the states will then be free to try all sorts of novel hurdles to fair voting. In the summer of 2005, Georgia passed the nation's most restrictive voting law, requiring every citizen to purchase a state-approved photo i.d., which must be shown by every would-be voter. Such a measure—"clearly a poll tax," as John Conyers has observed—would handily disenfranchise countless Georgians who are not Republicans.[44] A similar law is pending now in Indiana; and in Arizona, Proposition 200, ostensibly intended to prevent illegal immigrants from voting, would clearly force poll workers to reject some eligible voters (primarily Hispanics).[45] Such laws will pop up all throughout the nation if the Voting Rights Act is "re-authorized" as Bush & Co. intend.

There have been other danger signs, most of them reported quietly if at all. On March 4, 2005, the Supreme Court refused to hear an appeal brought by nine black Virginians who were seeking to invalidate the redistricting plan forced on their state in 2001. The lawsuit "focused on the 4th District, contending that the GOP-controlled General Assembly deliberately 'packed' majority-black voting precincts into the adjacent 3rd District, where black voters were already dominant," reported the AP.[46] "Instead of creating two districts where candidates who appeal to black voters could be effective, plaintiffs argued, the GOP plan concentrated blacks in one Democratic-voting district, making the other largely white and Republican-oriented." In other words, the plan was meant to thwart Virginia's non-Republicans as Tom DeLay bushwhacked the Texas Democrats when he engineered the gerrymandering of that state in 2003. The Manichaean purpose of such tactics is to racialize our politics, with one big all-white party permanently riding herd on a much weaker second party, mostly black (and brown, and red). The GOP's electoral intentions have been lately reconfirmed by Bush's nomination of John Roberts to the Supreme Court. Back in 1981, when Roberts was a frisky junior lawyer on the Reagan team, he fought quite hard to get the president to deal the Voting Rights Act a tremendous blow. The act was up for renewal in 1982, and Roberts wanted Reagan to insist that plaintiffs suing over violations of the act be required to prove that there was a deliberate *intention* of disenfranchisement—a stroke that would have made the measure unenforceable.[47]

All this is bad news, of course—as any news that has been long suppressed must come as quite a shock to those who finally hear it; and quite a lot of news has been kept from us in the Age of Bush. Without our noticing (for who would tell us it was happening?), the two great corporate entities of government and media have unified against us, when each of them should be assisting us as we attempt to live our lives, enjoy our liberties, and, most of all, pursue our happiness. All of this will be increasingly at risk until we get our country back; for our lives and liberty and happiness depend on our ability to rule ourselves—that is, our right to vote. We must start working to reclaim that right, and to do that, we must know all we can about our rights, our history and this government. We must, in short, be as intelligent as possible—even more intelligent than most of us were in this nation's polling-places on Nov. 2, 2004. Bush's seeming victory made us look stupid in the eyes of all the world. "How can 59,054,087 people be so dumb?" asked the front page of the British *Daily Mirror* on Nov. 4. It is past time for us to set the record straight; for the whole world is still watching as we drift ever further toward the brink.

The choice *is* finally ours. What Thomas Paine wrote in 1775 is actually still true today: "We have the power to begin the world over again." So how will America vote in 2008?

Appendix
The Bush campaign in Jacksonville, Oregon

Trish Bowcock is a retired attorney from Avotih, Texas, now living in Jacksonville. Debi Smith is a homemaker, who lives wih her husband and two children in Ashland, Oregon.

FROM TRISH BOWCOCK, 10/16/04

A few weeks before my father died, he woke me in the wee hours of the morning. He needed to talk. He was worried about Attorney General John Ashcroft and the destruction of American civil liberties. I comforted my father, believing he was delusional from medications. I was wrong.

I write this from my home in Jacksonville Oregon (population 2,226). President George W. Bush came here this week. The purpose of his visit was political. Southern Oregon has been deemed a "battle ground" area in the presidential race. John Kerry has made incredible inroads in this traditionally

Republican stronghold. President Bush's campaign stop was an attempt to staunch the slide.

Jacksonville is an old gold mining town. Our main street is only five blocks long, lined with restored storefronts. The sidewalks are narrow. We are a peaceful community. The prospect of an overnight presidential visit was exciting, even to me, a lifelong Democrat. My excitement turned to horror as I watched events unfold during President Bush's visit.

In the mid-1800s, when Indians invaded Jacksonville, citizens clambered upon the roof of the old library. It was the one building that would not catch fire when flaming arrows were shot. This week it was a different scene. Police armed with high powered rifles perched upon our rooftops as the presidential motorcade approached. Helicopters flew low, overhead. A cadre of motorcycle police zoomed into town. Black SUVs followed, sandwiching several black limousines carrying the president, his wife and their entourage as they sped to the local inn where they would eat and sleep.

The main street was lined with people gathered to witness the event. Many supported the president. Many did not. Some came because they were simply curious. There were men, women, young and old. The mood was somewhat festive. Supporters of John Kerry sported signs, as did supporters of George Bush. Individuals, exercising their rights of free speech began chanting. On one side of the street, shouts of "four more years" echoed in the night air. On the other side of the street, chants of "three more weeks" responded. The chants were loud and apparently could be heard by President Bush. An order was issued that the anti-Bush rhetoric be quieted. The local SWAT team leapt to action.

It happened fast. Clad in full riot gear, at least 50 officers moved in. Shouting indecipherable commands from a bullhorn, they formed a chain and bore down upon the people, only working to clear the side of the street appearing to be occupied by Kerry supporters. People tried to get out of their way. It was very crowded. There was nowhere to move. People were being crushed. They started flowing into the streets. Pleas to the officers, asking, "where to go" fell upon deaf ears. Instead, riot police fired pellets of cayenne pepper spray into the crowd. An old man fell and couldn't get up. When a young man stopped to help, he was shot in the back with hard pepper spray balls. Children were hit with pepper spray. Deemed "Protesters," people were shoved and herded down the street by the menacing line of armed riot police, until out of the president's earshot.

There the "Protesters" were held at bay. Anyone vocalizing anti-Bush or pro-Kerry sentiments was prohibited from venturing forward. Loud anti-Bush chants were responded to by the commanding officer stating: "FORWARD," to which the entire line of armed police would move, lock-step, toward the "Protesters," forcing backward movement. Police officers circulated, filming the crowd of "Protesters." Some were people like me, quiet middle-aged women. Some sported anti-Bush signs, peace signs, or Kerry signs. A small group of youth, clad in black with kerchiefs wrapping their heads, chanted slogans. A young woman in her underwear, sporting peace signs sang a lyrical Kumbaya. Mixed among the "Protesters" were supporters of the president. One 19-year-old man shouted obscenities at anyone expressing dissatisfaction with the president, encouraging the police to "tazar" the "Stinking Protesters." Neither the "Protestors [sic]" nor the police harassed this vocal young man. Across the street, individuals shouting support for the president were allowed to continue. Officers monitored this group but allowed them to shout words of support or hurl derisions toward Kerry supporters, undisturbed. Honking cars filled with Bush supporters were left alone. A honking car full of Kerry supporters was stopped by police on its way out of town.

The standoff with "Protesters" continued until the president finished his dinner and was secured in his hotel cottage for the night. Only then were the riot police ordered to "mount-up," leaping upon the sideboard of a huge SUV, pulling out of town, and allowing "free speech" to resume.

In small town America I witnessed true repression and intimidation by law enforcement. I saw small children suffering from the effects of being fired upon by pepper bullets. I felt legitimate fear of expressing my political opinions: a brand new feeling. Newspaper accounts state the chaos started when a violent "Protester" shoved a police officer. No one I talked to witnessed this account.

It is reputed that President Bush and his staff will not allow any opposition activity to occur within his earshot or eye sight. I can confirm, that in tiny Jacksonville, Oregon, this was true. Physically violent means were taken to protect the president from verbal insults. Freedom of speech was stolen.

My father was not paranoid as he lay dying. He was expressing great insight into the dangers of our current presidential administration and its willingness to repress personal freedoms. If I could talk to my father today, I would say, "I am sorry Daddy for doubting you." And, no matter what, I will continue to exercise my individual right to freely express my opinions. Americans cannot take four more years.

FROM DEBI SMITH, 10/21/04

Last week, both vice presidential nominee John Edwards and President George W. Bush visited Southern Oregon. Considering the area is relatively rural, sparsely populated, and Oregon is a state that usually gets little attention in a presidential election, it was an unprecedented and rather exciting occasion. I decided to try and get tickets to both events for my kids and myself.

Getting tickets from the Jackson County Democratic Party Headquarters for the Edwards event was pleasant and easy. They didn't ask me to declare a party, didn't ask who I was voting for, didn't ask me to provide personal information or a DNA sample.

Not so at the Jackson County GOP headquarters. First they wanted to know my name, address, phone number, email, and my driver's license number. "Do they really have the time, funds, and need to run all this data through some security check? What are they afraid of?" I asked myself. But hey, if it'll get me some tickets, I'll grudgingly fill out the application.

It didn't get me the tickets. "Are you a Bush supporter?" I was asked. I explained that I was a registered Independent and not necessarily a Bush supporter. "Are you going to vote for Bush?" I was asked. "No," I honestly, and out of curiosity to see what would happen, replied. I was summarily told that if I wasn't planning on voting for Bush, I wasn't welcome. "John" came over to make sure I got the message. I told him I'd taken my kids to similar events (we saw Clinton and Gore in 1996) and didn't he think it was good to get my kids involved in the democratic process early? To take them to events such as these and let them make up their own minds? I guess not. He just kept repeating, in a rather intimidating way, that if I wasn't a supporter, I wasn't welcome. (Funny how he wasn't worried about how this sort of attitude might affect the future of the Republican Party. Hmm.)

I initially found the whole thing absurdly funny even though I was shaking (intimidation will do that to you) as I walked out of GOP headquarters. As the day wore on and the more I reflected on the starkly different experiences I'd had at both head-quarters, the more frustrated and indignant I became. What is happening in this country that my children and I are kept out of a rally for the man who is currently our president? I had no intention whatsoever of causing any disturbances or protesting the event in any way. We're a homeschooling family that uses a variety of life experiences and opportunities as our classroom. This was simply just another unique event for my children and I to attend and learn from.

Incidentally, I observed nary a protest during the entire Edwards rally the following day, despite the fact there had been no effort to keep anyone out based on their viewpoints or political affiliations. Why couldn't the Bush Campaign and the GOP behave in the same congenial and democratic fashion, I wondered, and again asked myself, "What are they afraid of?" I even tried to come up with a new acronym for the GOP. Grand Old Paranoia came to mind.

Feeling more and more outraged by the sanitation of the Bush event, I decided to attend the unWelcome Bush rally to be held in Jacksonville. Jacksonville is a tiny little dot on the map (pop. 2,245). It's a well-preserved gold mining town that now houses museums, tiny boutiques, eateries, and small inns. Bush would be spending the night here following his presumptuous and premature "Victory Rally" being held a few miles away in Central Point. A politically active friend of mine had organized the peaceful demonstration and had spoken several times with local authorities, informing them of the event, and asking all the pertinent questions. She was told that as long as people remained on the sidewalks, there should be no problem and that they were there to protect the president as well as our right to peaceably assemble.

Our group started out small, 70 or so people carrying signs, water bottles, video cameras, and children. As the evening wore on more people began gathering—Bush supporters and protesters alike. There were several blockades, manned by security, at different intersections to the west of where we were. People, to my knowledge, were respecting the requests not to move beyond the blockades as well as continuing to respect the request to keep to the sidewalks. When a helicopter started making low passes overhead, a portion of the motorcycle motorcade came by, and a throng of riot cops made their appearance guarding the west end of the block, we assumed the president was on his way. Everything continued to remain fairly calm, even with the mixture of chanting from both sides.

Suddenly, an officer within the line of riot cops ordered the crowd to move back two blocks to 5th Street. They allowed about four seconds for this to sink in and then started pushing us back by moving forward in a line. The sidewalks could not contain the sudden movement of people, and subsequently the streets became crowded and chaotic. If their desire for us to move had been communicated earlier, or if that portion of the street had been blocked off to begin with, people probably would have, in general, respected it, even though we were in our legal right to be in the vicinity. But instead, the authorities in charge chose to create confusion and conflict instead of wisely diffusing it ahead of time. And the result was an unnecessary melee: sudden gunfire; people running, falling, being shot with pepper bullets; children upset by the gunfire, and coughing from the pepper; women who were carrying their children being grabbed and pushed violently; people daring to ask questions being forcibly pushed and intimidated. It must be reiterated, this event was organized to be peaceful, non-violent, and family friendly. And, even though there was a mixed demographic on the street, the event remained non-violent and relatively peaceful . . . except for the actions of a few of the less than restrained riot cops. Riot cops, who were, we have to remind ourselves, taking orders from a higher command.

I fully expected to see the presence of the secret service, the snipers, and a multitude of officers at this event. What I didn't expect to see was a completely unnecessary use of extreme force in a situation that clearly didn't warrant it. If there was, and to my knowledge there wasn't, anyone doing something illegal or outside their constitutional rights, then why couldn't a couple of these well-trained officers peacefully remove the offenders? I was at the front of the crowd when the mayhem broke out and I saw nothing that would warrant shooting pepper bullets, especially into a crowd so full of young children.

After returning home from this disturbing event, I turned on the news. The only thing that aired on my local NBC affiliate regarding the event was an interview with a Bush supporter in the darkened street. I did learn later that a couple other outlets offered a slightly more balanced, though still sanitized, viewpoint. Several independent video clips documenting the overuse of force have also been sent to various media outlets over the past few days, and to my knowledge, none have been aired. More sanitation. Could this be happening all over the country? How many valid stories are going unreported by the major media? Or are they so sanitized as to be a faint glimmer of the actual truth?

Afterword:
State of Denial

I

On the evening of October 28, 2005, I met briefly with John Kerry at a fundraiser in a Manhattan townhouse. The hardcover edition of this book had just been published, and I wanted to hand him a copy and hear his thoughts about the problem of election fraud in the United States. As I had written *Fooled Again* to throw a spotlight on that rising civic threat—a danger to democracy not only in this country but throughout the world—I hoped the senator would pay attention and help to put this all-important issue on the national agenda. (Someone close to him, sharing my concern, had set up the meeting.) We spoke for about ten minutes.

As there was not much time, I got right to the point: "You were robbed, Senator," I told him, handing him the book. "I *know!*" he shot back, with a look of frazzled outrage, and proceeded to deplore the strange disinterest of his fellow Democrats in Washington: "They won't talk about it!" Just the week before, he said, he had tried to broach the subject with his

Senate colleague Christopher Dodd (D-CT), telling him that something must be done about the computerized voting machines.[1] "I told him, 'Chris, these machines are dangerous.' And he got mad! He said, 'We looked into it, there's nothing there.'" Kerry looked at me, incredulous. "They're in denial!" he marveled. "So I need evidence. I need to show them evidence. Is there evidence in your book?"

I assured him there was. "In fact," I said, "there's actually no evidence that Bush *won*—aside from the official numbers. There's only evidence that *you* won." I recommended several works, my book included; and then made the pitch that I'd been pondering for days. After studying the evidence, I told him he should lead a major senatorial investigation of the state of the U.S. election system. Such an effort would both profit him politically and help save our foundering Republic. "There are a lot of Democrats out there who would be thrilled to see you take this on," I said. (This was a diplomatic way of saying that a lot of Democrats were still enraged by his concession in 2004.) Specifically, I urged him to attack election fraud as he had dealt with Iran/Contra and BCCI, spearheading strong investigations of both scandals—"the highlight of your senatorial career," I said in all sincerity. And then I added bluntly that there was, of course, far more at stake than his political career, and more than the survival of the Democratic Party—that the future of American democracy itself could be at risk, unless he helped to force this taboo subject out into the light of day.

"Yes, someone ought to do that," Kerry answered thoughtfully. "But I don't know if *I* can be the one—because of the 'sour grapes' factor." "Yes, that is a problem," I replied, "but it may not be as serious as you think. You'll be able to say, in good conscience, that you really did believe you'd lost; but that having looked carefully into the evidence, you must regretfully conclude that the official tally may be illegitimate. And that this is finally not about your own political career, but about the welfare of American democracy," etc. Thus, all fired up by his unexpected ardor, I was writing him a speech.

Kerry told me he was eager to go through the book, and that we'd keep in touch, and then he punctuated that assurance with a hearty little sequence of fraternal gestures: a go-get-'em sock on the arm, a chummy wink, a big thumbs-up. I left the townhouse greatly heartened—less by Kerry's jockstrap camaraderie (although I sure enjoyed it) than by his frank claim to have seen the light. In my view, his speedy cave-in had been just as catastrophic as the bogus "victory" that it seemingly confirmed; and so his new and darker view, and apparent willingness to look more deeply into that election, could spark just the sort of shattering re-assessment that must finally lead to genuine reform. After all, the press ignored the evidence of fraud in large part because Kerry had dismissed it. Once he had revisited that evidence, I felt quite sure that the journalists would also take another look at it.

Four days later, on Tuesday, November 1, my book tour started in New York. At the podium throughout that week, I told of my exchange with Kerry, as the question of his prompt surrender came up everywhere I spoke, and there was certainly no better way to answer it than to recount that conversation. On Friday morning, November 4, I told the story to a national audience, in the course of a debate with journalist Mark Hertsgaard on Amy Goodman's national radio show *Democracy Now!* Hertsgaard was the author of a recent piece in *Mother Jones* claiming that there was no solid evidence of fraud ixn the Ohio presidential race. (The piece disputed several works, including *Fooled Again*.) For all his doubts, Hertsgaard was audibly impressed by

Kerry's new position. "I think Mark Crispin Miller has given us a major news flash here, and kind of buried the lead!" he said. "If Kerry thinks that the election was stolen, that is big, big news!" He wondered, rightly, why it took the senator a year to question the results in Ohio, and then concluded: "It is entirely plausible that this election was stolen, and, above all, that what we need is a real investigation." On that point we agreed completely.

By noon the "big, big news" was all over the Internet, the show's producers having hurried out a press release: "Kerry Told Me He Now Thinks the Election Was Stolen."[2] The news incited maelstroms of e-commentary all that afternoon, with many posters thrilled at Kerry's willingness, at last, to raise his voice, and many more lambasting him for going AWOL in the first place. The former take struck me as more productive: "Believe me, I understand, and share, your feelings of impatience at the senator's long silence," I posted on one thread at DemocraticUnderground.com. "But if he'll champion the issue of electoral reform, we stand to gain much more than we can get from merely cursing him for his timidity. I therefore would advise you all to shower him with strong encouragement ASAP."[3]

It seemed to be a promising debate; and then, a few hours later, Kerry's office killed it. They issued a statement categorically denying that the senator and I had ever had our conversation. While it was true that I had given him a copy of my book, said Jenny Backus, one of Kerry's aides, the dialogue that I'd reported was my own invention, prompted by a craving for publicity and a near-psychotic zeal. "I know Mr. Miller is trying to sell his book, and he feels passionately about his thesis," she told John Byrne of Raw Story, "but his recent statements about his conversation with Senator Kerry are simply not true." Backus said that I should stop "misrepresenting" Kerry and start applauding his bold leadership in Congress on the issue of election reform. "Make no mistake," said Backus, in conclusion, "after pouring his heart and soul into the campaign and seeing George Bush continue the mess he created, if the election had been stolen, John Kerry would be fighting them today to reverse the outcome."[4]

II

I wrote this book to set the record straight—a daunting project, as the facts were scattered and submerged in oceans of disinformation; but a job that I felt certain I could manage, with the help of countless others who had witnessed crimes, or crunched the funny numbers, or examined the insane machinery, or discerned the partisan design in all those seeming random "glitches" and "mistakes," or scrutinized the ballots (if any), or filed lawsuits, or waylaid furtive bureaucrats, or otherwise exposed the continental crime spree that was Bush's "re-election." Such labors had produced an ever-growing body of clear evidence that Bush was "re-elected" not by any actual majority but through various and pervasive fraud. And yet that evidence had been ignored, or laughed off, by the very interests that, it would seem, had the most to gain from looking into it. You would, of course, expect mere snide dismissal from Bush/Cheney and their henchmen in the GOP. You would surely not expect it from the Democrats, who, if the system's rigged, can never be assured of winning even when they really win. And you would not expect the press to discount or jeer at the evidence without inspecting it, as newsfolk always love a scandal, and this one is, without doubt, the biggest scandal of them all.

And yet, far from studying the evidence, the press and Democrats alike were, from the outset, strangely adamant in their refusal even to admit that anything was wrong. As I note here in Chapter 2, the journalistic hooting started right after Election Day. The *New York Times*, *Washington Post*, *Boston Globe*, *Baltimore Sun*, *San Francisco Chronicle* and others snickered at the "rumors," "fantasy," "paranoia" and—above all—"conspiracy theories" allegedly Out There in "the blogosphere" and other crazy places. That sort of blunt derision soon subsided (in the corporate media), giving way to an all-but-total silence on the subject. As I point out here as well, the journalists, with very few exceptions, also suppressed the so-called Conyers Report, despite its wealth of solid evidence that there was something rotten in Ohio. From the date of its release—January 5, 2005—for many months, those Americans who didn't watch Keith Olbermann or tune in Amy Goodman (or get their news online) were unlikely ever to have heard of that report, so total was the blackout by the Fourth Estate.

For their part, most high-profile Democrats responded just as mutely to the evidence of Bush & Co.'s rampant fraud. The Kerry campaign didn't want to know about it even when it was ongoing. When Robert Hagan, a Democrat and state senator in Youngstown, Ohio, tried to cast his vote for Kerry, the machine kept flipping it into a vote for Bush. Hagan notified the Kerry/Edwards people. "Leave it alone," they told him. "Don't talk about it. It's not something we want to get out."[5] Evidently this was Kerry's attitude from that day on. The should-be U.S. president was noticeably absent from the fracas in Ohio and shunned the subject afterward for months (as we have seen).[6] This despite the fact the he still had some $15 million of campaign funds left—much of it raised precisely for the purpose of challenging a fishy outcome—and so he could have helped immensely with the post-election legal battles in Ohio, if he had only bothered to acknowledge them.

But it wasn't only Kerry who kept mum. From that Election Day until the next one two years later (and thereafter), few top Democrats would breathe a word about the ever-mounting evidence of fraud. It was only in the summer of 2006, with the midterm races looming, that some dared to broach the subject, once or twice. Speaking to an ACORN conference in Columbus on July 10, Hillary Clinton took a tacit shot at Blackwell: "I know there's been a problem here in Ohio, and I hope everybody in Ohio is watching this election like a hawk!" The place went wild, but if she ever brought it up again there is no public record of it. (That little flash of honesty was too much for the local press: "Clinton feeds theory of election vote tampering," ran the headline in the *Cincinnati Enquirer.*)[7] Howard Dean was slightly bolder, noting his concern about election fraud in a few interviews, once even going so far as to declare the e-voting machinery "a serious problem that faces American democracy."[8] On Aug. 23, six weeks before Election Day, as chairman of the DNC Dean sent out a strong e-mail on "Republican efforts to disenfranchise voters and suppress Democratic turnout this November," soliciting donations to enhance the party's "voter protection operation."[9] It was, of course, a little late—especially for the computer-savvy Dean, who had known about the dangers of e-voting for some time. In April of 2005, guest-hosting *Topic A with Tina Brown* on CNBC, he himself had hacked a Diebold machine, right on camera, with the guidance of election reform activist Bev Harris.[10]

Thus Dean already knew enough, and was of course well-placed to push for strong corrective measures long before the next campaign, instead of issuing alerts (or one alert) two weeks before Election Day. For all we know, he may have tried—but if he did, he clearly had no backing from the party, which was no more inclined than the Republicans to deal forthrightly with the threat of fraud. As cautious as they were, both Dean and Sen. Clinton were obsessive babblers on the subject in comparison to their fellow Democrats, whose long and stony silence would have awed John Gotti. However liberal or partisan, and even if they had themselves been burned by Bush & Co.'s GOP, they would not mention the 2004 election or address the grievous problems that it raised. Aside from such rare birds as Conyers, Robert Wechsler, Barbara Lee, Stephanie Tubbs-Jones, Dennis Kucinich, the meteoric Cynthia McKinney, Rush Holt, Henry Waxman, Jan Schakowsky, Carolyn Maloney and (for a while) Barbara Boxer, as well as the Congressional Black Caucus, the Democrats have mostly been as silent as the tomb. Even though they have all been assailed with pleas for help from worried citizens, there's been no comment from such "losers" as Al Gore, John Edwards, Max Cleland, Walter Mondale, Tom Strickland or Joe Lieberman (who had no problem with Bush/Cheney's "win" but then went bonkers over his legitimate defeat by Ned Lamont in the Democratic primary in Connecticut). On Bush/Cheney's "re-election" and its implications, Bill Clinton spoke publicly in June of 2006 (a moment that the media ignored).[11] On the other hand, as of this writing there has been no comment from Barack Obama, Dianne Feinstein, Patrick Leahy, Robert Byrd, Chuck Schumer, Russ Feingold, Ted Kennedy, Dick Durbin, Joe Biden, Tom Harkin, Frank Lautenberg or any other infamously "liberal" senator, and none from Nancy Pelosi, Barney Frank, John Murtha, Rahm Emanuel, Bernie Sanders, Jerry Nadler and most other liberals and party stalwarts in the House.

The party's strange refusal to perceive Bush/Cheney's civic crimes became explicit and official on June 22, 2005, with the DNC's release of its report, "Democracy at Risk: The 2004 Election in Ohio."[12] Having reconfirmed the evidence of fraud, the report concludes that there's no evidence of fraud—an assertion based entirely on weird math and wishful thinking. The report's self-contradiction is astonishing. On p. 5 of Sec. 2, for example, the study notes that "scarcity of voting equipment caused long lines and deterred people from voting. These problems varied significantly by race and [by] type of voting machine." Those using DRE machines were forced to wait the longest—especially in urban Franklin County, where "there were also proportionally fewer voting machines in [the] minority neighborhoods than in its predominantly white neighborhoods." And statewide, "African-American voters reported waiting an average of 52 minutes before voting while white voters reported waiting an average of 18 minutes." Although those figures grossly understate the inequalities—such "averages" mislead, as countless Democrats, and few Republicans, were forced to wait in line for several hours—this overview agrees with every other source that those long lines were disproportionately evident at Democratic polling places.

And then, with Orwellian agility, the study's authors turn black into white. On p. 2 of Sec. 3, they come up, out of nowhere, with this reassurance: "Despite the problems on Election Day, there is no evidence from our survey that John Kerry won the state of Ohio." What about all those long lines?

Two (2) percent of voters who went to the polls on Election Day decided to leave their polling locations due to the long lines. This resulted in approximately 129,543 lost votes. However, these potential voters would have divided evenly between George Bush and John Kerry.

Since we already know, from the report itself, that far more Democrats were forced (or "decided") "to leave their polling places due to the long lines," it is not clear exactly *how* "these potential voters would have divided evenly" between the parties. The mystery deepens when we check the authors' methodology. All that very precise analysis, a footnote tells us, is based on a survey of 1,201 would-be voters. One might argue that that number is a bit too low to tell us much about the mass disenfranchisement in Ohio; and 2 percent of that wee sample is, of course, much smaller still. (On the next page, that percentage changes without explanation: "Three (3) percent of voters who went to the polls left their polling places and did not return due to the long lines.") This means that the DNC's analysts interviewed some 24 would-be voters, of whom 12 (or so) said they would certainly have voted for Bush/Cheney if they had not "decided" that they'd better go to work, or hurry home to nurse an ailing relative, or pick their kids up at the day-care center, or get back to the task of trying to find a job.

Although "Democracy at Risk" is dense with pages of equations, its purpose was apparently not scientific but political: i.e., to put a lot of miles between the Democratic Party and John Conyers, whose solid research on the crime spree in Ohio evidently irked the DNC or some factions in it.[13] For all its buried evidence of fraud, the DNC report purveys the far more comfortable notion that the problems in Ohio were inadvertent—simple glitches, random accidents and genuine mistakes. To that narcotic view the "liberal media" was noticeably more receptive than it had been to the Conyers study. As noted here, the latter never surfaced in the *New York Times*, which, on the other hand, reported bluntly that the DNC "did not find evidence of widespread election fraud that might have contributed to President Bush's narrow victory there" and that "Democratic officials could not conclude [that Kerry] would have won in Ohio even if voting had gone smoothly."[14] The Ohio press repeated the refrain: "The survey found those voters would have likely divided equally between Bush and Kerry," claimed the *Dayton Daily News*, and the *Cleveland Plain Dealer* invoked the DNC's "strong evidence against the claim that widespread fraud systematically misallocated votes from Kerry to Bush."

Meanwhile, the mighty propaganda organs of the right either re-echoed that faux-exculpation far and wide ("Dems Find No Vote Fraud in Ohio," blared NewsMax.com, in a punchy paraphrase of AP's coverage), or, typically, *attacked* the DNC for excessive partisan belligerence and failure to acknowledge *Democratic* "voter fraud." According to the *Washington Post*, RNC chair Ken Mehlman dismissed the report as "pure political fiction," pointing to widespread reports throughout Ohio, where Democratic campaign activists submitted thousands of bogus voter-registration cards in an attempt to tip the state into the Democratic column. And Fox News noted gleefully that Howard Dean was forced to "back off" his initial claim that Ohio's GOP engaged in "massive voter suppression."

One scholar involved in the study quickly backed away from that notion. "Where the partisan bias came from, where it went, we really have no basis for making any assertion about that and I don't believe the report makes any statements about that," said Cornell University professor of government Walter Mebane, Jr. Dean was forced to come back later and amend his statement. "While we certainly couldn't draw a proven conclusion that this was willful, it certainly has the appearance of impropriety," he said.[15]

Thus the whole Establishment—the two parties and the media, both "liberal" and "conservative"—had reached a mad consensus: that there was no evidence of fraud in the 2004 election. That is how things stood in the summer of 2005; and as fall approached, there was no change in that consensus, even as more evidence of fraud kept coming out from highly reputable sources. Although such evidence was well known to the few of us who knew to look for it, the general public was completely in the dark, because the press and Democrats alike ignored it, letting it bounce off their iron certainty that, in this great democracy, there is no need to fret about election fraud.[16]

In October, the Government Accountability Office came out with an ominous report—indeed, a shocker, notwithstanding its narcotic title: "Elections: Electronic Voting Systems Are Under Way, but Key Activities Need to Be Completed." (The report is available online at http://www.gao.gov/new.items/d05956.pdf.) Through an exhaustive study of the e-voting machinery produced by several different manufacturers, the GAO discovered a broad range of fatal flaws in the security of those devices, whose use was quickly spreading nationwide. (In 2004, 23 percent of the U.S. electorate had cast their votes, or tried to cast them, on paperless DRE machines. By the 2006 election the rate was 39 percent.) Contrary to the soothing claims of Diebold and ES&S, the GAO revealed a system so susceptible to fraud that even a non-paranoid might think it was designed that way.

Through it, a sly operative could secretly and quickly flip the vote-count, as the machines "did not encrypt cast ballots or system audit logs, [so that] it was possible to alter both without being detected." The GAO also discovered that some of the machines' supervisory functions were not password-protected, so that anyone with access to just one machine could play games with an entire network. The machines themselves could easily be programmed to flip individual votes: "It was possible to alter the files that define how a ballot looks and works so that the votes for one candidate could be recorded for a different candidate." These and other chilling revelations in the GAO report made it crystal clear that the machinery could be rigged precisely as the evidence suggested that it had been in the last election.

That fact probably explains the vast and eerie journalistic silence that followed the release of the report. Certainly it can't be that the source was unreliable or that the work was sloppy, as the GAO—the investigative arm of Congress—has long been widely hailed both for the excellence of its research and its non-partisan integrity. The report, moreover, was flagged urgently by a bipartisan assemblage of twelve congressmen, led by John Conyers, and including Henry Waxman, Sherwood Boehlert and James Sensenbrenner. Yet it might as well have come from Syria or the North American Man-Boy Love Association, for all the coverage it received. "*Not a single wire service* (AP, Reuters, UPI, AF, et al.) nor the *NY Times* nor the *Washington Post* has even run a single paragraph on the landmark GAO report or even the news release to our knowledge," BradBlog.com reported on November 1.[17] The AP finally broke the silence on November 30, mentioning the report in the fifth sentence of an article about the state of HAVA (Help America Vote Act) readiness throughout the nation. Otherwise, the only piece that dealt with the report appeared on the invaluable website (www.freepress.org) created by election reform activists Bob Fitrakis and Harvey Wasserman.

That very thorough article was posted on October 26, 2005, and so it edified about 9,000 unique visitors a day, here in our nation of 300,000,000 people.[18]

The story of the GAO report was not the only major vote-related news killed softly by the media that week. There was a shady victory for Diebold in North Carolina, where a court had ordered the evasive company to put its programming codes in escrow, or its machines could not be certified, as required by law. Diebold refused, threatening to pull out of the Tar Heel State—and then, within three days, the State Board of Elections simply waived the law and certified the company's wares anyway (despite fierce grass-roots opposition). In California, where Diebold's wares had been de-certified by Secretary of State Kevin Shelley, there was a grass-roots push to get Shelley's successor, Bruce McPherson, to extend the ban. (In retribution, Shelley had been forced from office by a hail of claims that he had violated ethics rules: charges that were groundless, as it turned out afterward.) Diebold showily agreed to a big public demonstration of the hackability of its machines, apparently to prove that this could not be done—and now that offer turned out to be fake, with Diebold stipulating that the hacker could touch only those machines that Diebold had prepared for him; and so the seeming deal collapsed. (McPherson shortly certified Diebold's machines, despite fervent grass-roots opposition.) And in Georgia, there was a legal setback for a law requiring voters to present state-issued photo IDs at the polls—a law that ultimately passed (despite fierce grass-roots opposition). Those were only some of the big vote-related stories of that week, and the next week there were several others, and many, many more throughout the weeks thereafter, but few of them made any news off-line.[19]

III

Such was the climate when *Fooled Again* came out. It was maddening to see the gravest news consistently ignored or buried, while the headlines and the anchors blared of trifles. In that last week of October 2005, the top stories in the mainstream media were Bush's trip to Mar del Plata, Argentina, for the fourth annual Summit of the Americas, the world premiere of *Harry Potter and the Goblet of Fire*, and, less trivial, an odd outbreak of tornadoes that took 20 lives in Indiana and Kentucky. (There was also word of high malfeasance by the Bush administration—broad and groundless FBI surveillance of U.S. citizens on U.S. soil; a DIA report that undermined the claims of an alleged "al Qaeda" witness to Saddam Hussein's vast secret weapons program—but that news was not prominent, although it got more play than anything concerning our elections.) And yet I was still optimistic, for I believed—and do believe—that once the people know what's really happening, they will tend to make the right decision; and I also thought that the Establishment's resistance to the story of election fraud was largely based on unawareness, fortified by a professional distaste for highly complicated problems and forbidding technical complexities. It seemed to me that one might break down that resistance with a lucid and compelling argument, fully documented, showing that Bush/Cheney's fraud was rampant nationwide and not just in Ohio. As I had tried, in *Fooled Again*, to do just that, I was hopeful that the book might at long last induce the media, the Democrats and principled Republicans to take a new look at the evidence, and help to get the word out to the people; for I was certain that the people, once they finally knew the story, would respond.

It was in that optimistic spirit that I spoke to Kerry on October 28[20] and then went on to talk about our conversation publicly throughout the week. When his aide denied it I was shocked (no doubt naïvely), and at first incensed. When Raw Story phoned me for a comment, I called Kerry's turnabout "contemptible," and, I must admit, felt meanly gratified by all the e-mails I received assailing Kerry for his "flip-flop" and calling him some very nasty names. The consensus was that Kerry's move reflected on his character, and that a politician less weak-kneed would not have caved (again).

At first I bought that judgment; but the more I thought about it, the less sense it made and the more irrelevant it seemed. There was something odd in Kerry's recantation—something that eluded the ad hominem interpretation of his public U-turn on November 4. According to that view, he had denied our conversation out of simple cravenness: a fear that the Establishment and/*or* the right would call him "paranoid" or "a sore loser" if he did not loudly foreswear his reported heresy. And that is surely how the senator himself perceived his situation. He had made this clear in mentioning "the sour grapes factor" as a reason why it might be hard for him to spearhead a congressional investigation; and those alleged qualms were soon corroborated by another witness.

Two days later, on November 6, the investigative journalist Robert Parry bolstered my account of Kerry's views with an article that quoted Jonathan Winer, a longtime Kerry adviser. Back in November and December of 2004, Winer said, Kerry had been deeply troubled by the evidence of fraud throughout Ohio: the countless e-votes flipping automatically from Kerry to Bush (while there were none that went the other way); the statewide shortages of e-voting machines in Democratic precincts only;

the exit polls that showed a Kerry win. Although he had grave doubts about Bush/Cheney's win, however, Kerry kept them to himself, apparently because he feared the right would bash him and the press would censure him (and the Democrats, no doubt, would run for cover). According to Winer, Kerry thought he couldn't find sufficient evidence to make a winning case; and he "was certain he would face withering criticism if he challenged the election results without strong evidence. 'The powers in place would have smashed him,' Winer said."[21]

That much was surely true. If Kerry *had* aired his misgivings on November 3—with or "without strong evidence"—"the powers in place would have smashed him," just as they had smashed Al Gore. And yet that likelihood itself does not sufficiently explain why he did not speak out, or even ask for just a bit more time to sort things out: as he would certainly have done had he entirely grasped the magnitude of what was happening, not just to him but to American democracy. This was (and is) a national emergency, and in emergency conditions you don't hesitate to yell, no matter what "the powers in place" or anybody else might think, unless you reassure yourself that things are really not so bad despite those rising waters or that thick smoke out there in the hall. And so John Kerry kept his mouth shut not because "the powers in place" would have gone after him, but because he could not, would not, see it as the *catastrophe* it was.

What was most striking, then, about his self-reversal was its demonstration of the very obtuseness that he had himself deplored in his own peers: "They're in denial!" That he was "robbed" the senator was smart enough to understand—but he understood it without really getting it. He saw enough of what had happened in Ohio to grasp intellectually that Bush & Co. had prevented or erased a lot of votes that ought to have elected him. Beyond that, however, Kerry could not go; for the implications of Bush/Cheney's "win" were far too monstrous for him to accept. That his silence was not really based on fear of censure is apparent too from his odd failure to lend even quiet assistance to those activists—David Cobb of the Green Party, and lawyers Susan Truitt, Bob Fitrakis, Cliff Arnebeck, Peter Peckarsky and John Bonifaz—who carried on the post-election legal struggle in Ohio. They got nothing from him—not one dollar from his bulging war-chest, nor a single word of interest or encouragement. Such aloofness seems to indicate that he just did not want to look too deeply into what had happened.

That Bush could "win"—*again*—despite the will of the electorate is not just one more Bush & Co. scandal, but a catastrophic crime that ought to shake us, and this system, to the roots. It means the United States is no democracy. And this means, at the very least, that the United States has no right to promote, or force, "democracy" abroad, or dictate anything to the United Nations, or pass judgment on the state of civil rights in Venezuela, Cuba or Iran. That the United States today is no democracy means also that our mainstream press has no right to look down, whether benignly or suspiciously, on the democratic throes of poorer countries. Indeed, this nation, under Bush, is now *below* the civic level of such states as Ecuador, Ukraine, South Africa and Senegal, where the democratic process is no joke. The system here is so corrupt that the Carter Center wouldn't even monitor U.S. elections, as Jimmy Carter noted on November 5, 2006, when he was in Managua to observe Nicaragua's presidential race.[22]

And once we face the truth about Bush/Cheney's "win," the implications become darker still. That this regime could thus extend itself means that the party ruling over us is neither democratic nor republican but radically opposed to popular self-government and both the letter and the spirit of the Bill of Rights. Bush/Cheney's program of electoral subversion is entirely of a piece with their systematic use of torture, mass surveillance, domestic covert propaganda, secret prisons, secret trials and other un-American devices. Under Bush, Americans no longer even have the right of habeas corpus—a Great Leap Backward that we never voted for and never would, just as we have never voted for Bush/Cheney.

This is quite a pill for any good American to swallow; and such hard truth must be especially troubling for the Democrats. If it is possible to swing U.S. elections through non-democratic means, in an anti-democratic spirit, and for anti-democratic purposes, then there is little point in all the tactical activity that now preoccupies the Democratic Party: whoring after millions, trolling for the perfect candidate, crafting a hot "message," polling all the time and everywhere, and otherwise preparing deftly for a war that has already been invisibly decided. Thus consumed with squandering their civic energy, most Democrats are just not built to battle openly and fiercely to protect democracy. Big money has long since disabled them as guardians of our revolutionary heritage—which we must now revive, or this great national experiment is over. How could any major Democrat consider such a movement? Rather than consider it, they tell themselves that there's no need for it, because "the system works."

Not all Democrats are in denial about the regime's war against American democracy. Within the party there are elements supportive of Bush/Cheney's programs, or, for venal reasons, quietly colluding with the local GOP machine. In some places—rural Ohio, Georgia, parts of Florida—there are Democrats not easy to distinguish from their nominal opponents, the parties often intermingling to preserve the status quo. Regardless of the voters' will. On January 24, 2007, two Cleveland poll workers were convicted for their part in subverting the post-election recount—a process that was "rigged," according to the prosecutor. Of those two felons working for Ken Blackwell, one was a Democrat, the other a Republican.[23] (As I note above, there are also "Democrats"—like the infamous Theresa LePore—who are really covert agents of the GOP.)[24]

Moreover, e-voting, although it's mainly a Republican obsession, has always had bipartisan support. Diebold and its bold compeers have long depended on the pliancy of Democrats, as those outfits have pockets deep enough to house whatever pol might be inclined to go along. Certainly one might assist such companies for reasons other than venality, although it's hard to figure out what those might be. Cathy Cox, the Georgia secretary of state who put Diebold in charge of that state's voting process, is a Democrat, and so, of course, is Rep. Steny Hoyer, who helped draft HAVA—a giant gift to the e-voting companies—and also has pushed Diebold's wares in Maryland (over fervent grassroots opposition). And then there is the larger fact of many Democrats' acquiescence in the face of gerrymandering, "the war on drugs," felon disenfranchisement, neo–Jim Crow laws, the post-Katrina mass detention of New Orleanians (over 70,000 by Election Day, 2006) and other measures to restrict the vote.

And yet, on the question of Bush/Cheney's "re-election," more Democrats are in denial than in collusion. This is clear from the absurdity of their main rationale for clamming up about Bush & Co.'s election fraud throughout the two years prior to the 2006 midterms: "We don't talk about it, because it might suppress the turnout." In other words, too much discussion of election fraud—or even mentioning the problem—might discourage grass-roots Democrats from voting.

As plausible as it may sound initially, that line, murmured off the record by innumerable Democrats and/or their staffers, makes even less sense than John Kerry's excuse for his long public silence. (Those two rationales, it should be noted, contradict each other, as Kerry feared that no one would believe there had been fraud, whereas, according to his fellow partisans, the danger was that *everybody* would believe it.) What if there's a massive Democratic turnout, and the Democrats "lose" anyway? All those voters will be devastated psychologically and maybe will never vote again, since no one ever spoke out loud about the possibility of fraud. (This is basically what happened after the election in 2004.) Not only is this rationale absurd and dangerous, it is profoundly cynical; for no Democratic Party worth the name should ever try to win by keeping its constituents in the dark. That sort of thing is doomed to fail in any case. We the People must be full participants in our own governance, or our elections are a waste of time. An informed electorate *will* turn out, no matter how dispiriting the news, as long as they believe in the ideals of their democracy. (This happened on Election Day 2006.)

The Democrats who used that rationale were surely smart enough to sense how dumb it was; and yet they used it anyway, because they very badly needed not to face the truth about our national predicament. In private, however, they did at least admit that there was a problem not to talk about. Others seem to have convinced themselves that there was simply not a problem, and therefore no need either to keep silent *or* speak out about it. In late November, on a late-night train back home from a bookstore event in Philadelphia, I ran into Rep. Jerry Nadler, a liberal New York Democrat, who was in the club car schmoozing with the Amtrak employees. I handed him a copy of this book. "Oh, yeah," he said, with a dismissive wave, "I've seen that." "No, no—I'm the author!" I said hastily (as I should have in the first place), and he made up for the inadvertent slight by snapping smartly into great-to-see-ya mode. "*Hey! Thanks!* I hope you signed it," etc.

I settled down to shoot the breeze with him and got right into it. "Say, what's happening down there, about the election? What are the Democrats doing about the fraud, and all that stuff?" We were leaning back against the window, chatting comfortably over the seat divider. He went vague. "Well, you know . . . Bush won Ohio by—what?—400,000 votes? So he would have won anyway. . . . " His voice trailed off, and he looked away. In my amazement I said something meant to get him to elaborate, but he was clearly not inclined to push the subject any further, so I changed the subject, and shortly went back to my seat.

I was amazed by his reply because I knew that Nadler was a member of the House Judiciary Committee and that he had participated fully in the Conyers inquiry. He therefore had to know that Bush had "won" Ohio by about 118,000 votes, not 400,000—a number crazily inflated far beyond the propaganda estimates of Bush's own most feral followers. Nadler is intelligent, progressive, well-informed. He made that weird mistake, I would suggest, because, right then and there, he needed some good-sounding reason not to care about Bush/Cheney's second coup. And so, in Nadler's mind, the Democrats weren't dealing with the fraud because there wasn't any fraud for them to deal with.

IV

After my apache dance with Kerry, I went on touring all across the country, drawing large and keenly interested crowds in states both "blue" and "red," and finding that it wasn't only Democrats who craved some truth about the last election. I got the same bipartisan—or, better yet, non-partisan—reception as an interviewee on the radio, doing countless (local) shows from Maine to Utah, from Florida to Oregon, thereby discovering further evidence that Americans are neither the apathetic boobs conceived by many liberals nor the foaming dittoheads exhorted daily by Rush, Hannity, O'Reilly and La Coulter. In short, I found the good news in this book—that there is no pro-Bush majority in these United States—confirmed by my experience promoting it.

It had been a year since the 2004 election—an eon in the culture of TV—and yet the subject was still fresh, as the news on the election front was always bad. By this I mean not only that the Bush machine was still committing brazen civic crimes from coast to coast but that the press continued to ignore them. Take the vote on Tuesday, November 8, 2005, on a proposed amendment of Ohio's constitution. It was an amazing feat that such a plan was even on the ballot, as the state GOP had gone all out to block it; but the coalition pushing it prevailed, with a momentous slate of four election reform propositions. Issue Two would allow all Ohioans to vote by mail (an innovation based on the successful mail-in vote program in Oregon); Issue Three would radically cap campaign contributions to political candidates; Issue Four would create an independent election commission, which would be empowered to create competitive legislative districts; and Issue Five would replace Ken Blackwell's wholly partisan machine with a new bipartisan board of supervisors that would henceforth administer Ohio's elections.

Although not perfect—the plan would still permit the use of DRE machines maintained by private vendors—"the amendments go a long way toward solving many of the problems encountered in the state's 2004 election," as Bob Fitrakis wrote in the *Columbus Free Press*.[25] On Issues Two and Three, the people of Ohio overwhelmingly agreed, and the other two amendments had a fighting chance, according to the *Columbus Dispatch*, which on November 6 ran the numbers from its pre-election polls:[26]

Issue Two: 59% yes, 33% no, 8% undecided
Issue Three: 61% yes, 25% no
Issue Four: 31% yes, 45% no, 25% undecided
Issue Five: 41% yes, 43% no, 16% undecided

Now imagine the surprise of rational Ohioans when they saw the official vote count, as posted on website of Sec. Blackwell:[27]

Issue Two: 36.66% yes, 63.34% no
Issue Three: 33.14% yes, 66.86% no
Issue Four: 30.30% yes, 69.70% no
Issue Five: 29.92% yes, 70.08% no

It was a staggering "upset"; and lest we think it was the pre-election polls that were all wrong and not Ken Blackwell's numbers, note what happened with another proposition—one that the Ohio GOP supported. Issue One called for an expenditure of some $2 billion, ostensibly for new state programs to attract high-tech employers to Ohio and otherwise create new jobs (actually to flood the coffers of the scandal-ridden ruling party).

In its poll published on November 6, the *Columbus Dispatch* showed that referendum passing with 53 percent of the vote. On Election Day it passed with 54 percent. (It was supported by Ohio's labor unions.)

And so the bold reformist package was "defeated" as decisively as everyone expected it to win. It was a proposal to reform the very system that was used to kill it—and that, of course, had just been used to fake a "victory" for Bush/Cheney: the same regime, the same machines, the same peculiar crashes, freezes, chaos and long lines at Democratic polling places. In short, it was another fraudulent election in Ohio, a sham as obvious as those fat history books that Bush so showily schleps around in public.

Astounding though it was, the "defeat" of those amendments in Ohio was less marvelous than the U.S. press's silence on it. The double standard is remarkable. If there had been a contest half that fishy on the West Bank or in Venezuela, the U.S. media would have been all over it, and vice versa. But it happened here; and so it evidently never happened. The national press ignored the story, while the state's big dailies quickly came out with all sorts of tidy "explanations" as to why Ken Blackwell "won": the voters were confused, or they were sick of scandal, or they wanted *real* reform and not the halfway measures on the ballot, etc. Even the *Columbus Dispatch* downplayed its own pre-election poll. "Opinion polls are a snapshot in time rather than predictive," noted the unnamed reporter, who did not mention the *Dispatch*'s strangely accurate call on Issue One.[28]

That is how "the system worked" from that point on, right through the 2006 election and beyond: the Bush machine would sabotage democracy, and the press would not report it. This has happened even when such crimes have been as brazen as a flasher at the Super Bowl. In San Diego on June 6, 2006, there was a special race to fill the empty seat of Rep. Randy Cunningham, a Bush Republican now doing time for bribery, mail fraud, wire fraud and income tax evasion. Although leading in some pre-election polls, the Democrat, Francine Busby, lost, apparently, to Brian Bilbray of the GOP. It then came out that poll workers had been asked to *take the e-voting machinery home with them* for up to 12 days prior to the race.[29] This was a jaw-dropping revelation, it being a very simple task to rig the final count by fiddling with the gadgets' memory cards. There were also many other whopping improprieties, any one of which could easily have changed the outcome, as Busby "lost" by only 4,732 votes out of a quarter million putatively cast.

At the news of those machine sleepovers, San Diegans called for an investigation and a new election. Among those outraged citizens was far-right radio host Roger Hedgecock, a frequent Limbaugh substitute and staunch Bilbray supporter. "It seems to me," he noted on his program on June 21, that "if we have *any* bedrock notion in this country, it ought to be that the votes ought to be fully and fairly counted!"[30] Meanwhile, one week after the election—and 17 days before the vote was even certified—Bilbray had flown to Washington, where Dennis Hastert, speaker of the house, summarily swore him in (when there were over 14,000 paper ballots still uncounted). Refusing to accept Hastert's anointed as their "representative," the people mobilized throughout the summer, calling for a full hand count of all the paper ballots *and* DRE receipts, while the county registrar, a Bush Republican, refused to do it. There was more organizing, a lawsuit filed, and other actions planned—and then, on August 25, the whole campaign was obviated by Superior Court Judge Yuri Hofmann, who, in his dismissal of the plaintiffs' lawsuit, tortuously argued, on the basis of Art. 1, sec. 5 of the Constitution, that the state of California had no jurisdiction once the House of Representatives had made the people's choice.

The scandal has some shocking civic implications. After all, if Dennis Hastert could choose Brian Bilbray for that seat, irrespective of the will of the electorate, why bother having House elections anywhere? Why bother with elections at all? Why not just have Congress's membership decided by the speaker of the house? Those Republicans who may not have objected to so radical a step back then would surely reconsider it, now that the Speaker is a Democrat—more evidence that Hofmann's judgment was a constitutional disaster. (The judge, moreover, ruled in Bilbray's favor after he received an ex parte communication from Paul Vinovich, Republican Counsel to the House Administration Committee, arguing for dismissal of the case.) And the San Diego scandal sheds much-needed light on the momentous question of how best to fix our voting system. Many Democrats and others have been calling for the use of "paper trails"—printers hooked up to the DRE machines, providing voters with receipts that would (apparently) record their choices, much like the receipts from ATMs. (Such is the gist of Rep. Rush Holt's bill, H.R. 811.) The Busby/Bilbray race suggests that such a fix can do no good, as San Diego's DRE machines have paper trails.

Here, then, was a story of supreme importance to the public interest, vital to the preservation of American democracy—and our free press ignored it. There was no national coverage of the sleepovers, which went unreported even in the California papers, other than the *San Diego Tribune*, the *San Francisco Chronicle* and the *Sacramento Bee*. The only national TV show to mention the sleepovers was *Lou Dobbs Tonight* on MSNBC. Nor did the left/liberal press report them. *The Nation*, Salon, *The Progressive*, *Mother Jones*, TomPaine.com, AlterNet, *The*

Village Voice and Slate, to name a few, all tuned out that news, which was scrupulously covered by Brad Friedman on his website, bradblog.com.

Thus the press was in denial,[31] like the Democrats; and, like the Democrats, the press stayed in denial right on through Election Day 2006—another day of rampant fraud and vote suppression by the Bush Republicans, as more Americans would know if our free press would report the facts instead of wishing them away. Regardless of the seeming Democratic sweep, there were, again, elections stolen in Ohio[32] and elsewhere—including San Diego, where Bilbray "won" again, after the DRE machines, again, slept over at the homes of GOP poll workers. And our elections will continue to be fraudulent until the press gets over its neurotic fear of naming the abusers of American democracy.

There was just one aspect of our electoral crisis that the press would dare to cover, and it did so far too late, and far too timidly, to provoke a timely public outcry. Starting in the spring of 2006, the press at last reported on the perils of e-voting, focusing primarily on Diebold's DRE machines. At first sporadic, the coverage steadily increased through the summer, fed by an ever-growing body of research, including an important study from the Brennan Center at New York University of the many insecurities in DRE technology; the book *Brave New Ballot* by Avi Rubin, a computer scientist at Johns Hopkins; and several other works that bolstered the longstanding verdict of all reputable experts that e-voting is a grave mistake. By Election Day there had been ample coverage of the issue, with Lou Dobbs in the forefront, and strong reports from, among others, Catherine Crier on Court TV and David Brancaccio on PBS.

It was a great breakthrough; and yet such exposés hid more than they revealed. Through excessive focus on the "glitches" in the DRE machines, they skirted all the larger questions that any thorough investigator must ask first: Have the machines miscounted Democratic and Republican votes equally? Has either party had particular relations with the companies that make and service the machines? Has either party used old-fashioned tricks and tactics to extend the disenfranchisement beyond the e-voting machinery: blocking voter-registration efforts, purging voter rolls, bullying and/or disinforming would-be voters, and so on? The answers to those questions (no, yes, yes) make clear that our democracy is under massive and sustained attack by activists committing conscious fraud, and not just plagued by random "glitches." As that fact is, so far, inadmissible, those questions are taboo. Until the press gets past that inhibition and finally speaks the f-word loud and clear, the whole debate will go astray. Our problem, finally, is not technical but civic and political; and so any high-tech fix will only make things worse, by giving us a false sense of security while leaving the offenders at the helm. We therefore must forget all nice "bipartisan" or "compromise" solutions, and steer as far as possible away from federal control. In short, the Bush Republicans, and those colluding with them actively or passively, cannot in any way help save American democracy because they themselves are the major threat to this democracy—and we can start to deal with that threat only by acknowledging that our elections have been fixed through systematic fraud.

It was, of course, to make that very point that I wrote *Fooled Again*—which, I soon discovered, wasn't going to spark the sort of national debate I'd had in mind, because the book did not officially exist. Aside from the early notices in *Publishers Weekly* and the like, the book received no national reviews in any U.S. magazine or newspaper. Of all the dailies in the country only

two—the *Columbus Dispatch* and the *Florida Sun-Sentinel*—
reviewed it; and *Fooled Again* was even scarcer on commercial
television, as I could get no interviews on any national program,
cable or terrestrial. (I did appear on *The Daily Show*, but not to
talk about the book.) The only corporate radio shows that had me
on were Michael Medved's—he being the only rightist willing to
discuss the book—and Jim Bohannan's late-night call-in show on
ABC, as well as Jesse Jackson's show on Sunday mornings.

I did not fare so well on public radio. No national NPR show
would receive me, although I had often been a guest on *Talk of the
Nation*, *The Connection*, *To the Point*, *On the Media* and *All Things
Considered*. Diane Rehm and Terry Gross both passed. I was similarly blocked by several local NPR affiliates—including Terry
Gross's station, WHYY-FM in Philadelphia, whose management
refused to broadcast paid ads for the book once they learned its
full subtitle: *How the Right Stole the 2004 Election & Why They'll
Steal the Next One Too (Unless We Stop Them)*. (As that "next one"
is now behind us, a timelier subtitle seemed appropriate for the
paperback edition.) After having given us the go-ahead, they
changed their minds once they had read the copy, nor would they
let us edit it for their approval. "We don't accept paid political
announcements," I was told by one of them. "I'm not running for
president," I answered. "I'm the author of a book." "We don't
accept paid political announcements," she replied.

And so it went for months. The book did garner many excellent reviews, online and in local weeklies; and I was often on the
air, on non-commercial radio and television: C-SPAN, Pacifica
Radio and numerous shows on independent local stations. I was a
frequent guest on Air America, with Thom Hartmann, Marc
Maron, Laura Flanders, Janeane Garofalo, Sam Seder, Randi
Rhodes, Peter Werbe and Peter B. Collins. (Al Franken, eyeing

public office, would not talk about election fraud.)[33] I did some XM radio with Dave Goodfriend, Keith Murphy and Michaelangelo Signorile. Online, I did as much as I could do without developing a stoop. Otherwise I had to hit the road, to talk about the book in person and, whenever possible, through local media.

This is no sob story, because that blackout was not a personal thing but strictly business; and the subject of election fraud is bad for business, since facing it, as noted earlier, would kill business-as-usual. This is why *all* studies of Bush/Cheney's bogus "re-election" slipped right down the memory hole. After *Fooled Again* had come and gone, much like the Conyers Report before it, several other works came out, corroborating both this book and Conyers's findings—and therefore just as quickly vanished, every writer having much the same experience as mine, or worse. Because such works could not be honestly refuted, the best way to stop them was to disappear them at their birth. Such universal silence is as sure a way to hide the truth as any bonfire or injunction.

For instance, there's the truth about Ohio. While thousands know the Conyers Report, very few Americans have even heard about the three essential books compiled by Bob Fitrakis, Harvey Wasserman and Steve Rosenfeld and published intermittently throughout the two years after the 2004 election. Conyers's investigation was enabled largely by the labors of Fitrakis and his team, who assembled the immense (and ever-growing) trove of evidence that *proves* Bush/Cheney stole Ohio. A great deal of that evidence—including much that Conyers's staff could not accommodate—is included in the team's first book, *Did George W. Bush Steal America's 2004 Election?* That doorstopper came out in May 2005, followed four months later by the slimmer and more reader-friendly sequel,

How the GOP Stole America's 2004 Election & Is Rigging 2008.
Then, just before the 2006 election, Fitrakis et al. came out with
their third and most important book (as well as their most read-
able), *What Happened in Ohio: A Documentary Record of Theft and
Fraud in the 2004 Election*, published by the New Press. Based on
scrupulous examination of the actual ballots, as well as many
other records heretofore unknown, this volume—-put together
largely by Steve Rosenfeld—nails Bush/Cheney with still further evidence of fraud—including scores of phantom ballots cast
for Bush in precinct after precinct. In short, as far as Bush's "victory" in Ohio is concerned, the work of the Fitrakis team has
clinched the case; or would, if anyone could learn that it exists.
The team's first book was glancingly attacked in *Mother Jones*
(about which more below), and their third was recommended by
MSNBC's Lou Dobbs. Otherwise, all three books have, as of
this writing, gone completely unreviewed.

So has Steve Freeman's *Was the 2004 Presidential Election
Stolen?: Exit Polls, Election Fraud, and the Official Count*, co-
authored with Joel Bleifuss (editor-in-chief of *In These Times*)
and published in June of 2006 by Seven Stories Press. The
blackout on that book was even heavier than the night that fell
on *Fooled Again*, and even more momentous than the blackout
on Fitrakis's work, which deals only with Ohio. Freeman's
book contends that Kerry won the national race, by 5 million
votes or more—a victory that was (inadvertently) revealed by
the national exit polls. The exit polls—*all* exit polls—were
then dismissed as "unreliable," at least in the United States (although not in Ukraine). Thus have the facts about those exit
polls, and exit polling generally, become illegible behind the
fog of propaganda long since settled over them. Freeman
clears the air, carefully disentangling fact from fiction and

demonstrating that those exit polls were evidently sound, and that there were, in fact, no valid arguments against them.

If there are any valid arguments against that book, they are so far unknown. Other than some passing shots fired in a *New York Times* review some six months after it was published, there have, as of this writing, been no national reviews of Freeman's book—in fact, no print reviews at all—nor any network radio or TV interviews with either author. Freeman taped an interview with Terry Gross for NPR's *Fresh Air*, but it was never broadcast.[34] Thus Freeman's book was disappeared as he himself had been after the 2004 election. As he notes in the preface, soon after Kerry's "loss" the author's qualms about the vote-count sparked the interest of reporters, and yet no press coverage resulted. Freeman's interviews with the *Washington Post* and *USA Today* did not see print, and his interview on CNN was never aired. His scheduled interview on MSNBC was canceled, because, the producers said, the jury in Scott Peterson's murder trial had reached a verdict, but they had no interest in rescheduling.

Such treatment would be understandable if Freeman, Bleifuss and the Seven Stories Press were all completely out to lunch; but in that case their thesis should have been demolished in the public interest. In any case, Freeman's lucid work has been extolled by experts of considerable standing—mathematician John Allen Paulos, political scientists Lance DeHaven-Smith, Jack Nagel and Kenneth Warren, technology consultant Bruce O'Dell, public opinion expert Michael X. Delli Carpini, dean of the Annenberg School of Communication, and others. Without a fair and cogent rebuttal, we must conclude that Freeman's argument adds up and that the refusal to discuss it makes no sense.

Also published in June 2006, Greg Palast's *Armed Madhouse* has been blacked out just like Freeman's book—a disappearance even more perverse, as Palast is an international celebrity, his publisher is not a plucky little independent but a major corporate player (Penguin) and *Armed Madhouse* is a runaway success. And yet *Armed Madhouse* has gone unreviewed—even by the *New York Times*, although it has ranked high on that newspaper's own Best Seller List. (Palast is a formidable publicist.) Certainly there could be many reasons to suppress the book, which ranges far and wide over explosive ground.[35] But its hottest pages deal with Bush & Co.'s penchant for election fraud—the theme that made Palast famous when he broke the biggest news about the theft of Florida in 2000. That crucial exposé looms large in his last bestseller, *The Best Democracy Money Can Buy*, which was also shunned throughout the corporate media, its revelations also turned out by "the liberal media."

Armed Madhouse is dangerous, not only to the Bush regime but to the press, because of Palast's thorough coverage of the theft of the 2004 election in New Mexico as well as his analysis of how the GOP plans to re-steal the White House in 2008. As we have seen, that line of inquiry is unacceptable to right and left alike. Here, in its entirety, is one of Palast's few mainstream interviews, on ABC's *Sean Hannity Show*:

SH: So this is Greg Palast?
GP: Yes. Hello, Sean.
SH: Greg Palast, the BBC Television reporter?
GP: Yes, BBC carries my reports.
SH: Well, Palast, you know what you are? You're a *putz*, Palast! You know what a *putz* is?! Well, you're a *putz!!* (Hannity hung up.)

Although the conversation was more cordial (and extensive),

Palast got essentially the same response on KQED, the NPR affiliate in San Francisco (and the only NPR affiliate to have him on), when host Michael Krasny opened with this courteous accusation of psychosis: "I'm really surprised to find that your book has a lot of very interesting information in between the unsupportable conspiracy theories."[36]

Thus we were at a standstill in our drive to get the press and/or the Democrats to break through their denial and fight the good fight openly. As all of us were academics, activists, real Democrats (like Conyers) or real investigative journalists, our work was much too easily dismissed as the weird science of some "special interest" (whatever that might be). What we needed was corroboration of the "theory" of election fraud by someone far more famous and respected than ourselves (and better-looking wouldn't hurt). Such a person joined the fray that June, when Robert F. Kennedy, Jr., came out with a devastating overview in *Rolling Stone* of what had happened in Ohio.[37] That essay was at once a careful synthesis of all the work that we and many other citizens had done and a piece of deft original reporting, including a broad range of fascinating interviews. It was scrupulously fact-checked both by Kennedy's own research team and *Rolling Stone*, whose editors also let the lawyers at it. Such precautions were a wise idea, as the piece was so much dynamite. Kennedy determined, and demonstrated, that Bush/Cheney had indeed committed massive fraud, robbing Kerry/Edwards of at least 350,000 votes—a total some three times bigger than Bush/Cheney's "win."

The media's response at first seemed promising. Kennedy got coverage far beyond our reach. He appeared on PBS with Charlie Rose, CNN with Wolf Blitzer, MSNBC with Tucker Carlson and Chris Matthews, Fox News with Neil Cavuto, Court TV with Catherine Crier, and Comedy Central with Stephen Colbert. After our long lockout by the media, that spate of national TV interviews was staggering—as was the apparent recognition by the *New York Times* that the 2004 election was a travesty. On June 12, Bob Herbert's column—"Those Pesky Voters"—was devoted to the article in *Rolling Stone*, which "leaves no doubt that the democratic process was trampled and left for dead in the Buckeye State. Kerry almost certainly would have won Ohio if all of his votes had been counted, and if all of the eligible voters who tried to vote for him had been allowed to cast their ballots." Herbert ended with a trumpet blast of patriotic outrage, calling on "Democrats, the media and ordinary voters . . . to fight back."

> The right to vote is supposed to mean something in the United States. The idea of going to war overseas in the name of the democratic process while making a mockery of that process here at home is just too ludicrous.[38]

So strong a statement was extraordinary for the *Times*, which from the start had largely whistled past the civic crisis, tuning out most news on the election front, and featuring no op-ed columns on the problems with the last election *or* the one to come. (The paper did, and does, run frequent unsigned editorials, by Adam Cohen, on election matters nationwide—excellent work, but far too circumspect.) Herbert's battle cry, we thought, portended a dramatic shift away from the repressive quietism of the paper that had urged Al Gore to quit the race before the votes were counted, obscured the fact that Gore had really won in Florida, then did the same with Kerry in Ohio. And if the *Times* had been enlightened by the piece in *Rolling Stone*, so, we hoped, would the other "liberal media." The day that Herbert's piece came out, Kennedy was a guest on Brian Lehrer's show on WNYC-FM, New York City's NPR affiliate—a hopeful sign that where the *Times* had finally gone, NPR et al. would follow. So we were pleased to see that Herbert's column evidently carried weight within the paper. Two days later, the *Times* ran three supportive letters (one written by myself) expressing hope that it would henceforth pay more attention to the rising threats against "the democratic process."

It was high time for an awakening by the media, and not just for the abstract reason that our democracy depends on dogged journalistic oversight. The *Rolling Stone* piece should have been much bigger news because it was a record-breaking popular success, that issue selling over twice as many copies as any other in the history of the magazine and reaching millions through the Internet. And yet such ardent public interest had no influence on the media—which, after all those cable shows and Herbert's piece, just dropped the subject. Kennedy's article received no serious coverage in any national daily or newsmagazine, or on national TV or radio. It was mentioned only to be ridiculed, as various comedians who had not read it played it for a laugh.[39]

"Does the president believe Kennedy has raised any new evidence of voter fraud?" rightist shock jock Les Kinsolving asked Bush & Co. press secretary Tony Snow at a White House briefing. "No," Snow chuckled. "What I think he *will* do is let *you*, Lester, be his emissary from *Rolling Stone!*" (The place broke up. "You funny man," Kinsolving deadpanned.)[40] "Did Pres. Bush steal the 2004 election?" Don Imus asked Prof. Michael Beschloss on June 13. "Not by the evidence so far," replied the telegenic scholar. "I think there's some people who are pretty un[re]constructed, especially in the Kerry camp. You remember that Japanese soldier in Okinawa who came out in 1965, came out of the jungle and finally confessed that they lost the war?"[41]

"Oh, I remember that! Yes!" barked Imus (and the place broke up). Some newspapers—the *Chattanooga Free Press*, the *Columbus Dispatch*—joined the chorus of derision, re-echoing the line that one Daytonian published in his local weekly: "Robert F. Kennedy, Jr. Joins the Barking Moonbats."[42]

Such mockery was not a marked departure from the main-stream coverage that Kennedy received. While Crier and Colbert each gave Kennedy a chance to say his piece, those other talking heads were patently inquisitorial, not letting Kennedy present his argument but trying to knock it down with talking points, and interrupting him repeatedly. When he told Tucker Carlson that election fraud is finally not a partisan concern, the host got nastier: "Your piece [. . .] is a purely partisan piece! You quote, again and again, Howard Dean, John Conyers, Dennis Kucinich, Ralph Neas—I mean, literally, Michael Moore and Ramsey Clark are about the only two leftists you don't quote!"[43] In fact, the piece quotes experts and observers of all stripes and either party (and neither Michael Moore nor Ramsey Clark believes that Bush's re-election was a fraud). Other, "liberal" interviewers were equally resistant, if less caustic. Charlie Rose, who had Kennedy on for over 15 minutes, changed the subject after only four.

Their intention, conscious or not, was to make his exposé appear so daft that no one would go out and read it; and that was also what the *Times* did in the end.[44] As if to atone for Herbert's column, the *Times* revisited the story on June 25, not by going through the evidence in *Rolling Stone* but with a scolding profile of Kennedy himself. Significantly placed in the Style section of the Sunday paper, Mark Leibovich's piece portrayed its subject as a sort of tragic flake—Camelot's mad-dest prince, doomed by his family history, unending money and an "intense metabolism" to a life of lone utopian crusades (and lots of really great vacations). Thus his social activism comes across as neurotic recklessness: Leibovich notes Kennedy's youthful proneness to "some kind of spontaneous, even daredevil" act, like "impatiently jumping off a chairlift" or "jumping off a cliff," and asks portentously, "At what point is he tempting fate?" Kennedy, hints Leibovich, has been thus leaping recklessly for years: into the green depths of environmentalism, into the "much-challenged" theory that childhood vaccines have increased autism—and, most dangerous of all, into the "accusation" of GOP election fraud in 2004. "Recently," writes Leibovich, "he has taken increasingly audacious leaps into political swamps that transcend the environment."

This is the unwisest leap of all, as it is dangerous not just to the bedazzled hippie types who follow Kennedy around like Jesus, or Jim Jones (he "has a certain Pied Piper quality about him," Uncle Ted observed to Leibovich) but, far more important, to his own career as a celebrity. "It is impossible to read the *Rolling Stone* article without wondering how Mr. Kennedy's audacious accusations might relate to his philosophical evolution or even affect his political viability." After all, he is by far the hottest of the younger Kennedys, "looked upon as the next potential vessel for Something Bigger." So he should climb out of that swamp, the article suggests, dry off, get dressed and join the party—because there is *no case for fraud*. It's clear that there is nothing to the *Rolling Stone* article because no "leading Democrats" have (publicly) endorsed it.[45] The theft of the 2004 election is "a cause that has largely been consigned so far to liberal bloggers, and which nearly all Democratic leaders and major news media outlets have ignored and which, unsurprisingly, Bush supporters have ridiculed. [RNC press secretary Tracy Schmitt] accused Mr. Kennedy of 'peddling a conspiracy theory that was thoroughly debunked nearly two years ago.'" In short, Bush's re-election was legitimate because we say it was, and if your facts say otherwise, they must be wrong. (A clear sign of the lunacy of Kennedy's campaign is its demented inspiration. After the election, Leibovich writes, "Mr. Kennedy spent Christmas skiing in Sun Valley, Idaho, at the home of [Laurie] David and her husband, Larry David, the *Seinfeld* creator and *Curb Your Enthusiasm* protagonist. Mr. David urged him to read a book on the 2004 election by the news media critic Mark Crispin Miller.")

Thus even Kennedy could not break down the firewall of denial that the media and political establishments have used to shield themselves, and us, from the intolerable truth. The profile ended with a view of Kennedy as a deranged utopian, quixotically intent on salvaging American democracy—a goal as mad, apparently, as a sustainable environment or any other hippie fantasy:

> "'It's all in God's hands,' he said on Wednesday night at Treasure Island, a lemony sun setting over the Golden Gate Bridge. He was surrounded by environmentalists swapping stories about protecting the earth's resources (and imbibing other liquid resources.)
>
> "I can only control my own conduct," Mr. Kennedy said, shrugging "And I plan to go down fighting."

V

In all fairness, it must be noted that the "major news media outlets" did not base their unanimous dismissal of the evidence on groupthink alone. The media and all those Democrats were also swayed by a particular delusion. They earnestly believed that the whole "theory" of election fraud had long since been debunked in every point by experts who had studied it with care. On this assumption right and left agreed, however crudely or politely they might put it. To the party propagandist, all that talk of fraud was "a conspiracy theory that was thoroughly debunked nearly two years ago." To the *Times*, the charge was a collective fantasy of "liberal bloggers," whose rantings on the Internet were answered by an equal force of savvier e-commentators. Since *Rolling Stone* had posted Kennedy's article on June 1, writes Leibovich, "the Web has been ablog with a split between those who believe this is the biggest unreported story ever and those who think it's old news, discredited long ago."

As an example of the latter, saner type, Leibovich quotes Farhad Manjoo of the liberal online magazine Salon: "If you do read the Kennedy article, be prepared to machete your way through numerous errors of interpretation and his deliberate omission of key bits of data." The line comes from Manjoo's ostensible dissection of the article in *Rolling Stone*—a screed accusing Kennedy of doubtful motives, sloppy research, glaring intellectual dishonesty, political extremism and even intimating plagiarism.[46] While Manjoo's piece was widely quoted among propagandists of the right, there is no truth in the *Times'* assertion that the Web was "split" between two equal armies, one backing Kennedy, the other one Manjoovian. On the contrary: After Salon posted Manjoo's diatribe on June 3, the magazine was overwhelmed with hundreds of corrective e-mails from readers—a good number of them experts—shocked by the reporter's many flagrant errors of fact and logic. Joan Walsh, Salon's editor, posted a defense of his performance, lauding Manjoo's "open mind"; and when I sent her a reply for publication, she refused to post it.[47] (In it I made several points, beyond addressing Manjoo's untrue claim that Kennedy took "everything [he] has to say" from *Fooled Again*.)[48] Her stance irked *Salon's* readers even more, with many canceling their subscriptions. Although she still appeared to back Manjoo, Walsh soon quietly removed him from the voting beat and had him back at work reporting on technology and business. Other than one later piece—a glowing review of the excellent HBO documentary "Hacking Democracy"— Manjoo left the field for good, so that the job could now be done by journalists whose minds were really open.

And so the web was not "split" between two equal and opposing sides. That claim was based not on reality but on the *Times'* need to reassure itself that the appalling truth about Ohio had somehow been "discredited long ago." In fact that very notion was *itself* a theory, and a wholly groundless one at that; and yet "the powers in place" had pushed *that* theory from the start. Within a few days of Bush/Cheney's "re-election," the common wisdom was that all the evidence of fraud had been debunked. It never was—indeed, the bulk of it had never even been acknowledged. And yet that highly confident assertion, based on nothing, sounded "rational" and "sensible," while every claim based on the facts sounded fantastic and extreme. According to that view, those who look into the evidence of fraud are chasing after something that just isn't there. And yet it's those who flog that view who are invoking phantoms, as a brief retrospective will make clear.

This brings us to the strangest aspect of this long postdemocratic nightmare: the key role of the left in the suppression, or evasion, of the awful truth. After laughing off the evidence of fraud right after the 2004 election, the corporate media largely stopped its jeering and chose instead to keep completely silent on the subject, uttering not one word except when Kennedy obliged them to respond (a little). For its part, the rightist media machine was even quieter, with Bill O'Reilly, Rush Limbaugh, Laura Ingraham, David Brooks, George Will, Glenn Beck, Ann Coulter, Pat Buchanan, Michael Savage, Michelle Malkin, the *Wall Street Journal*'s editors, *The National Review*, *The Weekly Standard*, the *Washington Times* et al. emitting not a peep of argument defending Bush & Co.'s re-election—nor can we call Sean Hannity's response an argument, as calling Greg Palast a putz and then hanging up on him was just another way to keep the issue buried. (Michael Medved kept away from it after his interview with me. Throughout the year after this book came out, moreover, neither *Hannity & Colmes* nor *The O'Reilly Factor* would have me on to talk about it, although I had done O'Reilly's show before.) While all "the liberal media," from center-right to far right, stayed as silent as the tomb, the only journalists purporting to *attack* the "theory" of election fraud were mostly seasoned troops of the left/liberal press.

After November 2, 2004, *The Nation* was largely hostile to the "theory" that Bush/Cheney stole it—a sharp turn from its prior course. Three months before Election Day, the magazine had published Ronnie Dugger's "How They Could Steal the Election This Time," a solid, chilling article about the threats posed by e-voting nationwide.[49] And then the chill was gone, as Washington editor David Corn, both in his magazine and on his blog, chastised his unbelieving readers. "The emails keep pouring in," he complained. "The election's been stolen! Fraud! John Kerry won!" Here were people charging that the exit polls were right, the outcome wrong, the process rigged. "Could this be? Or have ballot booths with electronic voting machines become the new

Grassy Knoll for conspiracy theorists?"[50] In his view, there was no fraud to speak of. "The evidence to date," he wrote on November 30, "is that the election results were not rigged but were produced by a flawed system."[51] The view dictated Corn's treatment of the issue and strongly tinged *The Nation*'s coverage overall.[52] Its editors and writers steered clear of fraud, focusing instead on less traumatic reasons why, presumably, the Democrats had "lost": the party wasn't left enough, John Kerry ran a poor campaign, etc. Starting in the spring of 2005, the magazine confirmed its long uninterest in Bush/Cheney's fraud by assigning the election beat to the British journalist Andrew Gumbel, who, although he does suspect that Bush stole the election in 2000, holds that we should "stop obsessing over conspiracy."[53]

Another writer for *The Nation*, though much further to the left, shared Corn's view that the e-voting machines have now "become the new Grassy Knoll for conspiracy theorists." In the issue of December 6, 2004 (and also in his own magazine, *CounterPunch*, November 20/21), Alexander Cockburn railed at length against the "conspiracy nuts" assailing him with pleas to deal with Diebold and Ohio. "My inbox is awash with their ravings," he complained, infuriated by such mass impertinence where David Corn was just annoyed.[54] Election fraud *could not* have happened, Cockburn claimed: it just wasn't possible. "As usual, the conspiracy nuts think that plans of inconceivable complexity worked at 100 percent efficiency, that Murphy's law was once again in suspense, and that 10,000 co-conspirators are all going to keep their mouths shut."[55]

Such fraud was just impossible—not that it mattered: "Do I think the election was stolen? No more than usual. The Democrats are getting worse at it and the Republicans better. Back in 1960 it was the other way round." (JFK's election did not hinge on Illinois, but that's another matter.) So election fraud *is* possible, but it doesn't matter since both parties do it. Well, okay, so it happened in 2004, but not that much. "So, for sure there's vote suppression in Ohio and Florida. I don't think it made the crucial difference," he declared, with no further explanation.

Cockburn's view was not based on the evidence, which he rejected out of hand.[56] Others who have fired off shots against the "theory" of election fraud have done it with a more professional attitude, claiming to have probed the story like Columbo, measuring and sniffing every piece of evidence before concluding that there wasn't any. Such was the method of Russ Baker, an independent liberal journalist who often posts on Tom-Paine.com, a progressive website. On January 7, 2005, Baker posted a long article defending Bush & Co.'s victory in Ohio: a victory based not on fraud but only "cluelessness," "dysfunction" and "incompetence."[57] Baker argued that the major documents alleging fraud—the Conyers Report and the extensive legal pleadings filed by Bob Fitrakis's team—were filled with paranoid inventions and exaggerations. He had discovered this, he wrote, when he "traveled to Ohio" and got the inside dope. There he found no evidence of tampering with the e-voting machines, nor any evidence that Diebold or any other private vendor was or even would have been involved in fraud. He found no evidence that the exit poll results were more accurate than the official vote count. He found no evidence that absentee ballots had been miscounted. Although he was convinced that there had been too few machines in Democratic precincts, he found no evidence that this had been intentional.

Thus Conyers et al., despite their "good intentions," were hobbled by "bad facts." Being "an old-fashioned investigative reporter," Baker had a civic obligation to correct them: "Half-baked conspiracy theories are damaging to the public confidence in democracy." While that is surely so, democracy is at far greater risk from half-baked journalistic efforts to deny election fraud: this piece, like others Baker wrote afterward, was nothing but a paraphrase of talking points from state officials working for the very system that should have been exposed, and not defended, on TomPaine.com. Like too many other journalists, Baker went about his task distrustful of the very people best equipped to help him with it—as he made clear in his first sentence: "Many of us fear that the Ohio election was stolen, because people— like talk show sleuths, blogger number crunchers, forensic attorneys, crusading professors and partisan activists—keep telling us so." Disdainful of such cranks (for who were *they*?), Baker sought out Democratic state officials, county bureaucrats and other "solid" sources—who, he thought, would give it to him straight—and treated everything they said to him as gospel.[58] Knowing nothing of Ohio politics, he figured that a local Democrat—any local Democrat—would quickly spill the dirt on the Republicans if there were any dirt to spill. He did not understand that many an Ohio Democrat is just a DINO— "Democrat In Name Only"—snugly bedded down with the apparent opposition and so unlikely to gainsay the party line.

Take, for example, Baker's rosy notion that the statewide shortage of machines—in Democratic precincts only—was probably an accident. The seasoned news-hound based that argument entirely on the say-so of Bill Anthony, chairman of the Franklin County board of elections, and in Baker's eyes an upright member of the opposition party: "an African-American and a Democrat himself (in fact, he is the county chairman and works as a union representative)." Asked by Baker if the fix was in, which might explain the shortage of machines throughout

Columbus, Anthony became indignant: "Anthony resents the suggestion that Franklin County authorities somehow worked to help Bush. 'I worked my ass off in those precincts,' he says of African-American areas of the county." Thus convinced, by Bill Anthony himself, that Bill Anthony was on the level, Baker blithely paraphrased Bill Anthony's long, complicated reason for the shortage of machines. The rationale is even less believable for coming from Bill Anthony, who is not the stout progressive Democrat evoked in Baker's column but a man distrusted by true party stalwarts for his ever-shifting loyalty. He has cut deals to allow Republicans to campaign unopposed and has also backed "bipartisan" tickets organized to thwart progressive Democrats. As chair of the Franklin County board of elections, he served Republican Secretary of State Ken Blackwell's interests, hence his own.

In denying any fell intent behind the shortage of machines, Anthony was covering for Blackwell. As chair of the board of elections, first of all, Anthony played no role whatsoever in the allocation of machines—a job wholly up to the *director* of the board, a solid Bush Republican named Matt Damschroder. In any case, Anthony knew plenty about Blackwell's plan to stiff the Democrats, not just in Franklin County but statewide; and when he spoke to Baker he was in the bag. A few months later, after Blackwell turned on him (blaming him for the disenfranchisement of black voters in Franklin County), Anthony was more forthcoming.[59] On a local radio show, he said that he had known before Election Day that the DRE machines would slow things down, and that he had even asked Blackwell for paper ballots. Blackwell, he said, refused—and Anthony, sharp henchman that he was, did not go public with the problem. (Even before Baker interviewed him, Anthony had doubts about the voting process elsewhere in the state: doubts that were made known to Baker, who seems not to have looked into them.)[60] Thus Anthony was not the best of sources to affirm the probity of Blackwell's operation; and yet the "old-fashioned investigative reporter" bought his tale without either checking out Anthony's background or looking up some other Democrat who might corroborate his story.[61]

Ordinarily, Russ Baker is a first-rate journalist (I quote his work in *Fooled Again*). Why so bald a failure on this most important story? I have to assume that, far too intelligent to buy Anthony's preposterous excuse, he accepted it because he wanted to accept it. All his pieces on Ohio are thus heavily stacked for the defense. Sometimes Baker just *asserts* his case, as if he were an oracle or Antonin Scalia: "As for Diebold and other vilified companies, in all probability, they didn't, and wouldn't, risk the ignominy and consequences of fixing an election." Period. The evidence that they both did and would does not come into it. More often, the reporter simply heaps scorn on the critic[62] and just as arbitrarily defers to the good judgment of whichever bureaucrat or pol supports Bush/Cheney's case— always making much of the person's being a Democrat, as if that in itself were proof of anything. Baker's hostile treatment of the evidence was sometimes staggering. To make his case that there was nothing to the exit polls, he invoked Steve Freeman's book, mocked Freeman's credentials, then quoted someone whose credentials were a total mystery: "I spoke with a source who, in the common parlance, is 'familiar with the thinking of' Warren Mitofsky, the 'father' of the exit poll." That that source could have been Mitofsky's wife, or psychoanalyst, was apparently beside the point, as Baker moved directly to the kill: "Asked about Freeman's analysis, my source told me that it is 'all wrong.'" So much for Freeman's careful work—which, like the Conyers Report, Baker evidently had not read.

Baker's case incited several strong rebuttals on the web, but they made not a dent in the quasi-Republican consensus that kept inexorably hardening throughout the left. Months later, *Mother Jones* contributed to the confusion with an article by Mark Hertsgaard, an excellent reporter and a staunch progressive, and the author of *On Bended Knee*, a classic work of media criticism dealing with the cave-in of the U.S. press throughout the Reagan years. It was therefore surprising to find Hertsgaard arguing in the November 2005 issue of *Mother Jones* that there was actually no evidence that Kerry won Ohio. Purporting to review the Conyers Report, Fitrakis's first compilation and this book (although *Fooled Again* deals only briefly with Ohio), Hertsgaard followed Baker's lead, offering up a random catalogue of what he claimed were misconceptions based on partial evidence and wishful thinking.[63] Here again, the counter-blast itself was flawed in just that way, as it was based entirely on the exculpatory claims of certain Democratic sources in Ohio. Hertsgaard believed them even when the evidence disproved them.

On the other hand, he seems to have misrepresented the position of those sources who confirmed, or reconfirmed, the case against Bush/Cheney. Sherole Eaton was a Democratic whistleblower who had worked on the Board of Election in Hocking County, where she witnessed fraud of several kinds and made her story public, testifying before the House Judiciary Committee. (For doing so she lost her job, and sued to get it back.) According to Hertsgaard, Eaton had essentially recanted, telling him, he claimed, that she really "[doesn't] know if there was fraud" in Hocking County. Eaton angrily denied Hertsgaard's contention, in an e-mail sent to *Mother Jones* on November 15:

I asked Mr. Hertsgaard to *not* quote me out of context. *He did!* The article in *Mother Jones* [. . .] was slanted and shallow with little or no investigative work by the infamous Mr. Hertsgaard. I suggest that you assign someone else to write an article on the same subject without any slant. The full story with depth[,] and the reporting of investigative interview[er]s with no slant[,] will prompt most of your readers to take a closer look at the possibility of fraud in our voting system.[64]

Bob Fitrakis had a very similar experience:

Hertsgaard, who is a friend of Harvey Wasserman's, called him and said that he had made a few phone calls and there was nothing to the stolen election story. Harvey had to lobby him in order to get him to do an interview with me before he ran the story. Steve Rosenfeld, after talking to Hertsgaard who seemed reluctant to talk to me, wrote to the Mother Jones editor and complained that Hertsgaard had already come to his conclusion without consulting anyone on our team. Hertsgaard's interview with me was incredibly arrogant and contemptuous. It was interesting because he had never come into Ohio and he knew absolutely nothing about Ohio politics and law. Yet, he was dismissive of everything I said and seemed little interested in checking out any facts.[65]

That "slant" distorted all of Hertsgaard's counter-arguments. Take his treatment of the sudden "terrorist alert" in Warren County on Election Night—a freak occurrence that allowed officials to eject reporters from the premises before the votes were counted. (Warren was among the last Ohio counties to report their tallies: see above, pp. 29–30.) That alert was *not* suspicious, Hertsgaard claimed: "a Democrat" who'd been there told him so. As credible as that source may have been, his mere word does not moot the contradictory evidence that Hertsgaard overlooked. There was the FBI's denial, on November 3, that that "terrorist alert" had been authentic; and there were e-mails proving that the plan to sound that false alarm had been in place for some nine days. (Both stories were reported in the *Cincinnati Enquirer*.) Hertsgaard also failed to note the affidavits of two eyewitnesses who, after the "alert," saw ballots stealthily carted off to an unofficial storage site managed by a GOP operative. He was told about those witnesses by Bob Fitrakis but evidently did not try to reach them.

Hertsgaard also leapt nimbly over several other scandals, always with a leg up from some helpful pol or bureaucrat. He claimed that the vote-flipping had occurred on only 18 out of 1,148 machines and that the problem was "quickly corrected" (a claim made by a lone "tech specialist" in Mahoning County and sharply contradicted by scores of affidavits and sworn statements). He claimed that all the gross mathematical anomalies throughout the state—thousands of votes missing, or thousands more votes cast than voters, and so on—were really just a few, and all were "caught and corrected." Such arguments have all been blown away by Bob Fitrakis, Richard Hayes Phillips and others who have actually spent months examining the evidence throughout Ohio; and yet the myth that there was no such evidence is still officially regarded as the truth, in large part thanks to *Mother Jones*.

Still, the article was not a total whitewash. Hertsgaard ended by conceding that "there was indeed something rotten" in Ohio. He noted certain scandals that he saw as genuine, such as the shortages of DRE machines, and Blackwell's purging of the voter rolls in urban areas. Although he cast most of the evidence as bogus or exaggerated, Hertsgaard finally did approve the basic effort to investigate all wrongdoing by Republican officials (only in Ohio, the only state where he thought any fraud had been committed). "This was not a fair election, and it deserves the scrutiny skeptics have brought to it," he admitted, thereby leaving room for more research and further argument.

That quiet acknowledgment of fraud, and the encouragement of further scrutiny, were wholly missing from the work of Salon's Fahrad Manjoo, the most influential of the faux-debunkers on the left. Throughout his meteoric tenure as the best-known critic of the critics of Bush/Cheney's re-election, Manjoo simply jeered at all efforts to discuss the evidence of fraud, which he dismissed as fantasies or outright lies by the "far left."[66] Later in November, a few weeks after the review in *Mother Jones*, Manjoo tore into *Fooled Again*, attacking it as "pseudo-journalism," a tissue of "half-truths and partisan theories," a "bad book," which apparently he felt besmirched by even having had to read.[67] He actually had no precise objections of his own, merely recommending that the reader looking for specific errors read Mark Hertsgaard's article, "a nice compendium of fraud claims that the author buys into too easily." This was not true, as Hertsgaard's piece dealt with three books, and only glancingly with mine; but then Manjoo's aim was not to deal in earnest with the facts but simply to deny that there were any facts to deal with: "Though I searched the contents, the index and the voluminous endnotes, I found no proof of Miller's theory. Like his claim that Kerry now believes he was robbed, Miller's many suggestions of fraud dissolve under close scrutiny. By the end, the only fraud you're sure of is the fraud perpetrated upon you, the reader, into bearing with this book."

This is precisely how the Bush Republicans in Congress

"answered" the Conyers Report—a work "without any evidence," as Tom DeLay and all his troops hallooed repeatedly on January 6, 2005 (see above, pp. 116–17). It was, to say the least, an odd position for a liberal magazine; and even odder that Fahrad Manjoo should be asserting that there is "no proof" in *Fooled Again*, since not a little of the evidence herein derives from Manjoo's own reporting prior to Election Day. (Indeed, I thank Manjoo in my acknowledgments, on p. 393.) Hence the exceptional ferocity of his attack; for it was clearly not the lack of evidence that so enraged him but his desperate eagerness to put as much daylight as possible between his own reporting and my "exaggerated and easily disputable theories of election theft."[68] In short, he was in denial—as he himself made clear in that review. He took particular exception to my argument that, at the grass-roots level, Bush's win depended heavily on the energies of Christianist extremists, who, as Manjoo (accurately) put it, "believe they must 'slaughter' their opponents in the same way that religious fanatics slaughter their holy foes." This idea, according to Manjoo, must never be expressed: "Even if you believe this to be true, *and even if it is in fact true, shut up about it*; this sort of unhinged rhetoric can't help, and can only hurt, our capacity to solve the problem of voting in America" (emphasis added).

There, in a nutshell, is the case that Manjoo and the rest have offered in defense of Bush & Co.'s re-election. It is, indeed, a case entirely worthy of the Bush regime itself, as it is based not on facts but on a mad refusal to acknowledge them. The madness gleams throughout that sentence in Salon, which breaks down right before our eyes. *If it is in fact true* that a ferocious anti-democratic movement has subverted our electoral system, to say so cannot be a flight of "unhinged rhetoric." And *if it is in fact true* that millions of Bush/Cheney's followers believe that God wants them to steal elections for Him, it cannot be right— either rational or moral—to "shut up about it" on the theory that our honesty about all this must do more harm than good. The implication is that keeping mum about that plot might somehow lull the plotters into helping us "to solve the problem of voting in America"—a "problem" they would like to "solve" by limiting the franchise to their own minority. Given such a game plan on the right, there's nothing to be gained from any nice bipartisan "reform"; and yet that tacit call for compromise is really not the point of Manjoo's sentence, which is not about resolving this unprecedented crisis but denying it. Even if it's true, the sentence says, we must pretend it's not—because, of course, it's not. How could it be? Thus Salon confronts, at last, the terrifying threat of a deliberate theocratic drive against American democracy, but it does so only to repeat that there is no such threat: "Even if it is in fact true, it can't be true," the sentence says. Or to put it in more familiar terms, "It can't happen here."

That woozy notion has been blinding countless good Americans for generations. Sinclair Lewis's *It Can't Happen Here* came out in 1935, by which time such calamitous political complacency was nothing new. And yet despite its durability, that notion is in fact profoundly un-American, as our whole civic system was based squarely and deliberately on the pragmatic view that "it" *can* happen here, just as it can happen anywhere. It was precisely in their hope of hindering this fatal national tendency that the republicans of yesteryear constructed such a government as ours was meant to be, with its separation of powers, checks and balances, and—most important—Bill of Rights, ensuring the complete and permanent divorce of church and state, the universal

right of habeas corpus, freedom of the press and other liberal institutions that now seem utopian (including state militias to avert
the need for a "standing army," which could turn our president
into an emperor). The idea that "it can't happen here" would
have astonished Jefferson and Franklin, Madison and Paine, and
quite a few less famed Americans who also saw the beauty of our
founding revolution.

And yet "it can't happen here" is a given nowadays—a fantasy
as dear to some of us as liquor to an alcoholic. The press has
leapt to its defense, tuning out or shouting down whatever facts
might threaten to dispel it. While always ready to deplore the
rising danger to democracy in Moscow or Caracas or Teheran,
the U.S. press ignored the subject here, precisely where it matters most to us—and where the press is both empowered and
obligated by the First Amendment to report such civic danger
loud and clear.

Of all Bush/Cheney's moves against American democracy,
their effort to subvert the voting process is the most explosive;
their other anti-democratic measures seem remote and hypo-
thetical by contrast with that drive, which hits us where we live,
as we have long been (wrongly) taught that voting is the only
civic action left to us. Thus the left/liberal press performed a
crucial task by certifying the myth that Bush & Co. was legitimately re-elected—a service that sheds a disturbing light on the
condition of the American left today. For that service was, of
course, not conscious or deliberate, but in large part the expression of a certain strange new hunger for mainstream approval
and a fear of seeming too far Out There "on the grassy knoll."
This new conformist angst arises largely from the dismal economic fact that many of us in the middle class are skating on
thin ice, just one misstep or accident away from poverty. Such

organs as *The Nation*, *Mother Jones*, Salon et al., and most of those who write for them, are middle-class and therefore just as risk-averse as everybody else in that weak stratum. In such a leaky vessel, even the most righteous of progressive journalists will naturally incline toward views that will not rock that sinking boat, and that might even get them hoisted onto some big ocean liner. You'll never get to serve as the House Leftist on, say, MSNBC or at *Time* magazine if your views smack of forbidden chat-rooms. (I can say all this, of course, because I am myself not in that tough professional position. If I were not a tenured academic, you certainly would not be reading this.) Nor will major advertisers want to rent your space if you're inclined to publish certain kinds of exposés.

Thus those organs were so quick to patch together such a feeble case for Bush & Co.'s re-election, and to push it with such ornery sincerity. Others on the left, of course, had no careerist interest and were therefore unconcerned with the consensus of the networks or the *New York Times*. For the most part, they ignored or minimized Bush & Co.'s election fraud for ideological not economic reasons—although they too were in denial. They ducked the issue mainly by assailing Kerry and the Democrats, discerning in the latter's putative defeat a vindication of their own far purer politics, as if the people too disdained both parties as identical and rejected Kerry as not "left" enough. Certainly it's often much too hard to tell the Democrats and the Republicans apart, but that fact is irrelevant to Bush & Co.'s crimes against democracy. In using the apparent outcome of the presidential race to kick at Kerry and his party, many leftists placed the exhibition of their own political acuity above the public interest. In any case, such purism is based on a naïve belief in the integrity of the official vote-count—it being unthinkable, apparently, that

Kerry would have "lost" no matter how far left he had run, or for that matter even if he had run a masterful campaign. (By and large his campaign was a dismal farce, but that too is beside the point.) According to the evidence, a clear majority took pains to vote against Bush/Cheney, and that expression of the people's will is sacrosanct, regardless of the other party's failures or corruption. That fact was evidently lost on, or pointedly denied by, those leftists who asserted mass lukewarmness toward the contest. Such was the view of Michael Moore (see p. 122) and the magisterial Noam Chomsky, who deemed election fraud a minor matter given the far deeper rot of U.S. politics.[69]

Meanwhile, the (as it were) commercial left accommodated the Establishment with the sort of loaded and selective case that would cost a lot of money if you had to hire, say, Hill & Knowlton to come up with it; and, like any able propagandist, the left devised that case through niggling over-emphasis on a few details plucked neatly from the flood of evidence and then subjected to a withering pseudo-analysis meant to demonstrate that they did not exist. This was an especially easy job, and not just because the journalists and their audience so badly wanted to believe that it could never happen here. The left's unwitting propaganda was also eased by the extraordinary—and deliberate—complexity of Bush/Cheney's national crime spree.

As this book demonstrates, the regime's re-electoral fraud was dizzyingly various, carried out through several different means on every front, so that there was no single covert measure at the heart of it. By and large the fraud was not spectacular, moreover, as the thievery did not exceed the margin of error; and Bush did not ostensibly prevail in any state where such a victory would have seemed peculiar. Where he was the expected victor, Bush "won" many more votes than he actually received (as in North

Carolina: see pp. 184–86); and where Bush was the likely loser, Kerry's winning margin was much smaller than it should have been (as in Wisconsin and New Jersey: see pp. 187–89). Such cautiousness, and the broad diversity of tactics, made for a near-perfect crime in that it left no single "smoking gun"—a crime that much more imperceptible because adept computer hacking leaves no trace. Bush/Cheney's fraud, in short, was no big secret, as the evidence lay right before our eyes, requiring only that we take a good hard look at the numbers that did *not* add up, the countless "glitches" that afflicted Democratic precincts only, the many tens of thousands of firsthand accounts by citizens who couldn't register, or couldn't vote, or couldn't vote as they had planned; at the exit polls that clearly show who won; and at whatever other inconvenient facts required erasure. All such hard facts were annihilated through that dogged over-focus on particulars. The best way not to see the forest is to focus only on a couple of trees, and then find experts who assert that those aren't really trees.

Those arguing that this regime was duly re-elected also set the bar of "proof" so high that only God could reach it. In other words, they voided the big picture not just by restricting their attention to Ohio. More fundamentally, they minimized Bush/Cheney's panoramic fraud by noting only certain kinds of evidence, all of it based wholly on the claims of just a few assertive sources. As noted earlier, the champions of Bush & Co.'s "win" relied primarily on the say-so of uncomprehending (or complicit) Democrats; and they also favored certain number crunchers who purported to find every argument for fraud *mathematically* unsound, as if this were a purely quantitative matter.[70] Thus they, and the reporters quoting them, implicitly ruled out all other types of evidence, which, although acceptable in court, are evidently useless in the civic sphere. A jury may consider circumstantial evidence (such as the vote-flipping from Kerry to Bush, or the inadequate machines in Democratic precincts only); inferential evidence (such as the fact that Bush's numbers don't add up); and, of course, the testimony of sworn witnesses. All such vital data simply did not figure in the work of the debunkers, who dismissed it all as "rumor," "anecdote" and "speculation"—a view as anti-democratic, and finally as irrational, as the Bush regime itself.

And so, by the end of 2005, the left was largely satisfied that Bush & Co. had been re-elected fair and square. The allied voices of *The Nation*, TomPaine.com, *Mother Jones* and Salon seemed to constitute a strong consensus: "we" had lost and "they" had won, and that was it, as there was "no proof" of the "theory" that Bush/Cheney stole (only) Ohio. By having certified that "win," the leftist press did not only help the left itself stay in bed (or under it). That quick consensus served to justify the acquiescence of the whole Establishment, which seized on those weak arguments to keep not doing what needed to be done. The arguments themselves were less important than the fact that they'd been made, and by reporters on the left—for if *they* saw no evidence of fraud, there obviously wasn't any (just as Kerry's concession stood as "proof" that his "defeat" was real). Thus it was not necessary even to have read, say, Hertsgaard's piece, or Baker's, to get the message: "There's nothing to see here, folks. Move along." When Jerry Nadler quickly waved this book away as if it were a copy of *The Turner Diaries*, he may himself have read in *Mother Jones* or on the web—or have heard from a colleague or a staffer—that all those claims of fraud had been shot down.

In the summer of 2006, the left consensus was explicitly deployed to tarnish Robert Kennedy's important overview in

Rolling Stone. Having slammed that piece in Salon, Manjoo was now the designated hitter for the media, which used him frequently to "balance" Kennedy, as if Manjoo's piece were not a mere reprise of other journalists' mistakes but a genuine expert analysis. Thus was he exalted by the *New York Times*, as we have seen; and his name kept popping up along with Kennedy's throughout the spectrum of permissible opinion. In interviewing Kennedy on Fox News, Neil Cavuto quoted Manjoo's piece at several points, forcing Kennedy to use his time correcting Manjoo's errors instead of making his own case.[71] On CNN, where Kennedy was "balanced" by Bush & Co. propagandist Terry Holt (who answered every claim with the assertion that the *Democrats* were perpetrating massive "voter fraud"), host Wolf Blitzer opened by parroting Manjoo's main point, that the DNC report itself had found no evidence of GOP fraud in Ohio. (Kennedy corrected him.)[72] And on Brian Lehrer's show on WNYC-FM, New York City's NPR affiliate, Kennedy was "balanced" by Manjoo himself.[73] Although callers noted some of Manjoo's bloopers, the host himself was left with the impression that Salon's reporter had come up with a "point-by-point disputation" of Kennedy's analysis, as Lehrer put it on his show a few months later.

Thus even Bobby Kennedy was blacked out like the rest of us; and at the worst of times, as the next election now was just four months away. The people needed more than ever to be told the truth: that Bush & Co. had never been elected, that the GOP's control of Congress too was probably illicit, that the same party now enjoyed an even tighter grip on the electoral machinery from coast to coast, so that it could maintain its hold on Congress, even with minority support; and, therefore, that the people *must* get out and vote—not because they could be certain that their choices would prevail but as a crucial protest on behalf of free and fair elections. The higher the national turnout, the harder it would be for Bush & Co. to spin its next amazing "victory" as legitimate; and if the people voted in too blithe an expectation of defeat for Bush's party and then appeared to lose, the psychological effect might cripple them for good. (Millions of Americans had only just recovered from John Kerry's concession.) In short, they must vote with their eyes wide open, and this time be ready not to fall apart if the Republicans should seem to win, but to *start* fighting on Election Day: not, surely, for the Democratic Party but for democracy itself.

The media, however, blocked that message right up through November 7. Having blacked out Bobby Kennedy, the press also ignored his second article for *Rolling Stone*—"Will the Next Election Be Hacked?"—which came out some three weeks before Election Day.[74] In it, Kennedy quotes Chris Hood, a Diebold whistle-blower who, along with other of the vendor's employees, took part in the surreptitious placement of a software "patch" in the company's machines in Georgia. (Just weeks before, that state's electoral system had been privatized through a secret contract with the secretary of state.)[75] The order came directly from Bob Urosevich, president of Diebold's e-voting machine division, who had quietly flown in from Texas to direct the operation personally. "We were told not to talk to county personnel about it," Hood told Kennedy. And what about that patch? "We were told that it was intended to fix the clock in the system, which it didn't do," Hood noted. "The curious thing is the very swift, covert way this was done."

This happened on one sticky day in August of 2002. On Election Day, some ten weeks later, the official vote-count baffled everyone: Senator Max Cleland, a Democrat whom polls showed had been leading his opponent, Saxby Chambliss, by five points, lost by seven points. In the race for governor, Democrat Roy Barnes, who had been leading Republican Sonny Perdue by eleven points, lost by five. Both losses were inexplicable, and Cleland's was especially poignant. A war veteran and triple amputee, and a Georgian born and bred, Cleland was quite popular throughout the state, whereas Chambliss (born in North Carolina, raised in Louisiana) was unknown—and a chickenhawk to boot, a "bad knee" having kept him out of Vietnam. (See pp. 94–95.) Chambliss's attack ads had cast Cleland as a traitor because he had voted against establishing the Department of Homeland Security. And now the people of the Peach State had apparently been shaken by their fear of terrorism into believing that those ads were right.

That, at least, was the conclusion of the press, whose watchdogs evidently found it more believable that Georgians would thus switch en masse at the eleventh hour because of the attack ads of a feeble challenger, than that there might be something wrong with the electoral machinery, which was now managed by a private firm linked closely to the winning party. Officially, that possibility was not just unbelievable but inconceivable—even though the same thing also happened that day in two other states deploying Diebold's wares: Colorado (where Republican Wayne Allard, down by nine points against Democrat Tom Strickland, won by five points) and New Hampshire (where Republican John Sununu, down by one point against Democrat Jeanne Shaheen, won by five points). Such miracles restored the Senate to Republican control.[76]

That Georgia's voters had been cheated electronically, and that Chris Hood's account was true, were all the likelier for the fact that Hood was not the first insider to go public with the story of

Urosevich's covert operation. Back in 2003, Rob Behler, a computer engineer, came out with a detailed and harrowing report on that affair and other crimes and improprieties throughout the Georgia program, which Behler knew from top to bottom, having temporarily served as Diebold's deployment manager in the summer of 2002. As Behler told Ronnie Dugger in the fall of 2004, Diebold's DRE machines were all completely insecure, with the memory cards all unencrypted and requiring the same password (1111). On Election Night 2002 67 memory cards disappeared from Fulton County, locale of Atlanta. "Running his laptop with a dual battery," Behler says, "in six or seven hours he could have changed the totals on those sixty-seven cards. 'There's no technical problem. There was absolutely zero protection on the card itself. You throw the card in, you just drill down into its files.'"[77] Before helping Dugger with that first-rate essay in *The Nation*, Behler also had appeared on ABC's *Nightline*, on Super Tuesday, March 2, 2004. After that brief encounter with the corporate press, Behler slipped into oblivion.

Aside from an appearance on MSNBC's *Hardball with Chris Matthews* (who steered clear of the Georgia story), Kennedy got no coverage for his second piece, despite its flood of troubling news about the companies—Diebold, ES&S, Hart InterCivic and Sequoia—whose wares were shortly to be used by over 80 percent of the U.S. electorate. Because his piece warned pointedly about the looming threat of fraud by Bush & Co.'s party, as opposed to mere snafus, mistakes and accidents, Kennedy's later revelations were ignored even more thoroughly than his prior survey of Ohio; for the press would not even face, much less report, that what was happening here was really happening.

Since Bush/Cheney's "re-election," such denial has had catastrophic consequences in Congress, where the Democrats, like the press, have stubbornly refused to note the evidence that Cleland "lost" to Diebold, not to Saxby Chambliss. In late September 2006, the House approved Bush/Cheney's Military Commissions Act by a vote of 232 to 191, with a dozen Democrats "[trying] to blunt election-year attacks by voting for the legislation," according to the *Wall Street Journal*.[78] Considering the extremism of that law, which lets Bush order warrantless surveillance on ourselves and actually repeals our right of habeas corpus—a cornerstone of free society since 1215—that anyone at all who calls himself a Democrat (or for that matter a Republican) would vote for it is staggering. Still more remarkable, however, was the motivation not just for those votes but for the party's general over-cautiousness.

While many Democrats made impassioned speeches against the military-tribunals legislation, they knew they had to tread carefully. They have been saying for weeks they don't want to step into another "Max Cleland moment," a reference to the former Georgia senator and Vietnam War veteran who lost his 2002 bid for re-election after campaign ads questioned his commitment on national security.[79]

As there's no evidence that Cleland "lost" at all, much less because of his alleged weakness on "national security," the Democrats' subdued response to that most un-American of bills was not a stroke of pragmatism but a crazy tragedy, the party struggling to placate a massive phantom bloc of pro-Bush voters.

Despite its devastating implications—or rather because of them—the Georgia story was denied by both the corporate and left/liberal press, despite its timely resurrection by Bobby Kennedy. The left's denial became clear to me a month before Election Day, on October 5, 2006, when I debated Andrew Gumbel at a meeting of the Berkeley chapter of the ACLU. The

Los Angeles correspondent for the British *Independent*, now reporting on election matters for *The Nation*, Gumbel is an able journalist, although fixated on legitimizing Bush & Co.'s "reelection." When, in our debate, I noted Cleland's curious defeat, Gumbel countered that the purpose of that covert patch was not to fix the pending race, but merely as a stealthy way for Diebold to attempt removal of the bugs from its malfunctioning machines, so that Georgia would not terminate the contract. Rob Behler, Gumbel claimed, had said so: "It's a matter of public record." In fact, Behler had said no such thing; and Cathy Cox herself, a month after Election Day, made clear that she did not believe the patch had any such innocuous purpose and asked Diebold for a fuller explanation.[80] (Diebold never sent her one, nor did she press for it; and she eventually revised the contract to keep Diebold operating in the state.)

Gumbel thus dismissed all contradictory research. Freeman's book, he told the audience, had been "laughed out of court"—a startling claim, since the book had not received a single print review, nor had it once been mentioned, much less challenged, in the corporate or left/liberal media. "Freeman doesn't know what he's talking about," Gumbel said, and that was that.[81] He just as categorically impugned the probity of Kevin Shelley, the California secretary of state who dared decertify Diebold's machines and was then punished with a slew of charges that he had violated ethics rules, so that he had to quit his post. Shelley was convicted on those charges, Gumbel said—although Shelley had, in fact, been wholly cleared, as noted earlier. Shelley was replaced by Bruce McPherson, who became acting secretary of state, and who, said Gumbel, had been admirably "tough on Diebold"—even though McPherson had, in fact, been very soft on Diebold, certifying their machines despite a massive grass-roots push against it. (Running to remain in office, McPherson lost to Debra Bowen in the 2006 election, primarily because he was too soft on Diebold, while Bowen promised radical electoral reform.) And having thus denied the rising danger of election fraud, Gumbel then denied that any-one denied that danger, claiming that the issue had been fully covered by the press and dismissing my contrary claims as "paranoid."

Gumbel's line helped harden the Establishment's conviction that *there is no evidence of fraud*—a fact so obvious to those confirming it that they perceive no need to offer any evidence at all. Such denial was especially pointed and ubiquitous throughout the last few weeks before Election Day 2006. In its October 16 issue, *The New Yorker* ran a column by Nicholas Lemann— "Paranoid Style: How Conspiracy Theories Become News"— that opened with a series of ostensible examples, including Kennedy's assessment of Ohio in 2004. Having roughly para-phrased the article in *Rolling Stone*, Lemann never bothered to revisit it, and so noted not a single error in it. (His piece dealt mainly with some theories about 9/11.)[82] On November 5, Michael Kinsley made the same point in the *New York Times Book Review*, in a long portfolio review that also brushed off all the evidence, enabling him to claim that "the whole stolen-election–2004 indictment has that echo-chamber sound of people having soul-searching conversations with each other." (Ironically, that shot applies to Kinsley and his peers, as he himself immediately demonstrated: "Richard Hofstadter's 'paranoid style,' exhibited mainly on the right when he coined the term in the 1960s, seems to have been adopted by the left, as Nicholas Lemann recently pointed out in *The New Yorker*.") The Democrats were no less certain that Bush/Cheney's fraud was just a mass delusion. On October 27, the *New York Times* reported on the possibility that blacks might sit out the election "because of disillusionment over past shenanigans." That public sentiment exasperated Donna Brazile, who saw such "past shenanigans" as figments of those voters' minds: "This notion that elections are stolen and that elections are rigged is so common in the public sphere that we're having to go out of our way to counter them this year," she said, implying that the party had to use some kind of therapy to snap folks out of it.[83]

Thus both "the liberal media" and the DNC dismissed the people's judgment; for the "notion" of election fraud was not the mere hobgoblin of a few warped minds out on "the left" but a fact now proved beyond all reasonable doubt and therefore recognized by the majority, which did the right thing on Election Day.

VI

The evidence was always more convincing than the sophistries deployed against it. Thus those who did, like Bobby Kennedy, finally (if briefly) penetrate the blackout opened and illuminated many minds, even if Wolf Blitzer, Charlie Rose or Tucker Carlson took cheap shots at him or changed the subject. And yet while Kennedy was surely the best-known reporter of Bush & Co.'s election fraud, he was only one of many who crisscrossed the country telling people what they had to know. Throughout the months preceding the 2006 election, many of us lectured endlessly in schools and churches, rented halls and private homes, spoke out on independent radio and posted pieces all over the Internet. There were websites spreading the forbidden news—Brad Friedman's bradblog.com, Bev Harris's blackboxvoting.com, John

Gideon's VotersUnite.com, Warren Stewart's VoteTrustUSA.com and Kathy Dopp's US Count Votes, among others—and other sites, like Truthout and Buzzflash, that often highlighted the bigger stories. There always was a wealth of new and vital information on Democratic Underground (http://www.democratic.com), many of whose numerous discussion groups have focused on election fraud, often with new data and original research.

Offline, meanwhile, there were independent voices on the air, their numbers growing as the story slowly spread throughout the nation. On their syndicated programs, Thom Hartmann, Stephanie Miller, Peter B. Collins and the Rev. Jesse Jackson were diligent and fearless in their coverage of the issue, as were Bev Smith, Mike Malloy, Peter Werbe and Meria Heller, Mike Webb in Seattle, Jon Elliott and Stacy Taylor in San Diego, Ray Taliaferro in San Francisco, Bishop Victor T. Curry in Miami, Santita Jackson in Chicago, Jim Hogue and John Barkhausen in Vermont, and Keith Murphy on XM. On Air America, the issue was covered thoroughly by Laura Flanders, Randi Rhodes, Sam Seder and (until her departure for *The West Wing*) Janeane Garofalo. Pacifica Radio paid close attention, especially at KPFA in Berkeley and KPFK in Los Angeles, and on Amy Goodman's *Democracy Now!* There was also frequent coverage by a range of smaller independent stations, including KBOO in Portland and KRLC in Salt Lake City. On independent cable, the International News Network (INN), which reaches some 25 million homes, reported on the problem of election fraud. Nor was such coverage limited to independent media, for as time went on there was a growing mainstream interest in the story. ABC's Bernie Ward, whose late-night show on KGO-AM enjoys the largest audience on the West Coast, became a keen observer of the problem.

Finally, the educative impact of such programs was immeasurably enhanced by several potent independent documentaries, including Dorothy Fadiman's *Stealing America: Vote by Vote*, Earl Katz's *Invisible Ballots*, Terry Murray's *Invisible Coup*, Laura Paglin's *No Umbrella: Election Day in the City*, David Earnhardt's *Eternal Vigilance*, Ian Inaba's *American Blackout*, Richard van Slyke's *The Right to Count*, Take Back the Media's *Electile Dysfunction*, the Votergate Project's *Votergate*, the Ecological Options Network's *Got Democracy?* and *Help America Vote on Paper*, and, not least, Earl Katz's *Hacking Democracy*, which very helpfully premiered on HBO just days before the 2006 election. And the movement also had strong champions in the world of print, including Bob Koehler of the Tribune Media Services, Chris Floyd at the *Moscow Times* and, online, Bernie Weiner at the Crisis Papers (www.crisispapers.org), Paul Craig Roberts at Counterpunch and lewrockwell.com, Michael Collins at Scoop (www.scoop.co.nz) Ray Beckerman on his own site (fairnessbybeckerman.blogspot.com), sociology professor Dennis Loo and the ubiquitous Oliver Dawshed.

All such effort gradually conveyed the truth about America's elections, and the crying need for genuine reform, to an ever larger, ever more receptive audience—which was, in fact, not just an audience but increasingly a citizenry mobilized to salvage and invigorate (or rather, realize) U.S. democracy. The nationwide campaign to spread the word encouraged, and in turn was strengthened by, the rise of grass-roots movements in state after state dedicated to democratizing the election system. Those many separate drives could not unite into a national force because there was no money for it (and little prospects of receiving any, as likely funders were inhibited by the delusion that Bush/Cheney really won). Within the ranks, moreover, there was at times division over strategy, with some endorsing "paper trails" (i.e., receipts from DRE machines) some calling for paper ballots counted by op-scan machines and some insisting on hand-counted paper ballots only. Yet despite such disagreements and its paltry funds, the movement did succeed in helping carry out the most important task, which was to tell the people that the system was at risk and getting worse.

And so the people got it, recognizing instantly the likelihood that (a) Bush & Co. stole its "mandate" in 2004, and (b) that the regime was not above attempting it again. Thus it did not matter that some groups were hesitant to come right out and charge the Bush Republicans with fraud, as such a stand might be dismissed as "partisan," "inflammatory" or "paranoid." Having finally heard the facts, or some of them, people drew their own conclusions, being smart enough to see that any regime wild enough to lie the nation into a disastrous war and let a major U.S. city drown would certainly not draw the line at stealing a few million votes. In any case, the people were persuaded not just by the evidence and their own common sense but by their own direct experience of disenfranchisement. In other words, by telling people what had happened, we were not so much revealing anything as certifying what they knew, or sensed, already, and so confirming that their own experience was not unusual or inadvertent but only one example of a scourge that had afflicted a majority of other voters.

The news hit hard not just because the press had so completely blocked the truth about Bush/Cheney's re-election. What made the news especially striking was its timeliness, for the regime's election fraud was not a one-shot deal but an ongoing drive that ought to have been covered daily by the press from left to right. Throughout the two years after the 2004 election, there were important stories on election matters breaking (or not breaking) every week—from those abortive referenda in Ohio on Election Day 2005 to the party's open intervention in the San Diego House race in the summer of 2006; from Diebold's shady little victories in North Carolina and California to Georgia's new requirement of a state-issued I.D. for voters—all of which occurred within the same week, in October 2005, that the GEO report came out and sank without a trace. In speaking publicly about the party's fraud, we were dealing not just with the last election but with the next one; for the same devices that had been deployed to re-elect Bush/Cheney were now being multiplied and strengthened for the party's benefit in state after state and throughout the federal government.

To do such preparations justice would take far more space than we have here. Suffice it to point out that most of those grass-roots campaigns to mend the voting process in so many states were steamrolled, improperly or illegally, by Diebold and Bush/Cheney's operatives. While there were some victories against the use of DRE machines, most notably in New Mexico and Connecticut, such civic efforts were sidetracked or blocked outright in California,[84] Illinois, New York, New Hampshire, Maryland and Pennsylvania—all "blue" states thus reddened artificially—and, as well, in North Carolina, Florida, Georgia, Arizona and Alaska. (In Volusia County, Florida, a poll worker was fired for expressing disapproval of the DRE machines.)[85] It was through dirty or illegal deals that e-voting spread nationwide, despite the overwhelming disapproval of computer experts, the growing outcry by the media and—most important—the near-total opposition of the people. According to a Zogby poll released on August 21, 2006, 92 percent of the American people believe the public has the right to view and verify the counting of their votes. (Six percent did not agree, while 2 percent were undecided.)[86] That fact too, of course, went unreported, except by the reform movement itself, which also worked to spread the word about those opposition movements nationwide, and the various tricks and tactics used to thwart them.[87]

While the party thus imposed its e-voting machinery throughout the country (with the help of certain Democrats), it also furthered mass disenfranchisement by passing neo–Jim Crow laws devised specifically to block the vote. On February 1, 2006, the Ohio legislature passed HB3, a law quadrupling the price of recounts, making machine audits near-impossible, hindering—indeed criminalizing—the registration of new voters, tightening partisan control of the election workforce and requiring voters to bring photo I.D.s to the polls.[88] Such state-issued documentation—a poll tax, in effect—was also suddenly required in Missouri, California, Arizona, Indiana, Florida and Georgia. (Most of those requirements had been declared illegal by Election Day 2006; but such judicial victories could not undo the harm, for they did not prevent poll workers in those states and others from demanding photo I.D.s anyway.)[89] Most remarkable of all, perhaps, was the state legislation patently devised to keep the people from inspecting the machines or challenging their numbers. Prior to the midterm races, Florida and Alabama passed laws declaring it illegal to hand-count paper ballots once they have been "counted" by machine—laws that are, as of this writing, still in force.

At the federal level, meanwhile, the Bush regime was also working quietly against democracy, by shattering the Justice Department's Civil Rights Division. At first, Bush/Cheney hobbled the division mainly through a program of malign neglect, overlooking rights abuses in employment, housing, law enforcement and access for the disabled. "It seems their goal is to do as little as possible, and in that they seem to be succeeding," complained one jurist in November 2003.[90] After Bush & Co.'s "re-election," however, the division's managers came out as overt agents of discrimination, especially in the area of voting rights—a U-turn that entailed a massive purge of the division's stressed Old Guard. In November 2005, the *Washington Post* reported it as "an upheaval that has driven away dozens of veteran lawyers and has damaged morale for many of those who remain, according to former and current employees."[91] Those civil servants were outraged by their office's decision to approve, over their objections, a range of Jim Crow measures beneficial to the GOP, including Tom DeLay's congressional redistricting plan in Texas and Georgia's law requiring voters to bring photo I.D.s to the polls. A few weeks later, according to the *Post*, the department "barred staff attorneys from offering recommendations in major Voting Rights Act cases, marking a significant change in the procedures meant to insulate such decisions from politics."[92]

Through such state and federal measures, Bush's party headed into the midterm elections technically and legally *more* capable of fraud than it had been two years before. The party leaders certainly did not intend to cede congressional control, regardless of the will of the electorate; for if they were to lose the House or Senate by a seat or two, or maybe three or four (Karl Rove did not foresee a larger loss), they planned to get such unacceptable defeats reversed after Election Day, much as they did after the rape of Florida in 2000. In the summer of 2006, a well-placed party operative told radio host Thom Hartmann, off the record, that the plan, if the Republicans should (barely) lose, was to raise a giant stink about the "fraud" that had been perpetrated by the *Democrats*, and then force a turnaround with the unknowing assistance of the media.

Whatever the credentials of that source, there were, before Election Day, clear signs that the regime planned not merely to defraud the people at the polls (again), but to get away with it by charging that such fraud had been committed by the Democrats—an ancient tactic and delusion of the right (see Chapter 4), but now the Bush Republicans were evidently getting ready for a major propaganda drive to make the accusation stick. Indeed, they seemed to be preparing such a gambit even if they won again. ("I kind of hope something happens," said a Fox News anchor early on Election Night.) A month before Election Day, the Department of Justice pulled an innovative move in Mississippi, "charging blacks with voting fraud," the *Times* reported, "in a state whose violent rejection of blacks' right to vote, over generations, helped give birth to the Voting Rights Act of 1965."[93] In late October, it was reported widely that the Treasury Department had been looking into possible Red infiltration of Sequoia: "Government Probes Electronic Machine Maker with Alleged Tries [*sic*] to Venezuelan President Chavez," as Foxnews.com put it on October 29.[94] The government was seemingly concerned about the purchase of Sequoia by Smartmatic, a corporation owned by Venezuelans, who had bought the company in December 2004 (and sold it two years later). As the inquiry had been ongoing since July, this news was evidently timed to strengthen the pre-propaganda drive against the Democrats, whose solidarity with Hugo Chavez (and Kim Jong-il and Fidel Castro) was, of course, a given.[95]

That drive entailed much livid repetition of the pro-Bush propaganda claims refuted in this book (see pp. 119–21).[96] It also made much of the "fact," now well established by the rightist media, that the Democrats had stolen the 2004 gubernatorial election in Washington, a race so close that it was not decided until the spring of 2005.[97] Ultimately, Democrat Christine Gregoire, on a third recount, beat Republican Dino Rossi by just 129 votes. Her win depended on 573 ballots that turned up in late December in Kings County, a heavily Democratic area. That stroke of luck, and the approval of those ballots by the state's top court, infuriated Rossi's backers, who continued to decry Gregoire's alleged fraud right up until, and after, the 2006 election. But while Republicans deplored those several hundred sudden ballots for Gregoire, they never said a word about the several *thousand* phantom votes for Rossi—votes concocted by Sequoia's e-voting machinery in Snohomish County (Hugo Chavez evidently favoring the GOP there). That faux-advantage was discovered by attorney Paul Lehto, whose lawsuit contributed to a decision by the county council to get rid of DRE machines.[98] This victory left the state of Washington almost entirely free of DRE machines. Because the Democrats persistently refused to set the record straight, the myth about Christine Gregoire's victory was excellent pre-propaganda for a larger drive against the Democrats after the 2006 election.[99] (More evidence of pro-Rossi mischief came to light in March 2007 when John McKay, former U.S. Attorney for Western Washington, revealed that he had been contacted by the office of Rep. Doc Hastings, R-WA, about investigating the Gregoire campaign for voter fraud. He demurred and was thereafter fired. "I was concerned and dismayed by the call," he said.)[100]

Meanwhile, from February 2005 up through the summer of 2006, the threat of Democratic "voter fraud" was broadly propagated by an outfit called the American Center for Voting Rights. In August of that year, the ACVR brought out a thick "report"

ostensibly detailing all the Democratic mischief that had jeopardized Bush/Cheney's re-election. A mere compendium of
rightist talking points, that document and all of ACVR's other
doings were meant to hide the fat hand of the GOP in the subversion of the U.S. voting system, and to make things even worse
by pushing for strict new I.D. requirements nationwide.

Although it called itself a "non-partisan" association, the "Center" was in fact a front group for far-rightist party operatives
intent on nullifying American democracy. Its president, Mark
F. "Thor" Hearne II, formerly a lawyer for the Bush/Cheney
campaign, had helped "observe" the vote-count in Broward
County in 2000, oversaw the GOP's gerrymandering of Missouri
in 2002 and in 2005 advocated for Bush/Cheney's appointment of
another far-right justice to the Supreme Court. The ACVR's
"Democratic" chairman, Brian Lunde, was not much of a Democrat. A former DNC official who supported Bush in 2000, and
then ran "Democrats for Bush" in 2004, Lunde also helped Jack
Abramoff defraud his Indian clients and lobbied in Washington
for Joseph Kabila, dictator of the Congo. ACVR spokesman
Jim Dyke was a party propagandist who had served as press
secretary first to the Christianist Don Evans, secretary of com-
merce, then to the RNC, in which capacity he claimed, after
the 2000 election, that all reports of Democratic disenfranchisement were "baseless." Finally, the ACVR served often as a
platform for the veteran party animal John Fund, whose talents
as an anti-democratic propagandist were on full display in his
faux-study, *Stealing Elections: How Voter Fraud Threatens Our
Democracy* (see pp. 100–02).[101]

In short, the ACVR was an appendage of the Bush regime, its
statements against "voter fraud" intended merely to legitimize
the party's drive to disenfranchise non-Republicans. As noted

here (pp. 119–21), Democratic "voter fraud" was virtually non-existent in 2004, nor has there been a shred of evidence that it somehow became a problem afterward. Indeed, in mid-June of 2006, Bush's own Election Assistance Commission (EAC) received a full report on voter fraud determining that there was "little evidence" that it was a problem, by contrast with the larger danger of *election* fraud. Under pressure from the ACVR, the EAC buried the report, which was unknown until October, when Richard Wolf of *USA Today* got hold of it and wrote an article— "Report refutes fraud at poll sites"—that exposed the groundlessness of all the tough new legislation meant to make it harder for citizens to vote.[102] Aside from Wolf's piece, the EAC report received no major coverage before Election Day. In December, the EAC released an expurgated version of the document, heavily revised by Hearne and other activists, including Ben Ginsberg, chief outside counsel to Bush/Cheney's 2000 and 2004 campaigns, Kathy Rogers, Georgia's director of elections, and Todd Rokita, who as Indiana's secretary of state purged over 1 million names from the voter rolls and, according to the *Ft. Wayne Journal Gazette*, "strongly supported an unnecessary voter ID law, and . . . refused to intervene in problems surrounding voting machines until it became politically expedient to do so."[103]

Thus purified, that final draft of the report obscured the crucial fact that "voter fraud" has posed no threat at all to "our democracy." That fact was only reconfirmed in the 2006 election, which was so clean, as far as the behavior of the voters was concerned, that there was nothing to "expose." Thus the "Center" was completely out of gas. (Their website disappeared a few months after the election.) And yet, thanks to the EAC, the propaganda myth of (Democratic) "voter fraud" remained intact; and it will surely resonate again.

Thus Bush & Co. approached the midterm races with high confidence despite the staggering unpopularity of Bush, Cheney and their fellow partisans in Congress. Such confidence appeared psychotic only to observers who were blind to the regime's extraordinary skill at self-election. Bush/Cheney had it all sewed up, what with the continental spread of e-voting machinery (including computerized poll books), the new state laws excluding people from the polls, the ready teams of "challengers," the vast disinformation apparatus and the arsenal of other tactics that had put, then kept, the Republican Party in control of both the Congress and the White House. Bush & Co. apparently had just one problem. This time, it would be much easier to steal the race than to *justify* so unexpected and improbable a win, as all polls clearly indicated that the regime had no broad support. Even Bush's base was softening, and more Republicans than ever were outspoken in their opposition (and that is saying something, as the party was already deeply riven prior to the 2004 election: see pp. 7–14).

A win despite all that would seem impossible, unless there were some rationale for it believable enough at least to satisfy the press; and so Bush & Co. recycled—and the press compliantly re-echoed—the same weak "explanations" that had seemed to validate their victory in 2004. The rationale was now known as the two T's. "Terrorism and turnout," as *The Hill* put it, "were the 'two t's' that have been credited with GOP dominance in the last three elections."[104] As they had assured Bush/Cheney's victory before, so would the two T's benefit the GOP again. In other words, the Bush Republicans would win again through fear, aroused by the eternal aftershock of 9/11 and by mobilizing the expansive legions of their Christianist supporters. And so the press was ready to explain away Bush/Cheney's next electoral triumph just as it had done two years before—even though these rationales were still demonstrably absurd. In 2004 the fear of terrorism had impelled only some 9 percent of the electorate, according to Pew's comprehensive poll; and, despite the Christianists' own propaganda, there were simply too few rightist evangelicals to have re-elected Bush (see pp. 4–6). Just as this regime could not be re-elected honestly, in other words, neither could it honestly retain its hold on Congress.

It would be interesting to know how stubbornly the media would have hammered on such rationales if Bush & Co. had "won" again. Certainly the people would have found that victory hard to swallow—for *they* did not dismiss the evidence or fail to see the likelihood of fraud by this regime. While the Establishment derided or ignored the issue, all those grassroots, independent and/or maverick efforts to report the story had a marked influence on public understanding. In retrospect, Bush/Cheney's re-election seemed increasingly unlikely to a growing number of Americans. In August 2006, Zogby did a poll of 1,018 likely voters and found that only 45.2 percent of them felt "very confident" that Bush/Cheney had been re-elected fair and square, while 32.4 percent were "not at all confident," and 20 percent were only "somewhat confident" (2.4 percent were "not sure").[105] According to a poll conducted by Michael Alvarez and others for USC's Annenberg Center of Communication, by Election Day 2006, one-quarter of likely voters were not confident that their votes had been accurately counted two years earlier—an "almost 13% decline in voter confidence," with a near-doubling of "the percentage of respondents expressing no confidence that their vote would be counted correctly." As for the 2006 election, the pollsters noted lowered confidence about the count especially among

Democrats, Independents, African-Americans and less likely voters—a trend suggesting that the national turnout might be low that year.[106]

VII

And yet the off-year turnout was, officially, the highest since 1970—and no doubt far higher than that, since countless citizens who came to vote could not, primarily (although not only) because so many DRE machines broke down. In any case, the regime failed to pull it off, despite their long and multifarious preparations. The Democrats took back the House and Senate, by a margin that made it politically impossible for the Republicans to charge foul play. This was, of course, good news to all Americans who still believe in the ideals of our democracy, however they may feel about the Democratic Party. And yet the news should have been better still—for the Democrats won even bigger than they think. The Bush Republicans once more perpetrated massive fraud of several kinds and were foiled not only by the people but by their own miscalculation—and apparently, as well, by certain elements of the Establishment itself. In short, although the outcome was a great relief and a signal victory against Bush/Cheney's one-party rule, it also demonstrated just how far we have to go before we can regard ours as a government of, by and for the people.

First of all, the evidence of fraud by the Republicans was once again both copious and well-documented. In fact, the disenfranchisement was noticeably more extensive than two years before, according to John Gideon, Brad Friedman, Warren Stewart and Bob Fitrakis, among many others.[107] The problem was much worsened by the more extensive use of DRE machines from coast to coast, the gadgets breaking down, primarily to the benefit of the Republicans, in Florida, Ohio, Maryland, New Jersey, Colorado, Virginia, Tennessee and Indiana. The expanded use of DRE machines meant more long lines and many more thwarted voters than in 2004 in, among other places, Baltimore, Chicago, Denver ("a voting nightmare," claimed the *Denver Post*), Cleveland, Pittsburgh, California, Mississippi and Miami (where "many would-be voters left, livid," reported the *Miami Herald*).[108] There was also, as ever, widespread vote-flipping by the DRE machines, mostly from Democratic to Republican, in Texas, Maryland, Missouri, New Jersey, Kentucky and, of course, all over Florida. Such flagrant "blips" were epidemic nationwide; and yet the overall toll of votes trashed electronically was probably far greater still; for those machines malfunction, or misbehave as programmed, undetectably. For every glitch that someone noticed, countless others surely passed unknown, so that there's literally no telling how we really voted.

Meanwhile, cruder tactics were employed to cut the vote still more: polling places that opened late or not at all; phone calls threatening arrest if you showed up to vote; large disinformation efforts to get would-be voters trekking to the wrong addresses. While such foul play was rampant in the last election (as this book notes), 2006 also saw the vote suppressed through innovative methods. The new I.D. requirements, or the rumors that you needed an I.D., worked exactly as intended, with would-be voters staying away in states like Arizona, Florida and Indiana, and polling personnel demanding I.D.s even where they weren't required, as in Missouri, Pennsylvania, Maryland, throughout the South and even in New Paltz, New York. (On the other hand, those voting in Ohio's nicer neighborhoods were often *not* required to show I.D.s despite the new state law.) There were other novel stratagems, or measures used more heavily than in the last election. The Bush Republicans deployed harassing robo-calls—obnoxious taped appeals, ostensibly from Democrats, that jammed people's phone lines, making them so livid that, theoretically, they'd vote Republican or not at all—in at least 53 House districts nationwide, and there were countless other criminal tricks, especially where Republicans were on the ropes (i.e., most places).[109] In Virginia, citizens confronted so egregious an array of vote suppression tactics—meant primarily to keep George Allen in the Senate—that the FBI was called in to investigate.[110]

This time, Bush & Co.'s operatives attacked the vote more openly than ever. In San Diego, where Francine Busby once again faced Brian Bilbray, the DRE machines "slept over" at the homes of poll workers for *three weeks* before Election Day. (Before the primary in June, they were thus housed for a week or two.) Despite an order from the California secretary of state, moreover, Mikel Haas, San Diego registrar of voters, ordered poll workers not to tell voters that they had a choice between machines and paper; and Haas also delayed counting the paper ballots—which represented 6.4 percent of the electorate and which, according to the Zogby exit poll, favored Busby by 58 percent to 39 percent. (Busby "lost" by 21,406 votes, or just under 10 percent.)[111] While such overt defiance might, in part, have been a sign of desperation, it was also clearly hardened by the ease with which the Bush Republicans had always got away with murder (so to speak). Haas et al. would certainly have cheated more discreetly if their antics of the previous June—and Bilbray's stealthy swearing-in by Dennis Hastert—had been properly reported. Long accustomed to the press's acquiescent silence, Bush & Co.'s special forces now got reckless. On Election Day, far-right shock jock Laura Ingraham urged her national radio audience to jam the Democrats' voter protection hotline: "This is what I'm thinking. Tell me if you think I'm crazy. This is what I'm thinking: I think we all need to call 1–888-DEM-VOTE all at the same time."[112]

It was especially brazen given that the GOP was then entangled in a lawsuit over its phone-jamming tactics in New Hampshire in 2002 (see p. 43). To help get John Sununu into office, the party paid four operatives to block the Democrats' get-out-the-vote drive in Manchester and other cities—an action that entailed 800 hang-ups, bolstering Sununu's narrow victory of less than 20,000 votes. (As noted earlier, Sununu had been trailing Democrat Jeanne Shaheen right up until Election Day.) When Ingraham called for similar tactics nationwide, the lawsuit was about to go to trial, with one of the defendants, Shaun Hansen, set to testify that the sabotage had been approved both by the Bush administration and the RNC (which had been paying the hefty legal bills of James Tobin, the plot's ringleader). Investigators had already traced several of the culprits' phone calls to RNC chair Ken Mehlman. It was therefore disappointing, if unsurprising, when the parties settled on November 29 for an undisclosed amount, the judge ruling that "the Democrats had the right to allege that the phone jamming thwarted their efforts to increase voter turnout."[113] Meanwhile, back in May, defendant Charles McGee, having served seven months in prison for his part in the affair, was already "back at his old job with a Republican marketing firm," reported the *Washington Post*, "and will be helping out at the firm's 'GOP campaign school' for candidates"—two days of seminars in Manchester.[114] (Such training clearly had an influence on the party's further efforts in New Hampshire. A few days prior to Election Day 2006, it was reported that the GOP had been illegally phoning private citizens with taped attack ads against Paul Hodes, Democratic candidate for Congress.)

Ingraham's criminal incitement made no news outside the blogosphere, even though Sen. Patrick Leahy (D-VT) urged the Justice Department to look into it;[115] and Busby's second loss in San Diego got less coverage even than her first, despite the several flagrant wrongs by Mikel Haas. Elsewhere, the party's fraud was so explicit that several races were contested by the Democrats who "lost" them—an unprecedented slew of challenges, which, by and large, the press ignored. The only one that garnered any national attention was Christine Jennings's challenge to the razor-thin majority—368 votes out of over 239,000 cast— won by Vern Buchanan in Florida's 13th district, for the House seat recently (and dubiously) held by Katherine Harris, who had vacated it to run for senator. Buchanan's victory was suspicious, as there were over 18,000 undervotes—votes cast for neither candidate—in Sarasota's Democratic precincts, according to ES&S's iVotronic DRE machines.[116] (Two years earlier, the same snafu enabled Bush to "win" New Mexico, where there were nearly 19,000 undervotes for president, all in Democratic precincts; and over 17,000 of them on DRE machines—mostly iVotronics from ES&S: see pp. 148–49. Four months after the 2006 election, Ellen Theisen came out with a study of the presidential contest in New Mexico, showing that the excess undervotes accumulated only in minority precincts using DRE machines, while those precincts with paper ballots saw no such anomaly.)[117]

Although the press under-reported it, the Sarasota mess attracted national attention, especially from Paul Krugman in the

New York Times and E.J. Dionne in the *Washington Post*, marking the first time that either of them had addressed the subject of possible election fraud by the Bush Republicans since 2000.[118] Refusing to concede, Jennings started jumping, or trying to jump, through many hoops: filing Notice of Contest with the House (on December 20), and, in Florida, petitioning for a revote, challenging the state's voting certification process and seeking to inspect the source code, software and hardware—all of it from ES&S—that had been used, ostensibly, to count the votes in FL 13. That last application was denied in court, and Jennings appealed. (That is where things stand as of this writing. The resolution of such matters ultimately rests with Congress.)

Jennings was not the only Democrat contesting the results of the 2006 congressional election. In Florida alone there were three others. Foremost among them was Clint Curtis, a skilled computer programmer and a cogent witness to the GOP's subversive efforts, which he had been trying to expose since September 2004. (Until he recognized the party's ways, Curtis was a lifelong registered Republican.) In a self-published book, and then in a sworn affidavit signed on December 6, 2004, Curtis reported that four years earlier, when he was head programmer at Yang Enterprises in Oviedo, Florida, he had been asked to "develop a prototype of a voting program that could alter the vote tabulation in an election and be undetectable."[119] The request came directly from Tom Feeney, then Yang's general counsel and a Republican state senator, and since 2002 the U.S. Congressman for Florida's 24th district, which covers the exurban sprawl east of Orlando. The prototype was for defensive uses only, Feeney said, asserting that "Democrats would try to use such a program to steal an election, and he wanted to be able to detect and prevent that if it occurred." Feeney became Florida's house speaker a month after that meeting.

Curtis designed the prototype and submitted it to Yang—discovering only then that it was not intended for defensive use. "You don't understand," Li Woan Yang, the company's CEO, told him. "In order to get the contract we have to hide the manipulation in the source code. This program is needed to control the vote in South Florida." Shocked, Curtis pulled out of the project and soon left Yang, but not before attending further meetings with Ms. Yang and Sen. Feeney where the latter "bragged" about other stealthy tactics that the Florida party had prepared to slash the vote.

Curtis's affidavit made no news outside the blogosphere, and even there the splash was minimal, although he was interviewed both on Air America and on Thom Hartmann's syndicated radio show. Brad Friedman carefully examined, and refuted, Tom Feeney's categorical denials.[120] (Curtis also took a lie detector test, arranged and paid for by film producer Earl Katz and administered by the retired chief polygraph operator for the Florida Department of Law Enforcement. Curtis passed that test "with flying colors," according to all those involved.) Yet beyond a few Florida newspapers, the press continued to ignore the story. To break through that silence, Curtis mounted an ambitious run for Feeney's seat in the 2006 election and used that forum to tell his story as well as demonstrate the ease with which his program could instantly and imperceptibly reverse the outcome of elections.

Although polls showed Curtis neck-and-neck with Feeney on the eve of the election, the latter "won" by nearly 16 percent. Curtis immediately started canvassing the voters in four precincts, collecting affidavits demonstrating a broad gap between the rate

of actual votes and the official numbers. "We are showing a difference of between 7 percent and 11 percent more votes for me
than we received, which is enough to affect the outcome of the
election," he told the *Tampa Tribune* in early January 2007.[121]
He also advised the two other Floridians who had been unac-
countably defeated by incumbent Bush Republicans. In the
state's 5th district, a sprawling mélange of eight counties on the
western coast of central Florida, John Russell lost to Ginny
Brown-Waite, apparently, by some 50,000 votes. Russell can-
vassed one precinct, Shady Hills in Pasco County, eventually
collecting affidavits from 40 voters claiming that their votes for
him were not recorded—a noteworthy find, since Russell had, in
that precinct, won only 35 votes to Brown-Waite's 46. (He based
his legal challenge on that discrepancy, and then continued
gathering evidence.)[122] In Florida's 21st district, comprising
much of western Miami–Dade County, Frank Gonzalez was officially defeated by 19 percent, or roughly 20,000 votes, in his bid
to unseat Lincoln Diaz-Balart. Under Curtis's guidance, Gonzalez too began collecting affidavits from voters, many claiming
that his name had not been on their ballots. Gonzalez also found
over 5,300 undervotes in Democratic areas, and, according to
one news report, "a disproportionate number of absentee votes
for Diaz-Balart in some precincts." On February 1, 2007, Gonzalez's campaign requested data on the absentee vote from the
office of the county's supervisor of elections, Bush appointee
Lester Sola, who at once refused Gonzalez's request.[123]

Beyond those four contested races in Florida (and a fifth, on
different grounds, in Louisiana),[124] there were still more races
nationwide whose outcomes *should* have been disputed—and
not just by Democrats, as we shall see. Take the Senate (as the
Democrats should probably have done by a more formidable

margin). Having evidently lost by 50,000 votes out of some 1,800,000, Democrat Harold Ford should have withheld his concession to Republican Bob Corker, as there was evidence of fraud both in Memphis and in Nashville, two Democratic strongholds, and elsewhere, especially in West Tennessee. In some precincts in Nashville, it took people over five hours to cast their votes, and on Election Day, Ford himself expressed some very reasonable qualms. "We got calls this morning from Madison County, which is Jackson, Tennessee, a heavily Democratic turnout, where the machines are down, and they've actually closed the facility and told all the poll workers to go home and all the election officials to go home without giving any real guidance to voters."[125]

As for the House, there were as many as fifteen races whose apparent losers, all Democrats, had strong grounds for refusing to concede but eventually conceded anyway, although several had, at first, vowed not to quit until all votes were counted and all anomalies resolved. (Francine Busby caved within the month.)[126] In Ohio, two leading Bush Republicans were barely re-elected even though the odds—and, evidently, the electorate—opposed them. In the 2nd district, Jean Schmidt beat Democrat Victoria Wulsin by 2,517 votes (out of 237,000-plus cast), although her approval had been sinking like a stone, primarily because of her notorious House speech attacking Rep. John Murtha, a decorated veteran, as "a coward" for his opposition to Bush/Cheney's war.[127] And in Ohio's 15th district, seven-term incumbent Deborah Pryce defeated Democratic challenger Mary Jo Kilroy by 1,062 votes, even though the latter was 12 points ahead on Election Day, and Pryce had polled no higher than 43 percent: an unsurprising showing, as Pryce ardently defended both the war and Bush & Co.'s plan to "save"

Social Security and was close pals with compulsive page-turner Mark Foley—whom she called "sick," "disgusting" and a "predator," although she also said he was "a friend of mine" and had taken quite a lot of money from him.

There were other questionable Republican victories in Ohio, what with the high volume of complaints and the impossibility of verifying electronic numbers—and, furthermore, there having been, in 2006, even *more* uncounted ballots statewide than there were two years before: an amazing 5.1 percent of the total official vote, versus 4.3 percent in the previous election. Thus it would make sense to look more closely into the apparent wins by Bush Republicans such as John Boehner in OH 8 and Steve Chabot in OH 1.

Throughout the nation there were other iffy rightist wins, all of which should have been contested: Patricia Madrid's loss by the tiniest of margins (861 votes) in New Mexico's 1st district, to incumbent Heather Wilson in a race fraught with egregious improprieties, especially (again) in Bernallilo County (see p. 148); incumbent Marilyn Musgrave's unexpected victory, by some 7,200 votes, over Angie Paccione in Colorado's 4th district; incumbent Jim Gerlach's remarkable last-minute victory over Lois Murphy in Pennsylvania's 6th district despite a rash of scandals that had dragged down his approval ratings. (Gerlach also held a controversial fundraiser starring Karl Rove and had given openly to Tom DeLay's defense fund.) That Democrats threw in the towel despite glaring indications of foul play attests not to the weakness of the evidence but to the feeble civic spirit of the Democratic Party, which offered no support to those who did contest their losses and pressured other Democrats to fold. In any case, the silence of those candidates who were most likely cheated is irrelevant; for the problem here is not the inconvenience to particular careers but the annulment of the people's right to vote.[128]

Nor was it only Democrats who shouldn't have conceded. Many of their victories were so close that their opponents had every right to challenge the results—and would have, if they were honestly committed to democracy. Having been unseated, officially, by just 2,847 votes out of nearly 400,000, Conrad Burns of Montana ought to have double-checked the victory of Democratic challenger Jon Tester. Such prudence would have been especially apt in those states rife with problems on Election Day. In Missouri, Sen. Jim Talent, ousted unexpectedly by Claire McCaskill, should have asked for a recount, as she won only by some 46,000 votes out of 2,000,000 in a statewide contest plagued by voter I.D. snafus, e-voting machine errors and "inadequate pollworker training," according to VoteTrustUSA.[129] Even more suspicious was the victory of Democratic challenger Jim Webb in Virginia, where Sen. George Allen lost by only 7,231 votes out of nearly 2,400,000. As noted earlier, Election Day was an exceptional disaster in the Old Dominion state, and so Allen was entitled to hang tough, as he initially seemed to do. "Stay strong for freedom," he told supporters in the wee hours Tuesday morning, "and accuracy in elections will prevail!" At that point his crew was clearly bracing for a fight: "We're looking forward to watching this process unfold," said consigliere Ed Gillespie.[130] It was therefore noteworthy that less than two days later, Allen called the whole thing off, waving an immense bouquet of olive branches. Any further fighting over this election, he said, would only "cause more rancor," more "personal animosity," more "bitterness"—bad vibes wholly inconsistent with George Allen's "purpose-driven life," and so he disavowed the recount, thanking God profusely.

It was remarkable to see the proud macaca-hunter thus decked out in beads and sandals, nor was it the only such surprising post-election metamorphosis. Way behind in Pennsylvania, where Democrat Bob Casey was apparently trouncing him by almost two to one, Sen. Rick Santorum also took a war-like stand, at first. On Election Night, his campaign charged Democratic interference with the DRE machines. The Republican State Committee faxed the secretary of state an emergency demand for the immediate impoundment of the e-voting machinery in 27 counties. The campaign charged that the machines were either nullifying pro-Santorum votes or flipping them to Casey, and hinted at a lawsuit: "We've got all options on the table at this point," threatened party officer Scott Migli. "We feel like the electoral system has been left up to computer technicians."[131] That feeling was, of course, entirely justified; and so it was unfortunate, although unsurprising, that the party withdrew its request a few hours after making it. Santorum suddenly conceded without a peep about all those malfunctioning machines,[132] and just like Allen, was now anomalously cooing like a dove while thanking God profusely.

It might be nice to think that such Republicans so quickly and politely caved because it was the "gracious" thing to do, as Nixon supposedly did in 1960. (That story is a propaganda myth of Nixon's own device: see p. 396. n. 24.) It is far likelier that Talent, Allen, Burns, Santorum et al. folded to protect themselves, as any real investigation of the civic crime wave in 2006 would probably land them, or their minions, in the slammer. In any case, the idea that the Bush Republicans would ever make a purely "gracious" move, or otherwise observe the common good, is ludicrous. As argued here (see esp. pp. 81–134), the party's recent dirty war against American democracy has been driven largely (although not only) by a fanaticism that plays a larger role in the regime's policies than Democrats and others have allowed themselves to see. The Christianists' complacency toward natural disaster, their blunt refusal to acknowledge global warming—and, above all, their policy of war throughout the Middle East—are ultimately based on an apocalyptic wish to "bring it on" and get it over with, the electorate (literally) be damned.

It is therefore no coincidence that all the doubtful "winners" in 2006 had been supported by the Christian Coalition,[133] and that most of the incumbents—including Tom Feeney, Marilyn Musgrave, Robin Hayes, Ginny Brown-Waite, Arizona's Rick Renzi, Idaho's Bill Sali—had received the highest ratings from that outfit. Musgrave also received a warm endorsement from the Arkansas-based Knights Party, an affiliate of the Ku Klux Klan.[134] Watching a condemned man's execution in 1999, Brown-Waite saw, in the blood gushing from his nose, a vision of the cross, which she took as "a message" of the Lord's approval, bolstering her belief in the death penalty.[135] That sort of spirit often had strong backing from local groups conceived to help elect the unelectable. In Ohio, Jean Schmidt and Deborah Pryce were fiercely championed by the Ohio Restoration Project (ORP), a diligent network of theocratic pastors eager to "ignite a new chapter in human history" and therefore heavily implicated in the machinations of Ken Blackwell (who, running for governor in 2006, proved too unpopular even to squeak by illegally). "The arteries of our culture," ORP claims, "have been infected with the toxin of dogmatic secularism which have sought to deny America's Godly heritage and undermine her God-given potential."[136] Eager for the Rapture, such crusaders want this nation absolutely cleansed ASAP, and to that end they have subverted our elections just as zealously as they have worked to ban contraception, "cure" homosexuality and close down the public schools.

Thus the Democrats appear to have been fooled again; for the elections of 2006 were really not so close. As dazzling as their victory was—and even though they were, of course, content with it and wouldn't dream of making any trouble—the Democrats may well have picked up over 50 House seats (as opposed to 29) and one or more Senate seats over the official number (51, including Independents Lieberman and Sanders). The evidence lies not just in the thousands of reports of e-voting mishaps and vote suppression tactics nationwide. The gist of such diffuse intelligence has been statistically corroborated in a study from the Election Defense Alliance, released on November 16, 2006.[137]

In "Landslide Denied," election reform activist Jonathan Simon and computer scientist Bruce O'Dell demonstrate that the Republican Party gave itself a 4 percent advantage nationwide—a useful handicap of some 3 million phantom votes, produced (and hidden) electronically. The analysts discovered this inhuman surge through a meticulous comparison of the "weighted" exit polls, released at 7:07 p.m. EST on Election Day, with the "adjusted" numbers that came out on Wednesday morning. The first polls are especially significant, as they asked respondents how they had voted in the presidential race two years earlier. As the answers to that question were consistent with the national exit poll results for that race, they indicate that there was no over- or under-sampling of either party's voters in the "weighted" polls. Those polls showed 55 percent of the electorate voting Democratic and 43.5 percent voting Republican—a Democratic margin of 11.5 percent. The "adjusted" polls inexplicably decreased that margin by 3.9 percent, with

52.6 percent voting Democratic and 45 percent now voting for the GOP. The analysts conclude: "In the process of adjustment (or 'forced weighting') to make the poll results equal or mirror the reported vote results, the sample had to be distorted, by giving less weight to the respondents who said they had voted for a Democratic candidate and more weight to the respondents who said they had voted Republican."

This analysis has major implications; or would have, if EDA's press release had not immediately vanished down the memory hole. (Outside the blogosphere, the story was reported only on the website of KXMA, a television station in Dickinson, North Dakota.) First of all, the only states where there was no bogus "red shift" were Maryland and Pennsylvania—the two states where the Bush Republicans were evidently poised to charge the *Democrats* with massive fraud (see p. 461, n. 99). And yet the Simon/O'Dell study also offers infinitely more important clues. Besides reconfirming the copious bad news from actual voters, or would-be voters, nationwide, the analysis includes a cogent explanation as to *why* the Bush Republicans lost so much ground. After all, if they could rig the vote, why would they not go all the way and "beat" the Democrats again?

According to the data, the phantom votes for Bush/Cheney's Republicans were, predictably, all clustered in those districts where the races were the most competitive. This fact, and the unvarying recurrence of that spectral 3.9 percent from race to race across the country, indicate a stealthy measure sometime prior to Election Day—probably a covert application to the memory cards installed in the machines. As the e-voting machinery was now often closely monitored by activists, the party's gremlins would have fixed the codes as early as they could so as to hide their actions all the more completely. Nor could they give themselves an artificial boost of more than 4 percent, which falls within the margin of error. Thus did they lock themselves into a lead that, while it may well have seemed sufficient at the time, was finally not enough to do the trick.

That miscalculation was compounded, first of all, by the tremendous turnout on Election Day—a genuine victory for American democracy, attesting to the people's resolution in the face of very powerful disincentives to get out and vote. Aside from their extreme and multifarious intimidation tactics (just as in 2004), the Bush Republicans went all-out in the Muck Department, sponsoring, in Jackson Thoreau's words, "the dirtiest campaigns in history."[138] While the Democrats, as ever, largely pulled their punches (although they had a lot to work with), Bush's party cooked up a vast steaming banquet of salacious lies: in Tennessee, that Harold Ford consorted with white hookers ("Call me!"); in Wisconsin, that Rep. Ron Kind was a voracious purchaser of porn ("Ron Kind pays for sex, but not for soldiers") because he would not vote to stop the NIH from funding academic sex research (an ad deployed as well against Rep. Brad Miller in North Carolina); in New York, that Democrat Michael Arcuri was into phone sex (because a staffer had misdialed a number, at a cost of $1.25); and so on.[139] The purpose of such ads is not to muster sympathetic votes but to depress the turnout overall; and in this case the gambit largely failed, as Miller, Kind, Arcuri et al. won handily. Voters, this time, could not be so easily turned off.

While the people largely rose above the stench, many of them also showed a new resolve, based on their growing awareness that they might be rejected at the polls, or that the e-voting machinery might flip, or trash, their votes. Such doggedness was evident both in the turnout and the number of complaints, as countless citizens now took it on themselves to monitor the process nationwide. Thus the people largely overcame the pessimism that was heavily, albeit inadvertently, encouraged by the press, which, as Election Day approached, repeatedly portrayed the voting process as a purely *technical* disaster—a gigantic crapshoot that might nullify the votes for Democrats, Republicans or any other party. By thus censoring all evidence of fraud or partisan intention, the press made voting seem about as safe as online gambling. As noted earlier, it was ostensibly the fear of just such mass discouragement that kept the Democrats from even mentioning election fraud. That the people voted anyway suggests that they are smarter, and a lot less apathetic, than either the Democrats *or* the press—both corporate and left/liberal—seem to think.

It would be naïve, however, to explain the Bush Republicans' defeat as a pure upshot of growing democratic nerve. The party's star was also lowered by some shattering revelations that came after Bush & Co. gave itself that 4 percent advantage—revelations that could only come from deep in the Establishment, which was now split much as it had been back when Joe McCarthy rumbled off the reservation and attacked the army. As Bush's team had made some potent enemies right there in Washington, and especially in Langley, the corporate media unloosed a few late thunderbolts that ripped immense new gashes in the party's hull. In late September 2006, the corporate press went hog wild over Rep. Mark Foley's e-flirtations with congressional pages: the first *Republican* sex scandal in our modern history, even though that hot new item was considerably tamer than, say, male prostitute Jeff Gannon's work for, and many visits to, the White House, to name just one of the "conservative" entanglements that have made zero news.[140] (That ABC News broke the Foley story is especially noteworthy, as the network's journalists had worked for months, throughout the spring and summer, on a major exposé of the dangers of e-voting—a story that was finally spiked when Disney's lawyers refused to clear it.) That blow alone was fatal— "Foley scandal is momentum changer for GOP," *Newsweek* noted on its website—but there was more to come.

A few days later, the CIA leaked portions of a National Intelligence Estimate that had been completed six months earlier, concluding that "the Iraq conflict has become the 'cause celebre' for jihadists" everywhere. While that bombshell was still resonating, Bob Woodward came out with the anomalous third volume of his trilogy, *Bush at War*. A harrowing portrayal of an almighty coterie unhinged, *State of Denial* shatters Bush's image as a resolute "decider" and his White House as a tightly run machine: an image that had been constructed with no little help from Woodward, whose prior two volumes quietly hailed the Caesar that this third book cuts to pieces. The book rocked the president and all his men, though not because it broke the story of their lunacy. That had been variously told by other journalists already. What made *State of Denial* so damaging to Bush & Co., rather, was the mandarin status of its author, who, with this book, had cleared the story for admission to, and endless retransmission by, the echo chamber of the corporate press. That he had suddenly reversed his view of "Bush at war" does not suggest a personal epiphany so much as a decision, by the author or others, to deal Bush/Cheney's party a hard blow; for Woodward is, as they say, well-connected, having started out, *before* his placement in the Fourth Estate, as an intelligence officer with the U.S. Navy (a history that the bending author will neither confirm nor deny).[141]

While the Democratic turnout would have been quite high in any case, the turnout on the right was slashed immensely by the

Foley scandal, the CIA's delayed report and Woodward's timely exposé. (Among Christianists, moreover, the dispiriting impact of Foley's plight was surely heightened by the news that theocrat Ted Haggard, head of the National Association of Evangelicals and a close friend of the president's, had paid for the services of prostitute Mike Jones, who also sold him crystal meth—a scandal that may also have been broken, or accelerated, from on high.) And so the Bush Republicans did not experience a setback on Election Day 2006—or "a thumpin'," as Bush himself so quaintly put it on November 8—but were dealt the sort of crushing blow that should have meant the party's total reconstruction, with the Christianists sent packing. The glaring prevalence of fraud, moreover, should have sparked some revolutionary changes, with all e-systems junked, the Gordian knot of registration rules eliminated and the voting system wrested from the grip of either party and handed over to the people, to be run and monitored by them alone at government expense. (Proportional representation should be on the table, too, so as to end the partisan duopoly on state and federal power.)

And yet such change is not, of course, on the agenda now, because the truth about Election Day 2006, was often buried even as it partly came to light. "On a bright note," ABC News reported in the early afternoon, "[Virginia] Board of Elections analyst Clay Landa reports to the AP that turnout could reach 65 percent, and there have been reported problems with touch screen voting."[142] That report came straight from Wonderland, as Virginia's DRE machines had been malfunctioning all day, and the FBI had been investigating in the state for several hours. "We've been running down reports of voting problems in several states," said NBC's Doug Adams around 3 p.m. EST. "None has been terribly serious, but here's an update."

Adams then noted a Republican report of Democratic rigging in New Jersey, adding that there'd been no evidence to back it up, and also mentioned two "glitches" in Indiana, which, he said, had caused no problems.[143] (That snap judgment echoed the blithe diagnosis of Bush Republican Todd Rokita, Indiana's secretary of state, who assured AP that "it's going to be one of Indiana's finest hours.")[144] On Election Night, Warren Stewart, head of VoteTrustUSA, appeared on Lou Dobbs's show on CNN and gave it to us straight, noting that reports of major system failure had been pouring in all day from precincts coast to coast. After Dobbs's show, Stewart stayed on at CNN throughout the night, assuming that he would be called upon for updates. And yet his news was of no interest whatsoever to Wolf Blitzer, Jeff Greenfield, Bill Schneider or any of the other wealthy players bloviating on the "meaning" of it all. When Stewart told CNN's producers of the latest questionable race, suggesting that such news ought to be aired, they'd put him off by saying, "Let's wait and see who wins."[145]

That answer was, of course, illogical, since it's impossible to "see who wins" when it is literally impossible to see who wins. And yet, although the answer was absurd, it made a sort of sense within the shadow world of the commercial media, where winning *images* are all that matter. Take Election Night. There's another victor beaming at the podium, backed by a quartet (or more) of happy kin, and thanking everybody in the room; and everybody out there's beaming, too, and doing jubilant high fives, and shouting, "YES!" Then there's the loser, grinning through the pain (and yet relieved that it's all over, you can tell), and his loved ones are behind him there, too, some smiling gamely while the young ones blubber openly as he thanks everybody in the room, and everybody out there's disappointed but still full of fight, and shouting "YES!" Each picture is a rich emotional confection, just the thing for topping off a portion of the evening's drama; and all such simple and familiar scenes, from the primaries to the conventions and beyond, comprise a larger and still more delicious spectacle of "our democracy at work." The subtext of that bright tableau—on TV and on radio, in print, online—is deeply reassuring: "Here, there are no tanks or troops out in the streets, coercing our assent. Here, the people make their sovereign choice, and it is duly honored. While evil governments worldwide routinely rig the vote, that just can't happen here in the United States, where what you see is what you get."

Outside that tacit propaganda pitch the corporate press is neither willing nor equipped to go. It cannot tell the truth about the state of our democracy, for it has no interest in democracy, nor does it want us taking civic action. What we call "the press" today, in other words, bears no relation to the common organ that once edified (and riled) the people, back when Jefferson and Madison et al. composed the First Amendment to protect those fractious papers—and, therefore, the people's rights and freedoms—from the government. Today, it is the blogosphere that serves this vital civic purpose, while what we call "the press" is just another facet of the media cartel, which wants us only to stay tuned and keep on buying everything, including the official bromide that "the system works." In short, a true republican *or* democratic press would cover politics as our concern and our responsibility: the proper sphere for our self-government. Contrarily, the media, across the board, sells "politics" as something that we ought only to watch addictively, just sitting back and taking it all in, tearing up or freaking out or snickering on cue, and letting, say, Chris Matthews do our shouting for us.

With very few exceptions, such celebrity "insiders" have ignored the Bush Republicans' campaign to disenfranchise the
majority, and, therefore, also ignored the Democrats' complicity
in that crusade. Rather than defend our right to vote by constant
hard reporting on this crisis (as Lou Dobbs has done), the major
talking heads prefer to jabber knowingly and endlessly about the
rising candidates—and not about those candidates' positions or
connections or financial backing, but, exclusively, about *how well
those candidates are doing on TV.* Does Hillary still come across as
strident? What's Obama's strategy for playing down (or up) his
inexperience? What about that gaffe of Biden's? How will Rudi,
or McCain, or Romney get the Christianists on board? By thus
fixating on "the horse race" as a purely televisual competition,
the bloviators only serve the media cartel itself, by casting politics as *nothing but* TV, thereby invalidating every action or
concern that gets no airtime.[146]

Thus they see the electorate not as citizens engaging in self-
government, but as the same impetuous and profitable mass that
watches some shows more than others and that buys (or not) the
goodies advertised throughout those shows. The U.S. press perceives the people not as the great engine of democracy, but
merely as a sort of inert substance acted *on* by others sharp
enough, and with sufficient funds, to make it boil. This is why
the people got no public credit whatsoever for the massive
turnout in 2006, as all the media's plaudits went to Sen. Chuck
Schumer and Rep. Rahm Emanuel, the so-called architects of
that apparent victory by and for the Democratic Party. The
media cartel could not perceive that it was actually a (partial)
victory by the people; and a victory achieved not for the Democratic Party but for our democracy itself, or what's now left of it
outside the gyre of corporate media.

How, then, will Americans vote in 2008? Will the next Election Day see another victory for the people, or will it bring us yet another "upset" for the ultra-right? We can prevent the latter only by acknowledging, and acting on, some hard realities. Certainly we have to face the fact that this regime was not elected, and that Bush's party represents a crackpot fringe whose purpose is as foreign to democracy as Mullah Omar's. To Bush & Co., therefore, we the people owe no more allegiance than a child owes to the criminal who stole her from her home and now abuses her while posing as her father. At the very least, we must push both the Democrats and sane Republicans to stop behaving like battered spouses and finally stand up for themselves and all the rest of us.

However, we must henceforth see ourselves not just as fed-up clients, hollering that our agents in the Capitol had better listen up, or else we'll vote them out. That huffy stance won't get us anywhere, because the voting process is corrupt, and so that ultimatum is about as threatening as a pile of angry letters, or a national day of marching in the streets. Rather than just try to force the hand of our apparent instruments in Congress, we must begin to see that Congress, and both parties, and the media, are *themselves* the problem now: a juggernaut that, in its own way, is as solidly opposed to the ideal democracy of Paine and Jefferson as any Soviet or Christianist elite. We need to break that juggernaut through radical reform: of our election process, and of campaign financing and, ultimately most important, of the media. Only through such long, hard work can we the people finally realize American democracy.

March 2007

Acknowledgments

For months after Bush & Co.'s apparent re-election in 2004 by some three million votes, it was all but impermissible to argue otherwise in public. Thus Bush/Cheney's victory recalled their case for war against Iraq—another shaky proposition that at first was questioned only by a few, who were then mocked and smeared for it, or, more often, totally ignored. And yet many more Americans spoke out against the regime's war plans than would later doubt, in public, Bush's "mandate." This book would therefore have remained a mad gleam in its author's eye, if not for the far-sightedness of certain editors.

I start by thanking Lewis Lapham and John R. MacArthur, respectively the editor and publisher of *Harper's*, for first hearing me out on the forbidden subject, and then soliciting an essay on it for the magazine. Their encouragement, and the research assistance they provided me, were crucial to the undertaking. Having learned of that assignment, William Frucht at Basic Books invited me to take the project further, and secured a contract for me, with the help of my inestimable agent, Emma Parry. For Bill's dedication to the enterprise, and for his expert guidance (and rare tact) as I labored on it, I thank him warmly. More generally, I thank all Bill's associates at Basic—John Sherer, Jamie

Brickhouse, Elizabeth Maguire, Marty Gosser, Joann Miller and David Shoemaker—for their enthusiastic dedication to this work. Holly Bemiss, my publicist at Basic, and veteran publicist Barbara Monteiro have gone well beyond the call of duty in their efforts to get the word out. I am most grateful also to Christine Marra, who supervised the very complicated preparation of the manuscript, and Kevin Goering, for his scrupulous attention to the legal issues that this book has inevitably raised. I also thank Jim Nicola and Linda Chapman of the New York Theater Workshop, for allowing me to do the one-man show *Hard Times* there in the spring of 2005—an exercise that helped me work through some of my ideas. For his collaboration on that piece, I must again thank Gregory Keller, my extraordinary director.

No single writer could even begin to tell the story of Bush/Cheney's strike against American democracy. Such an epic must be democratically assembled, out of the experiences, investigations, observations and analyses of countless others who went through the process. I have garnered so much information from so many of my fellow-citizens that I could not acknowledge all of them in this brief space, but must mention Bob Fitrakis, Cliff Arnebeck, Harvey Wasserman, Steve Rosenfeld, Ray Beckermann and Cynthia Butler, who have all worked heroically to find and publicize the truth about Ohio; Steve Freeman, who helped me greatly (and whose *Was the 2004 Presidential Election Stolen? Exit Polls, Election Fraud, and the Official Count*, co-authored with Joel Bleifuss, is a necessary complement to this book); Jonathan Simon, a statistician (and poet) whose acuity and generosity appear to be unlimited; the invaluable Greg Palast, who through the BBC and other media has broken scores of crucial stories; Greg's associates Leni von Eckardt and Matthew Pascarella; Thom Hartmann, who has worked journalistic wonders as a writer and broadcaster; ace blogster Brad Friedman; Robert

Glenn Plotner (aka "ignatzmouse"), for his lucid studies of the numbers in New Mexico and North Carolina (available online); Keith Olbermann, Janeane Garofalo and Laura Flanders, who have been all but alone in dealing with this story through the national media; Amy Goodman, who, as ever, has reported it according to the highest journalistic standards on "Democracy Now!"; Max Blumenthal and Esther Kaplan, for their extensive knowledge of the U.S. theocratic movement; John Conyers and the other Democratic members of the House Judiciary Committee, and their staffers, for their collaboration on the so-called Conyers Report; John Brakey and Dave Griscom in Arizona; Roxanne Jekot and Denis Wright in Georgia; Ian Whatley in South Carolina; Lisa Sarinelli in North Carolina; and, for both his research and his courage, the late Andy Stephenson.

What's left of our democracy would be quite lost without the Internet, especially the much-derided "blogosphere." I owe an incalculable debt of thanks to Mark Karlin at Buzzflash.com, Bob Fertik at democrats.com, David Brock at Media Matters, Micheal Stinson at Take Back the Media, the righteous multitudes at DemocraticUnderground.com, Arianna Huffington of the Huffington Post, Carolyn Kay at Make Them Accountable, Farhad Manjoo at *Salon*, Jerry Politex at BushWatch, my good friends at Fairness in Accuracy in Reporting, the folks at Bartcop and the Smirking Chimp, and Josh Marshall, DailyKos and Meria Heller. I also thank Danielle Holke, Stef Cannon, Josh Osersky, R. Miller, Oliver Dawshed, Joe Surkiewicz, Siva Vaidyanathan, Jeff Wallen, Maia Cowan, Bob Moser, Gene Gaudette, Liz Rich, Susan Dzieduszycka-Suinat, Catherine Root, William Betz, Joe Conason, Sidney Blumenthal, Morgan Pillsbury, Brett Rierson, Justin Hauley, the inimitable Fritz von Spüchen, my parents, Jordan and Anita Miller, my brothers Bruce and Eric, and my son Louis, for hot leads and helpful data of all kinds. I owe a special debt of gratitude to William Tucker for his understanding and support.

For this project I have been particularly blessed in my assistants. At *Harper's*, Emily Hyde worked briefly and efficiently with me until her re-assignment. She was then replaced by Emily Dische-Becker, who was my assistant there throughout her internship and also helped me afterward. From the spring throughout the summer of 2005, I leaned heavily on Jared Irmas, of whose meticulous hard work, high intelligence and sense of civic justice I could never say enough. A tireless researcher and very able critic (as well as a skilled mathematician), Jared was a godsend to me, often more collaborator than assistant. Especially for one so young (in 2004 he was my student as a sophomore at NYU), he has a formidable nose for news *and* for baloney, which he can spot a mile away, and refute like an old pro. I feel myself privileged by the partnership.

Finally, I thank my family still here at home—dearest Amy, and delightful Billy—who put up with the pressure of this most demanding project, even though they hadn't voted for it.

I could not possibly have handled all the research for the 2007 afterword without the expert help of Joyan Saunders and Sarah Beth Christensen, both of whom were kind enough to help me gratis. For their very helpful comments, moreover, I also want to than Bob Fitrakis, Brad Friedman, Paul Lehto, Kat L'Estrange, Bruce O'Dell, Steve Rosenfeld, Jonathan Simon and Harvey Wasserman.

I especially want to thank the excellent Martha Logan-Pearl, a California patriot whose generosity enabled me, eventually, to reach an audience far larger than I could have done without her timely help.

Notes

CHAPTER ONE

1. "Pat Robertson: God Told Him It's Bush in a 'Blowout' in November," Associated Press, 1/2/04.

2. With 99% of precincts reporting nationwide, the Associated Press reported Bush with 59,017,382 votes, an increase of 8.56 million from 2000 (Associated Press Election Wire, 11/3/04). The non-partisan Committee for the Study of the American Electorate (CSAE) released a report soon after that predicted Bush would have a net gain of 10 million votes once all were counted (CSAE, 11/4/04; PDF available at www.fairvote .org/reports/CSAE2004electionreport.pdf). In their final report, released two months later, CSAE calculated Bush won a solid 11.5 million votes more than he garnered in 2000 (CSAE, 1/14/05; PDF available at election04.ssrc.org/research/csae_2004_final_report.pdf).

3. David E. Sanger, "Polls Show Bush's Job-Approval Ratings Sinking," *New York Times*, 5/14/04.

4. Dan Balz, "Bad Signs for Bush in History, Numbers," *Washington Post*, 5/14/04.

5. Pre-Election Day polling data available at http://www.pollingreport. com/BushJob.htm.

6. "Swing States Lean to Kerry," *USA Today*, 10/31/04.

7. Edward McBride, "The American election: the 'silent majority' speaks," CatholicInsight.com, January 2005 (http://catholicinsight.com/online/political/amelect.shtml).

8. John C. Green, Corwin E. Smidt, James L. Guth and Lyman A. Kellstedt, "The American Religious Landscape and the 2004 Presidential

Vote: Increased Polarization," Pew Forum on Religion and Public Life. PDF available at pewforum.org/publications/surveys/postelection.pdf.

9. Ibid.

10. Ibid.

11. "Exit Poll Data Inconclusive on Increase in Evangelical Voters," *Washington Post*, 11/8/04.

12. Green et al., "The American Religious Landscape and the 2004 Presidential Vote: Increased Polarization."

13. Alan Cooperman and Thomas B. Edsall, "Evangelicals Say They Led Charge for the GOP," *Washington Post*, 11/8/04.

14. "Voters Liked Campaign 2004, But Too Much Mudslinging; Moral Values: How Important?" Pew Research Center for the People and the Press, 11/11/04 (http://people-press.org/reports/display.php3 ?ReportID=233).

15. "Where morality ranked for voters depends on the question asked," Associated Press, 11/11/04.

16. "American voters say urgent moral issues are peace, poverty and greed," Zogby International (http://www.zogby.com/soundbites/ReadClips. dbm?ID=10389).

17. Brian Faler, "Election Turnout in 2004 Was Highest Since 1968."

18. John McCormick, "Good News for Both Parties in Voter Rolls," *Chicago Tribune*, 10/29/04.

19. "New Voters Surge in 9 States," *San Francisco Chronicle*, 10/17/04.

20. For more information on Democrats out-registering Republicans, see Terry M. Neal, "What Poll and Registration Numbers Don't Reveal," Washingtonpost.com, 10/13/04; Ford Fessenden, "A Big Increase of New Voters in Swing States," *New York Times*, 9/26/04.

21. Bush won Montana by 20 points, although Brian Schweizer, the Democratic candidate for governor, won a decisive victory there, his party also winning four of five state offices as well as taking over the state senate.

22. Brian Faler, "A Polling Sight: Record Turnout," *Washington Post*, 11/5/04.

23. John Eisenhower, "Why I Will Vote for John Kerry for President," *Manchester Union Leader*, 9/9/04.

24. In 1960, after Nixon was defeated by John Kennedy in the presidential race, the former quietly used Morton, among others, to demand a recount, while publicly pretending to be above such ungracious politicking. "Three days after the election, party chairman Sen. Thruston

Morton launched bids for recounts and investigations in 11 states"—the notorious Illinois, as well as Texas, Michigan, Minnesota, Delaware, New Jersey, Nevada, Pennsylvania, South Carolina, Missouri and New Mexico. Morton could scare up no evidence of Democratic fraud nor could any other of Nixon's agents. Dan Greenberg, "Was Nixon Robbed? The Legend of the Stolen 1960 Presidential Election," *Slate*, 10/16/00, http://slate,msn.com/id/91350.

25. Ballard Morton, "Bush 'Goes Against Values I Treasure,'" *Louisville Courier Journal*, 10/14/04.

26. Four months later, Bandow wrote a piece for *Fortune* that assailed Bush/Cheney for their runaway extravagance: "In terms of real *domestic discretionary* outlays, which are most easily controlled, the biggest spender in the past 40 years is George W. Bush, with expenditure racing ahead 8.2% annually." The only viable solution, Bandow wrote, was to have a Democratic president confronted by a hostile Congress, on the theory that divided government inhibits federal spending (Doug Bandow, "The Conservative Case for Voting Democratic," *Fortune*, 4/10/04). The theory had been proposed, in May of 2003, by William Niskanen, chairman of the Cato Institute and former acting chairman of Reagan's Council of Economic Advisers. It figured prominently in right-libertarian critiques of Bush & Co. throughout the campaign year. See William Niskanen, "A Case for Divided Government," Cato Institute, 5/7/03, http://www.cato.org/dailys/05-07-03.html.

27. General Merrill A. McPeak, "Radio Address to the Nation," 7/30/04.

28. "Fukuyama Withdraws Bush Support," *Zaman* (Turkey), 7/14/04.

29. PNAC's purpose was to propagate the program for a worldwide Reaganite imperium, based on "anti-terrorism" and "free markets." Its members started lobbying for a U.S. re-invasion of Iraq in early 1998. Its "Statement of Purpose" may be found at http://www.newamericancentury.org/statementofprinciples.htm. For more on PNAC's aims and background, see http://home.earthlink.net/~platter/neo-conservatism/pnac.html and http://www.informationclearinghouse.info/article1665.htm.

30. For an archive of Roberts's many anti-Bush op-eds, see www.lewrockwell.com/roberts/roberts-arch.html; for an archive of Rockwell's many anti-Bush op-eds, see www.lewrockwell.com; and Bob Barr, "An Agonizing Choice: Conservatives Have Plenty of Cause to Abandon Bush," TruthOut.org, 10/7/04 (http://www.truthout.org/docs_04/101304G.shtml).

31. "ACLU Announces Collaboration with Rep. Bob Barr," American Civil Liberties Union, 11/25/02 (http://www.aclu.org/Privacy/Privacy.cfm?ID=11449&c=39). I have been unable to find any Democratic op-ed pieces backing Bush in the election. On November 2, *American Politics Journal* ran a pro-Bush editorial by Jeff Koopersmith, but it was satiric.

32. "The Conservative Case," *The American Conservative*, 11/8/04 (http://www.amconmag.com/2004_11_08/cover1.html).

33. For a more informal view of Bush's true repute among the non-fanatics in the GOP, see Philip Gourevitch, "Swingtime: Former Bush Voters Advertise Their Disaffection," *New Yorker*, 8/19/04. The article discusses filmmaker Errol Morris's treatment of the president's standing in his party. See also Dkospedia, at www.dkospedia.com/index.php/Republicans_for_Kerry_2004.

34. Eileen McNamara, "A Telling Shift in Allegiance," *Boston Globe*, 9/12/04.

35. Dan Simpson, "Born Republican, But Not Born Yesterday," *Pittsburgh Post-Gazette*, 10/27/04.

36. Joe Conason, "Diplomats Break Silence to Criticize White House," *New York Observer*, 6/21/04; David Thalheimer, "Why I'm Voting Against My Commander-in-Chief," truthout.org, 10/22/04 (http://www.truthout.org/docs_04/102704X.shtml).

37. This is from the group's first public salvo, released on June 16. DMCC published three more statements prior to Election Day, on July 28, September 28 and October 6. All were lucid and hard-hitting condemnations of Bush/Cheney's anti-terrorism policy, both in the war abroad and here at home. ("AMERICANS ARE LESS SAFE UNDER BUSH ADMINISTRATION POLICIES," the July statement asserted.) The texts are online at http://www.diplomatsforchange.com/project/statement.shtml.

38. Richard Kohn: "Bush Censure by Envoys May Be a First, Historians Say," Bloomberg.com, 6/18/04 (http://quote.bloomberg.com/apps/news?pid=10000103&sid=alMjDzShgJkQ&refer=us).

39. Jesse J. Holland, "Moderate Republicans Criticize Bush on Eve of Convention," AP, 8/29/04.

40. "Log Cabin Republicans Vote to Withhold Endorsement from President Bush," Log Cabin Republicans Press Release, 9/8/04 (http://www.lcrga.com/archive/200409081159.shtml).

41. Edmund L. Andrews, "Business Professors Criticize Tax Cuts," *New York Times*, 10/5/04.

42. Bush's ideological extremism had already been criticized on July 9, when 4,000 scientists, including several Nobelists, published an open letter backing Kerry: "But, they say, so much damage has been done that simply a new administration won't be enough—i.e., Kerry will have some serious 'reconstruction' to do," the statement concluded. "4,000 Scientists Join in Call to Expose and Correct Bush's Abuse of Science and Scientists," posted on the Environmental News Service, July 9, 2004; http://www.enn.com/news/2004-07-09/s_25704.asp.

43. Lee Iacocca: "Switching Candidates, Iacocca Backs Kerry," *New York Times*, 6/25/04.

44. Adam Klein, "Ed Koch: Why I'm Voting for Bush," WorldNet-Daily, 8/24/04.

45. Denis Staunton, "Economic Forum Ends in Gloom," *Irish Times*, 1/28/03; Peter Mackler, "US Takes Conciliatory Tone at Davos but Critics Still Wary," *Agence France Presse*, 1/25/04.

46. "Wall St. Republicans Grow Cool on Bush's Campaign," *Financial Times*, 8/27/04.

47. "The Bursting of the Bush Bubble: John Kerry Is a Better Choice for US President," *Financial Times*, 10/25/04.

48. "The Incompetent or the Incoherent?" *Economist*, 10/28/04.

49. Greg Mitchell, "Daily Endorsement Tally: Kerry Wins, Without Re-count," *Editor & Publisher*, 11/5/04; Greg Mitchell, "Daily Election Tally: Kerry Has Now Picked Up 41 Flip-Flops," *Editor & Publisher*, 10/29/04.

50. "The Tribune Recommends," *Albuquerque Journal*, 10/12/04.

51. "Kerry for President," *Orlando Sentinel*, 10/24/04. "The Herald Recommends: For U.S. President," *Miami Herald*, 10/17/04.

52. "Gazette Opinion: Bush Hasn't Earned 2nd Term in Office," *Billings Gazette*, 10/24/04.

53. "Kerry Will Restore American Dignity," *Lone Star Iconoclast*, 9/28/04.

54. Likewise, Bush was endorsed by Kerry's hometown paper, the *Lowell Sun*—which, although usually Democratic, had never favored Kerry in any race. "Endorsement: George W. Bush for President," *Lowell Sun*, 10/3/04. By and large, Bush was backed by smaller dailies like the *Sun*, although there were some major papers, like the *Denver Post*, that endorsed him after having backed Al Gore four years before. ("George W. Bush for President," *The Denver Post*, 10/24/04.) The *Post* readers strongly disagreed with the decision. "More than 700 readers have given us their

400 NOTES TO CHAPTER ONE

thoughts on Sunday's presidential endorsement, and they add up to a passionate dissent . . . Every letter we received was critical of the Post endorsement; we publish a sampling here today" ("The Open Forum— Letters to the Editor," *The Denver Post*, 10/26/04). It was Kerry who came out ahead, however, in both the number of endorsements and the reach of those newspapers backing him. Greg Mitchell, "Daily Endorsement Tally." As we shall see, the *national* media clearly favored Bush throughout the race and afterward.

55. Gromer Jeffers, Jr., "Crawford Mayor Is Kerry Supporter," *Dallas Morning News*, 6/1/04.

56. *The Situation with Tucker Carlson*, MSNBC, 7/14/05. Sports broadcaster Jim Lampley also noted those Vegas odds. "At 5:00 P.M. Eastern time on Election Day, I checked the sportsbook odds in Las Vegas and via the offshore bookmakers to see the odds as of that moment on the presidential election. John Kerry was a two-to-one favorite. You can look it up." Jim Lampley, "The Biggest Story of Our Lives," Huffington Post, 5/10/05 (http://www.huffingtonpost.com/theblog/archive/2005/05/biggest-story-of-our-live.html).

57. "Evaluation of Edison/Mitofsky Election System 2004," prepared by Edison Media Research and Mitofsky International for the National Election Pool (NEP), 1/19/05 (PDF available at http://www.ap.org/media/pdf/EvaluationEdisonMitofsky.pdf); "Response to the Edison/Mitofsky Election System 2004 Report," US Count Votes (PDF available at http://uscountvotes.org/ucvAnalysis/US/USCountVotes_Re_Mitofsky -Edison.pdf); Steven S. Freeman, "The Unexplained Exit Poll Discrepancy," 11/14/04 (http://www.truthout.org/docs_04/111404A.shtml).

58. A paperback edition, with an introduction by Gore Vidal, was published in early May of 2005 by Academy Chicago Publishers, with the title *What Went Wrong in Ohio* (ISBN 0-89733-535-X). No hardcover edition of the text was published by the government. Before Bush/Cheney, and Tom DeLay's dominion in the House, it was standard practice for congressional committees to come out with *two* reports after an investigation: a majority report and a minority report. In this case, the majority refused to let the Government Printing Office print, bind and publish the Democrats' report—even though it is required by law that "all reports" by congressional committees be thus made available; and even though the Republicans on the House Judiciary Committee had no majority report to publish, as they would not participate in the investigation. Conyers's staff photocopied the report, and sent it out, and also e-mailed it, to every member of

the House. Interview with Ted Kalo, General Counsel, Minority Staff, House Judiciary Committee, 5/12/05.

59. Anita Miller, ed., *What Went Wrong in Ohio: The Conyers Report on the 2004 Presidential Election* (Chicago: Chicago Academy Chicago Publishers, 2005), p. 2. (In the interests of full disclosure, I note here that Academy Chicago is owned and managed by my parents, Jordan and Anita Miller.)

60. Ibid., p. 2.

61. "Press Conference," Senate Radio/TV Gallery, 1/6/05.

62. "Lawmaker Says Bush Vote Should Be Contested," *Los Angeles Times*, 1/6/05.

63. "Bush's Victory Certified after Protest over Ohio," *Miami Herald*, 1/7/05.

64. The only evidence of Bush's victory is the ostensibly official vote count, which is to say, the mere assertion that he won. Granted, that assertion was immediately echoed by the Democrats and then the press. Such multitudinous agreement with the lie does not make that lie true.

CHAPTER TWO

1. Anita Miller, ed., *What Went Wrong in Ohio: The Conyers Report on the 2004 Presidential Election* (Chicago: Chicago Academy Chicago Publishers, 2005), p. 17.

2. Ford Fessenden, "A Big Increase of New Voters in Swing States."

3. Ibid., pp. 20–21.

4. Ibid.

5. Ibid., p. 19.

6. Arizona had the same arrangement, with Secretary of State Jan Brewer serving also as co-chair of the state Bush campaign. John Dougherty, "Election Eve Nightmare," *The Phoenix New Times*, 10/14/04.

7. Ibid., p. 30.

8. Ibid., pp. 24–25.

9. Paul Farhi, "In Fierce Contest for Ohio Vote, Secretary of State Feels Scrutiny," *Washington Post*, 10/27/04.

10. Miller, ed., *What Went Wrong in Ohio*, pp. 32–33.

11. Ibid., pp. 41–42.

12. "Voting Issues Keep Courts Busy up to Last Minute," *Cleveland Plain Dealer*, 11/3/04.

13. Interview with Sören Söndergaard, 3/11/05.

14. Miller, ed., *What Went Wrong in Ohio*, pp. 43–46.

15. Richard Hayes Phillips, Ph.D., "Warren County, Ohio: Most Successful Voter Registration Drive in American Political History, or Stuffing the Ballot Box," *The Free Press*, 12/1/04.

16. Miller, ed., *What Went Wrong in Ohio*, pp. 47–48.

17. Ibid., pp. 50–51.

18. Ibid. pp. 51–52.

19. Ibid., p. 53.

20. Ibid., pp. 46, 58.

21. Ibid., p. 58.

22. Ibid., p. 49. In 2004, Bush apparently won Mercer County by 75 percent—a seven-point increase over his victory margin in 2000. Ibid., p. 59.

23. Ibid.

24. "Kerry's Name Omitted from Some Ballots," *Columbus Dispatch*, 10/19/04.

25. Miller, ed., *What Went Wrong in Ohio*, p. 56.

26. Ibid., p. 56.

27. Ibid., p. 57.

28. Jo Becker and David Finkel, "Now They're Registered, Now They're Not," *Washington Post*, 10/31/04.

29. Miller, ed., *What Went Wrong in Ohio*, p. 56.

30. Ibid.

31. Scott Shane, "Never Shy, Bolton Brings a Zeal to the Table," *The New York Times*, 5/1/05.

32. Ibid., p. 75.

33. Ibid. In May 2005, Eaton was ordered by the Hocking County Board of Elections to resign her position—a retaliatory strike ordered by Blackwell, she determined. (All members of Ohio's boards of elections serve at his pleasure, regardless of their party affiliations.) Eaton sued for reinstatement, and also, on July 11, 2005, filed charges with the county Sheriff's Department against board of elections director Lisa Schwartze for having illegally shredded up to 10,000 documents in order to ensure Bush/Cheney's "victory." Ostensibly fired because she was not a "team player," Eaton replied, "Why should I be a team player if the director's doing illegal things? She took an entire rotating file cabinet of registration documents including brand new changes of addresses and shredded the hard copy and deleted items on a computer. Why should I keep my mouth shut? And I really don't understand the so-called Democrats [on the Board

of Elections] that fire me after I blow the whistle." Bob Fitrakis, "Ten Thousand Voter Registration Documents May Have Been Shredded in Hocking County, Ohio," *Free Press*, 7/13/05, http://www.freepress.org/columns/display/3/2005/1164.

34. Video available at http://video.lisarein.com/election2004/ohioreport/triadtech_100k.mov.

35. Miller, ed., *What Went Wrong in Ohio*, p. 79.

36. Ibid., pp. 77–78.

37. Ibid., p. 56.

38. Ibid., pp. 87–93.

39. Ibid., pp. 73–74.

40. Ibid., pp. 24–29.

41. Wayne Madsen, "Ohio GOP Secretary of State and gubernatorial candidate J. Kenneth Blackwell cannot certify how Federal election assistance money was spent," WayneMadsenReport.com, 8/15/05.

42. On November 17, apparently responding to complaints, the *Globe* ran "Media Accused of Ignoring Election Irregularities" (F1), a longer and less supercilious piece on the persistent "allegations" of electoral fraud. That piece quoted dissidents respectfully. It dealt not with electoral fraud per se, however, but with various explanations as to why that story had not broken from the blogosphere. It was cast not as a major civic story, in other words, but as a story on the media.

43. Wyatt Buchanan, "If It's Too Bad to Be True, It May Not Be Voter Fraud," *San Francisco Chronicle*, 11/11/04.

44. Dan Thanh Dang, "Conspiracy Theorists Focus on Voting Machines," *Baltimore Sun*, 11/5/04.

45. Interview with Michael I. Shamos, 2/23/05.

46. Interview with Will Doherty, 3/2/05.

47. Buchanan, "If It's Too Bad to Be True, It May Not Be Voter Fraud."

48. Interview with Thomas Patterson, 2/23/04.

49. Jules Witcover, "Ohio Recount Highlights Continuing Vote Trouble," *Baltimore Sun*, 1/2/05.

50. Dick Rogers, "Retaining Faith in Our Democracy," *San Francisco Chronicle*, 12/9/04.

51. Aside from Haddock's article, that news was not reported in this country. In late December 2004, Scripps Howard ran a similar story on the vote count in Ohio, where nearly one in fifty votes had not been counted. "Nearly 97,000 ballots, or 1.7 percent of those cast across the state, either did not record a preference for president or could not be

counted because the voter selected more than one presidential candidate." Michael Collins, "In Ohio, Almost 1 in 50 Votes for President Don't Count," Scripps Howard News Service, 12/22/04. That story too went unreported beyond a few Scripps Howard newspapers.

52. Leonard Pitts, Jr., "Memo to Kerry: The Election Is Over, and You Lost," *Baltimore Sun*, 1/23/05.

53. "Report Acknowledges Inaccuracies in 2004 Exit Polls," *Washington Post*, 1/20/05.

54. She had made the comments at a Democratic fund-raiser in Seattle, where one local daily ran a gleeful column on her talk: "'Two brothers own 80 percent of the [electronic voting] machines used in the United States,' Heinz Kerry said. She identified both as 'hard-right' Republicans. She argued that it is 'very easy to hack into the mother machines.' 'We in the United States are not a banana republic,' added Heinz Kerry. She argued that Democrats should insist on 'accountability and transparency' in how votes are tabulated. 'I fear for '06,' she said. 'I don't trust it the way it is right now.'" Although basically accurate (her point about the brothers Bob and Todd Urosevich, owners of Diebold and ES&S, was misstated slightly), Heinz Kerry's statement figured in the story not for its civic significance but as just one example of her wacky motor-mouth: "The sails of the philanthropist wife of Sen. John Kerry were not trimmed by November's narrow electoral defeat," the reporter giggled vis-à-vis her "spicy observations." Joel Connelly, "Teresa Heinz Kerry Hasn't Lost Her Outspoken Way," *Seattle Post-Intelligencer*, 3/7/05. On CNN, Dobbs took the same misogynistic line: "Another outspoken figure in American politics has not slowed down since November. Teresa Heinz Kerry gained a reputation for speaking her mind during the campaign, and she has not stopped. At a fund-raiser this weekend, she implied the results of the election were rigged. She was quoted in a Seattle newspaper saying that 80% of the voting machines in the United States are owned by hard-right Republicans. Heinz Kerry said it's easy for hackers to break into those machines. No comment from Senator Kerry." Lou Dobbs, *Lou Dobbs Tonight*, CNN, 3/8/05.

55. John Solomon, "GOP Pays Legal Bills in Vote-Thwart Case," AP, 8/12/05.

56. Steven Dyer, "Analysis Points to Election 'Corruption,'" *Akron Beacon Journal*, 4/1/05.

57. Interview with Jeff Rusnak, 6/26/05.

58. Robin Erb, "Burglars Left Plenty in Political Break-in," *Toledo Blade*, 10/14/04.

59. Ibid. Ohio Democrats are oddly subject to such sabotage. In the first week of July 2005, as the Ohio press was most aggressively investigating "Coingate"—a massive money-laundering operation by the state GOP, probably for off-the-books campaign expenses in 2004—there were two more nocturnal break-ins. Someone broke into the office of Denny White, chair of the Ohio Democratic Party, and stole only his laptop. Much the same thing happened to Dan Lucas, a close aide to Rep. Sherrod Brown (who was then heavily engaged in opposition to CAFTA, the "free-trade" agreement). Someone broke into Lucas's home, made his way to Lucas's study on the second floor, and stole his laptop. Interview with Jeff Rusnak, 7/22/05.

60. Interview with Denise Shull, 6/19/05.

61. In Stark County four years earlier, Nader threw the race to Bush, who won 78,153 votes to Gore's 75,308, with Nader taking 4,032. During Bush's first term, the county lost several large employers. On the other hand, there is an influential evangelical community in and around Canton. What happened in Stark County on Election Day may be especially significant, as it has long been a bellwether within Ohio (which has itself long been a bellwether in the United States). "If Ohio is a marker of the national mood, Stark County (population 377,519), in which Canton is the main town, is the best indicator of what Ohio is thinking, backing the right candidate for president every election bar one over the past 40 years. As Ohio goes, so goes the nation; as Stark County goes, so goes Ohio." Gary Younge, "Fading Picture of the American Dream," *The Guardian*, 10/13/04. This is an especially astute political portrayal of Stark County a few weeks before Election Day.

62. Interview with John Conyers, 5/21/05.

63. Paul Krugman, "Hack the Vote," *New York Times*, 12/2/03.

64. Video available at http://whatreallyhappened.com/IMAGES/peterking.mov.

65. In Congress, where the issue was debated in 1791/92, the decision to require a modest fee for mailing newspapers represented the "conservative" position. There was also considerable support for the more radical alternative of mailing newspapers for free. Elbridge Gerry was among the "anti-restrictionists": "Wherever information is freely circulated," that staunch Republican declared, "there slavery cannot exist; or if it does, it will vanish, as soon as information has been generally diffused." The so-called restrictionists, led by James Madison, were persuaded that a modest fee would make the postal system more efficient, by providing local postmasters with

a clear incentive to ensure delivery (as the fee was paid by the recipient). There was no argument based on a wish to lessen or impede the flow of news. See Richard R. John, *Spreading the News: The American Postal System from Franklin to Morse* (Cambridge, Mass.: Harvard University Press, 1995), pp. 33–37.

CHAPTER THREE

1. See David Brock, *The Republican Noise Machine* (New York: Three Rivers Press, 2004), p. 45, 50.

2. Mike Allen, "Bulge Under President's Coat in First Debate Stirs Speculation," *Washington Post*, 10/9/04.

3. Ibid.

4. Kevin Berger, "NASA photo analyst: Bush wore a device during debate," *Salon*, 10/29/04; Dave Lindorff, "Was Bush Wired? Sure Looks Like It," *Mother Jones*, 10/30/04. The *Times*'s treatment of the controversy was reported, after the election, by Dave Lindorff in "The Emperor's New Hump," *Extra!* Jan./Feb. 2005, pp. 6ff.

5. "Another Contested Contest?" *New York Times Magazine*, 10/31/04, p. 17.

6. David Hoffman, "Bush Takes Some Blame for Scandal," *Washington Post*, 12/21/1986.

7. J.H. Hatfield, *Fortunate Son*, Third ed. (New York: Soft Skull Press, 2002), p. 79.

8. Dan Balz, "Bush, Perot Lash Clinton," *Washington Post*, 11/2/92.

9. "What the President Knew," *The New York Times*, 10/19/1992.

10. Walter Pincus, "Bush Pardons Weinberger in Iran-Contra Affair," *Washington Post*, 12/25/1992.

11. Anita Miller, ed., *The Complete Transcripts of the Clarence Thomas–Anita Hill Hearings* (Chicago: Academy Chicago Publishers, 1994), p. 117.

12. Ibid., p. 118.

13. Ibid., p. 117, 120, 126, 139, 140.

14. Ibid., p. 139.

15. Ibid., p. 118.

16. Ibid., p. 120.

17. Ibid., p. 160.

18. Ibid., p. 140.

19. In response to the Terry Schiavo episode, Danforth called the GOP a "political arm for Christian conservatives." John C. Danforth, "In the Name of Politics," *New York Times*, 3/30/05.

20. John C. Danforth, *Resurrection: The Confirmation of Clarence Thomas* (New York: Viking, 1994), p. 89.

21. Ibid.

22. Ibid.

23. Ibid., p. 106.

24. Ibid., p. 107.

25. Ibid., p. 126.

26. Ibid., p. 129.

27. Ibid., p. 128–129.

28. Paul M. Barrett, "On the Right: Thomas Is Emerging as Strong Conservative Out to Prove Himself," *Wall Street Journal*, 4/27/93.

29. Jane Mayer and Jill Abramson, *Strange Justice: The Selling of Clarence Thomas* (Boston and New York: Hyperion, 1992); David Brock, *Blinded by the Right: The Conscience of an Ex-Conservative* (New York: Crown, 2002).

30. Ibid., p. 104

31. Anita Hill, *Speaking Truth to Power* (New York: Doubleday, 1997), pp. 196–197.

32. Lou Dubose and Jan Reid, *The Hammer: God, Money, and the Rise of the Republican Congress* (New York: Public Affairs, 2004), p. 143.

33. "Contesting the Vote: The Demonstrators; How the Troops Were Mobilized for the Recount," *New York Times*, 11/28/00.

34. "GOP Redistricting Expert Calls Proposed Map Unconstitutional," AP, 5/9/03.

35. The speech, "Be Not Afraid," is online at http://www.majority leader.gov/news.asp?FormMode=Detal&ID=131.

36. Danforth, *Resurrection*, p. 130.

37. Ibid.

38. "EPA Cuts Defeated in House," *Washington Times*, 7/29/1995.

39. "New Stars Emerge on GOP's Right," *Washington Times*, 5/16/1991.

40. "House Democrats Rescue D.C. Budget, Heading Off GOP at the Pass, *Washington Post*, 8/6/1989.

41. "House Rejects Statehood, But Backers See Gains," *Washington Times*, 11/22/1993.

42. "DeLay vs. Dean," *Washington Times*, 9/3/03.

43. "Election vitriol subsides," *Houston Chronicle*, 11/1/02; "Nobel 'Appeasement Prize,'" *Washington Post*, 11/8/1995; "DeLay Revels in

GOP Strength with Bush in the White House," *Washington Times*, 3/9/01.

44. Dubose and Reid, *The Hammer*, p. 264.

45. See "GOP Tightens Grip on K Street Leaders Send Message to Associations," *Roll Call*, 3/12/01.

46. "Business Group Backs Democrat Whose Hiring Irked GOP Leaders," *Washington Post*, 10/15/1998. There is, of course, a tactical dimension to such disingenuous ripostes. To charge the other with the very crime that you yourself have just committed, are committing or will soon commit is an exquisitely disarming move, at once distracting your accuser and obscuring your own criminality. "The propagandist must insist on the purity of his own intentions and, at the same time, hurl accusations at the enemy," notes Jacques Ellul. "But the accusation is never made haphazardly or groundlessly. The propagandist will not accuse the enemy of just any misdeed; he will accuse him of the very intention that he himself has and of trying to commit the very crime that he himself is about to commit" (*Propaganda: The Formation of Men's Attitudes* [New York: Vintage Books, 1973], p. 58). It is a most effective tactic—insofar as it *is* a tactic, and not instead, or also, an "honest" paranoid projection. Although a masterful manipulator, Hitler was, as well, a true believer, dying in the iron conviction that the Nazis had been waging a *defensive* war against "world Jewry," which had finally beaten them. Goebbels also was a cynical fanatic, simultaneously functioning as both devoted missionary and disinterested technocrat. Although their cases are extraordinary, that pathology per se is not unique to them, but figures in all anti-liberal revolutionary movements that rely on modern propaganda methods. Lenin was divided thus, so was Joe McCarthy, and so are Grover Norquist and Paul Weyrich today.

47. "DeLay's Reply," *Washington Times*, 4/7/05.

48. "Barton Denies Favoring Westar," *Roll Call*, 6/22/04; Laylan Copelin, "DeLay's Texas PAC Investigated," *Roll Call*, 12/8/03; "Diverting the War on Terrorism," *New York Times*, 6/10/03.

49. Larry Margasak, "House GOP Embraces Change in Membership Rules to Insulate Delay Against Possible Indictment," AP, 11/17/04.

50. "A 3rd DeLay Trip under Scrutiny," *Washington Post*, 4/6/05, A1; Mike Allen, "House Rescinds GOP Ethics Charges," *Washington Post*, 4/28/05.

51. Ibid.

52. "DeLay: 'I Came Here to Limit Government,'" *Washington Times*, 4/14/05.

53. "Parties Sharpen Their Political Rhetoric over Terri Schiavo Case," AP, 3/24/05.

54. "GOP: Soros Behind DeLay Attacks," NewsMax.com, 3/24/05 (http://www.newsmax.com/archives/ic/2005/3/24/91823.shtml).

55. "Ads Hit Reynolds on Ethics Issue," *Buffalo News*, 4/3/05.

56. Jill Zuckman, "DeLay Blames Conspiracy in Appeal to Senate Republicans," *Chicago Tribune*, 4/12/05.

57. Rep. Wilson's statement is no longer available on his official website. It can be found reposted at "Media repeat anti-Soros propaganda by DeLay defenders," MediaMatters.org, 4/19/05 (http://mediamatters.org/items/200504190004).

58. Barbara Comstock on *Crossfire*, CNN, 4/11/05.

59. William Kristol on *Special Report with Brit Hume*, FOX News, 4/7/05.

60. Richard Lessner, "DeLay Is All About Politics," *Washington Examiner*, 4/13/05 (http://www.conservative.org/columnists/lessner/04132005rl.asp).

61. Phyllis Schafly, "Urgent Alert from Phyllis!! Tom DeLay Needs Our Help Now!" EagleForum.org, 4/12/05 (http://www.eagleforum.org/alert/2005/04-12-05.html).

62. "Watch for the Religious Left Sock Puppets on TV and Radio!" TraditionalValues.org, 2/17/05 (http://www.traditionalvalues.org/print.php?sid=2144).

63. Richard Poe, "Soros Shadow Party Stalks DeLay," FrontPageMag.com, 4/12/05 (http://www.frontpagemagazine.com/Articles/ReadArticle.asp?ID=17686).

64. "DeLay Not Worth the Fight," *Rocky Mountain News*, 3/31/05.

65. Juan Williams on *Day to Day*, National Public Radio, 4/8/05.

66. Gail Russell Chaddock, "Historic Parallels as DeLay's Woes Deepen," *Christian Science Monitor*, 4/12/05.

67. "GOP: Soros Behind Delay Attacks," NewsMax.com.

68. "Report That Group Which Filed Delay Ethics Charge Received Soros Money False," RawStory.com, 3/24/05.

69. "Watchdog Groups Urge House Leaders to Resolve Unprecedented Ethics Crisis," The Campaign Legal Center, March 2005 (http://www.campaignlegalcenter.org/press-1583.html).

70. The projectivity of the DeLay campaign was manifest not only in the scale and vehemence of the operation overall but also in the conduct of certain of the drive's participants, who were required to denigrate *themselves* as well as Soros. The campaign's tacit anti-Semitism was especially

striking for the fact that some of the campaigners were Jews themselves: William Kristol and David Horowitz. The Reverend Lou Sheldon, head of the Traditional Values Coalition, is a Jewish convert to evangelical Christianity, while Robert Novak—a commentator prone to anti-Jewish gibes—was, as he puts it, "born in the Jewish faith," and is a Roman Catholic convert. Jewish self-loathing has long loomed large in the psychology of anti-Semitism at its most virulent, from the notorious career of Tomás de Torquemada, Spain's first Grand Inquisitor (and a descendant of *conversos*), to the case of radio hatemonger Michael Savage, whose anti-Semitic diatribes are sometimes reminiscent of the Nazis (and who was born Michael Wiener in the Bronx). See Mark Crispin Miller, *Cruel and Unusual: Bush/Cheney's New World Order* (New York: W. W. Norton, 2004), pp. 236–37.

71. Once Bush/Cheney had been chosen as the nation's president, Ginni Thomas went to work as a Senior Fellow at the Heritage Foundation, where her many tight connections at the top served her extremely well. She is now Heritage's major liaison with the Bush White House. "In her current position, Thomas works to advance Heritage's policy recommendations on a range of foreign and domestic issues among decision-makers in the executive branch" (http://www.heritage.org/About/Staff/VirginiaThomas.cfm).

CHAPTER FOUR

1. "Aids Cuts Threatened by US over Tribunal," *Boston Globe*, 12/5/04; "GOP's Power Play," *Washington Post*, 7/26/03.

2. Jon Brown, "Tom DeLay's New World Order," CounterPunch. org, 6/28/03 (http://www.counterpunch.org/brown06282003.html).

3. Ron Hutcheson, "Bush-Rove bond faces ultimate test," *Miami Herald*, 7/31/05.

4. Condoleeza Rice, *CNN Sunday*, 9/8/02.

5. Peggy Noonan, "Just the Facts," *Wall Street Journal*, 1/27/03.

6. Laura Bush on *20/20*, ABC, 12/13/02.

7. Mark Hosenball, Michael Isikoff, and Evan Thomas, "Cheney's Long Path to War," *Newsweek*, 11/17/03.

8. During an October 27 campaign rally in Kissimmee, Florida, Cheney asserted that Saddam was "a man who had produced and used chemical weapons against his own people and against the Iranians and

had other robust WMD programs." Ten months earlier, the U.S. Weapons Inspector reported his findings on WMD in Iraq—"It turns out we were all wrong, and that is most disturbing." "Ex-Iraq Inspector: Prewar Intelligence Failure 'Disturbing,'" CNN.com, 1/29/04 (http://www.cnn.com/2004/US/01/28/sprj.nirq.wmd.kay/).

9. Ann Imse, "Dark Suit, Earpiece and 'Come with Me,'" *Chicago Sun-Times*, 3/31/05.

10. "White House Weighs in on Ouster," *Rocky Mountain News*, 5/28/05.

11. Ibid.

12. "No Charges in Ouster," *Rocky Mountain News*, 7/30/05.

13. At the moment when John Ellis made his call, there was something funny happening to the numbers down in Florida. Suddenly, according to the Voters News Service, Gore's 16,000-vote lead in Volusia County disappeared, the total inexplicably distributed among the election's third-party presidential candidates. Other numbers in the state had also changed dramatically. After Gore told Bush he would concede, and as he made his way to Democratic headquarters to tell the world he was conceding, the numbers shifted to their prior levels, favoring Gore again. "Nick Baldick, his chief operative in Florida, saw that something was seriously amiss. V.N.S. had guessed that 180,000 votes were still outstanding. In fact, there were 360,000 votes that hadn't been counted—from precincts in Palm Beach, Broward, and Miami-Dade Counties, which were largely Gore country. And what was this? Negative 16,000 votes for Gore in Volusia County? A computer glitch, it turned out. Baldick watched the Bush lead wither with each new report." David Margolick, Evgenia Peretz and Michael Shnayerson, "The Path to Florida," *Vanity Fair*, October 2004.

14. Henry Waxman, "Did NBC Make Call with Welch in the Backfield?" *Los Angeles Times*, 8/13/01.

15. Robert Novak on *Evans, Novak, Hunt & Shields*, CNN, 11/11/00.

16. Nick Smith, "Faith-Based Initiatives," TruthNews.com, 8/24/03 (http://truthnews.com/world/2003080052.htm); "FBI agents reportedly are investigating allegations that Rep. Nick Smith (R-Mich.) was offered 'significant financial support' for his son's House campaign in exchange for a vote in favor of the Medicare legislation (HR 1), *Roll Call* reports (Bresnahan, *Roll Call*, 2/26). In December, Smith, who is retiring this year, said that unnamed Republican leaders promised to donate $100,000 to his son's congressional race in exchange for his support on the Medicare bill. However, Smith later backed away from that comment, saying that

suggestions he was bribed are 'technically incorrect.' Smith would prefer a nicer word, like 'gift' or 'good will payment.'" "FBI Examining Smith Medicare Allegations," *Roll Call*, 2/26/04.

17. "Weldon Introduces the 'Incapacitated Persons Legal Protection Act," Press Release, 3/8/05 (http://weldon.house.gov/News/DocumentSingle. aspx?DocumentID=23321); In the organization's brochure, Rep. Weldon is thus quoted: "Principle Approach International deserves our whole-hearted support and utmost respect." The brochure has been taken off-line (it was once available at www.face.net/PAIconferenceBrochure.pdf). As of this writing, there is a slightly garbled HTML/PDF version at http://64.233.161.104/search?q=cache:IG4VuRe5Bx0J:www.face.net/ PAIconferenceBrochure.pdf+%22Principle+Approach+International+ deserves+our+wholehearted+support%22&hl=en&client=safari.

18. William Bennett on *The O'Reilly Factor*, FOX News, 11/28/00.

19. David Grann, "Quiet Riot: Bush Rides the Tiger," *The New Republic*, 12/25/00.

20. Ibid.

21. *Hannity & Colmes*, Fox News, 12/15/00. Niger Innis is the national spokesman for the Congress of Racial Equality (CORE), the onetime civil rights advocacy group that had collapsed by 1968. What remained of it was taken over by Roy Innis, Niger's father. Since then, CORE has been a small but stalwart lobby for pro-corporate interests, and otherwise allied with the Republicans. For more on CORE, see http://www.gmwatch.org/profile1.asp?PrId=174.

22. Ibid.

23. The most informative accounts of that election are Jeffrey Toobin, *Too Close to Call: The Thirty-Six-Day Battle to Decide the 2000 Election* (New York: Random House, 2001); Greg Palast, *The Best Democracy Money Can Buy: An Investigative Reporter Exposes the Truth about Globalization, Corporate Cons and High-Finance Fraudsters*, rev. ed. (New York: Plume, 2004); John Nichols and David Deschamps, *Jews for Buchanan: Did You Hear the One About the Theft of the American Presidency?* (New York: New Press, 2001). See also Robert Greenwald's film *Unprecedented: The 2000 Presidential Election*, available on DVD (and updated after the election of 2004).

24. "Horowitz: It's the War Stupid!" NewsMax.com, 11/7/02 (http:// www.newsmax.com/archives/articles/2002/11/6/193824.shtml).

25. The U.S. press did not look into the bizarre electoral results of 2002. On July 30, 2003, AlterNet posted Thom Hartmann's excellent

overview of the computer glitches that had favored Bush Republicans throughout the nation: "The Theft of Your Vote Is Just a Chip Away," http://www.alternet.o/story/16474. This article is indispensable, as is the website electionline.org, which identifies the type of electoral technology used in every state and every county: http://www.electionline.org/index.jsp?page=ElectionLineToday2.

26. Allard's interest group ratings available at http://www.vote-smart.org/issue_rating_category.php?can_id=H0632103.=category&category=Conservative. "[A] Zogby International survey released Sunday morning on NBC's *Meet the Press* [showed] Strickland leading Allard 53 percent to 44 percent. A *Rocky Mountain News*/News 4 poll Friday showed Strickland leading 42 percent to 38 percent." "Strickland Hits the Western Slope," *Rocky Mountain News*, 11/4/02.

27. "Colorado County Voting Equipment Inventory" available at www.sos.state.co.us/pubs/ hava/cty_vtg_inv_2004_09_13.pdf.

28. For Marriage Protection Amendment, see "Wayne Allard—Federal Marriage Amendment" (http://allard.senate.gov/features/Marriage/). Full text of Constitution Restoration Act available at http://www.renewamerica.us/commandments/legislation/s2082.htm.

29. "Polling on 2002 Key Senate Races" (http://www.realclearpolitics.com/Congressional/Senate_02_Polls.html).

30. Coleman's interest group ratings available at http://www.vote-smart.org/issue_rating_category.php?can_id=CMN26428.

31. "Minnesota Poll: Wellstone slightly leads Coleman," AP, 10/19/02; Coleman, who had been mayor of St. Paul for eight years, was personally urged by Bush to run against the charismatic Wellstone, who was easily the boldest liberal in the Senate and harbored presidential hopes. Bush may also have imbibed some of his father's animus against the senator, whom Poppy termed a "chickenshit" for his outspoken opposition to the first Gulf War. Edward Walsh, "Wellstone Faces Fallout of Anti-War Offensive," *Washington Post*, 4/7/1991.

32. "Because of Wellstone's sudden death and Mondale's late entry, all the ballots in that race were hand-counted. For more on the surprising outcome, see above, pp. 93–94.

33. "GOP House Members Urge No Funds for U.N. Without Documents Probe," AP, 12/2/04.

34. "Minn. Senator Teams with Giuliani in Prescription Drug Probe," AP, 3/17/04.

35. Chambliss's interest group ratings available at http://www. vote-smart.org/issue_rating_category.php?can_id=CNIP7909. Also "U.S. Senate Race Draws National Interest," *Chattanooga Times Free Press*, 8/26/02.

36. "Pollsters Defend Their Surveys in Wake of Upsets," Cox News Service, 11/6/02.

37. "VFW Endorses Chambliss," *Atlanta Journal Constitution*, 10/10/02.

38. "Bin Laden Debuts in Chambliss Spot," *Roll Call*, 10/14/02.

39. "Campaign Kicks It up a Notch," *Atlanta Journal Constitution*, 8/5/02.

40. Myra MacPherson, "The VA's Max Cleland: A New Kind of Battle," *Washington Post*, 4/18/1977.

41. "Chambliss Stops in Hometown to Celebrate," *Atlanta Journal Constitution*, 11/8/02.

42. See Al Franken, *Lies and the Lying Liars Who Tell Them: A Fair and Balanced Look at the Right* (New York: Plume, 2004), pp. 186–214.

43. The original contract, the First Amendment, and a host of other raw documentation obtained from open records requests, are indexed and available to download in PDF format at http://www.countthevote.org/ga_contract/list.htm. Note that responsibilities appropriated to county officials in the original contract, such as writing the ballots and creating the election databases, had been reassigned to Diebold officials in the First Amendment. The First Amendment was signed on July 31, 2002, the day on which the original contract stipulated Diebold would complete training poll workers to undertake such tasks. By amending the contract on this day and reassigning these responsibilities, Diebold narrowly avoided a contract violation which, in accordance with their original contract, would have resulted in a compromise of their ultimate fee. See also Ronnie Dugger, "How They Could Steal the Election This Time," *The Nation*, posted on 07/29/04 (http://www.thenation.com/doc.mhtml?i=20040816&c=7&s=dugger).

44. This was probably a reference to John Fund's *Stealing Elections: How Voter Fraud Threatens Our Democracy*, whose publication date was five weeks later. See pp. 101–102.

45. Alan Keyes on *Judy Woodruff's Inside Politics*, CNN, 8/30/04.

46. "Jesus Wouldn't Vote for Obama, Keyes Says," *Chicago Tribune*, 9/8/04.

47. Dana Canedy, "As TV Cameras Roll, Haitians Dash from Stranded Boat to the Florida Shore," *New York Times*, 10/29/02.

48. *Rush Limbaugh Show*, Premiere Radio Networks, 10/31/02.

49. "Haitian Fury Grows; 6 Held in Plot," *Miami Herald*, 10/31/02.

50. *Rush Limbaugh Show*, Premiere Radio Networks, 10/31/02.

51. Ibid.

52. Michael Scott, "Dead Man On Voter Rolls Sparks Inquiry," *Cleveland Plain Dealer*, 9/23/04. At the time, there was reportedly a criminal investigation of the mischief in Lake County. However, there were no further press reports about the matter, and several messages left at the office of Lake County's chief prosecutor, who might shed some light on the alleged investigation, were not answered.

53. Charles Hurt, "Missouri Voter Drive Under Attack," *Washington Times*, 6/29/04.

54. "Inside Report: Dems Have Secret Plan to Steal Election," NewsMax.com, 9/27/04 (http://www.newsmax.com/archives/articles/2004/9/27/153454.shtml).

55. "Democrats Preparing to Steal Iowa Too?" NewsMax.com, 9/28/04 (http://www.newsmax.com/archives/ic/2004/9/28/84629.shtml).

56. "Colorado to Tackle Voter-Fraud Fears," *Washington Times*, 10/14/04.

57. Ibid.

58. "Racicot Asks Kerry to Fight Voter Fraud," *Washington Times*, 10/21/04.

59. "Judge Rebuffs GOP Effort to Contest Voters in Ohio," *Washington Post*, 10/28/04.

60. Mark Weaver on *The Abrams Report*, MSNBC, 11/1/04.

61. Mark Weaver on *CNN Live Sunday*, CNN, 10/31/04.

62. For more on Fund, see www.opinionjournal.com/diary/bio.html.

63. For more on the Bradley Foundation, see http://www.media transparency.org/funderprofile.php?funderID=1.

64. Sidney Blumenthal, *The Clinton Wars* (New York: Farrar, Straus and Giroux, 2003), pp. 427–3; Paul D. Coffard, *The Rush Limbaugh Story: Talent on Loan from God* (New York: St. Martin's Press, 1993), p. 189; interviews with Morgan Pillsbury and Melinda Pillsbury-Foster.

65. John Fund, *Stealing Elections: How Voter Fraud Threatens Our Democracy* (San Francisco: Encounter Books, 2004), p. 28.

66. Ibid., p. 13.

67. Joshuah Bearman, "The Ground War," *LA Weekly*, 10/29/04.

68. *Hannity & Colmes*, Fox News Channel, 7/16/04.

69. Ibid.

70. *Congressional Record—House*, 7/15/04.

71. *The Big Story with John Gibson*, Fox News Channel, 9/27/04.

72. Mark Foley on *News from CNN*, CNN, 9/27/04.

73. *Wolf Blitzer Reports*, CNN, 9/28/04.

74. "Colorado Election Day Manual: A Detailed Guide to Voting in Colorado," November 2004; PDF available at http://herren4georgiarnc.org/RNC_COManual.pdf.

75. Ibid.

76. Tucker Carlson on *Crossfire*, CNN, 10/14/04.

77. "Democrat Playbook Opened to Criticism," *Rocky Mountain News*, 10/15/04; "Parties clash on election procedures," *The Denver Post*, 10/15/04.

78. Anti-Bush registration drive stirs fraud concerns," *The Washington Times*, 10/15/04.

79. Dick Cheney on *Hannity and Colmes*, FOX, 10/20/04.

80. "Hood Refuses to Meet with U.S. Reps," *Tampa Tribune*, 10/16/04.

81. *Hannity and Colmes*, FOX, 10/26/04.

82. Rich Lowry on *The Point*, CNN, 3/3/01.

83. Fred Barnes on *Special Report with Brit Hume*, FOX, 8/8/01.

84. *Congressional Record—House*, 1/6/05, pp. H85–H127.

85. Rep. Jindal's father and daughter were not deceased. The congressman was harking back to "one of the proudest weeks in my life," when his dad and daughter had been present *in the House* to watch his swearing-in. For an overview of Jindal's theocratic extremism, see Francis C. Assisi and Ellizabeth Pothen, "The Agony and Ecstasy of Bobby Jindal" (http://www.indolink.com/Living/America/a91.php).

86. "Sheriff: Man says he was hired to provide phony voter registrations," AP, 10/18/04.

87. "Election Coverage," truthout.org, 11/2/04; http://www.truthout.org/eblog.shtml.

88. "Congresswoman's son, four others charged with slashing Republican van tires on Election Day," AP, 1/24/05.

89. Gretchen Elke, "Congresswoman's son, four others charged with slashing Republican van tires on Election Day," AP, 1/24/05.

90. "Investigation reveals potentially fraudulent voter forms," AP, 10/12/04.

91. Mary Perea, "Candidates seek voter forms of woman who registered teen," AP, 9/14/04.

92. "Election Fraud Cases Under Review," WBNS-TV (http://www.10tv.com/Global/story.asp?S=2458796).

93. For a savvy take on the whole ACORN controversy, see the exchange between Jack Hitt and GOP spokesman Scott Hogenson on Hitt's radio show, transcript available online at http://www.blogthevote.org/blog/archives/reports_by_state/az_voting_problems.

94. Michael Moore, "Just One Senator . . . An Open Letter to the U.S. Senate from Michael Moore," MichaelMoore.com, 1/4/05 (http://www.michaelmoore.com/words/message/index.php?messageDate=2005-01-04).

95. "As I recall, the facts are these: On election night we won. And then there was a recount and we won. And there was a selected recount as a result of different legal maneuverings, and we won that. And I believe one of these days, that all this is going to stop, and Dick Cheney and I will be the president and the vice president" (Bush campaign press conference, 11/30/00). What the Democrats had asked for, and never received, was a *hand* recount of the vote in Florida, either in those largely Democratic southern counties where there had been evidence of fraud, or in all the counties in the state.

96. Thomas Crampton, "Not a simple election, global vote monitors say," *International Herald Tribune*, 11/3/04.

97. Hugh Hewitt, *If It's Not Close, They Can't Cheat: Crushing the Democrats in Every Election (And Why Your Life Depends on It)* (Nashville: Nelson Books, 2004), p. 11. Gore made that notorious avowal—"I'll do anything to win"—in a private conversation with an aide in 1999. From the context it was clear that Gore was *not* boasting of his amorality, like Shakespeare's Richard III, but responding to a callow statement by his rival. "'I'm not like George Bush,' Al Gore told an aide in 1999, when campaign was just gearing up. 'If he wins or loses, life goes on.' Bush may not have been quite as driven. 'If this doesn't work out, I've got a life,' he told a *Newsweek* reporter in December 1999, when his campaign seemed to be dragging.'" "The Battle After the Bell," *Newsweek*, 11/20/04.

98. Hewitt, *If It's Not Close, They Can't Cheat*, p. 55.

99. Ibid., p. 109.

100. Quoted in Karen Armstrong, *Holy War: The Crusades and Their Impact on Today's World* (New York: Anchor Books, 2001), p. 210.

101. Ibid., p. 440.

102. Richard Slotkin, *Gunfighter Nation: The Myth of the Frontier in Twentieth-Century America* (Norman: University of Oklahoma Press, 1998), pp. 12–13.

103. Joseph Doddridge, *Notes on the Settlement and Indian Wars of the Western Parts of Virginia and Pennsylvania from 1763 to 1783* (1912; rpt. Parsons, W. Va: McClain, 1989), p. 43.

104. George Armstrong Custer, *My Life on the Plains: or Personal Experiences with the Indians* (1876; rpt. Norman, OK: University of Oklahoma Press, 1977), p. 13.

105. Kennedy spoke thus of communism in Salt Lake City on September 23, 1960, in the course of his campaign for president. See http://www.jfklink.com/speeches/jfk/sept60/jfk230960_saltlake01.html.

106. Shu Guang Zhang, *Mao's Military Romanticism: China and the Korean War* (Lawrence: University of Kansas Press, 1995).

107. Report on the Covert Activities of the Central Intelligence Agency, also know as the Doolittle Report, 9/30/54, Appendix A.

108. Stephen Ambrose, *Ike's Spies: Eisenhower and the Espionage Establishment* (Jackson, Miss.: University Press of Mississippi, 1999), p. 188.

109. No longer available on the Chalcedon Foundation website, Finnell's essay may be found reposted on http://theunjustmedia.com/America/Vote%20fraud/How%20George%20W.%20Bush%20Won%20the%202004%20Presidential%20Election.htm.

110. Biography available at http://www.natreformassn.org/statesman/01/confront.html.

111. Chalcedon's full mission statement available at http://www.chalcedon.edu/ministry.php.

112. Val Finnell, "Slash and Burn Politics."

113. Frederick Clarkson, "Inside the Christian Coalition," Institute for First Amendment Studies, January/February 1992) http://www.publiceye.org/ifas/fw/9201/coalition.html).

114. Texas Tommy's blog entry available at http://texastommy.blogspot.com/2005_02_01_texastommy_archive.html.

115. E-mail from John Brakey, 2/24/05.

116. "About Patrick Henry College" (http://www.phc.edu/about/default.asp).

117. Rosalind S. Helderman, "Outfitted With Placards and Prayer," *Washington Post*, 10/20/04.

118. Hanna Rosin, "God and Country," *The New Yorker*, 6/27/05 (http://www.newyorker.com/fact/content/articles/050627fa_fact).

119. Rosalind S. Helderman, "Outfitted with Placards and Prayer."

120. Campaign finance records available at http://www.opensecrets.org/parties/expenddetail.asp?txtName=WALKER%2C+LEEANN&Cmte=RPC&cycle=2004 and http://www.opensecrets.org/parties/expenddetail.asp?txtName=WALKER%2C+LEANN+C&Cmte=RPC&cycle=2004.

121. "Democrats Blast GOP Lawmaker's 'Suppress the Detroit Vote' Remark," AP, 7/21/04.

122. "Facts on the Ground War," *US News & World Report*, 11/1/04.

CHAPTER FIVE

1. Burdish had no theocratic motives: on the contrary. He is "a gay man who has been in the same relationship for 30 years, leaving him with a deep disdain of the religious right and its anti-homosexual agenda. Burdish calls himself a libertarian-conservative-Republican, a multihyphenated creation that speaks to his anti-tax leanings and his dislike for the intrusive social policies of the Christian Coalition. . . .'I believe they have done a disservice to the country as well as their religion,' Burdish says. 'They believe or profess to believe that God cares whether a Republican or Democrat is elected. It is my belief that God cares about how you treat your fellow man, not any label you might have after your name.'" Dan Burdish sits in gray area on some issues but is unrelenting in opposing governmental growth," *Las Vegas Review-Journal*, 2/15/04; http://www.reviewjournal.com/lvrj_home/2004/Feb-15-Sun-2004/news/23227491.html.

2. "Sides debate registrations," *Las Vegas Review-Journal*, 10/10/04.

3. "GOP fails in effort to move polls," *The Philadelphia Daily News*, 10/18/04.

4. Janklow was now out of politics, having been convicted, on December 8, 2003, of vehicular manslaughter, and then imprisoned for 100 days.

5. "AP Exclusive: Janklow criticizes GOP vote effort," AP, 10/12/04.

6. Terry Woster and David Kranz, "Workers who left in ballot flap join Bush," *Argus Leader*, 10/15/04.

7. A week earlier, Jeff Thune—nephew of John Thune, who was then running to defeat Senator Tom Daschle's bid for re-election—was implicated in a similar scandal at South Dakota State University, where he was participating in a campus drive to sign up student voters and/or provide them with applications for absentee ballots. The youth claimed to have "absenteed" 75 voters—a process that requires certification. "As long as you have a notary, which I am a notary, and they witness you filling out one of those requests you're good to go." However, a reporter at KELO-TV in Sioux Falls discovered that young Thune was *not* a notary, so that those applications were invalid. "Absentee Voting Awareness," 10/6/04,

http://www.keloland.com/NewsDetail2817.cfm?Id=22,35129. (A few weeks later, a Dashle volunteer was fined for the same misdemeanor. "GOP Workers Plead Guilty, Daschle Staffer Charged with Violation," Associated Press, 10/29/04).

8. Carlos Campos, "Election 2004: Vote raises red flag on potential for fraud," *The Atlanta Journal Constitution*, 9/30/04.

9. Roxanne Jekot and Emily Dische-Becker, "Secret ballot compromised in Georgia." *News from the Underground*, 6/24/05 (http://markcrispinmiller. blogspot.com/2005/06/secret-ballot-compromised-in-georgia.html).

10. Ibid.

11. That dangerous computer glitch was by no means the only indication of Republican chicanery in Georgia. In early October, state Democrats charged that the Republicans had sent Georgians "hundreds of thousands" of absentee ballots with pro-Bush literature attached to them. The mailing clearly broke a law passed by the Georgia legislature in 2001. "Dems Complaint Calls GOP Mailing Illegal," Associated Press, 10/6/04; http://www.tallahassee.com/mld/tallahassee/news/local/9851556.htm.

12. "Christian Political Soldier Helps Revive Movement," *The Washington Post*, 9/10/1993.

13. "Pat Robertson is back," *St. Petersburgh Times*, 5/26/1990.

14. Bill Salisbury, "Election officials criticize glitches," St. Paul Pioneer Press, 10/1/04.

15. Matt Brunswick, "Kiffmeyer takes flak, pushes on," *Star Tribune*, 9/25/04.

16. "Minnesota E-Voting Equipment: Standard" (http://www. verifiedvoting.org/verifier/map.php?state=minnesota&topic_string=5estd).

17. David Erickson, "Minnesota Secretary of State Kiffmeyer Under Fire," MNPolitics.com, 10/4/04 (http://mnpolitics.com/political-news/ news.asp?story=837).

18. The Republicans in Minnesota played very rough—more like rock-throwing than hardball. On September 9, Rep. Bill Kuisle sent an e-mail out to Olmstead County Republicans, alerting them to an event in Rochester featuring Carole King and the group Minnesota Women for John Kerry. "If anyone can go and harass it would be appreciated," Kuisle wrote. "DFL Criticizes GOPer's E-Mail Urging Harassment at Kerry Event," Associated Press, 9/11/04. On September 10, Ron Eibensteiner, chairman of the Minnesota GOP, publicly demanded that the Minneapolis *Star-Tribune* fire Rob Daves, long-time director of the

Minnesota Poll, charging that the poll had "underestimated Republican results by an average of 5.2 points since 1987." Anders Gyllenhaal, the paper's editor, rejected Eibensteiner's figures, and Daves's work was powerfully defended "Harry O'Neill, chairman of the National Polling Review Board, said that the Minnesota Poll and Daves enjoy a strong reputation nationally and that the poll uses proper methodology and obeys all ethical rules." "GOP Chairman Urges Firing of Newspaper Poll Director," *Star Tribune* (Minneapolis), 9/11/04. No doubt Eibensteiner's challenge was intended to promote the view that Norm Coleman was really doing much better against Walter Mondale than the Minnesota Poll suggested.

19. "The secretary of state's voter registration office was listed as an official sponsor of the recent Luis Palau evangelical crusade at the state capitol. Her husband, Ralph Kiffmeyer, a former state representative, is remembered by some for an ill-fated crusade to ban the sale of dildos and other sex toys." Mike Mosedale, "Some Things About Mary," *City Pages*, 9/8/04.

20. Alan Elsner, "Millions Blocked from Voting in U.S. Election," *Reuters*, 9/22/04.

21. Mary Jacoby, "It will be worse than in 2000," *Salon*, 10/28/04 (http://www.salon.com/news/feature/2004/10/28/julian_bond/index_np.html).

22. Greg Palast, "An Election Spoiled Rotten," TomPaine.com, 11/1/04 (http://www.tompaine.com/articles/an_election_spoiled_rotten.php).

23. "Blacks in Waller County file civil rights suit," AP, 8/17/04.

24. Waller County statistics available at http://quickfacts.census.gov/qfd/states/48/48473.html.

25. "Letter by Waller County DA Spurs Criticism from Blacks," *Houston Chronicle*, 12/10/03.

26. "Attorney General: Students Have Right to Vote," Associated Press, 2/4/04.

27. "Prairie View Students File Voting Rights Suit," Associated Press, 2/5/04.

28. "Alderman Wants State to Investigate Waller County DA; Prosecution of Black Officials at Issue," *Houston Chronicle*, 2/19/04.

29. "Waller County DA Apologizes in Vote Flap," *Houston Chronicle*, 2/25/04.

30. "NAACP, election officials caution voters of bogus letters," AP, 10/29/04.

31. "Campaigns condemn political flier," *Milwaukee Journal Sentinel*, 10/29/04.

32. Ibid.

33. "Kerry Has Strong Advantage Among Latino Voters," *The Washington Post*, 7/22/04.

34. Ibid.

35. Ron Fournier, "Cracks showing in GOP's Cuban-American base," AP, 6/7/04.

36. Ibid.

37. "Kerry Has Strong Advantage Among Latino Voters," *The Washington Post*, 7/22/04.

38. Ibid.

39. "Hispanic Vote in Florida: Neither a Block Nor a Lock," *The New York Times*, 10/17/04.

40. Ibid.

41. "Polls give Hispanics vote edge to Kerry," *Chattanooga Times Free Press*, 10/31/04.

42. Ibid.

43. "New, young and Latino votes emerge," *The Sacramento Bee*, 11/3/04.

44. CNN Exit Polls available at http://www.cnn.com/ELECTION /2004/pages/results/states/US/P/00/epolls.0.html.

45. Greg Palast, "Kerry Won . . ." TomPaine.com, 11/4/04 (http://www.tompaine.com/articles/kerry_won_.php).

46. Ibid.

47. Ibid.

48. Ibid.

49. "Bush's Hispanic Vote Dissected," *The Washington Post*, 12/26/04.

50. Ibid.

51. Bernalillo County statistics available at http://quickfacts.census. gov/qfd/states/35/35001.html.

52. Shea Andersen, "Judge eyed on ballots," *The Albuquerque Tribune*, 11/10/04.

53. Robert Glenn Plotner, "A Guide to Irregularities in the 2004 New Mexico General Election" (http://www.yu-gyo.com/Election/ GuideIrregularitiesNMElection2.htm).

54. Ibid.

55. Ibid.

56. New Mexico statistics available at http://quickfacts.census.gov/qfd/states/35000.html.

57. Jo Becker, "Indian Health Agency Barred New-Voter Drive," *The Washington Post*, 10/6/04.

58. "Government backs off on IHS voting drive prohibition," *Native Times*, 10/11/04.

59. South Dakota statistics available at http://quickfacts.census.gov/qfd/states/46000.html.

60. Hanna Rosin, "Right with God," *The Washington Post*, 3/6/05.

61. See Joe Conason, "Gannon: The early years," *Salon*, 2/18/05.

62. Carson Walker, "Judge partially grants Daschle's request to limit activity of GOP poll watchers," AP, 11/2/04.

63. David Melmber, "Thune campaign flyer upsets Lakota people," *Indian Country Today*, 10/30/04.

64. Ibid.

65. Katha Pollitt, "FOX Hunts Student Voters," *The Nation*, 9/23/04.

66. Mitra Taj, "Students Angry at Report on Registration Practices," *Arizona Daily Wildcat*, 9/9/04 (http://www.fairvote.org/righttovote/taj.htm). There are over 34,000 students at the University of Arizona, 17 percent Hispanic and 3 percent African American. If every one of them voted, they would account for roughly 7.5 percent of the electorate in Pima County, which is also 29.3% percent Hispanic. Figures used to calculate these numbers available at http://daps.arizona.edu/daps/factbook/factbook.html; http://www.recorder.co.pima.az.us/search/voter_totals.html, and http://quickfacts.census.gov/qfd/states/04/04019.html.

67. *NARAL*: "NARAL-WI Reports Fraudulent Calls," DailyKos.com, 11/1/04.

68. "Text of call Democrats say is misleading," AP, 11/1/04.

69. E-mail from Lynne Orengia, 6/2/05.

70. Beth DeFalco, "GOP operative under fire over voter-registration tactics," AP, 10/28/04. Pillsbury's full mission statement is online at http://www.pillsbury.edu/history.htm.

71. Ibid.; Sen. Kyl's interest group ratings available at http://www.vote-smart.org/issue_rating_category.php?can_id=H0121103; for more on Sen. Kyl's relations with defense contractors, see http://rightweb.irc-online.org/ind/kyl/kyl.php.

72. "Education (Roles); States Can't Resist the Lure of Federal Abstinence Money," *AIDS Weekly Plus*, 8/11/1997.

73. Bill Sizemore and Liz Szabo, "Reorganization is planned; political clout could wane," *The Virginian-Pilot*, 6/11/1999.

74. "Untangling political strands in anti-Clean Elections effort," *Arizona Republic*, 6/28/04.

75. E-mail from Linda McNeil, Professor of Education at Rice University, 7/1/05; "Gothbaum Calls on Chancellor Klein to Justify Use of Untested Reading," Press Release, 5/6/03 (http://pubadvocate.nyc.gov/news/releases_5_6_03.html).

76. Chip Scutari, "Clean Elections Law Under Attack," *Arizona Republic*, 6/20/04.

77. Jane Ann Morrison, "Signers of petitions register surprise at having party affiliations switched," *Las Vegas Review-Journal*, 7/31/04.

78. "GOPers rip up Demo registrations," KLAS-TV, 10/12/04 (http://www.sunmt.org/oct13chron04.html).

79. Adam Goldman, "Executive denies voter forms destroyed in Nevada," AP, 10/13/04.

80. Ibid.

81. Farhad Manjoo, "Sproul Play: RNC Funded Group Destroying Democratic Registrations," *Salon*, 10/21/04.

82. George Knapp, "Knappster: Voter fraud charges generate denials, threats, new questions," *The Las Vegas Mercury*, 10/21/04.

83. Ibid.

84. "Voter registration drive 'misleading,'" *Charleston Gazette*, 8/20/04.

85. The state's 42 One Stop stores are owned by Michael R. Graney and Patrick C. Graney, III, who had donated to the RNC and Bush campaign, as well as other Republican causes. Patrick is also president of Petroleum Products Inc., and administrator of PCG Inc., a West Virginia power company. The Graney family's political contributions have been published by the Center for Responsive Politics, and may be studied online at http://www.opensecrets.org/indivs/search.asp?NumOfThou=0&txtName=Graney&txtState=WV&txtZip=&txtEmploy=&txtCand=&txt2006=Y&txt2004=Y&txt2002=Y&Order=N.

86. Farhad Manjoo, "Sproul Play: RNC Funded Group Destroying Democratic Registrations."

87. The groups included the NAACP, NARAL, MoveOn, the Sierra Club and ACORN, among many others. The people at America Votes were not amused, telling the Associated Press that they would file a lawsuit to stop Sproul from misusing their name. "This organization absolutely has nothing to do with America Votes," said Kevin Lopper, the organizing

director for AV in Oregon. "Librarian Bares Possible Voter Registration Scam," Associated Press, 9/21/04.

88. "Voter Registration Workers Cry Foul," *Pittsburgh Post-Gazette*, 10/20/04.

89. Mark Brunswick and Pat Doyle, "Voter Registration; 3 former workers; Firm paid pro-Bush bonuses," *Star Tribune*, 10/27/04.

90. Farhad Majoo, "Sproul Play: RNC Funded Group Destroying Democratic Registrations"; Dennis B. Roddy, "Students Have Parties Switched by Bogus Petitions; Registration Changed to Republican Without Consent," *Pittsburgh Post Gazette*, 10/22/04.

91. Edward Walsh, "Deceptive Tactics Inflate GOP Voter Registration," *The Oregonian*, 10/30/04.

92. David Karp, "Students complain of false party swap," *St. Petersburgh Times*, 10/23/04; Garrett Therolf, "Voter Drives Investigated," *Tampa Tribune*, 10/22/04.

93. Arno's "grass roots clients" include Howard Jarvis's Taxpayers Association, U.S. English, the National Rifle Association and the Tobacco Institute.

94. For more on Arno Political Consultants, visit their official website at http://www.apcusa.com.

95. Although Arno declined to say how much the RNC was paying him, campaign finance records show that the committee paid the firm $450,000 in one reporting period in September. *St. Petersburg Times*, 10/23/04.

96. Jo Becker and Thomas B. Edsall, "Registering Voters: Add One, Take Away Two," *The Washington Post*, 10/14/04; "Campaign Roundup," *The San Francisco Chronicle*, 10/23/04.

97. "Allegations of Electoral Crimes," *The New York Times*, 10/18/04.

98. Dennis B. Roddy, "Students Have Parties Switched by Bogus Petitions." *Pittsburgh Post Gazette*, 10/22/04.

99. Ken Ritter, "Nevada judge declines to reopen voter registration in Vegas area," AP, 10/15/04.

100. Deborah Hastings, "Voter drive funded by GOP accused of deception," AP, 10/22/04.

101. Ibid.

102. Christina Almeida, "Lawsuit over missing voter registration forms filed in Nevada," AP, 10/21/04.

103. Mark Brunswick and Pat Doyle, "Voter Registration; 3 former workers; Firm paid pro-Bush bonuses."*Star Tribune*, 10/27/04.

104. "Librarian bares possible voter registration dodge," *Mail Tribune* (Jackson County, OR), 9/21/04.

105. Interview with Larry Noble, 6/30/05.

106. All RNC campaign finance filings available at http://query. nictusa.com/cgi-bin/fecimg/?C00003418 and ftp://ftp.fec.gov/FEC.

107. Interview with Carla Corbin, Compliant Specialist at the State's Elections Division, 6/28/05.

108. David G. Savage and Richard B. Schmitt, "Bush Seeks Limit to Suits over Voting Rights," *The Los Angeles Times*, 10/29/04.

CHAPTER SIX

1. "Paid Bush Supporters Cause Uproar," *The Dartmouth*, 11/1/04; http://www.thedartmouth.com/article.php?aid=2004110101010& action=print.

2. "With all precincts reporting, Bush wins Colorado, 41–34 percent, paper reports—except election hasn't started yet!" PrisonPlanet. com, 11/2/04 (http://www.prisonplanet.com/articles/november2004/ 021104bushwins.htm).

3. Jeffrey Cohan, "Probe of Vote Scam Widening," *Pittsburgh Post-Gazette*, 10/28/04; Julia Malone, "Civil Rights Groups, GOP Trade Charges of Dirty Tricks," *Cox News Service*, 11/1/04; Ian Hoffman, "Locals descend on swing states," *The Oakland Tribune*, 10/31/04; Richard Byrne Reilly, "Election day has its (dirty) tricks, too," *Pittsburgh Tribune-Review*, 10/28/04.

4. Garret Young, "Fake news story circulates to suppress voter turnout," *The Daily Pennsylvanian*, 11/1/04 (http://www.dailypennsylvanian.com/ vnews/display.v/ART/2004/11/01/4186fe33d7739).

5. "Local News: Philadelphia & Its Suburbs," *The Philadelphia Inquirer*, 11/2/04.

6. "Officials, GOP Fight over Vote-Fixing Claims in Philly," NBC-10, 11/2/04 (http://www.nbc10.com/news/3883063/detail.html).

7. David B. Caruso and Michael Rubinkam, "Pa. Voters wait hours at polls, but few major problems reported," AP, 11/2/04.

8. Brian Gottstein, "Back up! We need back up!" *The Roanoke Times*, 11/1/04 (http://www.votersunite.org/article.asp?id=3793).

9. "Officials Field Pa. Election Complaints; Some Polls Stay Open," Associated Press, 11/2/04.

10. Ibid.

11. "Shortfall of Special Ballots Is Glitch in County Voting," *Pittsburgh Tribune-Review*, 11/3/04.

12. "Officials Field Pa. Election Complaints; Some Polls Stay Open," Associated Press, 11/2/04.

13. Ibid.

14. "Preliminary Statement on the November 2004 Election," Count Every Vote, 11/5/04; PDF available at http://www.counteveryvote2004.org/forms/prelimstatement.pdf.

15. "Minorities Bear Brunt of 'Subtler' Bias at US Polls, Report Says," *Reuters*, 8/26/04.

16. WISC-TV.com (http://www.channel3000.com/politics/3886074/detail.html).

17. "Tuscaloosa County Election Incidents—EIRS 1.0.5 (https://voteprotect.org/index.php?display=EIRMapCounty&state=Alabama&county=Tuscaloosa&cat=ALL&tab=ED04).

18. E-mail from Ian Whatley, 11/29/04.

19. "Anderson County Election Incidents—EIRS 1.0.5" (https://voteprotect.org/index.php?display=EIRMapCounty&state=South+Carolina&county=Anderson&cat=ALL&tab=ALL).

20. "Greenville County Election Incidents—EIRS 1.0.5" (https://voteprotect.org/index.php?display=EIRMapCounty&state=South+Carolina&county=Greenville&cat=ALL&tab=ALL).

21. Ibid.

22. In January 1995, the Voting Section at the Department of Justice started filing lawsuits against California, Michigan, Vermont, Virginia, Pennsylvania, Mississippi, Illinois, New York and—an especially fierce resister—South Carolina.

23. E-mail from Ian Whatley, 11/29/04.

24. In July, 2005, it was reported that a group called Christian Exodus was planning a mass movement to the Upstate, with the aim of creating a theocracy. Christian Exodus, reported Fox Carolina, is "a non-profit group organizing Christians to move to the Palmetto State to concentrate the number of Christians in one location with the intent to influence how the state governs. A plan that some residents say we need. 'I think it's fantastic, I think we need more of that actually. I don't know which direction our government is heading in, but I think they need Christian influence, it would go a long way, I really think so,' says Mauldin resident, Reggie Brown. Percy Croft of Greenville agrees, 'America was founded on

Christian principles . . . people with different views about Christianity, you have them getting into the elected positions and they don't want to see this country stay the way it is, they want it to change . . .They're getting away from what they were founded on.'" "Christian Exodus Planned for South Carolina," FOX Carolina, posted 7/18/05; http://www.fox21.com/Global/story.asp?S=3592505&nav=2KPpc7ZV.

25. "Lexington County Election Incidents—EIRS 1.0.5" (https://voteprotect.org/index.php?display=EIRMapCounty&state=South+Carolina&cat=ALL&tab=ALL&county=Lexington).

26. Ibid.

27. Ibid.

28. "Lexington County Election Incidents—EIRS 1.0.5" Such fearmongering was epidemic in Lexington County. From Gilbert: "Caller phoning to repeat report that her son had knowledge of flyers being distributed in his neighborhood suggesting that people would be arrested if they tried to vote and they had not paid child support arrears." From Spartanburg: "People are passing out flyers in the Black community saying they are going to arrest people for child support at the polls."

29. "Horry County Election Incidents—EIRS 1.0.5."

30. WISC-TV.com (http://www.channel3000.com/politics/3886074/detail.html).

31. State panel to study voting machines" AP, 11/15/04; Gaston County statistics available at http://quickfacts.census.gov/qfd/states/37/37071.html; Mark Johnson, "GOP plaintiffs lose in court," *The Charlotte Observer*, 11/30/04; Carteret County statistics available at http://quickfacts.census.gov/qfd/states/37/37031.html.

32. Craven County statistics available at http://quickfacts.census.gov/qfd/states/37/37049.html.

33. Sue Book, "Election problems due to a software glitch," *The New Bern Sun Journal*, 11/5/04.

34. The week before Election Day, the Mecklenburg County commissioners, "led by Republicans," tried to block acceptance of a state grant for early voting, "because officials planned to use part of the money for voting this Sunday," the *Charlotte Observer* reported. The gambit's purpose clearly was to cut the Kerry vote: "Voter-turnout advocates say early voting and Sunday voting make it easier for people with busy schedules to cast ballots." The move inspired a bitter set-to fraught with racial and class politics: "Tuesday's action has sparked a partisan, racially charged debate and interrupted the plans of many groups—including several black churches—for a

'Souls to the Polls' effort after services on Sunday." The Republicans relented. "Board Rethinks Sunday Voting," *Charlotte Observer*, 10/21/04.

35. Plotner used the cyber-handle "ignatzmouse." His report, "Unofficial Audit of NC Election: A Comprehensive Case for Fraud," is online at Democratic Underground (http://www.democraticunderground.com/discuss/duboard.php?az=view_all&address=203x45003).

36. Richard A. Webster, "Nov. 2 NO election called 'catastrophe,'" *New Orleans CityBusiness*, 11/15/04.

37. Ibid.

38. Brett Martel, "Voting frustrations mount in New Orleans—again," AP, 11/3/04.

39. Max Standridge "Arkansas in 2004: Did Bush Really Win?" *Columbus Free Press*, 1/24/05 (http://www.votersunite.org/article.asp?id=4704).

40. Initially, there seemed to be an epic glitch in Oklahoma. On November 3, the pro-Bush *Tulsa World* ran a county-by-county breakdown of the unofficial statewide vote results, with 70 percent of the vote counted. The *World* showed Bush with 565,967 votes to Kerry's 441,220; and yet it also showed that Kerry led the president in 57 rural counties. However, when all the votes were counted, Bush, it seemed, had swiftly gained another 393,825 votes—more than six times what Kerry seemingly had gained—while Kerry was defeated in *all* 77 of Oklahoma's counties, evidently *losing* votes to pull off a remarkable defeat. In McCurtain County, he lost 2,766 votes, while Bush gained 5,632; in Canadian County, Kerry lost 1,806 votes, while Bush gained 16,917; and so on. It all turned out to be the *World*'s mistake: "The *Tulsa World* mistakenly placed 2002 countywide returns from the vote on State Question 687 on cockfighting into a form to be used for county-by-county election returns in the 2004 presidential race." "Corrections, Clarifications," *Tulsa World*, 12/2/04. A study of the vote on State Question 687 corroborates that explanation.

41. Lynn Campbell, "Hundreds of Iowa voter forms rejected," *The Des Moines Register*, 10/13/04; Lynn Campbell, "Republicans threaten lawsuit over voter registration issue," *The Des Moines Register*, 10/25/04; Lynn Campbell, "Voters mistakenly identified as felons," *The Des Moines Register*, 11/2/04.

42. Lynn Campbell, "Republicans threaten lawsuit over voter registration issue."

43. Amy Lorentzen, "Story County cancels extra day of satellite voting," AP, 10/30/04.

44. Bill Lueders, "Madison, Wisconsin, 4:16 P.M.," *The New Republic Online*, 11/2/04 (http://www.tnr.com/blog/election?pid=2299).

45. Greg J. Borowski, "GOP demands IDs of 37,000 in city," *Milwaukee Journal-Sentinel*, 10/30/04; Meg Jones, "GOP, City Reach Deal on Voter List," *Milwaukee Journal-Sentinel*, 11/1/04.

46. Aaron Nathans, "GOP fliers give wrong voting info," *The Capital Times*, 10/30/04.

47. Bill Lueders, "Madison, Wisconsin, 4:16 P.M."

48. "New Jersey: Kerry 53% Bush 41%," Rasmussen Reports, 10/31/04 (http://www.rasmussenreports.com/New%20Jersey_Fall%202004.htm).

49. "Erie County Election Incidents—EIRS 1.0.5" (https://voteprotect.org/index.php?display=EIRMapCounty&state=New+York&county=Erie&cat=ALL&tab=ALL).

50. "Albany County Election Incidents—EIRS 1.0.5" (https://voteprotect.org/index.php?display=EIRMapCounty&state=New+York&county=Albany&cat=ALL&tab=ALL).

51. "Westchester County Election Incidents—EIRS 1.0.5" (https://voteprotect.org/index.php?display=EIRMapCounty&state=New+York&county=Westchester&cat=02&tab=ED04).

52. Ibid.

53. "Westchester County Election Incidents—EIRS 1.0.5."

54. Ibid.

55. E-mail from Megan Demarkis, 11/12/04.

56. See pp. 238–239.

57. Farhad Manjoo, "Seeing Red in Florida," *Salon*, 10/15/04.

58. Ibid.

59. In early 2003, Gov. Jeb Bush tried stealthily to make those ballots disappear, by wiping out the budget of the Florida Division of Library and Information Services, the entity responsible for state archives and recordkeeping. With no funds for their storage, the ballots would have vanished into bureaucratic limbo—or a bank of shredders. By dismantling the Division, the state would have saved an estimated $5.4 million. The governor's effort met with strong resistance from the public and the legislature, leading him to drop the plan, at least temporarily. "One of Gov. Bush's worst ideas," *Sarasota Herald-Tribune*, 2/8/03. There had already been a flap in August of 2001, when Theresa LePore, Palm Beach County supervisor of elections, was assailed for destroying a computer file of ballot images from 2000. "LePore: Erased File Not Public Record," *Palm Beach Post*, 8/3/01.

60. P. Douglas Filaroski, "State's Voting Systems and Laws Sure to Come in for Close Scrutiny," *Florida-Times Union*, 11/19/00.

61. Rosewood Financial Inc., Caroline Rose Hunt's instrument, bought a 6 percent stake in Cronus Industries in January 1988. "In a Securities and Exchange Commission filing, Rosewood said it had purchased the shares 'to obtain a significant equity interest' in Cronus, which provides computing and micrographic services to county and municipal governments." "Rosewood Buys 6% Stake in Cronus," *New York Times*, 1/21/88.

62. Hagel and Nelson were neck-and-neck going into the 1996 election. "We have to say it's a dead heat," said David Moore, managing editor of the Gallup Poll. "Nelson-Hagel Race Called a Dead Heat," *Omaha World Herald*, 11/3/96. Hagel's 15-point win was therefore a surprise, to say the least. That victory was small change, however, by comparison with Hagel's defeat of Charlie Matulka in 2002. Apparently the senator won that race by 69 points (83 percent to 14 percent), or 322,991 votes. Conspicuous among his triumphs in both races was his unexpected popularity in African-American and Native American precincts.

63. Alexander Bolton, "Hagel's ethics filings pose disclosure issue," *The Hill*, 1/29/03.

64. Filaroski, "State's Voting Systems and Laws Sure to Come in for Close Scrutiny." The brothers Todd and Bob Urosevich founded AIS in 1979. Todd Urosevich is still at ES&S, as vice president for Aftermarket Sales. In 1995, Bob started I-Mark, which offered a sophisticated touch-screen voting system. In 1997, I-Mark was acquired by Global Election Systems, Inc. On January 22, 2002, Diebold—the second-largest U.S. manufacturer of voting machines—bought GES for $24.7 million. GES was thenceforth known as Diebold Election Systems, Inc. Bob Urosevich is president of Diebold.

65. "Rent Voting Machines, Harris Says," *St. Petersburg Times*, 2/23/01.

66. Mike Salinero, "Elections Chiefs Push High-Tech," *Tampa Tribune*, 5/9/01.

67. "State Approves First Touch Screen Voting System," AP, 8/16/01.

68. "County Will Spend Up to $4.6 Million on Voting System," *St. Petersburg Times*, 8/22/01. In 2000, Gore had been the victor by fewer than 1,000 votes, with 69,564 to Bush's 68,582. In 2004, Bush won by almost 30,000 votes, with 103,320 to Kerry's 84,749. However many people there supported Kerry, the county was a most Bush-friendly place, where Republicans were free to do overt electioneering right outside the polling booths (in one polling place, the Christian Coalition Voter Guide was handed out

to those in line, while in another, people waiting to cast votes were on their cell phones, loudly urging other voters to go out and vote Bush/Cheney). Over 93 percent white, with a black population of 2.1 percent (and 5.7 percent Hispanic), Pasco is racially uneasy. In Zephyrhills, the county's second-largest city, there was an ugly public clash in May of 2004, when the city council voted to rename Sixth Avenue "Martin Luther King Avenue." The move provoked such rage among the city's whites that the council soon reversed itself. All throughout Election Day, the residents of one black precinct felt intimidated by the presence of a Zephyrhills police car parked outside a polling place, with a sign that warned the passing motorists that their speed was being monitored. Data on Pasco County at epodunk.com (http://www.epodunk.com/cgi-bin/genInfo.php?locIndex=8834); election incidents in Pasco County are online at the site for the Election Incident Reporting System (https://epc.voteprotect.org/index.php?display=EIRMapCounty&tab=ALL&state=Florida&county=Pasco); "Honor for Dr. King Splits Florida City, and Faces Reversal," *New York Times*, 8/9/04.

69. Rebecca Wakefield, "Rage Against the Machines," *Miami New Times*, 9/23/04. The contract was a bad one for Miami-Dade, Wakefield reports. It "was written in such a way that the company would be almost completely paid off right after the November election, and likely before any major problems could be discovered. The county initially dismissed this criticism. "They said, 'Bollocks. You sweet little folks don't know what you're talking about,' laughs [voting activist] Dan McCrea" (Wakefield).

70. "No Recount for Reno; Statewide Check Denied Despite Missing Votes," *Palm Beach Post*, 9/14/02.

71. "Jeb Bush Makes History in Florida," CBS News, 11/6/02 (http://www.cbsnews.com/stories/2002/11/04/politics/main527998.shtml). This is not to suggest that Reno, or anybody else, would or could have been elected in a race so imperceptibly and tightly orchestrated. However, she would probably have made a tougher candidate than Jim McBride, as a favorite daughter, and maybe stood a better chance of winning mass support enough to make it that much harder to misrepresent the numbers. It is conceivable, moreover, that her long prosecutorial experience could have made it somewhat riskier for the Republicans to break election laws, however stealthily.

72. Farhad Manjoo, "Seeing Red in Florida," *Salon*, 10/15/04.

73. Glenda Hood on *Newsnight with Aaron Brown*, CNN, 9/29/04.

74. "A Critical Audit, a Fired Inspector," *St. Petersburg Times*, 9/29/01.

75. "Harris Left Department's Inspector General Post Unfilled," *Tampa Tribune*, 9/25/02.

76. "Harris Resigns Two Weeks After Law's Deadline Date," *Washington Post*, 8/2/02.

77. "Conspiracy Theories Swirl After McElyea Defection," *Sarasota Herald-Tribune*, 10/28/04.

78. Theresa LePore had in fact been a Republican before she ran for the position of elections supervisor. By her account, she switched parties prior to her first campaign "because the incumbent was Democrat and the county registration is predominantly Democrat." Her use of that locution "Democrat" (instead of "Democratic") and, of course, her flagrant pro-Bush bias indicate that she has staunchly served as a Republican in Democratic clothing. (She was defeated in her bid for re-election in 2004.) For more on Theresa LePore, see http://en.wikipedia.org/wiki/Theresa_LePore.

79. Larry Lipman, "Harris Joining House Leadership," *Palm Beach Post*, 12/7/02.

80. "Republican Congressman Tom Feeney of Oviedo asked a computer programmer in September 2000, prior to that year's contested presidential vote in Florida, to write software that could alter vote totals on touch-screen voting machines, the programmer said," reported the *Seminole Chronicle* exactly four years after Feeney was appointed an assistant whip. "The programmer was Clint Curtis, who testified before John Conyers and his associates. Former computer programmer Clint Curtis made the claim Monday in sworn testimony to Democrats on the House Judiciary Committee investigating allegations of voter fraud in the 2004 presidential election involving touch-screen voting in Ohio." "Feeney Implicated in Vote Fraud," *Seminole Chronicle*, 12/6/04. This story was also reported in the *St. Petersburg Times*—and nowhere else in the United States.

81. Not entirely unremarkable. A week before Election Day in 2004, viewers of C-SPAN were diverted by the spectacle of Rep. Harris necking with her colleague Rick Renzi (R-AZ) in the House, while, at the podium, Rep. Rob Simmons (R-CT) held forth about the growing global threat posed by Iran. (Both Renzi and Harris have 100 percent approval ratings from the Christian Coalition.) While it made no news off-line, the moment got a lot of play in cyberspace, even prompting the creation of a website. "Lawyers at C-SPAN are miffed about the devious Democratic operatives who created the web site thecanoodle.com, dedicated solely to an intimate moment in time between Reps. Katherine Harris (R-FL) and Rick Renzi (R-AZ), who, according to the web site, were canoodling on

the House floor." "The Canoodle Cabal," *Roll Call Online*, 10/28/04. It may or may not have been Harris's indiscretion that impelled the Bush brothers to stop supporting her. When she announced, in June of 2005, that she planned to run for Democrat Bill Nelson's Senate seat in 2006, they made it clear that they preferred some other candidate, apparently because they did not think that she could win. Brian Montopoli, "Jilted: The Bush Brothers Kick Katherine Harris to the Curb," *Slate*, 6/30/05, http://slate.msn.com/id/2121746/.

82. "Florida's secretary of state in the spotlight," Palm Beach Post, 8/8/04; "Candidates Fishing for Compliments," *Tampa Tribune*, 6/21/98.

83. "Orlando Is Home to a Growing Number of Christian Institutions," AP, 1/9/1999.

84. George Bennet, "Incumbent Shaw Faces Unusual Set of Opponents," *Palm Beach Post*, 10/28/04.

85. On September 8, in response to a lawsuit filed by Florida's Democratic Party, Circuit Judge Kevin Davey issued a temporary restraining order to prevent Hood from certifying Nader's place on the presidential ballot. (The Democrats had argued that the Reform Party was not a legitimate political party, but merely Nader's vehicle.) Hood announced that she would comply with Judge Davey's order and then, on September 13, reversed herself, filing an appeal. She then sent out a memo to all Florida counties, instructing them to put Nader's name on 50,000 overseas absentee ballots. In thus acting precipitously, Hood assailed the judge for acting too slowly. "Davey is scheduled to hear arguments Wednesday from the Reform Party and Nader before making his final ruling. Hood blasted him for not acting more quickly. 'We really should be outraged,' she said." Considering the perfect cynicism of the party's relationship with Nader, Hood's indignation was incredible (and typical). "Nader Back on Florida Ballot—for Now," Associated Press, Sept. 13, 2004.

86. "Box May Prevent Hundreds of Votes," *St. Petersburg Times*, 10/5/04.

87. "Florida Flooded with Pre-Emptive Election Lawsuits," *San Francisco Chronicle*, 10/14/04.

88. "Pushing to Be Counted in Fla.," *Washington Post*, 10/13/04.

89. The plaintiffs were the Advancement Project, AFL-CIO, American Federation of State, County, and Municipal Employees (AFSCME), People for the American Way Foundation and Service Employee International Union. The suit is detailed in "State of Florida sued to prevent the disenfranchisement of thousands of voters," a press release from the People for

the American Way Foundation, posted on 10/13/04 at http://www.pfaw.org/ pfaw/general/default.aspx?oid=17240.

90. From Section 302 of HAVA (http://www.fec.gov/hava/law_ext.txt).

91. "Federal Judge: Provisional Ballots in Wrong Precinct Don't Count," AP, 10/21/04; A federal judge in Michigan also ruled that "jurisdiction" should be liberally construed. In Colorado and Missouri, federal courts ruled otherwise. "Appeals Court Reverses Lower-Court Ruling on Provisional Ballots in Michigan," AP, 10/26/04.

92. Ibid.

93. "Historic Vote Count Is Over," *Miami Herald*, 11/6/04.

94. "Two-thirds of Florida's Provisional Ballots Rejected," AP, 1/3/05.

95. For more on Wexler's legal battles, see "Congressman Sues, Wants Voting Machines to Create Paper Printouts," AP, 1/17/04; "Wexler Suit over Voting Paper Trail Tossed Out," *Palm Beach Post*, 2/12/04; "Paperless Voting Unconstitutional, Suit Says," *Palm Beach Post*, 3/9/04; "Bill Would Exempt Electronic Votes from Manual Recount," *Palm Beach Post*, 4/1/04; "Congressman's Suit Seeking Touchscreen Voting Printouts Dismissed," AP, 5/24/04; "Appeals court approves dismissal of Wexler's voting suit," AP, 8/6/04 ; "Rage Against the Machines," *Miami New Times*, 9/23/04; "Federal court abstains from ruling on Florida e-ballot suit," AP, 9/27/04; "Secretary of State Okays Hand Recount," *St. Petersburg Times*, 10/16/04; "Court Denies Bid to Require Paper Trail for Touch Screens," *Palm Beach Post*, 10/26/04; "Voting Machine Recount Ruling Challenged," *Palm Beach Post*, 11/2/04;" "Congressman Sues, Wants Voting Machines to Create Paper Printouts," AP, 1/17/04.

96. Farhad Manjoo, "Seeing Red in Florida."

97. Florida Statute IS-2.027 available at http://www.leg.state.fl.us/ statutes/index.cfm?App_mode=Display_Statute&Search_String=& URL=Ch0102/Sec166.htm.

98. PDF of 1S-2.031 Recount Procedures available at election.dos. state.fl.us/ laws/ProposedRules/pdf/1S2031.pdf.

99. "Bill Would Exempt Electronic Votes from Manual Recount," *Palm Beach Post*, 4/1/04.

100. "Court rules against Limbaugh on records," *Palm Beach Post*, 10/7/04.

101. Special Emergency Ruling 04-1 available at http://election. dos.state.fl.us/ laws/ProposedRules/pdf/1SER04-1.pdf.Text available at http://www.flsenate.gov/statutes/index.cfm?App_Mode=Display_Statute &Search_String=&URL=Ch0102/Sec141.htm&StatuteYear=2003.

102. Text available at http://www.flsenate.gov/statutes/index.cfm?App
_Mode=Display_Statute&Search_String=&URL=Ch0102/Sec141.htm&
StatuteYear=2003.

103. Joni James, "State: Hood Agrees to Manual Recount," *St. Petersburg Times*, 10/16/04.

104. PDF of "Memorandum Opinion" available at http://www.flsd.
uscourts.gov/default.asp?file=cases/index.html#.

105. Florida Supreme Court Docket available at http://jweb.flcourts.org/
pls/docket/ds_docket?p_caseyear=2004&p_casenumber=2072&psCourt=
FSC&psSearchType=.

106. Steve Bousquet, "GOP Flier Questions New Voting Equipment,"
St. Petersburg Times, 7/29/04.

107. Ibid.

108. "Florida GOP Apologizes for Warning," United Press International, 7/30/04.

109. It was also mentioned passingly in several articles: "From Chad to
Worse: Absentee Fla. Voting," *Daily News* (New York), 8/3/04; "New
Election Disputes Hit Florida," *Austin American-Statesman*, 8/6/04; "Senate Primary a Test for Florida's Altered Election Process," *Washington Post*,
8/28/04; "Never Again!" Washingtonpost.com, 7/30/04; and Paul Krugman alluded to it in his column "Triumph of the Trivial," *New York Times*,
7/30/04.

110. See Greg Palast, "The Great Florida Ex-Con Game," *Harper's
Magazine*, 3/1/02.

111. Database Technologies (DBT), the Boca Raton company that had
been paid $3 million to purge the voter rolls, was bought up by Choicepoint in May 2000.

112. Jim Krane, "U.S. drug and immigration probes suffer after vendor
stops selling Latin American citizen data," AP, 8/31/03.

113. "Florida Democrats Put Heat on Katherine Harris," *Orlando Sentinel*, 2/23/01.

114. "New Voter Rolls Arouse More Fears," *St. Petersburg Times*, 12/2/01.

115. All such information is online at the website whitehousefor
sale.org.

116. "New Voter Rolls Arouse More Fears."

117. For more on Accenture and Halliburton, see Accenture's official
website at http://www.accenture.com/xd/xd.asp?it=enweb&xd=industries
%5Cresources%5Cenergy%5Ccase%5Cener_halliburton.xml.

118. "Election.com Sold to Group Tied to Saudi National," *Newsday*, 2/27/03.

119. "Pentagon Drops Plan to Test Internet Voting," *Washington Post*, 3/31/04.

120. "Accenture Launches eDemocracy Services Business," press release, 6/30/03; http://www.accenture.com/xd/xd.asp?it=enweb&xd=_dyn%5Cdynamicpressrelease_624.xml.

121. "Email on Felon List Contradicts Governor," *Sarasota Herald Tribune*, 10/16/04.

122. "System to Clean Up Voting Lists," *St. Petersburg Times*, 5/7/04.

123. "State Wants Felons Purged from Voter List," AP, 5/6/04.

124. Ibid.

125. "Florida Hoping to Avoid Problems as Voting Rolls Purged of Felons," AP, 5/25/04.

126. Jim Ash, "Groups: Publicize Criminal Voter List," *Palm Beach Post*, 5/27/04.

127. William March, "Ineligible Voter List Revives Concern," *Tampa Tribune*, 5/18/04.

128. That the list had been "approved" by the NAACP, as Hood's spokesperson had asserted earlier, thus seemed extraordinarily cynical in retrospect. In any case, it has been impossible to verify that claim. There is no NAACP headquarters in the state of Florida, just branch offices in some cities.

129. "Florida Scraps Felon Vote List," *St. Petersburg Times*, 7/11/04.

130. Ibid.

131. "Bush Dumps Request Form for Clemency," *St. Petersburg Times*, 7/23/04.

132. Jacksonville statistics available at http://quickfacts.census.gov/qfd/states/12/1235000.html.

133. Greg Palast, "New Florida Vote Scandal Exposed," BBC, 10/27/04.

134. "Republicans Claim Democrats Are Behind Office Attacks," *New York Times*, 10/26/04.

135. "GOP: Florida Felons Already Voting," *St. Petersburg Times*, 10/29/04.

136. "Miami-Dade Election Incidents—EIRS 1.0.5" (https://voteprotect.org/index.php?display=EIRMapCounty&state=Florida&county=Miami-Dade&cat=07).

137. Ibid.

138. Ibid.

139. Ibid.

140. "Broward County Election Incidents—EIRS 1.0.5" (https://voteprotect.org/index.php?display=EIRMapCounty&state=Florida&county=Broward&cat=ALL&tab=ALL).

141. "Palm Beach County Election Incidents—EIRS 1.0.5" (https://voteprotect.org/index.php?display=EIRMapCounty&state=Florida&county=Palm%20Beach&cat=ALL&tab=ALL).

142. "Orange County Election Incidents—EIRS 1.0.5" (https://voteprotect.org/index.php?display=EIRMapCounty&state=Florida&county=Orange&cat=02&tab=ED04). Such malfunctions occurred overwhelmingly in five Democratic precincts: 215 (63 percent black), 314 (10 percent black), 337 (27 percent black), 604 (87 percent black) and 616 (96 percent black). (These figures are available online at http://www.ocfelections.com/Public%20Records/2004%20Primary%20and%20General%20Turnout/2004_Gen_Turnout.txt.) There was also reportedly a marked unhelpfulness among the personnel in those precincts. (See, for example, the report on Orange County by EIRS, at https://voteprotect.org/index.php?display=EIRMapCounty&state=Florida&cat=02&tab=ED04&county=Orange.) Kerry just squeaked by in Orange County, with a margin of 827 votes (193,217 to 192,390).

143. Jo Becker, "Pushing to Be Counted in Fla.," *Washington Post*, 10/12/04.

144. "New Duval Elections Supervisor Quickly Adds Early Voting Sites," AP, 10/19/04.

145. Volusia County statistics available at http://quickfacts.census.gov/qfd/states/12/12127.html.

146. Medea Benjamin and Deborah James, "Florida's Palm Beach County Bracing for the Electoral Storm," truthout.org, 11/2/04 (http://www.truthout.org/docs_04/110204I.shtml).

147. Ibid.

148. Clay County statistics available at http://quickfacts.census.gov/qfd/states/12/12019.html; "Many Clay Early Voters Face Long Drive to Polls," *Florida Times-Union*, 10/29/04.

149. Greg Palast, "New Florida vote scandal feared."

150. Stephen Hegarty, "Election chief warns of absentee scam," *The St. Petersburgh Times*, 10/22/04.

151. Ibid.

152. The tension was extraordinary throughout South Florida. Two days before Election Day in Palm Beach County, the outrageous "Democrat" LePore imposed a new rule forbidding members of the press to interview or photograph Floridians lined up outside the polls. One journalist who dared to talk to early voters was assaulted by a cop, who tackled him and knocked him to the ground. Jane Daugherty, "Deputy tackles, arrests journalist for photographing voters," *Palm Beach Post*, 11/01/04.

153. "Broward County Election Incidents—EIRS 1.0.5" (https://voteprotect.org/index.php?display=EIRMapCounty&state=Florida&county=Broward).

154. See John Nichols, "The Beat Bush Brigades," posted http://www.furnitureforthepeople.com/brigades.htm. (This was posted pre-election but is undated.)

155. "Rules Set for Voter Challenges," *St. Petersburg Times*, 10/30/04.

156. Polls Bulge as Voters File in Early," *St. Petersburg Times*, 10/31/04.

157. "Broward County Elections Incidents—EIRS 1.0.5"; "Poll goal: Make hard day look easy," *St. Petersburgh Times*, 8/20/04.

158. This refers to Florida's Senate race. Thanks to ES&S, the caller's vote for Democrat Betty Castor turned into a vote for Mel Martinez, who had been the regime's Secretary of Housing and Urban Development (and "a leader in implementing President Bush's faith-based initiatives," according to the White House website). The polls gave Castor a slight lead on October 29 and 30, and had the two statistically tied by Election Day. Officially, Martinez won by 82,633 votes, beating Castor by 3,672,864 to 3,590,201. As Bush/Cheney's increased domination of the Senate was a goal almost as important as the regime's "re-election," there can be little reasonable confidence that Martinez's victory was legitimate, considering Florida's electoral practices.

159. "Postal Experts Hunt for Missing Ballots in Florida," *Reuters*, 10/27/04.

160. "Florida Outcry over Missing Absentee Ballots," AP, 10/28/04.

161. Broward County election results available at http://www.browardsoe.org.

162. "Polls Hint at Key Role for State Again," *Palm Beach Post*, 11/1/04.

163. "Volatile Numbers Push States to Front of Race," *USA Today*, 10/31/04.

164. Susan Page, "Swing States Lean to Kerry," *USA Today*, 10/31/04.

CHAPTER SEVEN

1. No exact census of Americans living outside the United States exists, but it is generally estimated that they number between 3 and 10 million, and 6–7 million is an average figure often cited.

2. Richard Pérez-Peña, "Counting the Vote: The Overseas Ballots; Floridians Abroad Are Counted, or Not, as Counties Interpret 'Rules' Differently," *New York Times*, 11/18/00.

3. *Florida Voter Fraud Issues: An FDLE Report and Observations*, Florida Department of Law Enforcement, 1/5/1998.

4. Pérez-Peña, "Counting the Vote."

5. Brian Whitmore. "Both Parties Reaching for Votes from Abroad," *Boston Globe*, 5/3/2004.

6. De Fouloy is a former senior research fellow at the neoliberal European Enterprise Institute. Expatica—a site of "news and information for Expats in Europe"—ran a story on de Fouloy in June 2004. http://www.expatica.com/source/site_article.asp?subchannel_id=19&story_id=8137&name=The+conscience+vote.

7. There are roughly 500,000 military personnel stationed abroad, and 7 million citizens.

8. Zogby International, 8/15/04.

9. Connie Borde, "Letter: Americans in Paris Involved in US Politics," *Boston Globe*, 6/6/04.

10. First reported by Jennifer Joan Lee, "Pentagon Blocks Site for Voters outside U.S.," *International Herald Tribune*, 9/20/04, and by *AP Worldstream* ("Pentagon Restricts Overseas Access to U.S. Voter Registration Site"), 9/20/04, after the block had been in effect for a month.

11. Ibid.

12. Jennifer Joan Lee, "Pentagon Lifts Block on Voter Site," *International Herald Tribune*, 9/23/04.

13. Department of Defense, "DoD Announces Broader Access to FVAP Web Site," at defenselink.mil/releases/2004/nr20040922-1313.html, 9/22/04.

14. Jennifer Joan Lee, "Pentagon Lifts Block on Voter Site."

15. www.fvap.gov.

16. Overseas Vote Foundation, 2004 Post-Election Survey Results, June 2005, at overseasvotefoundation.org/surveys.

17. Don Farthing. E-mail to overseasvote2004.com, 10/29/04.

18. Alix Christie, "Suppressing the Overseas Vote," *Salon.com*, 10/21/04.

19. "Press Release: Service Men and Women Upbeat on Bush, War in Iraq, Economy and Intend To Vote, Annenberg Data Show," *2004 National Annenberg Election Survey*, The Annenberg Public Policy Center of the University of Pennsylvania.

20. *World News Tonight* with Peter Jennings, ABC, 7/15/03.

21. Two days earlier, an anonymous e-mail from the killing ground was all over the Internet: "Our morale is not high or even low," it said. "It is nonexistent."

22. Robert Collier, "Pentagon may punish GIs who spoke out on TV," *San Francisco Chronicle*, 7/18/03.

23. Joseph R. Chenelly, "Free Speech at a High Cost," *The Army Times*, 7/26/04.

24. Gary Strauss, "'Farenheit' soldier in hot water," *USA Today*, 7/29/04.

25. Mark Harrington, "Election.com Sold to Group Tied to Saudi Nationals," *Newsday*, 2/27/03.

26. Reps. Maloney (D-NY) and Waxman (D-CA), House of Representatives Committee on Government Reform, Letter to GAO, 10/19/04.

27. Ibid.

28. Michael Moss, "Company Hired for Overseas Ballots Faced Lawsuit over a Bill," *New York Times*, 9/16/04.

29. Reps. Maloney (D-NY) and Waxman (D-CA), House of Representatives Committee on Government Reform, Letter to GAO, 10/19/04.

30. Overseas Vote Foundation, 2004 Post-Election Survey Results, June 2005, at overseasvotefoundation.org/surveys.

31. "U.S. Voters in Foreign Nations Could Decide the Election," *NewsMax.com*, 8/16/04, at www.newsmax.com/archives/articles/2004/8/16/112451.shtml.

EPILOGUE

1. "Bush wins. What's next for conservatives?" E-mail from Heritage Membership, 11/3/04.

2. Ibid.

3. "Texas Governor George W. Bush and Dick Cheney Meeting with Reporters at the Governor's Ranch," *Federal News Service*, 11/11/01.

4. Julia Malone, "Parties' voter drives generate outcry," Cox News Service, 10/15/04.

5. "6 to 1 Conclude Reagan was a Better President than Bush," AP, 6/27/04; "Americans see Reagan as a better president than Bush," *Salt Lake Tribune*, 6/27/04. Local polls told the same story. In Oregon, for example, "[a] survey of 770 businesses conducted for the July issue of Oregon Business magazine showed presumptive Democratic candidate John Kerry unseating President Bush by 47 percent to 43 percent in a two-way race." *Salem Statesman Journal*, 6/25/04. There was no way for such regional stories to penetrate the national consciousness.

6. Paul Gilfeather, "American Duty: Bush wants Blair to accept the Congressional Medal," *Sunday Mirror*, 8/22/04.

7. Sidney Blumenthal, "Turnout will be key," *Salon*, 10/20/04.

8. Ruy Teixeira, "New Voters for Kerry," The Emerging Democratic Majority, 10/24/04 (http://www.emergingdemocraticmajorityweblog.com/donkeyrising/archives/000849.php).

9. "Young Mobile Voters Pick Kerry over Bush," Zogby International, 10/31/04 (http://www.zogby.com/news/ReadNews.dbm?ID=919).

10. Michelle Goldberg, "They fought the law and the law won," *Salon*, 9/3/04.

11. Jennifer Moroz, "Woman arrested at '9/11' film," *The Philadelphia Inquirer*, 6/28/04.

12. Jennifer Bundy, "Trespass Charges Dropped Against Bush Protestors," AP, 7/15/04; Tara Tuckwiller, "'We weren't doing anything wrong': Couple in anti-Bush T-shirts were arrested at president's speech," *Saturday Gazette-Mail*, 7/15/04 (http://www.veteransforpeace.org/Couple_in_antiibush_tee_071504.htm).

13. Ian C. Storey, "Ticket ripped because of sticker," *Traverse City Record-Eagle*, 8/17/04.

14. "Credentialed columnist denied access to Cheney speech," Reporters Committee for Freedom of the Press, 8/27/04 (http://www.rcfp.org/news/2004/0827syndic.html).

15. "Grieving Mom Heckles Laura Bush," CBS News, 9/17/04 (http://www.cbsnews.com/stories/2004/09/17/politics/main644005.shtml).

16. "Soldier, Democratic supporter among those barred entrance," *The Citizens Voice*, 10/23/04 (http://www.citizensvoice.com/site/news.cfm?newsid=13207582&BRD=2259&PAG=461&dept_id=455154&rfi=6).

17. "Bush fires up party faithful in Southern Oregon," *The Oregonian*, 10/15/04.

18. "Resident Says Confusion Cost Her Tickets to Republican Rally," *Bucks County Courier Times*, 10/28/04.

19. Robert Schlesinger, "Reporters in chains," *Salon*, 6/15/04.

20. "Inter-American Press Association criticizes U.S. press restrictions," AP, 10/24/04;

21. "US Authorities Sieze IMC Servers in UK," IndyMedia.org, 7/10/04 (http://www.indymedia.org.uk/en/2004/10/298741.html).

22. Mike Francis, "Ordered to Just Walk Away," *The Sunday Oregonian*, 8/8/04.

23. Dave Lindorff, "The Emperor's New Hump."

24. Robert Scheer, "Bush suppresses damning CIA report on 9/11," 10/20/04.

25. See Benjamin DeMott, "Whitewash as Public Service," *Harper's*, October 2004. Appearing as it did right at the height of the enchanted time before Election Day, this excellent critique went unreported by the national press.

26. "The 180-page report written by commission staff says Bush 'has neither exhibited leadership on pressing civil rights issues, nor taken actions that matched his words' on the subject. Among other criticisms, it finds fault with Bush's funding requests for civil rights enforcement agencies; his positions on voting rights, educational opportunity and affirmative action; and his actions against hate crimes." "Civil Rights Panel to Wait to Discuss Bush," AP, 10/8/02.

27. John Files, "Bush Replaces Head of Panel on Civil Rights," *The New York Times*, 12/7/04.

28. "Culture of Fear at Interior," HonestChief.com, 8/2/04 (http://www.honestchief.com/nj/CultureofFeara.htm).

29. "Did Bush lie to become a member of the American legion?" AmericaBlog.org, 9/13/04 (http://americablog.blogspot.com/archives/2004_09_12_americablog_archive.html#109513040392425776).

30. Charles Laurence, "Kerry campaign attacks President over 'war honour he did not earn,'" *The Daily Telegraph*, 8/29/04 (http://www.telegraph.co.uk/news/main.jhtml?xml=/news/2004/08/29/wbush129.xml&sSheet=/news/2004/08/29/ixworld.html).

31. Gary Younge, "George Jr sent out of Texas by father as a 'drunken liability,'" *The Guardian*, 9/3/04 (http://www.guardian.co.uk/uselections2004/story/0,13918,1296350,00.html).

32. Russ Baker, "Why Bush Left Texas," *The Nation*, 9/14/04 (http://www.thenation.com/doc.mhtml?i=20040927&s=baker).

33. Ibid.

34. Matt Kelley, "Bush's Air National Guard file missing some required records," AP, 9/5/04.

35. Susan Cooper Eastman, "Fear of Flying: A Duval County Woman Says Nerves Ended W's National Guard Service in Texas," Citizens for Legitimate Government, 9/23/04 (http://www.legitgov.org/essay_eastman_bush_fear_of_flying_in_guard_092304.html).

36. Kit R. Roane, "The Service Question," *U.S. News & World Report*, 9/20/04 (http://www.usnews.com/usnews/news/articles/040920/20guard.htm).

37. Pablo Pardo, "In Twenty Years, the American Welfare State Will No Longer Be Needed," *El Mundo*, 9/12/04; English translation available at http://people-link5.inch.com/pipermail/portside/Week-of-Mon-20040920/014094.html.

38. "Pennsylvania School Board Votes to Include Intelligent Design," Center for Inquiry, posted online on 10/29/04 (http://ga1.org/center_for_inquiry/alert-description.tcl?alert_id=1009084).

39. Chris Floyd, "Pinheads," *Moscow Times*, 3/12/04 (http://context.themoscowtimes.com/index.php?aid=131199). Full text of the bill available at http://www.yuricareport.com/Dominionism/HR3799z ConstitutionRestorationAct.html.

40. Bill Berkowitz, "Bush's faith-based parks," WorkingForChange.com, 12/26/03 (http://www.workingforchange.com/article.cfm?Item ID=16200).

41. Frank Rich, "Now on DVD: The Passion of the Bush," *New York Times*, 10/03/04.

42. "As part of an Ambassadors for Peace ceremony, Rev. Moon was one of several dozen honorees at a ceremony at the Dirksen Senate Office Building on March 23, 2004. In what both church insiders and media commentators have called a 'coronation ceremony,' Moon and has wife were given bejeweled crowns by Rep. Danny K. Davis, D-IL. Moon announced that he would save everyone on Earth as he had saved the souls of even such murderous dictators as Hitler and Stalin, who he claimed had received 'the Blessing' through him. Moon said the reformed Hitler and Stalin vouched for him from the spirit world calling him 'none other than humanity's Savior, Messiah, Returning Lord and True Parent.' The media ignored the event at the time except for Moon's *Washington Times*, but freelance journalist John Gorenfeld spent the next three months reconstructing the details of the event. His writings forced a sheepish *Washington Post*, scooped

by web sites, to cover the Senate ritual, which the *New York Times* editorial page compared to an act of the Roman emperor Caligula." (http://en.wikipedia.org/wiki/Rev._Moon#Moon_Crowned_by_ U.S._Congressmen); Robert Parry, "Mysterious Republican Money," ConsortiumNews.org, 9/7/04 (http://www.consortiumnews.com/2004/ 090704.html).

43. *NBC Nightly News*, 9/24/04.

44. John Conyers, "Outrageous New Georgia Voter ID Law Must Be Stopped," ConyersBlog.us, posted online on 4/23/05 (http://www. conyersblog.us/archives/00000068.htm); see also "Feds should kill voter ID law," *Atlanta Journal-Constitution*, 7/31/05.

45. "Contentious voter ID bill heads to governor," AP, 4/12/05; "Election officials express concern about plan to implement Prop 200," AP, 7/18/05.

46. Bob Lewis, "High court refuses to hear appeal of Va. redistricting suit," AP, 4/4/05.

47. Robin Toner and Jonathan D. Glater, "Roberts Helped to Shape 80's Civil Rights Debate," *New York Times*, 8/4/05.

AFTERWORD

1. I was glad to hear that Kerry now opposed the use of those machines—a marked advance over his earlier indifference to the problem. Thanks to the intercession of an officer in Kerry's New York campaign, the senator and I had had a very brief exchange in December of 2003, when he was merely a contender for the Democratic nomination. At that event (a fundraiser at George Plimpton's house), I warned Kerry of the risks posed by computerized voting systems. At that time he was politely unresponsive; and, some months later, was among the last of the contenders for the Democratic nomination to speak out against the e-voting machinery. (Howard Dean was the first to bring it up, followed by Dennis Kucinich.)

2. Mark Crispin Miller, "Kerry Told Me He Now Thinks the Election Was Stolen," *Democracy Now* radio show transcript, 11/04/05; http://www.democracynow.org/article.pl?sid=05/11/04/1532222.

3. Mark Crispin Miller, "More on my exchange with Kerry," originally posted as thread on http://www.democraticunderground.com, 11/04/05; http://markcrispinmiller.blogspot.com/2005/11/more-on-my-exchange-with-kerry.html.

4. John Byrne, "Senator Kerry rebuffs claim he said election was stolen," *Raw Story*, 11/04/05; http://rawstory.com/news/2005/Senator_Kerry_rebuffs_claim_he_said_1104.html. As for Kerry's efforts on behalf of election reform, the senator had co-sponsored the Count Every Vote Act of 2005, introduced into the Senate by Barbara Boxer and Hillary Clinton on February 17. The legislation called for paper trails on DRE machines, mandatory recounts of paper ballots in 2 percent of all precincts or polling places in each state, and other anodyne requirements.

5. Hagan tells this story in Dorothy Fadiman's documentary, *Stealing America: Vote by Vote* (2006), available on DVD at http://www.directcinema.com/dcl/title.php?id=473.

6. On the subject of Ohio, Kerry finally bit the bullet almost two years later, in a statement on behalf of Rep. Ted Strickland's run for governor. "He used the power of his state office to try to intimidate Ohioans and suppress the Democratic vote," he wrote about Ken Blackwell (Strickland's opponent), in an e-mail sent out to 100,000 Democratic donors on Aug. 29, 2006. Blackwell's spokesman, Carlo LoParo, answered that mild criticism from his office on Bizarro World: "Some people will do anything for money," he said. "Fortunately, the historical record contradicts Senator Kerry." David Hammer, "Kerry Revives 2004 Election Allegations," AP, 8/28/06. How Kerry could have made a nickel from his statement, or why so rich a man would need it, were questions that LoParo did not address.

7. Jon Craig and Allison D'Aurora, "Clinton feeds theory of election vote tampering," *Cincinnati Enquirer*, 7/11/06.

8. Brad Friedman, "Howard Dean on Electronic Voting Machines, Diebold and Otherwise ...," *The Brad Blog*, 4/22/06. (David Grossman asked Howard Dean about Electronic Voting Machines; complete transcript of Dean's answer is below.) http://www.bradblog.com/?p=2724.

9. This mass e-mail was entitled "Stop Election Hijacking."

10. Transcript and Video: "Howard Dean Guest-hosts Topic [A] With Tina Brown," *CNBC*, 8/8/04. Available online at http://www.crocuta.net/Dean/Dean_Host_TopicA_Aug8_2004.htm#blackbox.

11. On June 17, 2006, in Little Rock, keynoting at the annual convention of the Association of Alternative Newsweeklies, Clinton publicly acclaimed Robert F. Kennedy, Jr.'s recent article about Ohio in 2004, which had just appeared in *Rolling Stone*. Kennedy made "a very persuasive case," he said and strongly urged the audience to read the piece. "This is without regard to party," he said. "I just don't think we ought to be suppressing voters. We ought to be getting them to the polls and letting them have

their say." The text of his full remarks is at http://aan.org/alternative/Aan/
ViewArticle?oid=oid%3A166649.

12. The report is available for download at http://www.democrats.
org/a/2005/06/democracy_at_ri.php.

13. On July 15, 2006, I received a call from Susan Turnbull, vice chair
of the Committee and formerly a Democrat without the slightest interest
in the problem of election fraud. She called to talk about the possible recurrence of Republican malfeasance in the next elections, especially in
Ohio. After I briefed her on the issue, she told me that some party lawyers
in Ohio would get back to me. Although I never heard from them, it was a
very heartening exchange. "I've seen the light," she said, and she also said
that Howard Dean was very much concerned about the danger.

Not all the members of the DNC are so receptive to such democratic
give-and-take. On Saturday, Aug. 19, 2006, the DNC met in Chicago,
where there were also several grass-roots activists who had been asked to
come and brief the group. (For more on that exchange, see
http://www.bradblog.com/?p=3308#more-3308.) At one point, John
Brakey, a seasoned activist from Arizona (and an ebullient soul), encountered Donna Brazile. "Donna, what happened with the Ohio report?" he
asked her. "That report really hurt the election integrity movement."
"Fuck you!" she replied. E-mail from John Brakey, 11/20/06.

14. James Dao, "In Ohio Vote, Woes, Yes, Fraud, No," The *New York
Times*, 7/23/05.

15. *www.NewMax.com* staff, 6/23/05; Dan Balz, "Democrats Say '2004
Election System Failed in Ohio,' Party Concedes No Evidence of Fraud;
Republican Decries 'Political Fiction,'" *Washington Post*, 6/23/05, A10;
"Dean Charges Black Vote Suppressed in Ohio," *Fox News*, Thursday,
6/23/05. (www.FoxNews.com).

16. That the Democrats actually knew better came out long after the
fact, and so quietly that no one heard it. On Jan. 25, 2007, for instance,
Sen. Harry Reid, now Senate majority leader, casually informed Chris
Matthews of his view that Kerry had won Ohio in 2004:

CM: Do you think he got a good count in Ohio […] at the end of that
election?

HR: Well, I think the Ohio count was bad, but he is a good American.
He realized that it was time to end the election and not drag this on. I think
some votes could have been changed in the state of Ohio, but John Kerry
did the right thing. He just pulled the plug.(http://www.msnbc.msn.com/
id/16826322.)

17. "Silence: Mainstream Media Completely Ignores GAO Report, Joint Congressional News Release on E-Voting!" BradBlog.com, 11/1/05, http://www.bradblog.com/?p=1965. That was a slight exaggeration, as the Federal News Service—a government facility—had noted the report. Thanks to its coverage, there were stories in the *Pasco Times* (in Florida), the *Dayton Daily News* and the *Eureka Times-Standard*.

18. Brian Bergstein, "E-Voting Under Scrutiny as Federal Compliance Deadline Looms," *Associated Press*, 11/30/05; Bob Fitrakis and Harvey Wasserman, "Powerful Government Accountability Office report confirms key 2004 stolen election findings," *The Free Press* (Departments, Election Issues), 10/26/05; http://www.freepress.org/departments/display/19/2005/1529.

19. On North Carolina, see Matt Zimmerman, "Diebold, North Carolina, and the Immaculate Certification," Electronic Frontier Foundation (EFF), 12/1/05; http://www.eff.org/deeplinks/archives/004223.php; on California, see Brad Friedman, "California Scheming: About McPherson's Diebold About-Face," bradblog.com, 2/21/06; http://www.bradblog.com/?p=2455. For further backgound, see "The Diebold Persuasion Machine," BlackBoxVoting.com, n/d, http://blackboxvoting.org/diebold-prmachine.pdf. On Kevin Shelley's exoneration, see "Criminal Complaint Against S.F. Housing Authority Commissioner Unsealed," KGO-TV, San Francisco, 4/8/05; http://www.abclocal.go.com/kgo/story?section=News&id=2952060; on the federal injunction on the Georgia law, see Darryl Fears, "Voter ID Law Is Overturned," *Washington Post*, 10/28/05, A3.

20. My optimism was dimmed slightly in the course of our exchange, when he asked me about evidence, and I mentioned other works—including the GAO report, which had been out for over a week. Kerry was impressed, because he hadn't heard of it until I brought it up.

21. Robert Parry, "Kerry Suspects Election 2004 Was Stolen," *Consortiumnews.com*, 11/6/05; http://consortiumnews.com/2005/110505.html. As they illuminated Kerry's true beliefs about the previous election, Winer's comments should have resonated far beyond his website. That Parry's news went nowhere is, of course, another clear example of the U.S. press's staunch refusal to approach the issue of election fraud.

We may learn more about the current state of U.S. journalism by considering Robert Parry's own career. An excellent reporter, he broke several of the major Iran/contra stories for *Newsweek* back in the eighties. Like many other great investigative journalists of the post-Watergate era,

Parry came to feel himself impossibly constricted by the bullying decorum of the corporate media and left in 1990. In 1995 he started Consortium News—"A Website Dedicated to Independent Investigative Journalism"— which subsists mainly on book sales and individual donations. The site (http://www.consortiumnews.com) averages about 10,000 unique visitors a day. *Newsweek*'s U.S. circulation is 3.1 million, with another million readers globally.

22. "There's no doubt in my mind that the United States electoral system is severely troubled and has many faults in it. It would not qualify at all, for instance, for participation by the Carter Center in observing. We require, for instance, that there be uniform voting procedures throughout an entire nation. In the United States procedures are fragmented not only from one state to another but also from one county to another. There is no central election commission in the United States that can make a final judgment. It's a cacophony of voices that come in after the election is completed, thousands or hundreds of lawyers contending with each other. There's no uniformity in the nation at all. There's no doubt that there is severe discrimination against poor people because of the quality of voting procedures presented to them.

"Another thing in the United States that we wouldn't permit in a country other than the United States is that we require that every candidate in a country in which we monitor the elections have equal access to the major news media, regardless of how much money they have. In the United States, as you know, it's how much advertising you can buy on television and radio. And so the richest candidates prevail, and unless a candidate can raise sometimes hundreds of thousands or millions of dollars, they can't even hope to mount a campaign, so the United States has a very inadequate election procedure." That statement, made on NPR's *All Things Considered*, received no further coverage. (http://www.npr.org/templates/story/story.php?storyId=6439233&ft=1&f=1001.)

23. "Ohio pollworkers convicted," AP, 1/25/07; Bob Fitrakis and Harvey Wasserman, "Do new Ohio recount prosecutions indicate unraveling of 2004 election thjeft cover-up?" *Columbus Free Press*, 1/24/07; http://www.freepress.org/departments/display/19/2007/2362.

24. This is actually an ancient Daley trick. According to the Illinois Election Code, there must be a bipartisan panel of election judges in every precinct. Daley got around this rule by having Democrats pose as "Republicans."

25. Bob Fitrakis, "Can there be real election reform in Ohio?" *The Free Press* (columns section), 11/3/05; http://www.freepress.org/columns/display/3/2005/1248.

26. Darrell Rowland, "3 Issues on Way to Passage, Poll Finds: Plan to Draw Legislative Districts Gets Little Support," *The Columbus Dispatch*, Sunday, 11/6/05.

27. http://www.sos.state.oh.us:80/sos/ElectionsVoter/results2005.aspx?Section=1225.

28. There was some controversy over the newspaper's treatment of its own poll numbers, begun by syndicated columnist Bob Koehler. See Dave Astor, "Columnist and Editor Differ on Why Columbus (Ohio) Dispatch Election Poll Was Wrong," *Editor & Publisher*, 11/28/05.

29. This account of the San Diego race is based on interviews with Paul Lehto, the attorney hired by those contesting the legitimacy of that election, and on Brad Friedman's coverage. See Friedman's invaluable update on 1/10/07; http://www.bradblog.com/?p=4002.

Lehto elaborated on the sleepovers: "The (literally) flimsy excuse for allowing sleepovers was the existence of thin removable plastic seals. Those seals, which would theoretically disable any tampering, could be removed and replaced quite easily by a committed cheater. However, when those plastic seals were missing—they were 'accidentally' removed very early on Election Day (according to two of the elections officials responsible for the sleepovers)—and this breach was reported to the Registrar of Voters [Mikel Haas], the proper steps weren't taken. The machines should have been taken off line and emergency paper ballots used. Instead, Haas told the poll workers who had removed those seals on the memory cards: 'Just keep an eye on the voters and the machines'—as if the voters posed the major risk of fraud. If the poll-workers took this 'solution' seriously, they would have had to keep the voters under actual surveillance, close enough to violate their right to cast a secret ballot. In doing so, the Registrar completely disregarded the conditional certification requirements for the Diebold machines, and also ignored the procedures that require the memory cards to be zeroed and re-sealed before allowing the machines could be used for recording votes.

"Haas then went on to choose precincts for the 1% California audit prior to the conclusion of the first count, thus knowing in advance which 99% of the precincts did NOT need to audit out correctly. In other words, it was open season on elections in November 2006 in the 50th Congressional District. (Ultimately there was almost a 6% exit poll discrepancy.)" See http://www.bradblog.com/?p=3772. E-mail from Paul Lehto, 3/5/07.

30. Brad Friedman, "Far Right San Diego Radio Host Agrees with Brad on Busby/Bilbray Mess During On-Air Appearance," *The Brad Blog*, 6/21/06; http://www.bradblog.com/?p=2988.

31. There is convincing evidence that certain journalists did not reflexively avoid the subject of election fraud but were informed by their superiors that stories on that subject would be most unwelcome. The word "lockdown" has been used by some observers, speaking off the record. Clearly there was, and still seems to be, some such policy at NPR, as the refusal to discuss the possibility of fraud has been remarkable at NPR from coast to coast. And according to several sources at *The New York Times*, the paper's all-but-total silence on the subject, both in its news coverage and its op-ed columns, reflects a policy dictated by Arthur Ochs Sulzberger, Jr., the *Times*'s publisher. Even if such claims are true, however, any such taboo would still bespeak denial, whatever rationales the media's top managers might feed each other, and themselves, behind closed doors.

32. As of this writing (March 2007), there is good reason to suspect the victory of incumbent Rep. Deborah Pryce over Democratic challenger Mary Jo Kilroy in Ohio's 15th congressional district. (According to a Kilroy pollster, Pryce was trailing by 12 points in the final pre-election poll, and never polled more than 43 percent.) Also doubtful was incumbent Rep. Jean Schmidt's defeat of Democrat Paul Hackett in Ohio's 2nd. (Schmidt had already "beaten" Hackett in a special election in August, 2005—a victory due in part to the last-minute breakdown of the DRE machines in Clermont County, a glitch that wiped out Hackett's lead. See Bob Fitrakis and Harvey Wasserman, "Did the GOP steal another Ohio Election?" *The Columbus Free Press*, 8/5/05; http://www.freepress.org/departments/display/19/2005/1398.) There is also some question about Democrat Barbara Sykes's failed run for state auditor. In Franklin County, the epicenter of election fraud in Ohio, the campaign of Carol Squire, Democratic candidate for common pleas judge, requested a recount of those precincts where some 30 DRE machines malfunctioned.

33. As Franken hopes to be a Democratic senator from Minnesota, his posture is in sync with, and was probably determined by, the official posture of the Democratic Party. The same would seem to be the case with liberal talk show host Ed Schultz, whose program airs daily on the Democracy Radio Network (and, in some markets, Air America). Schultz's views hew closely to the Democratic Party's, and he too will not discuss election fraud.

34. This happened several months after we tried to get WHYY-FM in Philadelphia, Gross's station, to run ads for *Fooled Again*. When they

refused to do it, Josh Mitteldorf, the local activist who was negotiating with the station, urged Tim Roll to consider an alternative idea. Roll's response was startling. "I suggested to him," writes Mitteldorf, "that Steve Freeman's book on a similar theme would be coming out in the near future, and I might approach them again with an ad for that book. He replied that they couldn't accept ads for just any book—and raised the analogy of *Mein Kampf*!" E-mail from Josh Mitteldorf, 1/9/06.

35. Its subtitle: *Who's Afraid of Osama Wolf?, China Floats, Bush Sinks, The Scheme to Steal '08, No Child's Behind Left, and Other Dispatches from the Front Lines of the Class War.*

36. E-mail from Greg Palast, 10/2/06. His exchange with Hannity is also online in "'I Had to Leave the Country': An Interview with Greg Palast," gregpalast.com, 10/9/06; http://www.gregpalast.com/an-interview-with-greg-palast.

37. Robert F. Kennedy Jr., "Was the 2004 Election Stolen?: Republicans prevented more than 350,000 voters in Ohio from casting ballots or having their votes counted—enough to have put John Kerry in the White House," *Rolling Stone*, 6/15/06; http://www.rollingstone.com/news/story/10432334/was_the_2004_election_stolen.

38. Bob Herbert, "Those Pesky Voters," *New York Times*, Monday, 6/12/06.

39. The propaganda drive against the piece in *Rolling Stone* popped up in some odd places. In its archival description of the video of Kennedy's appearance on CNN's *Hardball with Chris Matthews* (Sept. 27, 2006), the Video News Service editorialized overtly (probably the furtive doing of some worker with an axe to grind): "Interview—Robert Kennedy, Jr., article writer in Rolling Stone, offers his substantiveless [*sic*] narrative conspiracy theory about how the GOP are going to steal the Presidential election in 2008." http://ezproxy.library.nyu.edu:2073/universe/document?_m=508675cf6178e41325870c612f6d36be&_docnum=1&wchp=dGLzVlz-zSkVb&_md5=836f7fb2c368aa11c3da99cb53898005.

40. Les Kinsolving, "Snow offers no response on McKinney, Kennedy, Jokingly su ggests reporter serve as 'emissary from Rolling Stone,'" WND Exclusive, *WorldNetDaily.com*, 6/8/06; http://worldnetdaily.com/news/article.asp?ARTICLE_ID=50564.

41. *Imus in the Morning*, MSNBC, 6/12/06.

42. David H. Landon, "Robert F. Kennedy, Jr. Joins the Barking Moonbats," "Forum: Focus," *Dayton City Paper*, 6/14–20/06, 7.

43. "The Situation with Tucker Carlson," *MSNBC*, 6/1/06; http://www.msnbc.msn.com/id/13100049.

44. Mark Leibovich, "Another Kennedy Living Dangerously," *New York Times*, 6/25/06, Style, 1; http://select.nytimes.com/search/restricted/article?res=F60D14FC3D540C768EDDAF0894DE404482.

45. The only "leading Democrats" whom Leibovich contacted for a comment were John Kerry and Christopher Dodd. As we have seen, Bill Clinton certainly did not ignore the piece in *Rolling Stone* but had praised it publicly on June 17.

46. Farhad Manjoo, "Was the 2004 election stolen? No." *Salon*, 6/3/06; http://www.salon.com/news/feature/2006/06/03/kennedy/index.html.

47. Joan Walsh, editor, "Salon answers its critics," *Salon*, 6/6/06; http://www.salon.com/opinion/feature/2006/06/06/salon_answers/index.html.

48. Mark Crispin Miller, "Some Might Call It Treason: An Open Letter to Salon," Huffington Post, 6/16/06; http://www.huffingtonpost.com/mark-crispin-miller/some-might-call-it-treaso_b_23187.html.

49. Ronnie Dugger, "How They Could Steal the Election This Time," *The Nation*, 8/16/04; http://www.thenation.com/doc/20040816/dugger.

50. David Corn, "A Stolen Election?" *The Nation*, 11/2/04; http://www.thenation.com/doc/20041129/corn.

51. David Corn, "More on the 'Stolen Election'," *The Nation Blog*, 11/30/04; http://www.thenation.com/blogs/capitalgames?bid=3&pid=2037.

52. After the 2004 election, *The Nation* now and then addressed the likelihood of fraud but never with the prominence and urgency that had marked Dugger's article. In the Jan. 5, 2005, issue, there appeared "The State of US Elections," a short piece by John Nichols on the Democrats' indifference to the Conyers Report. (Corn never dealt with that report.) Six months later, in the June 27 issue, the magazine ran "Something Rotten in Ohio," a version of Gore Vidal's introduction to the paperback edition of the Conyers Report. (Vidal raised the issue again, in passing, in his incendiary essay "President Jonah"—which ran not in the magazine itself but on its website, on January 26, 2006.) Finally, in the issue of July 3, 2006, *The Nation* ran "The Death of News," my own brief contribution to the 10-year anniversary issue on the scourge of corporate media ownership. The final sentence of the piece is worth quoting here: "Whether it's such tawdry fare as Jeffrey Gannon's many overnights at Bush's house, or graver matters like the Patriot Act, or the persistent questions about 9/11,

or the President's imperial 'signing statements' or—most staggering of all—the ever-growing evidence of coast-to-coast election fraud by Bush & Co., the press has failed in its constitutional obligation to keep us well informed about the doings of our government."

53. Andrew Gumbel, "Fixing Elections," *The Nation*, 11/27/06; http://www.thenation.com/directory/bios/andrew_gumbel.

54. Alexander Cockburn, "The Poisoned Chalice," *The Nation*, posted 11/18/04 (Dec. 6, 2004, issue); http://www.thenation.com/doc/20041206/cockburn.

55. Alexander Cockburn, "Sapping the Empire—The Poisoned Chalice," *CounterPunch*, 11/20–21/04; http://counterpunch.org/cockburn11202004 .html. All subsequent Cockburn quotes from this source.

56. Four years earlier, fresh from the Counter-Inaugural gala protesting Bush's first "election," Cockburn had a very different attitude: "There should be some formal, legally based venue now in which evidence about the stolen election can steadily pile up, day by day." Alexander Cockburn, "Beat the Devil: Let's Get Our Show on the Road!" *The Nation*, 1/8/01; posted on *The Nation*'s website on 12/21/00; http://www.thenation.com/doc/20010108/cockburn.

57. Russ Baker, "Election 2004: Stolen Or Lost," *TomPaine.com*, 1/7/05; http://www.tompaine.com/articles/election_2004_stolen_or_lost.php.

58. Fitrakis and his associates hosted Baker's visit to Ohio and chauffeured him around to his appointments (which included a visit to the gym and dinner with some friends). Fitrakis had collected quite a lot of crucial documentary material, much of it unpublished, and he tried to show it to the journalist, to no avail. "Baker refused to look at data that I had in my possession" (e-mail from Bob Fitrakis, 3/24/06).

59. On Anthony's falling-out with Blackwell, see the former's press release in Robert J. Fitrakis, Steven Rosenfeld and Harvey Wasserman, *What Happened in Ohio? A Documentary Record of Theft and Fraud in the 2004 Election* (New York: The New Press, 2006), 101.

60. "I also told Baker that Anthony had told me that I shouldn't be focusing on Franklin County and the machines, where Kerry had won, but that he felt there was evidence in 'the Republican southwestern counties,' that the numbers didn't make any sense." E-mail from Bob Fitrakis, 12/19/06. Kennedy confirmed those doubts in *Rolling Stone*—a good example of the fresh news broken in that article.

61. The background on Bill Anthony is based on interviews with Bob Fitrakis. Also see Bob Fitrakis, "The new face of apartheid:

J. Kenneth Hackwell," *The Free Press*, 3/30/06; http://www.freepress.org/columns/display/3/2006/1343; and Bob Fitrakis and Harvey Wasserman, "Why can't the left face the Stolen Elections of 2004 & 2008?" *The Free Press*, 10/18/05; http://www.freepress.org/departments/display/19/2005/1502.

62. When I debated Baker in New York on July 12, 2006, on WBAI-FM, he belittled Bob Fitrakis—or rather, someone he'd mistaken for Fitrakis. At one point I extolled Fitrakis's knowledge of Ohio politics. Baker then chucklingly recalled his meeting with "Bob Fitrakis," who, he said, had wanted to talk only about music. "He has a nice record collection. He showed me his guitar." I pointed out to him that that was not Fitrakis, who is not a musician, but his associate Richard Hayes Phillips, a gifted singer/songwriter—but, more to the point, Fitrakis is a skilled researcher who spent months examining the ballots in Ohio and coming up with crucial documentary evidence of fraud. (See Phillips's "Another Stolen Election," http://web.northnet.org/minstrel/provisional.htm.) Baker was annoyed, and unconvinced, by my correction: "It was Fitrakis," he insisted.

63. Mark Hertsgaard, "Was Ohio Stolen in 2004 or Wasn't It?" *Mother Jones*, 11–12/05; http://www.markhertsgaard.com/Articles/2005/RecountingOhio.

64. This e-mail was sent to me by Sherole Eaton. *Mother Jones* did not publish it, either in its pages or on its website.

65. E-mail from Bob Fitrakis, 3/2/07.

66. Farhad Manjoo, "'Hacking Democracy,'" *Salon*, 11/2/06; http://www.salon.com/ent/tv/review/2006/11/02/hacking/index_np.html.

67. Farhad Manjoo, "Don't get 'Fooled Again'," *Salon*, 11/14/05; http://archive.salon.com/books/review/2005/11/14/miller/index.html.

68. In fact, Salon itself had, right after the election, published my own comments on Manjoo's strong pre-Election Day reporting. I was one of many people interviewed for a survey of immediate reactions that was posted on Nov. 4, under the title "What do we do now?" After noting that we had to see some solid evidence that Bush had really won, I tore into the press for having largely failed to deal with "the integrity of the electoral system," and added this: "I worked and worked and worked to get that story into the media, and no one touched it until your guy did." (There were many others working on that story too, of course, but I was speaking extempore, in high dudgeon.) See http://dir.salon.com/story/opinion/feature/2004/11/04/election_reactions/index1.html. As this was my first public statement on the likelihood of fraud in the 2004 election, Salon might appear to have

encouraged my career in pseudo-journalism—or so the editors of Salon may have feared.

69. "There's a lot of fuss on the left about election irregularities— like, you know, the voting machines were tampered with, they didn't count the votes right, and so on. That's all accurate and of some importance, but of far more importance is the fact that elections just don't take place, not in any meaningful sense of the term 'election.' And so, it doesn't matter all that much, if there was some tampering." Thus spake Chomsky at a conference in Boston on Dec. 16, 2006, http://www.democracynow.org/article.pl?sid=06/12/19/1433244, although his position had not changed since the election. (See his essay on ZNet.org, 11/29/04, at http://www.zmag.org/content/showarticle.cfm?ItemID=6751.)

While there was almost *no* "fuss on the left" about election fraud, Chomsky's basic point is surely sound, as our elections have indeed been rendered largely meaningless by the two parties and the media: i.e., by the big money behind all of them. However, Bush & Co.'s grand election fraud is not a mere detail on that appalling landscape, but a crime based on and continuous with the process that Chomsky deplores; and since the people *can* and *do* to some extent resist the efforts to manipulate them, the regime's blunt fraud is still more heinous than those other, more systemic strokes against democracy, as it has directly nullified the will of the electorate. Chomsky obfuscates this fact by minimizing the offense ("there was some tampering") and, more important, by denying that the issue matters greatly to the people. "The population doesn't get much exercised over it," he asserts. "The concern over stolen elections and vote tampering, and so on, is mostly an elite affair. Most of the country didn't seem to care very much." While that may be the case with some of Chomsky's readers, there is no evidence to back his claim about "the population" overall.

On the left, there is one serious effort to address the problem of election fraud: the International Endowment for Democracy (IED), founded by the Marxist Bertell Ollman, and with other eminent figures on its board, including Howard Zinn and Gore Vidal (http://www.iefd.org). Chomsky refused to join the board because of what he saw as the IED's over-emphasis on the issue of election reform. (E-mail from Bertell Ollman, 12/20/06.)

70. The most vocal of such figures was Mark Blumenthal, a Democratic pollster employed by Polimetrix, Inc., and a frequent poster on his

website, mysterypollster.com. Blumenthal has had a lot to say about the exit poll discrepancies in 2004, serving as Steve Freeman's main antagonist, questioning the latter's findings both on his own site and in his comments to reporters. His commentary on Freeman's research should, perhaps, be taken with a grain of salt, as his own work has been refuted in the latter's book. Moreover, Blumenthal apparently has no experience with exit polls per se. (His bio is online at http://www.pollster.com/about.)

71. "Explosive Charges," *Your World with Neil Cavuto, FoxNews,* 6/6/06; http://www.foxnews.com/video2/launchPage.html?060606/060606_cav _kennedy&Explosive%20Charges&Your_World&Was%20the%202004% 20presidential%20election%20stolen%20from%20Sen.%20Kerry%3F& Politics&–1&Explosive%20Charges&Video%20Launch%20Page.

72. "RFK Jr.: GOP Stole 2004 Ohio Presidential Vote," "The Situation Room," *CNN,* 6/2/06; http://transcripts.cnn.com/TRANSCRIPTS/0606/ 02/sitroom.02.html.

73. "Where Every Vote Didn't Count," *The Brian Lehrer Show,* WNYC, 6/12/06; http://www.wnyc.org/shows/bl/episodes/2006/06/12.

74. Robert F. Kennedy Jr., "Will the Next Election Be Hacked?" *Rolling Stone,* 10/5/06; http://www.rollingstone.com/politics/story/11717105/ robert_f_kennedy_jr__will_the_next_election_be_hacked/print.

75. Cox was a conservative Democrat. (See pp. 95–96.) There is no evidence that she was privy to the corporation's interference in the 2002 election. On the other hand, there is no evidence that she was much concerned about it, either.

76. There was also an upset victory in Minnesota, where Republican Norm Coleman, who had been running 5 points behind Democrat Walter Mondale, won by 2.2 points. Although Minnesota used no DRE machines, they did reportedly use op-scans, both from Diebold and ES&S. However, the op-scans were not used in 2002, as Paul Wellstone's sudden death, and his 11th-hour replacement by Mondale, left too little time to program them. The votes for senator were therefore all hand-counted.

Still, Coleman's upset victory, by over 49,000 votes, is not beyond suspicion, as over 11,000 absentee ballots for Wellstone were uncounted, and election analyst Bruce O'Dell has found high undervotes in at least heavily Democratic urban precincts—an incidence especially peculiar, as the Senate contest drew more votes than any other race that year, including the gubernatorial election. In any case, there is no reason to believe that Coleman won, against the odds, just because the rightist press so noisily decried Wellstone's memorial (see p. 95).

77. Ronnie Dugger, "How They Could Steal the Election This Time," *The Nation*, 8/16/04.

78. Sarah Lueck, "Detainee Bill Advances As House Debates Surveillance," *The Wall Street Journal*, 9/29/06.

79. Ibid.

80. In a "punch list" of concerns that Cathy Cox sent Diebold on December 3, the state requested "[c]onfirmation that '0808' patch was applied to all systems; confirmation that *patch was not grounds for requiring system to be recertified at national and state level;* as well as verifiable analysis of overall impact of patch to the voting system" (emphasis added). Office of the Georgia Secretary of State, "Punch List," 12/30/02, p. 1, Item 6; http://www.countthevote.org/cynthia2005/ga_dec_02_punch_list.html. The patch was a concern to Cox for technical not civic reasons: "State experienced 'freezing' and other problems after patch applied."

81. A few weeks later, I e-mailed Gumbel asking for specifics. He referred me to Mark Blumenthal's website, mysterypollster.com, and David Moore's book, *How to Steal an Election*, which is about Bush/Cheney's theft of Florida in 2000. As Freeman's book explodes the claims of Blumenthal, the latter certainly is not a useful critic of the former; and in any case one website, and a minor one at that, does not comprise a "court" of expertise. Moore's important book, on the other hand, deals not at all with Freeman's argument. And yet Gumbel found their judgments of the book decisive, without saying why: "Both are professional political pollsters who, unlike Freeman, know what they are talking about" (e-mail from Andrew Gumbel, 11/13/06).

It is worth noting here that Moore's book too has been ignored completely since its publication in October 2006. Despite his excellent credentials (a senior editor at Gallup, he was right there in the trenches on Election Night, 2000) and the book's considerable news value (Moore refutes the claims of Warren Mitofsky), *How to Steal an Election* was reviewed only on buzzflash.com and was reported only by a few press outlets in New England. (Moore lives in New Hampshire.) E-mail from David Moore, 3/5/07.

82. Nicholas Lemann, "Paranoid Style: How Conspiracy Theories Become News," *New Yorker*, 10/16/06.

83. Ian Urbina, "Democrats Fear Disillusionment in Black Voters," *New York Times*, 10/27/06.

84. On Aug. 9, 2006, Bruce McPherson, acting secretary of state, refused to certify Vote-PAD—a non-computerized voting system for the

handicapped—for use in California, notwithstanding its clear merits, modest cost and popular support. (The system had been used successfully in the Wisconsin primary election.) McPherson's testing process had been patently illegal. On October 16, Vote-PAD filed suit against him. For more details, see http://www.vote-pad.us/CA-BOEClaimAttachment.asp.

85. Ray Weiss, "Poll worker fired over touch-screen comment," Daytona Beach News, 8/29/06; http://www.news-journalonline.com/NewsJournal Online/News/Local/newEAST01POL082906.htm.

86. Michael Collins, "New Zogby Poll on Electronic Voting Attitudes," Scoop, 8/21/06; http://www.scoop.co.nz/stories/HL0608/S00220.htm. The poll was commissioned by attorney Paul Lehto, whose own observations are worth reading at http://www.democraticunderground.com/discuss/duboard.php?az=view_all&address=203x446445.

87. Mass disenfranchisement was also eased considerably by the use of computerized poll books, which became commonplace from coast to coast after Election Day, 2004. The process of switching to that system has entailed the "accidental" purging of countless Democratic voters. See "Vote Suppression in 2006: Rule Changes Threaten to Disenfranchise Hundreds of Thousands of Eligible Voters," Pacifica Radio, Democracy Now!, 10/31/06; http://www.democracynow.org/article.pl?sid=06/10/31/150218; and Jason Leopold, "Severe Election Problems Seen in 10 States," truthout.com, 10/26/06; http://www.truthout.org/docs_2006/102606Z.shtml.

88. The text of the Ohio legislation is online at http://www.legislature.state.oh.us/BillText126/126_HB_3_EN_N.html.

89. The party wanted to make such impediments a national requirement, and to do so by Election Day 2007. On September 20, the House passed HR 4844, the Federal Election Integrity Act, which had been introduced by Henry Hyde in early March. The bill, which passed by a vote of 228–196 ("with a small number of lawmakers crossing party lines," as The Hill reported later), required all would-be voters to carry photo I.D.s and proof of citizenship: a measure that would disenfranchise countless citizens of color and the poor in general, students, the disabled, young voters and the elderly. The Senate never took it up, because top Democrats immediately sent Majority Leader Bill Frist a letter threatening a fierce response—presumably a filibuster—if the GOP attempted to impose "a twenty-first century poll tax" on the people. "GOP voter-ID legislation may be casualty of Dems' takeover," The Hill, 11/15/06;

http://www.hillnews.com/thehill/export/TheHill/News/Frontpage/
111506/voterid.html. This clash received no coverage in the corporate or
left/liberal press.

90. Shannon McCaffrey, "Justice Dept.'s Civil Rights Division
Retreating from Activist Roots," Knight-Ridder, 11/21/03.

91. Dan Eggen, "Civil Rights Focus Shift Roils Staff At Justice," *Washington Post*, 11/13/05, A1.

92. Dan Eggen, "Staff Opinions Banned in Voting Rights Cases,"
Washington Post, 12/10/05, A3.

93. Adam Nossiter, "U.S. Says Blacks in Mississippi Suppress White
Votes," *New York Times*, 10/11/06.

94. *Foxnews.com*, 10/29/06, http://www.foxnews.com/story/0,2933
,226142,00.html.

95. The investigation of Sequoia had been sparked by the concerns of
Democratic Rep. Carolyn Maloney, who formally requested it in May.
However, Sequoia's ownership was only one of that lawmaker's many worries about electronic voting—and the only one that Bush & Co. bothered to
address, since only that one gave them a political advantage. (See http://mal-
oney.house.gov/index.php?option=com_content&task=view&id=267&
Itemid=61.) Earlier, another Democrat, Chicago Alderman Edward
Burke, had raised the issue of Sequoia's ownership in terms more paranoid than civic: "We've stumbled across what could be the international
conspiracy [*sic*] to subvert the electoral process in the United States of
America," he said on April 7, some three weeks after Illinois's primary
elections—the first electronic races in that state, and a major technical
disaster. Burke evidently found it easier to blame Chavez for that meltdown than the quartet of Republicans and Democrats who had imposed
the bad new system in the first place. "Alderman: Election Day troubles
could be part of 'international conspiracy,'" WLS-TV, Chicago, 4/7/06;
http://abclocal.go.com/wls/story?section=local&id=4065162.

96. There were two others not included here because I had not yet
heard about them. First, there was the news that countless New York
Democrats with second homes in Florida were voting in both places, by
sending absentee ballots down South. This claim was based on an exposé
by Russ Buettner in the *New York Daily News* nine weeks before the 2004
election, finding that some 46,000 New Yorkers were thus doubly registered, and that 68 percent of them were Democrats. It is unknown how
many of them double-voted in 2000, nor did Buettner revisit the issue
after the 2004 election, to determine how such double-voting figured in

that race. Whether or not such voters actually cast two ballots, double registration is itself a crime. "Exposed: Scandal of Double Voters (68% are Democrats)," *New York Daily News*, 8/21/04.

While there is no doubt that many Democrats were perpetrators, Buettner's piece makes clear that members of both parties were involved, as two out of the three he interviewed were staunch Republicans. The point here, however, is surely not to exculpate all Democrats but to point out how the Bush Republicans reflexively deny their own enormous crimes by over-focusing on the far slighter wrongs of their opponents. Those New York Democrats who cast illegal votes in Florida not only broke the law—for which they should be prosecuted—but they were also playing a loser's game, as the Bush machine in Florida routinely interfered with Democratic efforts to vote absentee, and no doubt threw those ballots out. (Indeed, it is surprising that so many New York Democrats were able to receive absentee ballots from Florida: see pp. 236–37, 248–49.) In any case, such Democratic crimes appear to have been wholly independent of the national party, whereas the crimes of the Republicans were evidently organized and/or subsidized directly by the GOP.

We ought to note the clear anti-Semitic subtext of the propaganda drive against the double voters, with Buettner's article appearing on such ultra-rightist websites as Free Republic and the neo-Nazi outfit Stormfront ("WHITE PRIDE WORLD WIDE"). "Interesting," one poster noted on the latter site, "since these were New York snowbirds wintering in Florida, I can guess their ethnicity (no they aren't Eskimos)," 8/22/04; http://www.stormfront.org/forum/showthread.php/exposed-scandaldouble-voters-florida–149375.html?p=1230455#post1230455.

97. For a good summary of the Rossi/Gregoire race, see Steve Freeman and Joel Bleifuss, *Was the 2004 Presidential Election Stolen?*, pp. 75–79. Freeman demonstrates that the 19 DRE machines retired for freezing or vote-flipping favored the Republicans in every case, and by more than 50 percent.

98. Lehto estimates that the emachines grave Rossi an advantage of at least 3,000 votes. E-mail from Paul Lehto, 3/8/07.

99. It is also possible that Maryland was meant to be a major flashpoint of the post-election drive to cast the Democrats as the sole perpetrators of election fraud. There the governor, a stalwart Bush Republican named Robert Ehrlich, made quite a show of his distrust of Diebold's DRE machines, especially after Maryland's disastrous primary

election on Sept. 12—and Maryland's Democrats reflexively (some might say stupidly) *defended* the machines, accusing Ehrlich of trying to suppress the turnout on Election Day, and actually opposing his advice that Marylanders use paper ballots. (Rep. Steny Hoyer, a powerful Democrat and now the House majority whip, was an especially ardent champion of e-voting technology and had been since he helped get HAVA passed in Congress in 2002.) Thus Maryland's Democrats played right into their adversaries' hands, as it seems quite unlikely that the governor's position was sincere. On and before Election Day 2006, the Maryland GOP mounted a large disinformation effort, aimed primarily at Baltimore, on behalf of Michael Steele's campaign for Senator against Democrat Ben Cardin. See, for example, "At Steele Rally, All Is Not Quite What It Appears," *Washington Post*, 9/24/06, C4; http://www.washingtonpost.com/wp-dyn/content/article/2006/09/23/AR2006092300889.html; and "Reid: Robo Calls Make Legislative Hit List," tpmmuckraker.com, 11/16/06, http://www.tpmmuckraker.com/archives/cats/michael_steele.

For further evidence of plans to charge the Democrats with fraud in Maryland (as well as Pennslyvania), see p. 382.

100. "McKay: Hastings' office called about probing Gregoire's election," *Seattle Post-Intelligencer*, 3/6/07.

101. On ACVR, see Joseph Cannon, "Indicted GOP Moneyman Tied To ACVR, the Phony GOP 'Voting Rights' Group," bradblog.com, 8/15/05; http://www.bradblog.com/?p=1708. Cannon's blog is a good synthesis of several sources, including the Democratic Party's response to the Center's report: "ACVR Report Riddled with Errors and Partisan Spin," posted on 8/9/05, at http://www.democrats.org/a/2005/08/acvr_report_rid.php.

102. Richard Wolf, "Report refutes fraud at poll sites," *USA Today*, 10/11/06; http://www.usatoday.com/news/washington/2006–10–10-poll-fraud-report_x.htm.

103. *Ft. Wayne Journal Gazette* editorial quoted on "Masson's Blog: A Citizen's Guide to Indiana," 5/30/06; http://www.masson.us/blog/?p=1468. For an authoritative essay on the myth of "voter fraud," see Tova Wang, "Where's the Voter Fraud?" bradblog.com, 12/8/06, http://www.bradblog.com/?p=3891. Wang co-authored the initial draft of the expurgated EAC report.

104. Ben Goddard, "Bush, post Labor Day," *The Hill*, 9/7/06.

105. Michael Collins, "Zogby Poll: Voters Questions Outcome of 2004 Presidential Election," Scoop, 9/25/06; http://www.scoop.co .nz/stories/HL0609/S00346.htm.

106. Michael Alvarez, Thad E. Hall and Morgan Llewellyn, "American Confidence in Electronic Voting and Ballot Counting: A Pre-Election Update," 11/3/06; http://www.annenberg.edu/files/2006-Voter-Confidence-Survey.pdf.

107. Interviews with Friedman, Stewart, Gideon and Fitrakis, all of whom had closely monitored both the 2004 and 2006 elections. (Fitrakis and his team were focused on Ohio, while the others kept track of reports nationwide.) This time, there were considerably more voter hotlines and trouble-shooting organizations than there had been on the previous Election Day. This range of services reaped an immense amount of data, on which I have largely based my overview of the 2006 election. That trove of data is, as of this writing, still under review by activists and scholars. (Once again the Election Incident Reporting System—EIRS—was operating, with the toll-free number 1-866-OUR-VOTE, but this time it malfunctioned temporarily, failing to record a single call for some three hours early on Election Day.)

108. George Merritt and Katy Human, "Voting problems overwhelm city," *The Denver Post*, 11/8/06; Susan Miller Degnan, "Ballot problem delays voting 90 minutes in Deerfield Beach," *Miami Herald*, 11/07/06.

109. See "Robo-calls in the 2006 campaign," Pew Internet and American Life Project, Washington, DC, 12/20/06; http://www. pewinternet.org/pdfs/PIP_Robocalls06.pdf; "Robo-Calls and Other 2006 Election Irregularities," Center for Media and Democracy, Madison, WI, 11/21/06; http://www.prwatch.org/node/5494; Paul Rogat Loeb, "Think Globally, Protect the Vote Locally," *Free Press*, 12/1/06; http://www.freepress.org/departments/display/19/2006/2266. The use of robo-calls and other dirty tricks was so egregious that Sen. Harry Reid promised swift legislative action from the Democrats. "'We need to make these criminal penalties,' Reid said, saying that civil liability was apparently not enough to deter what happened in the run-up to last week's election." Tim Grieve, "War Room: Reid vows legislation on robo-calls, phone sample ballot," *Salon*, 11/16/06; http://www.salon.com/ politics/war_room/2006/11/16/voting/index.html.

110. Jeff E. Schapiro, "FBI looks into voter intimidation," TimesDispatch.com (website of the *Richmond Times-Dispatch*), 11/7/06.

The FBI's investigation in Virginia received widespread press attention on Election Day.

111. On the Busby/Bilbray race in 2006, see Brad Friedman's excellent coverage in bradblog.com, especially his update posted on 1/10/07; http://www.bradblog.com/?cat=2, as well as Ken Simpkins's guest blog on that site, "Complaint Filed with New CA SoS Against San Diego's County Registrar Mikel Haas," 1/10/07 (ibid). On this subject I also interviewed Friedman and Paul Lehto.

112. "Can you imagine what those people look like?" she added. "Halloween all over again!" Ingraham, who has a law degree from the University of Virginia, clerked for Clarence Thomas in the early nineties. "Laura Ingraham Tells Listeners to Jam Voter Protection Hotline," thinkprogress.com, 11/7/06; http://thinkprogress.org/2006/11/07/ingraham-voter-line.

113. Caitlin Price, "New Hampshire GOP phone jamming case settles," *The Jurist: Legal News and Research*, 12/2/06.

114. Thomas B. Edsall, "GOP Official Faces Sentence in Phone-Jamming," *The Washington Post*, 5/17/06.

115. "Leahy Calls on Justice Department to Investigate Laura Ingraham's Phone Jamming," ThinkProgress, posted 11/17/06; http://thinkprogress.org/2006/11/17/leahy-ingraham-vote.

116. Officials claimed that all those under-votes were simply a result of the excessive nastiness of the Buchanan/Jennings race, which, they argued, moved those 18,000 citizens to vote for neither candidate. Why the Democrats alone were thus affected is a question that that argument does not address. In any case, a comprehensive count of all the under-votes in FL 13 devastates that talking point. As John Gideon pointed out a few days after the election, the rate of under-votes was not 13 percent, as the media had been reporting, but a little over 16 percent, with 2.6 percent of them on absentee—and therefore paper—ballots.

"The fact that the under vote is 2.6 percent for absentee ballots reveals the fallacy of the argument that the race was very ugly, turning off voters, [so that] a whole bunch of people did not vote in the race. How can it be that the nasty campaign only affected voters who voted on touch screen voting machines and not their neighbors who voted on paper? (And it can't be explained away by any late and particularly vicious ads, since voters were early voting—or 'not voting' according to the results—for two weeks before the election on the touch screen machines as well.)" John Gideon, "The Sarasota Triangle," VoteTrustUSA, 11/12/06;

http://www.votetrustusa.org/index.php?option=com_content&task=view& id=2025&Itemid=113.

117. "Paper Ballots Are Better (NM Case Study)," ePluribus Media, 2/26/07; http://scoop.epluribusmedia.org/story/2007/2/26/205229/794. This blog by Ellen Theisen is a version of her study, "2004 and 2006 New Mexico Canvass Data Shows Undervote Rates Plummet in Minority Precincts When Paper Ballots are Used," which is posted on the website of VotersUnitet.org, at http://www.votersunite.org/info/NM_ UVbyBallotTypeandEthnicity.pdf. Theisen worked on the data with Warren Stewart and Theron Horton. E-mail from Theron Horton, 3/4/07.

118. Paul Krugman, "When Votes Disappear," *New York Times*, 11/24/06; E.J. Dionne, Jr., "An Electronic Canary," *Washington Post*, 11/24/06.

119. Curtis's affidavit is online at http://www.bradblog.com/Docs/ ClintCurtis/CC_Affidavit_120604.pdf.

120. Curtis's foremost champion online, Friedman has covered the story scrupulously from the start. For a good overview of his reportage, see the update that he posted on his site on Aug. 28, 2006, http://www.bradblog.com/ClintCurtis.htm. For his refutation of Feeney's claims, see http://www.bradblog.com/?page_id=3980. My account is also based on interviews with Friedman and with Curtis himself.

121. Catherine Dolinski and Christian M. Wade, "3 Democrats Contest Wins by Incumbents," *The Tampa Tribune*, 1/12/07.

122. Christian Wade, "Russell Contests Brown-Waite's Election Victory," *Tampa Tribune*, 1/5/07. My account is also based on interviews with John Russell.

123. Catherine Dolinski and Christian M. Wade, op. cit. My account is also based on interviews with Frank Gonzalez.

124. In the state's 4th district, Democratic challenger Patti Cox contested the re-election of incumbent Jim McCrery, on the grounds that he was not a resident of Louisiana when the race occurred, as required by law. Formerly a resident of Shreveport, McCrery had moved his family to Washington, DC, some 18 months before Election Day 2006, and he did not maintain a residence in Louisiana. See http://louisianafourth.blogspot.com, for the text of Cox's lawsuits.

125. "Rage Against the (Voting) Machine," *Red Herring*, 11/7/06; http://www.redherring.com/Article.aspx?a=19610&hed=Rage+Against+th e+(Voting)+Machine. The machine problems in Tennessee were, as ever,

downplayed by the corporate press. "There were some reports this morning of problems with voting machines, glitches at least, but there were also reports at least some of those problems were fixed," CNN's Joe Johns told Kyra Phillips at 3 p.m. EST. CNN.com, 11/7/06; http://transcripts.cnn.com/TRANSCRIPTS/0611/07/cnr.07.html.

126. In North Carolina's 8th district, the very narrow "loss" by Larry Kissell to incumbent Robin Hayes—a margin of 339 votes—was identical to Christine Jennings's razor-thin "defeat" by Vern Buchanan in Florida's 13th district. Michael Collins argued that both contests were decided by extraordinary rates of Democratic under-votes cast on the iVotronic DRE machines provided by ES&S, and also that, as the under-votes in Florida cropped up in largely Democratic Sarasota, those in North Carolina were oddly concentrated in largely Democratic Mecklenburg County, which includes Charlotte, the state's largest city. Michael Collins, "Wrong Winner Chosen Twice by Same Voting Machine," *Scoop*, 1/15/07; http://www.scoop.co.nz/stories/HL0701/S00173.htm.

However, Collins's data was soon rigorously questioned by other reputable students of that race. See "NC08 Dist Election to Florida 13th—Facts 'Scoop' Missed," BlackBoxVoting.com, 1/16/07; blackboxvoting.com/s9/index.php?/archives/ 179-NC–08th-Dist-Election-to-Florida–13th-Facts -Scoop-Missed.html; "Time to Doff the Tin Foil—No Suspicious Undervote in NC–08," *The Southern Dem*, 1/18/07; and Joyce McCloy, "NC: Why NC 08 is not the same as FL 13 even though the iVotronic was used in both races," Oregon Voter Rights Coalition, 1/20/07; http://www.oregonvrc.org/2007/01/nc_why_nc_08_is_not_the_same_as_fl_13_even_though_the_ivotronic_was_used_in_both_races. As McCloy notes, the case for fraud in the Hayes/Kissell contest must be made as carefully as possible.

127. The late surge of ballots putting her on top recalled the late surge that had let her beat the well-liked Democratic challenger Paul Hackett in the district's special election on Aug. 2, 2005. See Bob Fitrakis and Harvey Wasserman, "Did the GOP Steal Another Election?" *Free Press*, 8/5/05; http://www.freepress.org/departments/display/19/2005/1398.

128. We must therefore look not only at those races where the rightful winners "lost," but also at those races that the rightful winners won by fewer ballots than were really cast for them. In Sheridan County, Wyoming, for example, Democratic challenger Gary Trauner unseated

GOP incumbent Barbara Cubin by 1,012 votes. As the county uses ES&S op-scanners, and Trauner's margin seemed surprisingly low, a trio of local citizens demanded a recount on principle, and as a check on the e-voting system. (Although he recognized the dangers of e-voting—he runs an Internet Service Provider—Trauner stayed out of it.) Such initiatives should always be encouraged. Michael Collins, "Three Wyoming Democrats Take a Stand for Democracy," Scoop Independent News, 1/22/07; http://www.scoop.co.nz/stories/HL0701/S00247.htm.

129. Robert Brandon, "Re-Cap of Election Day Problems and Solutions for Future Presidential Elections," *VoteTrustUSA.org*, 11/10/06; http://www.votetrustusa.org/index.php?option=com_content&task=vie& id=2020&Itemid=26.

130. Michael Shear, "Webb Has a Slim Edge Over Allen, But Recount Likely," *Washington Post*, 11/08/06; http://www.washingtonpost.com/ wp-dyn/content/article/2006/11/07/AR2006110701844.html.

131. "GOP Officials Call to Impound Voting Machines," *KDKA/AP*; KCKA.com, 11/7/06; http://kdka.com/topstories/local_story_311194635 .html.

132. The party's charge of pro-Casey vote-flipping was reconfirmed by no one else. See "GOP Officials Call to Impound Voting Machines," KDKA/AP, Pittsburgh, 11/7/06, 8:21 p.m.; http://kdka.com/topstories/ local_story_311194635.html; nor, as of this writing, have any such claims come to light. Not that the machines worked properly. "Pennsylvania was another state that saw extremely widespread problems with electronic voting machines across multiple counties." Jon Stokes, "Electronic voting: the silent catastrophe," Ars Technica, 11/14/06; http://arstechnica.com/news.ars/ post/20061114-8223.html. Pennsylvania was likewise bedeviled in the 2004 election: see pp. 175–77.

133. A few of those endorsements were lukewarm—as in San Diego, where the staunchest Christianists were troubled by the fact that Brian Bilbray is pro-choice. A canny operator, he campaigned not as a champion of "moral values" but as a dogged hunter of illegals sneaking in from Mexico.

134. "As of Friday afternoon, the Colorado Republican was featured prominently on a Web site representing the Harrison, Ark.-based Knights Party, described as 'America's Largest, Oldest and Most Professional White Rights Organization—We Love You.'"

"The Knights introduce Musgrave this way:

"'During her eight years in the Colorado Legislature, Musgrave, the mother of four and grandmother of five, co sponsored a successful 2000 bill that defined a marriage as a union between one man and one woman. She has also pressed the legislature to pass laws expanding the right to carry concealed weapons, requiring doctors to provide brochures and a videotape to women seeking abortions, lowering the tax burden for families, more stringent immigration laws, making adoption of children by homosexuals illegal, upholding the rights of ranchers and farmers, and she opposes slave reparations. She now serves as a U.S. Representative.

"They also reference her work to pass a constitutional amendment to outlaw same-sex marriage. According to the Web site, 'Musgrave points out that the homosexual movement is now making use of the many liberal judges appointed during the Clinton administration. Homosexuals are going to unelected judges to get their way rather than going through the legislative process.'" Mary Ann Akers, "What What What?" *Roll Call*, 5/22/06.

135. Mary Jo Melone, "A Switch is Thrown, and God Speaks," *St. Petersburg Times*, 7/13/99, 1B.

136. Ohio Restoration Project, http://www.ohiorestorationproject.com/overview.php.

137. Jonathan Simon and Bruce O'Dell, "Landslide Denied: Exit Polls vs. Vote Count 2006; Under-sampling of Democrats in the House Exit Poll and the Corruption of the Official Vote Count," *Election Defense Alliance*, 11/16/06; http://www.electiondefensealliance.org/landslide_denied_exit_polls_vs_vote_count_2006.

138. Jackson Thoreau, "Republican puds of today run dirtiest campaigns in history," dailykos.com, 10/27/06; http://www.dailykos.com/story/2006/10/27/175358/42.

139. Michael Grunwald, "The Year of Playing Dirtier," *The Washington Post*, 10/27/06, A1; "Attack ad claims Rep. Miller voted to fund sex research but not body armor," FactCheck.org (Annenberg Political Fact Check), 9/27/06; http://www.factcheck.org/article442.html.

140. An entire book could be written on that journalistic double standard, which, pre-Foley, always savaged Democrats—Gerry Studds, Gary Hart, Barney Frank, Bill Clinton, Gary Condit—while largely leaving rightist "deviates" alone. It is instructive to compare the coverage of any of the former stories with the press's general silence on Rep. Buz Lukens's (R-OH) frolic with a 16-year-old girl in 1989 (a bit of sport for which he'd paid her mother), the *Washington Times*'s exposé of the vast male

prostitution ring in Bush/Quayle's White House, also in 1989, and the tragic mess at rightist Hillsdale College—that pious institution's president having had a long affair with his own daughter-in-law, who killed herself when he decided to remarry—in 1999, right after the hysterical brouhaha over Clinton's brief consensual fling with Monica Lewinksy. William Bennett, *Wall Street Journal* writer John Fund, Henry Hyde, Newt Gingrich, RNC chair Ken Mehlman, and Rick Perry, governor of Texas, have been more recent beneficiaries of our media's selective blindness, as has George W. Bush himself.

141. Years before he went to work as a reporter and then hitched his star to Watergate, Woodward knew the inner workings of the White House fairly well. As a liaison officer for the Joint Chiefs of Staff under Adm. Thomas Moorer, Woodward paid weekly visits to the White House Basement, where he formally briefed Al Haig, who at that time was a top aide to Henry Kissinger (and who moved up to White House Chief of Staff in 1973, once Haldeman and Ehrlichman had been let go). These facts have been fully documented by Len Colodny and Robert Gettlin, *Silent Coup: The Removal of a President* (New York, 1991) and, in particular, Adrian Havill, *Deep Truth: The Lives of Bob Woodward and Carl Bernstein* (New York, 1993). While *Silent Coup* includes some highly controversial claims, especially about John Dean, the book deals soundly with Bob Woodward's background, as does Havill's book.

142. ABC News, 11/7/06, 1:35 p.m. EST.

143. "First Read: The Day in Politics" msnbc.mcn.com, 11/7/06, 3:09 p.m. EST; http://firstread.msnbc.msn.com/archive/2006/11/07/12137.aspx. On MSNBC, during Tucker Carlson's interview with Rick Santorum on Election Day a little after 4 p.m. EST, this caption appeared on the bottom of the screen: "Vote Democrat and get nuked?"

144. Cliff Brunt, "2 Ind. Counties have machine woes," Associated Press, 11/7/06; http://www.fortwayne.com/mld/newssentinel/15950441.htm.

145. Interview with Warren Stewart.

146. By thus obsessing on the "horse race," moreover, the TV pundits indirectly serve the interests of their parent companies; for it is the media cartel itself that ultimately gets the billions raised by all those candidates in their respective efforts to improve their "image" and/or "get their message out." "This biannual financial windfall is why the commercial broadcasters steadfastly oppose any viable form of campaign finance reform, or any system that would allocated broadcast time for free to candidates," writes Robert W. McChesney. "They claim that it is

their First Amendment right to do whatever they want to maximize profit." While thus protecting that enormous stream of revenue, the media cartel has also served itself by reporting almost nothing of importance throughout the campaign season. "Broadcasters have little incentive to cover candidates, because it is in their interest to force them to purchase time to publicize their campaigns. And as TV ads become the main form of information, broadcast news has little or no interest in examining the claims made in these ads, as that might antagonize their wealthy benefactors." McChesney, *Rich Media, Poor Democracy: Communication Politics in Dubious Times* (Urbana and London: University of Illinois Press, 1999), 263–64.

Index

Mark Crispin Miller is a professor of culture and communication at New York University and a well-known public intellectual. His writings on film, television, propaganda, advertising and the culture industries have appeared in numerous journals and newspapers the world over. His show *A Patriot Act* ran at the New York Theater Workshop in the summer of 2004, with a film version released a few months later. He is the author of *Boxed In: The Culture of TV* (1988), *The Bush Dylsexicon: Observations on a National Disorder* (2001) and *Cruel and Unusual: Bush/Cheney's New World Order* (2004). He lives in New York City.